GLOBAL LOGISTICS

GLOBAL LOGISTICS

New directions in supply chain management

6TH EDITION

EDITED BY
DONALD WATERS

The Chartered Institute of
Logistics and Transport (UK)

KoganPage

LONDON PHILADELPHIA NEW DELHI

Publisher's note

Every possible effort has been made to ensure that the information contained in this book is accurate at the time of going to press, and the publishers and authors cannot accept responsibility for any errors or omissions, however caused. No responsibility for loss or damage occasioned to any person acting, or refraining from action, as a result of the material in this publication can be accepted by the editor, the publisher or any of the authors.

First published in Great Britain and the United States in 2010 by Kogan Page Limited
Reprinted 2010, 2011

120 Pentonville Road	1518 Walnut Street, Suite 1100	4737/23 Ansari Road
London N1 9JN	Philadelphia PA 19102	Daryaganj
United Kingdom	USA	New Delhi 110002
www.koganpage.com		India

© Donald Waters, 2010

The right of Donald Waters to be identified as the author of this work has been asserted by him in accordance with the Copyright, Designs and Patents Act 1988.

ISBN   978 0 7494 5703 7
E-ISBN   978 0 7494 5936 9

British Library Cataloguing-in-Publication Data

A CIP record for this book is available from the British Library.

Library of Congress Cataloging-in-Publication Data

Global logistics : new directions in supply chain management /
[edited by] Donald Waters. — 6th ed.
    p. cm.
   Includes bibliographical references and index.
   ISBN 978-0-7494-5703-7 — ISBN 978-0-7494-5936-9 (ebook)   1. Physical distribution
of goods.   2. Business logistics–Management.   I. Waters, C. D. J. (C. Donald J.), 1949–
   HF5415.6.G55 2010
   658.7–dc22
                                                                                      2010000351

Typeset by Graphicraft Limited, Hong Kong
Printed and bound in India by Replika Press Pvt Ltd

Contents

Contributors

Julian Allen is a Research Fellow at the Transport Studies Group, University of Westminster. His major research interests are urban freight transport, the impact of manufacturing and retailing techniques on logistics and transportation systems, the relationship between policy measures and freight transport operations, and the market structure of the freight transport industry. He has done many projects in these areas and has widely published the results.

Grzegorz Augustyniak was a faculty member of the Department of Logistics at the Warsaw School of Economics (SGH) and held visiting positions at Carleton University, University of Calgary, University of Minnesota and the University of British Columbia. He is now an assistant professor in the Department of Management Theory at SGH and is also coordinator of the student exchange programme within the Community of European Management Schools, and Deputy Director of the Polish-Japanese Management Center. He has been a consultant to many companies in manufacturing and distribution, and is currently working on improving productivity and quality in Poland.

Colin Bamford is Professor of Transport and Logistics at the University of Huddersfield. His interest in transport issues originated in the early 1970s when he was one of Ken Gwilliam's researchers at the University of Leeds. At Huddersfield he has been responsible for the development of a pioneering suite of undergraduate courses in transport and logistics management. More recently he has been involved in setting up a new distance-learning training programme for logistics managers in Hungary. He has written many articles and supervised research on a variety of supply chain management topics and published text books in the field of transport economics.

Adrian Beesley is the Head of Product Development for DHL Exel Supply Chain within its Consumer Sector. Before this he was Director of the Academy of Logistics and Director of Client Operations at BAX Global covering EMEA solutions and business development. He has been a Senior Research Fellow with the University of Warwick's Manufacturing group where he worked on a number of projects for leading companies in the area of time compression. During this time he developed Time Based Process Mapping for supply chain re-engineering. Adrian started his career as a management trainee for Unilever, and his other experiences include Director of DLR Consulting in the Far East, Senior Consultant at PriceWaterhouse and Company Logistics Manager for B&Q.

Alan Braithwaite is the Chairman of LCP Consulting, which he founded in 1985. In more than 20 years the company has become a leading independent consultancy in supply chain management, working internationally and receiving worldwide recognition.

Alan has worked with the LCP team to develop innovative new analytical and design tools including Cost-to-Serve®, Time-to-Serve® and Carbon-to-Serve®. In his career he has consulted for more than 300 clients across every industry sector, applying key principles of supply chain management to manufacturing, purchasing, retailing, logistics and customer satisfaction.

Alan is a Visiting Professor at Cranfield University and holds an MSc in Business Administration from the London Business School and a BSc in Chemical Engineering from Birmingham University. He is a regular speaker at conferences, and the author of many papers and articles.

Michael Browne worked in international shipping and aviation before becoming an academic in 1985. He is now Exel Professor of Logistics at the University of Westminster, where he has been Head of the Transport Department and Director for the Graduate Centre for the Built Environment. His current focus is on research and consultancy projects concerned with freight transport and logistics, specializing in urban logistics, logistics and energy issues and international developments in logistics. Michael's work is widely recognized through, for example, the European Commission, Department for Transport, Research Councils and commercial organizations. He is the Assistant Editor of the journal *Transport Reviews*, and on the editorial boards of several journals.

Simon Chan is a research member of the Logistics Management Research Centre, Hong Kong Baptist University. He earned his bachelor degree in business administration (information systems management) from the same university, and is currently a PhD candidate at the Department of Finance and Decision Sciences. His research interests are enterprise resource planning systems, information systems and technologies application, logistics and supply chain management. He has published research papers in international conferences, journals and book chapters, and is active in several academic and professional bodies.

Martin Christopher was Professor of Marketing and Logistics at Cranfield School of Management and chaired the Centre for Logistics and Transportation, where his work in supply chain management gained international recognition. He is now Emeritus Professor at Cranfield University. He has published widely, with recent books including *Logistics and Supply Chain Management* and *Marketing Logistics*. Martin is also co-editor of the *International Journal of Logistics Management* and is a regular contributor to conferences and workshops around the world.

Martin is an Emeritus Fellow of the Institute of Logistics on whose Council he sits, and was awarded the 1988 Sir Robert Lawrence Gold Medal for his contribution to logistics education. He continues to do research and teach with colleagues at a number of universities around the world.

Robert Duncan is a Director of B & C Business Services Limited and operates as an independent consultant in the field of supply chain management. He has over 35 years of global supply chain management experience as both an executive and a consultant in many industry sectors. Robert has particular expertise in the area of outsourced supply chain resources. His recent work has been in the areas of supply chain process improvement and the use of IT to support those process changes both within outsourced and in-house supply chain environments. Robert has contributed to a number of publications and conferences relating to supply chain management.

John Fernie is Professor of Retail Marketing and was Head of School of Management and Languages at Heriot-Watt University. He has written and contributed to numerous textbooks and papers, concentrating on the field of retail logistics and the internationalization of retail formats. He is editor of the *International Journal of Retail & Distribution Management*, and received the award for Editor of the Year in 1997 and Leading Editor awards in 1994 and 1998 and 2000. He is on the editorial board of several marketing and logistics journals, is an active member of the Institute of

Logistics & Transport and the Chartered Institute of Marketing in the UK and has held offices in the American Collegiate Retail Association. He is a member of the Logistics Directors Forum, a group of leading professionals in supply chain management.

John Gattorna is a former Professorial Fellow in Supply Chain Management and Co-Director of the Supply Chain Research Centre at the Sydney Business School, University of Wollongong. He holds Adjunct Professorial positions at universities in Australia, the UK and France, and is a prolific writer on the topic of logistics and supply chains, including his most recent book, *Dynamic Supply Chain Alignment* (Gower Publishing, Farnham, UK, 2009).

John is a highly innovative and insightful thought–leader on global logistics and is much sought after as a speaker at international conferences. Apart from a busy teaching and research schedule, he advises several multi-national companies in Asia Pacific, the Middle East, Europe and South America. He is also on the Global Advisory Board of Arshiya International, a new Indian 3PL registered on the Mumbai Stock Exchange.

David Grant is Professor of Logistics and Director of the University of Hull Logistics Institute. Previously he was Senior Lecturer and Deputy Director of the Logistics Research Centre at Heriot-Watt University in Edinburgh and Lecturer at the Universities of Calgary, Lethbridge and Edinburgh. David is also an adjunct faculty member at Mannheim Business School and Vienna University of Economics and Business Administration and has been a visiting professor at University of the Mediterranean-Aix-Marseille.

David's doctoral thesis was awarded the James Cooper Memorial Cup from the Chartered Institute of Logistics and Transport (UK) in 2003. His research interests include customer service, sustainable logistics, and the integration of logistics and marketing. He has published widely on these topics, is on the editorial board of several journals and is a member of the British Retail Consortium's Storage and Distribution Technical Advisory Committee.

Markus Hesse graduated in geography from the University of Münster, received his PhD in regional planning from the University of Dortmund (Faculty of Spatial Planning), and completed a post-doctoral degree in human geography from the Faculty of Earth Sciences of the Freie Universität Berlin. Since 2008, he has been Professor of Urban Studies at the University of Luxembourg, Geography and Spatial Planning research centre.

His research is concentrated on principles of urban and regional development, European urban policy, globalization and the flows of materials – especially the impact of global logistics on Western Europe and North America.

Heikki Holma is a senior lecturer in Seinäjoki University of Applied Sciences. Before this, he worked as a researcher and project manager in the Department of Marketing in the University of Oulu, and then as a special researcher in the Department of Logistics. He has over 25 years of experience in business-to-business marketing, and his main research interests are focused on industrial marketing, networks and business relationships in supply chains. Heikki is also a specialist in the forest industry, starting research with The Finnish Forest Research Institute in the early 1980s and consequently completing a dissertation on moderating business cycles in the Finnish sawmill industry.

Jacques Leonardi is Senior Research Fellow in the Department of Transport Studies, University of Westminster. His research specialties are related to freight transport, energy and carbon footprint, surveys and survey methods, new technologies, data management, and policy impact evaluation. Recent work in these areas includes research for Green Logistics (www.greenlogistics.org), SUGAR (www.sugarlogistics.eu), Data and Knowledge Centre of TfL freight unit and COST SHANTI (a European network on transport data). He has published widely on these topics and also teaches at the University of Westminster.

Chris Lonsdale taught at the University of Hull and in 1993 moved to The University of Birmingham, Department of Political Science and International Studies and the Institute for Local Government Studies. The following year he moved to the Business School, from where he was awarded a PhD. He is now a senior lecturer in the Centre for Business Strategy and Procurement the School's supply chain management group, and was Programme Director of the MBA (Strategy and Procurement Management). In 2000, he was awarded honorary membership of the Chartered Institute of Purchasing and Supply.

Heimo Losbichler is Professor of Finance and Control and Chair of the Department of Accounting, Control and Financial Management at the University of Applied Sciences Upper Austria in Steyr. He was the elected Dean at the School of Management for the last three years and is an elected member of the board of the International Controller Association. Heimo's research and teaching interests include value-based management, financial performance analysis, and financial performance measurement within the supply chain. He has published his research widely in academic and professional journals. He also has extensive experience in industry, serving as the CEO of Baudatentechnik GMBH (an Austrian IT company) and consulting for leading Austrian companies.

Farzad Mahmoodi is Professor of Operations Management and Director of Clarkson University's Global Supply Chain Management Program. He has been actively involved in executive education and has served as a consultant for several Fortune 500 companies. His research interests focus on design and control of manufacturing and logistics systems, where he has published over 40 articles. Farzad has won several awards, including the Professor of the Year Award, the Commendable Leadership Award, the Distinguished Teaching Award, and the John W. Graham, Jr. Faculty Research Award. He serves on the editorial boards of the International Journal of Industrial Engineering and the International Journal of Integrated Supply Management.

Kirstie McIntyre leads Hewlett-Packard's environmental compliance responsibilities in Europe, Middle East and Africa. Her remit covers all product-related environmental laws and agreements on energy efficiency, chemical and material restrictions and end-of-life considerations. She has a particular interest in the development of waste electronic management systems. She liaises with government, industry partners, supply chain members, business customers and consumers on the implementation of environmental directives and the takeback and recycling of HP's products. Kirstie has worked for a number of years in the strategic development of end-of-life programmes for various companies in the electronics sector. She has an engineering doctorate in environmental technology and has published widely on sustainability and supply chain issues.

Alan McKinnon is Professor of Logistics and Director of the Logistics Research Centre at Heriot-Watt University, Edinburgh. A graduate of the universities of Aberdeen, British Columbia and London, he has been researching and teaching in freight transport and logistics for 30 years. He has published extensively on these subjects and was the European editor of the International Journal of Physical Distribution and Logistics Management.

Alan has conducted studies for numerous public and private sector organizations and has been an adviser to UK government departments, parliamentary committees and various international agencies. He is also a member of the World Economic Forum's Global Agenda Council on the Future of Transportation. He is a fellow of the Chartered Institute of Logistics and Transport, chairman of their Professional Development

Policy Committee and a founder member of its Logistics Research Network. He received the 2002 Herbert Crow Memorial Award from the Worshipful Company of Carmen of London and the 2003 Sir Robert Lawrence Award from the CILT.

Arnfried Nagel studied Industrial Engineering and Management at the Berlin Institute of Technology focusing on finance, controlling and supply chain management. He successfully completed international internships in France and worked as a consultant in Germany. Since 2005, Arnfried has been working as a doctoral assistant at the Berlin Institute of Technology with a focus on eco-efficiency in supply chain management.

Hildegunn Kyvik Nordås is a senior trade policy analyst at the OECD Trade and Agriculture Directorate where she is currently managing a project on measuring trade restrictiveness in services. Before joining the OECD she was a researcher in the WTO secretariat, a senior research fellow and research director at Chr. Michelsen Institute in Norway and at the University of Bergen. She has held visiting positions at Stanford University, University of Durban Westville and the University of Western Cape. She has published articles, book chapters and reports on international trade, trade and growth, trade and investment and macroeconomic management, and has served on the board of several programmes for the Norwegian Research Council.

Helen Peck is a senior lecturer at The Resilience Centre, Cranfield University. She joined Cranfield in 1983, from a major UK clearing bank, initially within the University's library and information service, and then completing a PhD and transferring to the academic staff. She now works at the Defence Academy, MOD.

Since 2001 Helen has been at the forefront of Cranfield University's government-funded programme of research into all aspects of supply chain related risk and resilience. Her publications include the Department for Transport's report on Creating Resilient Supply Chains and numerous academic and practitioner articles. She is co-editor and author of several books and an award-winning writer of management case studies.

Daniel Rief studied Information Engineering and Management at Universität Karlsruhe and Concordia University, Montreal, focusing on information systems, business processes and e-business supply chains. He completed internships in the financial sector and consulting and worked for international companies before becoming a doctoral assistant at the Berlin Institute of Technology (Technische Universitaet Berlin). He initially worked at the Competence Center for International Logistics

Networks focusing on logistics in the context of internationalization, and since 2009 works at the Kuehne-Foundation Chair of International Logistics Networks which focuses on global supply chain design.

Stephen Rinsler has extensive industrial experience including senior positions in Unilever (UK and European procurement and supply chains), Exel Europe (Services Director with a brief that included procurement, risk, health and safety), Volt Europe (SVP Operations), and Procurement and Supply Chain Director for Storehouse (Bhs and Mothercare). He is currently Director of Bisham Consulting, a vice president and trustee of the Chartered Institute of Logistics and Transport, a past chair of the CILT (UK) Board and the Supply Chain Faculty and a visiting Fellow of the Defence College of Management and Technology. He is commissioned as a colonel in the Engineer and Logistics Staff Corps RE(V) where he sits as the Non-Executive Director of the Defence JSCMB, an honorary Professor of Logistics and Engineering at the University of Nanjing, PR China and a Court Assistant of the Worshipful Company of Carmen.

Stephen was educated at Bristol University and attended Wharton Business School, Pennsylvania and is currently studying Mathematics at the Open University.

Jean-Paul Rodrigue received a PhD in transport geography from the Université de Montreal in 1994 and is now an associate professor in the Department of Global Studies and Geography at Hofstra University, New York. His research interests cover issues related to freight transportation, transport terminals, logistics and globalization, particularly as they relate to the economies of North America and Pacific Asia. His recent work focuses on the integration of maritime and inland freight distribution and the impact of intermodal transport on freight distribution. Jean-Paul's website – The Geography of Transport Systems – has been adopted internationally as a tool for education and research on transport issues. He is on the international editorial board of the Journal of Transport Geography, the Journal of Transport and Land Use and acts as a researcher in transport and logistics for the Van Horne Institute.

Krzysztof Rutkowski is Professor and Chair of the Department of Logistics, Warsaw School of Economics, Lecturer at the Community of European Management Schools, and Adjunct Professor of International Studies at the Carlson School of Management, University of Minnesota. He studied at Warsaw University, the Warsaw School of Economics, Rayerson Polytechnic University in Toronto and Scuola Superiore Enrico Mattei, Milan.

Krzysztof has worked in logistics for many years with a professional career that began in Plastics Kanada in Toronto and continued in IPEX,

Pomaton EMI, UPS, and PEKAES Group. His current research interests are in development trends in supply chain management, demand-driven supply networks, global logistics and best practices in supply chain management. He has published widely in these areas.

Krzysztof was Vice Rector of the Warsaw School of Economics and has been an advisor and expert to governments, international organizations, and international companies. He is currently President of the Association of Polish Logistics Managers.

Jari Salo was a professor of ICT business at the University of Oulu in Finland and is now an assistant professor of Marketing at the Helsinki School of Economics. His research interests include business relationship digitization, electronic commerce including mobile marketing, and new product development and innovation. He has published widely in these areas and is the editor-in-chief of the Journal of Digital Marketing.

Jari has worked as a consultant and organized research projects in many companies, and has raised funding from companies such as Nokia, Rauruukki, Outotec, Metso Paper and Outokumpu.

Joe Sanderson is a senior lecturer at the Centre for Business Strategy and Procurement at the University of Birmingham. He is currently working on a project to map the structural characteristics of supply and Value chains in a range of service and industrial sectors. He has a BA in politics from the University of Hull and is writing his doctoral thesis on the regulatory and organizational drivers of procurement efficiency in the UK utilities after privatization. His principle research interests are in international business and supply management, power in supply chains, and the impact of national, regional and international regulation on procurement practices.

Xinping Shi is the Director of the Logistics Management Research Centre, and Associate Professor in the Department of Finance and Decision Sciences, Hong Kong Baptist University. Xinping has taught widely on business management subjects, and has supervised many research projects and published widely in information system and supply chain management. His research interests include logistics and supply chain management, decision making in organizations, enterprise resource planning, knowledge management, and international business negotiations. He is a visiting professor of Logistics Management at the College of Logistics, Beijing Normal University, and is an independent director of logistics firms in Hong Kong and China.

Lars Stemmler is Deputy Head of Structuring/Analysis Transportation Finance Europe of HSH Nordbank AG. Prior to joining HSH he worked for BLG Consult GmbH (the consultancy branch of the BLG Logistics Group) Deutsche Schiffsbank AG (a leading ship and financial company) and the Oldenburg Chamber of Industry and Commerce. In these jobs he has been involved in several international projects concerned with port finance and logistics.

Lars is a guest lecturer at various universities and holds a PhD in economics and MSc in logistics from Cranfield University.

Frank Straube is Director of the Department of Technology and Management and Chair of Logistics at the Berlin Institute of Technology (Technische Universitaet Berlin). He is active as an international teacher at the CDHK of Tongji University, Shanghai, University of St. Gallen, Switzerland and University Paris II (Pantheon-Assas).

Frank is a member of the advisory board at the German Logistics Association, European Logistics Association, Bremer Logistics Group, and Deutsche Bahn AG. For the past 12 years he has also been chairman and board member of an internationally active consulting and planning company specializing in logistics and corporate planning. He is the founder of the International Transfer Center for Logistics, which implements innovative planning and professional development operations for companies.

Rolando Tomasini is Programme Manager for the Humanitarian Research Group at the INSEAD Social Innovation Center. His work focuses on public–private partnerships between humanitarian organizations and corporate multinationals. Through numerous secondments to various UN agencies and NGOs he has acquired an extensive knowledge of emergency relief operations and corporate social responsibility. He is the author of several case studies at INSEAD, academic articles, and books on humanitarian logistics. He has a Master of International Business degree from Florida International University and is working on his PhD at Hanken School of Economics.

Remko van Hoek was a supply chain improvement director for Nike, CPO at Nuon (a major Dutch utility company) and is now Chief Procurement Officer at Cofely (part of GDF Suez) in the Netherlands.

Remko is a visiting professor of supply chain management at the Cranfield School of Management, having previously been a professor of supply chain management. He has also taught at the Rotterdam School of Management and the University of Ghent/Vlerick School of Management. He is on the board of directors of CSCMP, and serves on editorial boards of several international academic journals. He is a frequent speaker in boardrooms and executive events, and his work is widely published.

He is co-author of the best selling textbook on Logistics Management and Strategy, and he has won 10 awards for academic work in the supply chain domain.

Luk Van Wassenhove holds the Henry Ford Chair of Manufacturing at INSEAD and is also the Academic Director of the INSEAD Social Innovation Centre. Before joining INSEAD he was on the faculty at Erasmus University Rotterdam and Katholieke Universiteit Leuven.

Luk's research and teaching are concerned with operational excellence, supply chain management, quality, continual improvement and learning. His recent research focus is on closed-loop supply chains (product take-back and end-of-life issues) and on disaster management (humanitarian logistics). He is senior editor for Manufacturing and Service Operations Management and departmental editor for Production and Operations Management, and publishes regularly in academic journals. He is the author of several award-winning teaching cases and regularly consults for major international corporations. In 2006 he won the EURO Gold Medal for outstanding academic achievement.

James Jixian WANG is Associate Professor in the Department of Geography, University of Hong Kong. He has a Bachelor in Economics from the People's University of China, MPhil from the University of Hong Kong, and PhD from University of Toronto. Currently he is a council member of Hong Kong Society for Transport Studies, and a Fellow of The Chartered Institute of Logistics and Transport. His research area is Transport Geography, particularly port development and port-city relations. He has published widely in many international journals and is on the editorial boards of the Journal of Transport Geography and Transportmatrica. As a port-city specialist, James has participated in planning projects and strategic studies for more than 25 cities in China and the rest of Asia.

Glyn Watson obtained a PhD from the University of Birmingham Business School in 1996 and is now a senior lecturer at the Centre for Business Strategy and Procurement. He was Programme Director of the MBA in Strategy and Procurement Management and recently became Director of Education for the Business School. He has done research in the broad area of integration and on European business issues, and his current interests include supply chain, supply chain typologies and supply chain management.

Allan Woodburn is a senior lecturer in Freight and Logistics in the Transport Studies Group of the Department of Urban Development and Regeneration at the University of Westminster. He was previously a lecturer in the School of the Built Environment at Napier University, where he completed his Doctorate in 2000. His areas of interest and experience include freight transport (particularly rail), transport policy, and public transport planning and operations. Allan has also worked for Colin Buchanan and Partners (CBP), where he managed a number of projects relating to rail/bus operations and freight transport and other policy-based studies.

Preface

The first edition of *Global Logistics and Distribution Planning: Strategies for Management* appeared in 1988. Since then the whole field of logistics has changed. Of course, there is still agreement about the basic principle of a supply chain as 'the series of activities and organizations that materials – both tangible and intangible – move through on their journeys from initial suppliers to final customers' (Waters, 2009). Then logistics – or supply chain management – becomes the function that 'plans, implements and controls the efficient, effective forward and reverse flow and storage of goods, services and related information between the point of origin and the point of consumption in order to meet customers' (CSCMP, 2006). But the way that managers control the movement and storage of materials has changed dramatically.

Not long ago, logistics would hardly be mentioned in the long-term plans of even major companies; now its strategic role is clear and virtually every organization recognizes that it can only succeed by improving the management of its supply chains. There are many reasons for this change. Communications and information technology offer new opportunities and ways of working; despite recent economic problems, world trade continues to grow; new markets and sources of materials appear; costs of materials and operations change; new types of operations appear; customers become more demanding; there is increasing concern for the environment; and so on.

In response to these pressures for change, logistics managers have changed the way they work, forming a single integrated function that is responsible for all aspects of material movement and storage all the way from initial suppliers through to final customers. Within this function there are dominant trends towards globalization, e-business, improving communications, lean and agile strategies, environmental concern, risk management, customer satisfaction – and all the other ideas that have become essential parts of logistics.

This book discusses the latest developments in this dynamic business function. The sixth edition builds on the success of earlier editions and follows the same general format. It is not an encyclopaedia of logistics that gives an exhaustive review of every aspect of a very broad subject. Instead it is a forum in which a number of key issues are addressed. It focuses on areas that are of particular current interest, and emphasizes changes that have occurred in recent years.

The contributors are acknowledged experts in their fields with a wealth of experience and knowledge. Each gives an authoritative view of current thinking. Of course, this does not mean that they present the only view, and we hope that the material will encourage informed discussion.

This new edition has been completely rewritten. To keep its contemporary focus we have removed some of the previous chapters and replaced them by new ones. The remaining chapters have all been updated. And so the book continues to evolve, maintaining its focus on current issues that are relevant to an international readership.

The book will appeal to everyone with an interest in logistics. This includes academics and students doing a variety of courses that have some logistics content. It also includes logistics professionals, consultants – and managers from different backgrounds who want an appreciation of current thinking about the supply chain. It is important for all managers to realize the importance of logistics, the way that it crosses organizational and disciplinary boundaries – and the way that it fundamentally affects the way that an organization works. The success of every organization depends on its ability to deliver products to customers – and this is precisely the role of logistics. To put it simply, an organization cannot succeed without good logistics – and if it does not get its supply chains sorted out, it may as well put the lights out and close the door.

James Cooper edited the first two editions of this book and summarized the pleasures of editing the contents:

> In my role as editor, I have already had the opportunity to read the thoughts and ideas expressed in each of the chapters. Indeed, one of the greatest pleasures of being editor was to be the first to enjoy the riches of the chapters as they converged into this book. I now leave it to new readers to explore the chapters that follow, in the anticipation that they too will benefit, both professionally and personally, from the wealth of knowledge and expertise that they contain.

References

CSCMP (2006) Publicity material, Council of Supply Chain Management Professionals, Oak Brook, IL, and website at www.cscmp.org

Waters, D (2009) *Supply Chain Management: An introduction to logistics*, Palgrave Macmillan, Basingstoke

Donald Waters
Penzance

1

New directions in logistics

Martin Christopher,
Cranfield School of Management

In recent years there has been a growing recognition that the *processes* whereby we satisfy customer demands are of critical importance to any organization. These processes are the means by which products are developed, manufactured and delivered to customers and through which the continuing service needs of those customers are met. The logistics concept is the thread that connects these crucial processes and provides the basis for the design of systems that will cost-effectively deliver value to customers.

Accompanying this recognition of the importance of process has been a fundamental shift in the focus of the business towards the marketplace and away from the more inwardly oriented production and sales mentality that previously dominated most industries. This change in orientation has necessitated a review of the means by which customer demand is satisfied – hence the dramatic upsurge of interest in logistics as a core business activity.

THE EMERGENCE OF THE VALUE-CONSCIOUS CUSTOMER

Recession in many markets, combined with new sources of competition, has raised the consciousness of customers towards value. 'Value' in today's context does not just mean value for money – although that is certainly a critical determinant of the purchase decision for many buyers – but it also means perceived benefits. Customers increasingly are demanding products with added value, but at lower cost, and hence the new competitive imperative is to seek out ways to achieve precisely that.

Michael Porter (1980, 1985) was one of the first commentators to highlight the need for organizations to understand that competitive success could only come through cost leadership or through offering clearly differentiated products or services. The basic model is illustrated in Figure 1.1. Porter's argument was that a company with higher costs and no differential advantage in the eyes of the customer was in effect a commodity supplier with little hope of long-term success unless it could find a way out of the box. His prescription was that the organization should seek to become either a *low-cost producer* or a *differentiated supplier*.

However, in reality it is not sufficient to compete only on the basis of being the lowest-cost supplier. The implication of this is that a competitor in the bottom right-hand corner has to compete on price – if a company is only a cost leader, how else can it compete? Competing solely in terms of price will merely reinforce the customer's view that the product is a

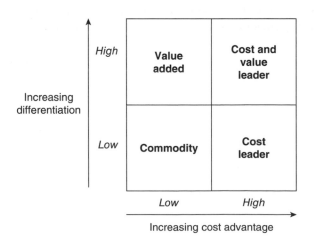

Figure 1.1   The competitive options

commodity – the very thing the company wishes to avoid. On the other hand, a strategy based upon differentiation will make it possible to compete on grounds other than price. While value for money will always be an issue, the aim is to increase customers' perception of the value they are receiving and hence their willingness to pay a higher price.

Organizations create value for their customers either by increasing the level of 'benefit' they deliver or by reducing the customers' costs. In fact customer value can be defined as follows:

$$\text{Customer value} = \frac{\text{Perceived benefits}}{\text{Total cost of ownership}}$$

Perceived benefits include the tangible, product-related aspects as well as the less tangible, service-related elements of the relationship.

The key point to note is that these benefits are essentially perceptual and that they will differ by customer. The 'total cost of ownership' reflects all the costs associated with the relationship, not just the price of the product. Hence the customer's cost of carrying inventory, ordering costs and other transactions costs all form part of this total cost concept.

Because logistics management, perhaps uniquely, can impact upon both the numerator and the denominator of the customer value equation, it can provide a powerful means of enhancing customer value.

An argument that is being heard more frequently is that logistics is a *core capability* that enables the firm to gain and maintain competitive advantage. More and more the view is expressed (Stalk, Evans and Shulman, 1992) that it is through capabilities that organizations compete. These capabilities include such processes as new product development, order fulfilment, marketing planning and information systems. There can be little doubt that companies that in the past were able to rely upon product superiority to attain market leadership can no longer do so, as competitive pressure brings increasing technological convergence. Instead these companies must seek to develop systems that enable them to respond more rapidly to customer requirements at ever lower costs.

LOGISTICS AND SUPPLY CHAIN MANAGEMENT

Logistics management is essentially an integrative process that seeks to optimize the flows of materials and supplies through the organization and its operations to the customer. It is essentially a planning process and an information-based activity. Requirements from the marketplace are translated into production requirements and then into materials requirements through this planning process.

It is now being recognized that, for the real benefits of the logistics concept to be realized, there is a need to extend the logic of logistics upstream to suppliers and downstream to final customers. This is the concept of *supply chain management*.

Supply chain management is a fundamentally different philosophy of business organization and is based upon the idea of partnership in the marketing channel and a high degree of linkage between entities in that channel. Traditional models of business organization were based upon the notion that the interests of individual firms are best served by maximizing their revenues and minimizing their costs. If these goals were achieved by disadvantaging another entity in the channel, then that was the way it was. Under the supply chain management model the goal is to maximize profit through enhanced competitiveness in the final market – a competitiveness that is achieved by a lower cost to serve, achieved in the shortest time-frame possible. Such goals are only attainable if the supply chain as a whole is closely coordinated in order that total channel inventory is minimized, bottlenecks are eliminated, time-frames compressed and quality problems eliminated.

This new model of competition suggests that individual companies compete not as company against company, but rather as supply chain against supply chain. Thus the successful companies will be those whose supply chains are more cost-effective than those of their competitors.

What are the basic requirements for successful supply chain management? Figure 1.2 outlines the critical linkages that connect the marketplace to the supply chain.

The key linkages are between procurement and manufacturing, and between manufacturing and distribution. Each of these three activities, while part of a continuous process, has a number of critical elements.

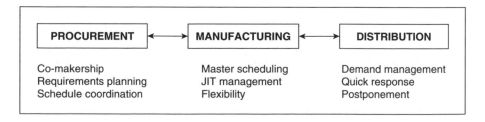

Figure 1.2 Critical linkages in the supply chain

PROCUREMENT

Typically in the past, supply management has been paid scant attention in many companies. Even though the costs of purchases for most businesses are the largest single cost, procurement has not been seen as a strategic task. That view is now changing, as the realization grows that not only are costs dramatically impacted by procurement decisions and procedures but also that innovation and response-to-market capability are profoundly affected by supplier relationships.

The philosophy of *co-makership* is based upon the idea of a mutually beneficial relationship between supplier and buyer, instead of the more traditional adversarial stance that is so often encountered. With this partnership approach, companies will identify opportunities for taking costs out of the supply chain instead of simply pushing them upstream or downstream. Paperwork can be eliminated, problems jointly solved, quality improved and information shared. By its very nature, co-makership will often involve longer-term relationships, but with fewer suppliers.

A fundamental feature of this integrated approach to supply chain management is the adoption of some form of alignment and synchronization of the customer's and the supplier's processes.

The aim should be to view your suppliers' operations as merely an extension of your own. Companies like Nissan, in their UK manufacturing facility, have developed closely linked systems with all of their suppliers so that those suppliers have full visibility not only of the production schedule at Nissan's Washington plant, but also of the real-time sequence in which cars are moving down the assembly line. By the use of electronic data interchange (EDI) and open communications, Nissan has been able to reduce lead times, eliminate inventories and take costs out of the supply chain. Other companies may have introduced similar just-in-time (JIT) systems, but often, in so doing, have added to their suppliers' costs, not reduced them.

MANUFACTURING

There has been much talk of 'lean' manufacturing in recent years (led by Womack, Jones and Roos, 1990). The idea of leanness in this sense is that wasteful activities are reduced or eliminated and that value-creating processes are performed more quickly. However, just as important as leanness is agility. Agility is a wider supply chain concept that is more concerned with how the firm responds to changes in marketplace requirements – particularly requirements for volume and variety. Leanness is undoubtedly a desirable feature of a supply chain unless it leads to a misplaced emphasis on manufacturing costs. It may be preferable, for example, to incur a cost penalty in the unit cost of manufacture if it enables the company to achieve higher levels of customer responsiveness at less overall cost to the supply chain.

The key word in manufacturing in today's environment is *flexibility* – flexibility in terms of the ability to produce any variant in any quantity, without significant cost penalty, has to be the goal of all manufacturing strategies. In the past, and even still today, much of the thinking in manufacturing was dominated by the search for economies of scale. This type of thinking led to large mega-plants, capable of producing vast quantities of a standardized product at incredibly low unit costs of production. It also has led many companies to go for so-called 'focused factories', which produce a limited range of products for global consumption.

The downside of this is in effect the possibility of hitting the 'diseconomies' of scale: in other words, the build-up of large inventories of finished product ahead of demand, the inability to respond rapidly to changed customer requirements and the limited variety that can be offered to the customer. Instead of economies of scale, the search is now on for strategies that will reduce total supply chain costs, not just manufacturing costs, and that will offer maximum flexibility against customer requirements. The goal must be 'the economic batch quantity of one', meaning that in the ideal world we would make things one at a time against known customer demands.

One of the lessons that the Japanese have taught us is that the route to flexibility in manufacturing does not necessarily lie through new technology, eg robotics, although that can help. A lot can be achieved instead through focusing upon the time it takes to plan, to schedule, to set up, to change over and to document. These are the classic barriers to flexibility and if they can be removed then manufacturing can respond far more rapidly to customer requirements. In a factory with zero lead times, total flexibility is achieved with no forecasts and no inventory! While zero lead times are clearly an impossibility, the Japanese have shown that impressive reductions in such lead times can be achieved by questioning everything we do and the way in which we do it.

DISTRIBUTION

The role of distribution in the supply chain management model has extended considerably from the conventional view of the activity as being concerned solely with transport and warehousing. The critical task that underlies successful distribution today is *demand management*.

Demand management is the process of anticipating and fulfilling orders against defined customer service goals. Information is the key to demand management: information from the marketplace in the form of medium-term forecasts; information from customers, preferably based upon actual usage and consumption; information on production schedules and inventory status; and information on marketing activities such as promotions that may cause demand to fluctuate away from the norm.

Clearly, while forecasting accuracy has always to be sought, it must be recognized that it will only rarely be achieved. Instead the aim should be to reduce our dependence upon the forecast by improved information on demand and by creating systems capable of more rapid response to that demand. This is the principle that underlies the idea of *quick response* logistics.

Quick response logistics has become the aim for many organizations, enabling them to achieve the twin strategic goals of cost reduction and service enhancement. In essence, the idea of quick response is based upon a replenishment-driven model of demand management. In other words, as items are consumed or purchased, this information is transmitted to the supplier and this immediately triggers a response. Often more rapid, smaller consignment quantity deliveries will be made, the trade-off being that any higher transport costs will be more than covered by reduced inventory in the pipeline and at either end of it, yet with improved service in terms of responsiveness. Clearly information technology has been a major enabling factor in quick response logistics, linking the point of sale or consumption with the point of supply.

A further trend that is visible in distribution is the search for *postponement* opportunities. The principle of postponement is that the final configuration or form of the product should be delayed until the last possible moment. In this way maximum flexibility is maintained, but inventory minimized. The distribution function takes on a wider role as the provider of the final added value. For example, at Xerox the aim is not to hold any inventory as finished product but only as semi-finished, modular work in progress, awaiting final configuration once orders are received. Similarly, at Hewlett-Packard, products are now designed with 'localization' in mind. In other words, products will be designed for modular manufacture but with local assembly and customization to meet the needs of specific markets. In this way economies of scale in manufacturing can be achieved by producing generic products for global markets while enabling local needs to be met through postponed configuration.

What is apparent is that distribution in the integrated supply chain has now become an information-based, value-added activity, providing a critical link between the marketplace and the factory.

THE NEW COMPETITIVE FRAMEWORK: THE FOUR Rs

We began this chapter with a brief review of how today's customer is increasingly seeking added value and how logistics management can provide that value. In the past, the primary means of achieving competitive advantage were often summarized as the 'four Ps' – product, price, promotion and place. These should now be augmented with the 'four Rs' – reliability, responsiveness, resilience and relationships – and logistics strategies need to be formulated with these as the objectives. Let us briefly examine each in turn.

Reliability

In most markets and commercial environments today, customers are seeking to reduce their inventory holdings. Just-in-time practices can be found in industries as diverse as car assembly and retailing. In such situations it is essential that suppliers can guarantee complete order-fill delivered at agreed times. Hence a prime objective of any logistics strategy must be reliability.

Making logistics systems more reliable means that greater emphasis must be placed upon process design and process control. The processes that are particularly germane to logistics are those to do with order fulfilment and supply chain management. Because traditionally these processes have been managed on a fragmented, functional basis they tend to have a higher susceptibility to variability. These processes are typified by multiple 'hand-offs' from one area of functional responsibility to another and by bottlenecks at the interfaces between stages in the chain. One of the benefits of taking a process view of the business is that it often reveals opportunities for simplification and the elimination of non-value-adding activities so that reliability inevitably improves.

One of the main causes of unreliability in supply chain processes is performance variability. Recently, the use of so-called 'Six Sigma' methodologies has been adopted to reduce that variability. Six Sigma is the umbrella term applied to a range of tools that are designed to identify the sources of variability in processes and to reduce and control that variability.

Responsiveness

Very closely linked to the customers' demands for reliability is the need for responsiveness. Essentially this means the ability to respond in ever-shorter lead times with the greatest possible flexibility. Quick response, as we have seen, is a concept and a technology that is spreading rapidly across industries. For the foreseeable future, speed will be a prime competitive variable in most markets. The emphasis in logistics strategy will be upon developing the means to ship smaller quantities, more rapidly, direct to the point of use or consumption.

The key to time compression in the logistics pipeline is through the elimination or reduction of time spent on non-value-adding activities. Hence, contrary to a common misconception, time compression is not about performing activities faster, but rather performing fewer of them. The old cliché 'Work smarter, not harder' is particularly relevant in this context.

As Hammer and Champy (Hammer, 1990; Hammer and Champy, 1993) have pointed out, many of the processes used in our organizations were designed for a different era. They tend to be paper-based, with many – often redundant – manual stages. They are sequential and batch-oriented rather than parallel and capable of changing quickly from one task to another. Even though eliminating or reducing such activities may increase cost, the end result will often be more cost-effective. For example, shipping direct from factories to end customers may be more expensive in terms of the unit cost of transport compared to shipping via a regional distribution centre, but time spent in the distribution centre is usually non-value-adding time.

Resilience

Today's supply chains are more complex and vulnerable to disruption than ever before. In many cases, as a result of outsourcing and the increasingly global nature of supply chains, the likelihood of interruption to product and information flows has increased significantly.

Identifying, mitigating and managing supply chain risk is now a critical requirement to ensure business continuity. The idea of resilience in the context of supply chain management is that supply chains need to be able to absorb shocks and to continue to function even in the face of unexpected disruption.

The paradox is that in many cases, because companies have adopted 'lean' strategies and reduced inventories and, often, capacity, there is little 'slack' left in their systems. Resilient supply chains will typically incorporate strategic buffers at the critical nodes and links in their networks. These buffers could be in the form of inventory or capacity, possibly shared with competitors.

As uncertainty in the business environment continues to increase, organizations need to adopt a more systematic and structured approach to supply chain risk management. One way in which this can be achieved is by creating a supply chain continuity team whose job is to audit risk across the supply chain and to develop and implement strategies for the mitigation of any identified risk.

Relationships

The trend towards customers seeking to reduce their supplier base has already been commented upon. The concept of 'strategic sourcing' is now receiving widespread support. Strategic sourcing is based on the careful selection of suppliers whom the customer wishes to partner. The benefits of such an approach include improved quality, innovation sharing, reduced costs and the integrated scheduling of production and deliveries. Underlying all of this is the idea that buyer–supplier relationships should be based upon partnership. More and more companies are discovering the advantages that can be gained by seeking out mutually beneficial, long-term relationships with suppliers. From the suppliers' point of view, such partnerships can prove formidable barriers to entry to competitors. Once again, companies are finding that logistics provides a powerful route to the creation of partnerships in the marketing channel. Logistics management should be viewed as the thread that connects the inbound and outbound flows of channel partners.

A good example of logistics partnership is the growing use of 'vendor-managed inventory' (VMI). The underlying principle of VMI is that the supplier rather than the customer assumes responsibility for the flow of product into the customer's operations. Thus instead of the customer placing orders on the vendor – often at short notice – the vendor can directly access information relating to the rate of usage or sale of the product by the customer. With this information the supplier can better plan the replenishment of the product with less need to carry safety stock. In effect, VMI enables the substitution of information for inventory in the supply chain.

The challenge to marketing and strategic planning in any business is to construct a corporate strategy that specifically builds upon logistics as a means to achieving competitive advantage through a much stronger focus on the four Rs. It is still the case that many organizations have not fully understood the strategic importance of logistics and hence have not explicitly tailored logistics into their corporate strategies and their marketing plans.

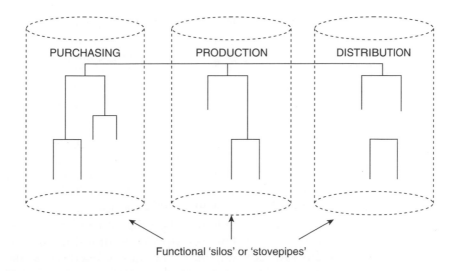

Figure 1.3   The vertical/functional organization

THE ORGANIZATIONAL CHALLENGE

One of the most significant changes in recent years has been the way in which we think of organization structures. Conventionally, organizations have been 'vertical' in their design. In other words, businesses have organized around functions such as production, marketing, sales and distribution. Each function has had clearly identified tasks and within these functional 'silos' or 'stovepipes' (as they have been called) there is a recognized hierarchy up which employees might hope to progress. Figure 1.3 illustrates this functionally oriented business.

The problem with this approach is that it is inwardly focused and concentrates primarily on the use of resources rather than upon the creation of outputs. The outputs of any business can only be measured in terms of customer satisfaction achieved at a profit. Paradoxically, these outputs can only be realized through coordination and cooperation *horizontally* across the organization. These horizontal linkages mirror the materials and information flows that link the customer with the business and its suppliers. They are in fact the *core processes* of the business. Figure 1.4 highlights the fundamental essence of the horizontal organization.

In the horizontal organization, the emphasis is upon the management of processes. These processes, by definition, are cross-functional and include new product development, order fulfilment, information management, profitability analysis and marketing planning.

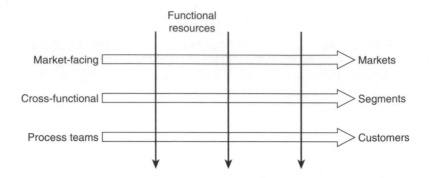

Figure 1.4 The horizontal/process organization

The justification for this radically different view of the business is that these processes are in effect 'capabilities' and, as we have observed, it is through capabilities that the organization competes. In other words, the effectiveness of the new product development process, the order fulfilment process and so on determine the extent to which the business will succeed in the marketplace.

How does a conventionally organized business transform itself into a market-facing, process-oriented organization? One of the major driving forces for change is the revolution that has taken place in information technology and systems, enabling the supply chain linkage to become a reality. More and more, the business will find itself organizing around the information system. In other words, the processes for capturing information from the marketplace (forecasts, anticipated requirements, customer schedules and orders) will be linked to the processes for meeting that demand.

It is no coincidence that companies that have installed the new generation of 'enterprise resource planning' (ERP) systems have also been at the forefront of the change from vertical to horizontal organizational structures. These systems enable entire supply chains to become truly demand-driven through the use of shared information. They open up new and exciting opportunities to create true end-to-end pipeline management and the achievement of the ultimate business goal of high service to customers at less cost.

SUMMARY

- Businesses in all types of industries are placing far greater emphasis on the design and management of logistics processes and the integration of those processes upstream and downstream with those of suppliers and customers.
- The business of the future will undoubtedly be market-driven, with logistics processes providing a critical means for achieving corporate goals.
- It will be a highly coordinated network of outsourced flows of materials and supplies, integrated through an information system that reaches from the ultimate consumer to the far end of the supply chain.
- The era of logistics and supply chain management, which many have predicted for some time, seems finally to have arrived.

References

Hammer, M (1990) Re-engineering work: don't automate, obliterate, *Harvard Business Review*, July/August, pp 104–12

Hammer, M and Champy, J (1993) *Reengineering the Corporation*, HarperCollins, New York

Porter, M (1980) *Competitive Strategy*, Free Press, New York

Porter, M (1985) *Competitive Advantage*, Free Press, New York

Stalk, G, Evans, P and Shulman, LE (1992) Competing on capabilities: the new rules of corporate strategy, *Harvard Business Review*, March/April, pp 56–68

Womack, J, Jones, D and Roos, D (1990) *The Machine that Changed the World*, Macmillan, London

2

Best practices in logistics and supply chain management. The case of Central and Eastern Europe

Krzysztof Rutkowski, Warsaw School of Economics

THE ESSENCE OF THE PHENOMENON OF BEST PRACTICES IN BUSINESS

All talk about logistics and supply chain management practices – the best, the good, the bad, and the worst – seems to pervade logistics and supply chain managers (at least temporarily) on both sides of the Atlantic. The visibility of the widely publicized successes of companies such as Toyota, Wal-Mart, Dell, Apple, IBM, P&G or IKEA has encouraged supply chain managers from many other industries to benchmark against their practices and to try to apply some of the practices in their own organizations.

In management, are there practices which can contribute to the achievement of established business goals in the best possible way? The answer to this question has probably always been on the minds of management theoreticians and practitioners. The very notion of best business practices also seems to be nothing new. The best practice phenomenon has been widely regarded as a 'corporate miracle' and became popular among practitioners of various disciplines in the 1980s and 90s.[1] In the current global economy of the 21st century, where companies more than ever are being forced to optimize their operations as a matter of survival, the term (or buzzword) 'best practice' gains more relevance for, and more interest from, key management personnel every year. Everyone wants to know how their operations compare with those of their competitors, and best practice metrics is seen as one way of doing this.[2] More and more companies see value in copying such practices if they are shown to be more efficient or more effective than current methods. The ability to translate the successful experience of one organization for the benefit of another represents a core element of the operating philosophies of many leading companies from all continents, which integrate best practices into their operating philosophies.[3]

The term 'best practice' is widely, albeit unreflectively, used within any type of business, including logistics and supply chain management. Best practices come in many shapes and sizes. There are best practices around policy, concept, model, process, activity, initiative, information, organization, people and technology. Taken together, best practices provide a comprehensive framework for designing, implementing and operating at the optimal level of performance.[4] There is a plethora of 'best practice examples' everywhere, especially if they concern the presentation of a company, its business offer, its successes and its achievements. A closer analysis of these practices indicates, however, that the term is rarely precisely defined and in most cases it is not uniformly understood, while the cited examples rarely reflect those business achievements which deserve publicity and the notion of 'the best'. Looking at the posts and comments on websites, it appears that the term is either 'overused' or misunderstood. Unfortunately, companies often confuse the latest or trendiest with the best, and the best practices of one era are soon superseded by the ever more ludicrous fads of the next.[5]

Best practices might be concepts, processes, activities or procedures with demonstrated ability to achieve superior results, which have been shown in practice to be the most effective and are considered leading edge, or exceptional models for others to follow. The best practice cannot be an acceptance of mediocrity; it must be supported by an achievement of unique success, ensuring the company's competitive advantage and its ability to achieve better results than the competition. Only then can such practices become the basis for achieving success, the consequence of which is a practice worthy of imitation by others. Using proven patterns as a base saves us from running into problems that others have already experienced, and also prevents us from reinventing the wheel and wasting effort. It pays to work smart by leveraging and building on existing information or proven patterns to fit our need. So irrespective of the name we'd like to give them, we do need 'things' of the nature of best practices and patterns to help us do our job better.

To some extent it doesn't matter if the 'best practices' are really best or not. 'Best practices' is only the name we choose to call them. Maybe it's a bad name but the important thing is that they teach us something, even if we don't agree with them. Unfortunately, this entire discussion is based on a misunderstanding of the word 'best' in the context of the phrase 'best practice'. It does *not* mean 'better than all other practices in *all* contexts'.[6]

TRANSFERRING BEST PRACTICES – ONE SOLUTION FITS ALL?

Can best practices be moved across sectors? Is it possible to transfer successful solutions from a small company to a large organization and vice versa? Are there any generic solutions that can be used regardless of the context in which they are applied? What are the problems facing companies when they transfer practices and learn from each other? The mythology about best practices is that they universally improve every organization. The truth is more likely that firms are so idiosyncratic that any practice born elsewhere probably needs tailoring before it can be imported.[7]

Some of the best practices are universal by nature and may be applied in all organizations and regions of the world (therefore are easily transferable); some, however, are specific to given sectors, regions or firms, which may significantly differ from each other and which may require a completely different approach to achieve success. The Six Sigma concept could be applied to control of the manufacturing process in practically all areas of business, whereas the Quick Response concept in its original form was restricted to the textile industry. The concept of distribution structures based on fully automated distribution centres works well in countries and regions characterized by high land and labour costs but fails to do so where the cost of these resources is low.

According to C. Ashton, 'best' is always contextual, or situation specific. No practice is good or bad in itself.[8] A 'best practice' is best only in the precise, specific context in which it exists. Even if moved from one situation to another very similar one, the chances of the transfer being made with practice intact might be nil. A specific development history, evolution path, competition strategy, key competences, size, accessible resources, organizational structure, products, management style, company culture, condition of the market, competition, regulatory environment, governmental assistance/impediments, executive leadership, state of international trade, acts of God, technology life cycle, partnerships/ alliances, trendiness/hipness, inertia, effects of corruption or even luck may be decisive in ensuring that transferring best practices between firms as well as business lines and countries is not a simple task. One can learn from the practices of others, but copying them by rote without analysing the conditions within which they were developed and implemented and then comparing them to one's own particular situation and making requisite adjustments would lead to mistakes being made. The best practices should therefore be perceived more as models to be imitated than ready models to be copied by other companies. One size doesn't fit all! The Supply Chain 2020 research project provides an excellent example of this type of approach to best practices.

MIT Supply Chain 2020

What exactly is an excellent supply chain? The Center for Transportation & Logistics at the Massachusetts Institute of Technology (MIT) is striving to answer that question. In 2005, the Center undertook a long-term research effort, called Supply Chain 2020 (SC2020), with the aim of finding out what the characteristics of so-called perfect supply chains should be in future. It will also map out the process innovations that will underpin successful supply chains as far into the future as 2020.

'Beyond best practices' is one of the unifying themes behind the research to be conducted on identifying supply chain principles. It is predicated on the fact that a practice may be best for the supply chain of a specific company trying to achieve competitive advantage, but it may not be best for another company in another industry, nor even in its own. It is not MIT researchers' intent to dismiss the value of best practice benchmarking in the right context. But it concerns them that managers continue to search fruitlessly for the 'silver bullet' that they expect will transform their organization into the next Toyota or Dell.

The successes of global business leaders such as Toyota, Wall-Mart or Dell, which have been described in a transparent and convincing way, have inspired theoreticians and the managers of supply chains from many sectors to attempt to compare themselves with these leaders and to transfer the best practices of these businesses to their own organizations. In practice, however, such attempts at transferring outside solutions have rarely succeeded. The best practices of Toyota, Dell or Wall-Mart vary significantly as a result of their completely different approaches to the configuration and management of their supply chains.

According to SC2020, the companies with the best supply chains are those with a clear business strategy supported by a supply chain strategy and a complementary operational model, which enables the perfect realization of strategy. Their activities are driven by a limited number of 'tailor-made' supply chain practices.

A critical element determining the success of the supply chain is the 'operational goals' of the firm, which define the main aim of their supply chain. This supports the firm's competition strategy and measurement system, which it uses to assess the effects of managing its supply chain. The operational goals can be divided into three groups: customer responsiveness, typical for firms active in those sectors with high profit margins and short product life cycles (eg fashion apparel, pharmaceuticals, cosmetics, toys, computers); efficiency, required in companies active in those sectors with low profit margins (eg the food and beverage industry, basic-goods retail, industrial supplies); and asset utilization, typical for those branches characterized by high capital intensiveness (eg the automotive and petrochemical industries, semiconductor fabricators).

Some supply chains, such as those of Wall-Mart or Dell, must be extremely efficient in order to maintain low costs and remain price-competitive. Others are designed in such a way as to focus more on reactive capacity, less so on costs. IBM is a good example of a company which has to focus on its ability to react quickly to signals coming from its customers, for only such an approach can guarantee its long-term success in the sale of its high-profit-margin products and services (although certainly at the cost of maintaining greater stocks and higher operational costs).

In light of these assumptions, a perfect supply chain is characterized by a focus on a limited number of consistent and cross-optimized business practices, which mutually reinforce each other and are strictly tied to the operational goals of the company. Perfect supply chains avoid, according to SC2020, the trap of trying to do everything well, for as a rule this results in nothing being done properly. In order to be perfect, the supply chain must focus more of its resources on the most important tasks, and less on others which are not as important from the perspective of the company's strategy and operational model. Therefore, according to SC2020, perfect supply chain practices deserve such credit only when the entire package of practices strengthens the realization of the firm's competitive strategy and its operating model. This means that the term 'best' may only apply when the whole system of tailored practices is greater than the sum of the parts.

Source: www.sc2020.net; L. Lapide, MIT's SC2020 Project: the essence of excellence, *Supply Chain Management Review*, April 1, 2006; *Proceedings of the Supply Chain 2020 Project's European Advisory Council's Fall 2005 Meeting*, Frankfurt, 18 October 2005; T. Speh, *Key Criteria for Supply Chain Excellence: US experience*, BestLog Meeting, Paris, 16 May 2007.

The best practice of one company will not automatically become best practice in another unless it is adapted, successfully implemented and brings the expected results.[9] Yesterday's core capabilities embedded in best practices could become tomorrow's core rigidities. Institutionalization of 'best practices' by embedding them in information repositories may facilitate efficient handling of routine, 'linear' and predictable situations during stable or incrementally changing environments. However, when change is radical and discontinuous, there is a persistent need for continual renewal of the basic premises underlying best practices. Organizations in such environments need imaginative suggestions and inspiration more than they do best practices.[10]

THE BEST PRACTICES – BETWEEN THE HAMMER OF ECONOMIC DEMANDS AND THE ANVIL OF CORPORATE SOCIAL RESPONSIBILITY

In business, the principle of achieving various goals (understood to be economic, most frequently financial) is dominant. This is generally the basic and sometimes only criterion of best practice assessment. Undoubtedly, many such business goals can be found, but the basic role is played by various financial targets (eg costs, revenues, profit, profitability). A US research, consulting and publishing firm that is a world leader in the field of best practice benchmarking, Best Practices, LLC, defines them as verified tactics which maximize revenues and profits, increase productivity and optimize costs.[11] When aiming for specific mastery of business activities, can non-business targets be completely overlooked?

First of all, this means facing balanced development postulates, which involve not only ensuring the financial success of a business in the long run, but also simultaneous involvement on the part of economic and social development, environmental protection, protection of social stability and assisting clients and suppliers in the fulfilment of the same targets. A balanced development has three, intrinsically linked, dimensions: economic, ecological and social.

A given practice may potentially lead to business success, but fail to find success for political, social or ecological reasons. Examples of such unacceptable practices are: building lasting business relationships with raw material suppliers from a country that is politically unstable; enforcing advanced technology in production or distribution that eliminates the need for a larger workforce in countries and regions with a high unemployment rate; and building distribution systems based on frequent road transport supplies in regions affected by heavy traffic congestion and/or in ecological danger. For non-business targets one must undoubtedly include various aims, such as meeting the challenges of social responsibility and/or balanced development.

Such a perspective refers to the guru of green business, J Elkington, who claimed that the success of a company influences its achievement in three respects: economic, ecological and social. He proposed a simultaneous consideration and balancing of three key dimensions (the Triple Bottom Line) observed from a micro perspective.[12] From the perspective of the organization, sustainable development is not only a question of good corporate citizenship based on collecting bonus points by reducing harmful emissions from its factory or ensuring healthcare for its workers, but becomes a fundamental principle for intelligent management. This concept emphasizes that combining social, ecological and economic activities not only has a positive influence on the natural and social environment, but also has its expression in economic benefits and the building of a competitive edge in the long term. In light of this concept, the exclusive realization of economic (financial) objectives is not the best of practices, but it is difficult to acknowledge that such practices realize ecological and social objectives but without any success in the economic sphere. Undoubtedly, good practices have the object of achieving economic and ecological, or economic and social, objectives, while the best practices focus on realizing economic, ecological and social objectives at the same time (see Figure 2.1).

It is believed that orientation towards sustainable development helps today's companies increase their market share, build customer loyalty, positively distinguish their brand, improve employees' morale and loyalty, and increase the effectiveness and productivity of their activities. Attention is also paid to the fact that such an orientation lessens risk by way of avoiding negative social opinions, taking a proactive approach towards new regulation and avoiding future safety threats of the supply

Figure 2.1 The best practices in light of the Triple Bottom Line concept
Source: devised on the basis of Carter and Rogers, 2008

chain. The BestLog project, described below, illustrates how logistics and supply chain management might combine economic, ecological and social dimensions in best practice assessment.

BestLog Project

The European BestLog research project is an ambitious attempt to undertake ecological and social topics with reference to logistics and supply chain management. A particular aim of the project principal, the Directorate-General for Energy and Transport (DG TREN), is an elaboration of the concept that will meet the challenge of sustainable land transport. From a long-term perspective, within the scope of the BestLog project is an attempt to overcome many of Europe's problems in the areas of transport, logistics and supply chain management, such as: a 30 per cent increase in transportation volume in the past decade, which has not been accompanied by suitable development of the transport infrastructure; underutilized intermodal transport; road congestion and environmental pollution; shortage of qualified supply chain management personnel; unsatisfactory exchange of supply chain management knowledge and practice; a gap in strategies for harmonizing efficiency and sustainability; and stakeholders' increasing sensitivity with regard to social responsibility. Failure to tackle these problems may mean that economic growth and effective development of the continent are threatened. The project is part of the EU policy context and the DG TREN transport policy context.

The first context draws particular attention to: the 'Transport White Paper' subordinating transport to economic interests as well as those of European citizens (transport at the service of European industry and citizens); Lisbon strategy assumptions leading to the creation of jobs by making Europe the most competitive and knowledge-based region of the world; sustainable development goals establishing the harmoniza-tion of economic growth and transport (decoupling economic growth and transport growth); and EU enlargement – continual integration of new Member States.

The DG TREN political transport context aims to pay particular atten-tion to the following: intermodal transport needs 'door-to-door' logistics solutions to be successful and compete in real terms; co-modality, with the assumption improvement of efficiency of all modes separately and together in intermodal chains; and shippers, who should take all modes of transport (not just road transport) into consideration.

Although the BestLog project concentrates on the promotion of 'green' transport solutions in logistics and supply chain management, it is closer in its assumptions to J Elkington's concept (a parallel consideration of three key microeconomic goals), which is illustrated in Figure 2.2.

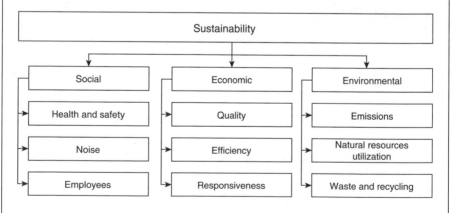

Figure 2.2 The scope of best practice assessment in the BestLog project – with benefits analysed in social, economic and ecological categories
Source: http://www.bestlog.org/; Department of Logistics at WSE, 2009

WHERE DO CENTRAL AND EASTERN EUROPE COUNTRIES COME FROM? FROM THE WORLD OF WORST PRACTICES!

Accepting the existence of best practices brings with it the necessity of accepting the thesis that their opposites also exist, namely – worst practices. 'Worst practice' is the synergistic combination of many elements of bad practice. Having just one or two elements of bad practice does not lead to worst practice status, but a range of bad practices that can 'support' and 'multiply' each other does. The economic and business environment of Central and East European countries before 1990 was a breeding ground for the emergence of worst practices in various business activities, including logistics.

With the end of the Second World War in 1945, Europe found itself divided into two spheres of power. Decades of separation during the Cold War resulted in different logistics systems and management attitudes in Western and Eastern Europe.[13] There is an obvious danger in generalizing about Central and Eastern Europe (CEE) as if it had been one place. CEE countries were not homogenous either in political or economic dimensions. Typically, however, under the centrally planned system, control over the entire economic system resided with state-owned enterprises (SOEs), which had dominance over raw material supplies, manufacturing, wholesaling and retailing, as well as warehousing. Government control of the economy meant that industry structures and management practices were not focused on efficiency. A persistent imbalance between demand and supply caused constant shortages.[14] Production was based on available raw materials, instead of customer orders. Because of shortages, managers' purchasing behaviour was inconsistent with the basic rules of logistics. Customer service was an unknown field. In fact, centrally planned economies did not need logistics. Therefore, logistics as a function was immaterial under the old system because whatever and whenever goods were available, they were sold.[15] Achieving legendary worst practice business and logistics practices in CEE must have exceeded expectation in a number of areas!

Logistics, if any, was oriented towards purchasing, not towards selling, and its characteristics were:

- no or poor customer focus;
- no or poor sales forecasting/order processing (customers went 'shopping' in production);
- lack of information systems;
- no or poor management of finished goods;
- no or poor material flow structures (internal and external);

- no or poor quality focus on warehouses and transportation;
- no third party available (either own truck fleet, or customers' trucks);
- very high stocks of raw materials (... if available, buy as much as you can);
- very high stocks of packaging materials;
- very long lead times, with loading times up to 12 hours;
- scarce palletization of products, leading to double and triple handling;
- people not familiar with Western logistics management tools, but with very good technical preparation.

Centrally planned economies generally put little emphasis on the retail sector. The communist government in Poland, for example, worked with an 'economy of shortages', where demand for most goods was greater than supply and there was no incentive to develop an efficient distribution system.[16] Furthermore, physical distribution of goods was primarily the responsibility of a government-run railroad and over-the-road carriers. Where more efficient private enterprises existed, they were very limited in both their operations and their influence on the overall system. Because of the overwhelming role of SOEs, this was a major hindrance not only for domestic firms, but also for most foreign companies wishing to develop business opportunities in Poland.[17]

WHERE ARE CEE COUNTRIES GOING? THE CASE OF POLAND

The fall of the Berlin Wall in 1989 served as both a literal and a symbolic catalyst for communism's decline in Europe and the emergence of social and economic freedom throughout Eastern bloc countries. The sudden collapse of the centrally planned institutions initiated the transition of Central and Eastern Europe into a market economy. New market forces transformed logistics structures and created a competitive environment for distribution services. Government regulations on developing sales and distribution networks did not exist beyond those needed to establish a business. Poland's new retail sector played a major role in bringing the country through a period of transition and into the subsequent period of growth. During this period the retail sector changed from having no power at all, simply following central government plans, to becoming a major force in the economy with increasing control of supply chains. Though the logistics revolution in Poland began in the retail industry, its relevance to other businesses has become ever more apparent. The appearance in Poland of global businesses with long supply chains has created new logistics challenges. As multinationals started expanding in the region, so did the global logistics firms. They were hoping to pick up business from the grocery, automotive, electronics, pharmaceutical and furniture sectors, now playing an important role in Poland. Global competition also poses a big challenge to Polish firms. If they are to find a place in the new pan-European supply chains that have begun to straddle Central and Eastern Europe, they will need to bring their logistical organization and technology up to the standards of multinationals. And, more generally, they will only stay competitive if they can keep pace with the state-of-the-art concepts and techniques now revolutionizing logistics and supply chain management in the West.[18]

The results of this transformation and privatization in Poland created a rapid expansion of logistics business opportunities. In the 1990s logistics was barely considered in the long-term plans of even major companies: now its strategic role is recognized in almost every organization. In the past decade, logistics in Poland has undergone a Cinderella-like transformation. This is hardly surprising. Recent years have seen a growth in international trade, strategic alliances, e-commerce and increased outsourcing of non-core activities. Add to this the increased emphasis on customer satisfaction, flexible operations, time compression and concern for the environment, and it becomes clear why organizations are concentrating on getting their logistics and supply chain management right. They are fast becoming a real focal point, as companies come to see them as a key battleground for gaining competitive advantage.[19] Meanwhile, logistics and supply chain management have become a fully fledged 'science', complete with their own vocational schools, university departments, research institutes, consulting firms, journals and newspapers.

Poland is the largest of the CEE countries. It has the largest landmass, the largest population and the largest economy. Poland's integration with the global economy has been highly dependent on foreign capital. Since the beginning of the 1990s there has been a huge increase in foreign direct investment in Central and Eastern Europe, with Poland topping the list of investment destinations.[20] This should be no surprise bearing in mind Poland's geographical location and the shift of production to this part of the world. According to the latest European Attractiveness Survey prepared by Ernst & Young, in 2007, Poland ranked as the most attractive destination for new foreign investment in Europe.[21]

Direct foreign investment in Poland involved not only the transfer of capital, but also machines, devices and technology, as well as modern systems of management and technological, marketing and organizational knowledge. These spread through the economy and were also incorporated by native companies with Polish capital. This contributed to the increase of competitiveness and innovation of all Polish enterprises, which at the same time improved their organizational culture and business ethics. The worst business practices were replaced by good and acceptable ones. This allowed Polish firms to enter European and global markets. Their practices became not just good, but the best, unique on a global scale, and worthy of being copied abroad.

The research projects carried out by the Department of Logistics at Warsaw School of Economics (WSE) have covered many of the latest examples of leading-edge companies and practices. In the authors' view, the content of the cases developed within these projects perfectly reflects the spirit of the smart opinion of D Blanchard on best practices' essence: '"Best practices" don't just happen by throwing a lot of money at your supply chain problems. ... It takes money, but it also takes time, talent, energy, focus, commitment from senior management, and a lot of guts to pull off a supply chain transformation. Those are the qualities that the best-run companies in the world share, and it's why they're on top.'[22] The knowledge and abilities of huge global corporations, together with entre-preneurship, imagination and an innovative approach to the business practices of corporations on the part of Polish managers and employees, led to an unexpected effect – the best practices 'Made in Poland'.

The benefits that Poland has gained from being a late entrant have enabled it to skip many interim best practices that were implemented by companies before the collapse of communism in the region. This quantum leap has allowed Polish logistics and supply chain managers to develop their own best practices. Moreover, no longer is Poland an importer of best practice. It is now an exporter, with its examples holding their own and available to the rest of the world.[23] The Polish small car producer Fiat Tychy provides an excellent example of how Polish best practices can influence automakers of other countries and continents.

Chrysler comes to Poland to learn the secrets of small-car production

American car companies never knew how to build a good small car. After a decade in which Detroit automobile companies depended on sales of big sport utility vehicles and pickup trucks for their profits, high gasoline prices are sending consumers flocking to small cars. Therefore, Detroit companies are rushing small cars into development and making deals with foreign companies to supply them.

Fiat, one of Europe's oldest and largest car companies, effectively took over Chrysler in 2009. Instead of buying the equity with cash, it will put up capital to retool part of Chrysler's production capacity to build smaller cars. The deal is the latest manoeuvre by Fiat's chief, Sergio Marchionne, who has pulled the Italian company back from the brink of collapse since taking over in 2004. The partnership will provide each company with economies of scale and geographical reach at a time when both are struggling to compete with larger and more global rivals like Toyota Motor Corp., Volkswagen AG and the alliance of Renault SA and Nissan Motor Co.

For many years, carmakers searching for the secret to small-car success would travel to Japan's Toyota City. Today, the destination is Poland's Tychy. Ever since the car manufacturer Fiat took over, Chrysler engineers from Detroit have been voyaging all the way to this Polish town, up until now more famous for its beer, to discover a car factory employing workers and managing to make a tidy profit! Fiat's plant in Tychy has hit a new production record. As of the end of October 2009 the facility rolled out 500,000 cars – up from the 492,000 produced in all of 2008. The plant is expected to exceed 600,000 units in 2009. At plants like Tychy, standards have been raised and the art of building smaller, fuel-efficient cars has been mastered. Chrysler has high hopes and believes that Fiat can do the same since assuming control.

At Tychy, the latest robotic technology is balanced by workers who can quickly shift models to match given demand. Today, the factory is running six full days a week. By contrast, most other car plants in Europe and the United States are running at a fraction of capacity. Fiat executives have several goals: to produce subcompact European models at Chrysler's North American plants and to teach Chrysler managers how to introduce smaller cars in the United States that Americans will want to buy, while increasing efficiency the way Fiat has done at its Tychy plant.

Mr Zdzislaw Arlet, the Tychy plant director, is always on the lookout for time- and money-saving improvements, adding that he himself looks to Toyota's famous Kaizen system for inspiration. For example, instead of filling up cars at different production points with brake fluid, petrol, water and other liquids, one machine on each of Tychy's three lines fills each vehicle. A car comes off the assembly line in less than a minute, half of what it took about 10 years ago. A new focus on quality has also been developed. About three years ago, workers were assigned an individual identification number that is stamped on whatever sections of the car they assemble so any problems at the end of the line can be traced to the source. *'At the moment, Tychy is the best of Fiat as far as quality is concerned'*, said Giuseppe Volpato, a professor of economics at the University of Venice who has long studied the company. *'I think Poland is becoming the reference point for the whole organization, even in Italy.'*

Source: ND Schwartz (2009) To shrink a US car, Chrysler goes to Poland, *The New York Times*, 14 July; Auto profits in Tychy, *Warsaw Business Journal*, 9 November 2009; Small cars, *The New York Times*, 22 November 2009; Fiat: Facts, Discussion Forum, and Encyclopedia Article, http://www.absoluteastronomy.com/topics/Fiat [accessed 22 November 2009].

THE BEST PRACTICES – THE HOLY GRAIL OF CONTEMPORARY BUSINESS?

Does the search for best practices place too much hope on discovering something new, something extraordinary, which does not exist? Many theoreticians and practitioners of management formulated and attempted to implement the 'Zero Inventory' or the 'Zero Defects' theory. From the beginning they were all too aware that they were striving to realize an unachievable goal, but this aim brought them closer to achieving better results than others. They failed to reach the absolute goal, perfection, but did become role models for others. The same goes for best practices. The comparison of the quest for best practices to the quest for the Holy Grail might also be a useful one. Striving to discover best practices is similar to the legendary search for the Holy Grail. To this day, nobody knows what the Holy Grail actually was or whether it actually existed. Despite long-term searches it has never been found. The same goes for the best practices.

Nevertheless, in the search for unique company success, business leaders allow themselves to discover all those things that lead to their achievement, which gives the company or institution an edge over the competition and proves its ability to achieve better results. Why, therefore, should one not aim to discover the basis for all these successes and make further attempts to transfer such experiences to the company? Such a shift may bring great benefits.

One can imagine a Sir Lancelot of the logistics and supply chain industry seeking the ultimate best practice without knowing what it is and whether it actually exists!

Notes

1 Axson, DAJ (2007) *Best Practices in Planning and Performance Management. From Data to Decisions*, 2nd edn, pp 59–60, John Wiley & Sons, Hoboken, NJ
2 http://www.allbusiness.com/company-activities-management/management-change-management/11796678-1.html [accessed 5 February 2009]
3 Axson, p 61
4 Axson, p 30
5 http://www.johnsmurf.com/jargon.htm [accessed 21 April 2009]
6 http://www.satisfice.com/blog/archives/27 [accessed 22 April 2009]
7 Brenner, R, *Worst Practices*, http://www.chacocanyon.com/pointlookout/071024.shtml [accessed 10 May 2009]
8 Ashton, C (1998) *Managing Best Practices*, p 12, Business Intelligence, London
9 http://en.wikipedia.org/wiki/GxP [accessed 30 October 2007]
10 When 'Best Practices' Become 'Worst Practices', http://www.brint.com/advisor/a110398.htm [accessed 13 May 2009]
11 http://www3.best-in-class.com/database [accessed 30 October 2006]
12 Elkington, J (1998) *Cannibals with Forks: The triple bottom line of the 21st century*, New Society Publishers, Stoney Creek, CT; and Elkington, J (2004) Enter the triple bottom line, in *The Triple Bottom Line: Does it all add up?*, ed A Henriques and J Richardson, pp 1–16, Earthscan, London
13 Peters, M (1996) The missing link, *Logistics Forum*, **4** (9), p 9
14 Spillan, JE, Vyas, BJ and Ziemnowicz, C (2004) Determinants of Poland's competitive advantage in the logistics sector, *Journal of East-West Business*, **9** (2), p 55
15 Spillan *et al*, p 55
16 Waters, CDJ (1999) Changing role of the retail sector in Poland during a period of economic transition, *International Journal of Retail & Distribution Management*, **27** (8), p 319
17 Spillan *et al*, p 53
18 Spillan *et al*, p 46
19 The new science. A survey of logistics, *Business Central Europe*, February 2001, p 45
20 See: http://www.paiz.gov.pl/index/?id=59112692262234e3fad47fa8eabf03a4
21 Ernst & Young (2008) *European Attractiveness Survey 2008*, Ernst & Young, London
22 Blanchard, D (2007) *Supply Chain Management Best Practices*, p 15, John Wiley & Sons, Hoboken, NJ

23 See real-life Polish case studies designed and developed in the Department of Logistics at WSE in: *Best Practices in Logistics and Supply Chain Management. The Case of Poland*, ed K Rutkowski, chapters 3–6, Warsaw School of Economics, Warsaw 2009; and *Najlepsze praktyki biznesowe w zarządzaniu łańcuchem dostaw*, ed K Rutkowski, Warsaw School of Economics, Warsaw 2008, Part II. Case studies completed by WSE and its partners during the BestLog project are available on the project webpage: www.bestlog.org

References

Carter, CR and Rogers, DS (2008) A framework of sustainable supply chain management: moving toward new theory, *International Journal of Physical Distribution and Logistics Management*, **38** (5), pp 360–87
Department of Logistics at WSE (2009) *Best Practices in Logistics and Supply Chain Management*, ed K. Rutkowski, Warsaw School of Economics

3

Trends and strategies in global logistics

Frank Straube, Arnfried Nagel and Daniel Rief,
Technische Universitaet Berlin

INTRODUCTION

Internationally successful companies have identified the importance of logistics as a management function. Public awareness of logistics has increased significantly, and its influence on strategic corporate decisions is strong. However, many companies are still in the process of defining the specific scope of responsibility for their logistics function and gearing their service networks towards the needs of their customers.[1] Reduced delivery times and adherence to defined delivery dates as well as completeness and accuracy of delivery are important criteria for increasing customer satisfaction through logistics services.

At the same time, worldwide megatrends such as internationalization of procurement, production and sales, increasing resource scarcity and energy costs are challenges for logistics managers and lead to new and changing requirements on the network competence of companies. As a result, overriding macroeconomic and social trends have an ongoing effect on the development of logistics. More than ever before, today's logistics managers are confronted with dynamic trends in corporate development, and dynamic trends are difficult to forecast. Future-oriented strategies must be able to adapt to nascent trends as early as possible, and logistics goals must be geared towards these trends. This is the only way to ensure the long-term success of a company. Besides globalization, other major logistics challenges are continuously arising, especially in the form of internationalization, increased security requirements and an increasing demand for ecological sustainability. Within the framework of this chapter, we discuss the evolution of megatrends in general and analyse the effects of three identified megatrends on logistics and supply chain management.

TREND RESEARCH

A challenging market environment paired with modern information and communication technology as well as continuously increasing global linkages and dependencies of economic systems lead to higher dynamics on enterprise levels. In addition, the increasing complexity of value chain systems makes future developments appear more uncertain than ever before.

Accordingly, companies are constrained to react to these constantly changing influences. Studying the past in order to make a future projection is suitable only to a limited extent. Rather, early detection of emerging developments and their influencing factors as well as anticipatory estimation of possible impacts is required.

Logistics in particular has been subjected to extensive change in the past four decades in order to meet the changing requirements and influences. This process is not yet complete, and in the future logistics will assume more tasks that go beyond its current scope. To face these changes in an efficient way and to stay competitive, future developments have to be forecast and understood. Then strategies can be adjusted to allow for and take advantage of upcoming trends.

The expression 'trend' is not to be considered as a temporary fashion or short-term fad; rather it can be understood as the tendency towards substantial changes in economic and social structures and processes that will take effect in the near future. Core characteristics of trends are their duration and the scope of their effects. For duration, the shortest trend interval is a season. Assuming a certain stability in the development of trends, research is limited to five years of observation. The scope of their effect differentiates the sectors of our society in which changes show up. Three types of trends can be distinguished:

- social trends that describe cultural and social changes;
- consumption trends that show the impact of social trends on goods and services;
- industry trends that reveal developments within an industry sector.

Based on the combination of duration and scope, different types of trend can be outlined. 'Hype' is when the scope of effects increases in a very short time, followed by an equally fast decrease. In comparison, a 'niche trend' has changes that do not reach a certain threshold or advance beyond a defined range of scope. These can have varying intensity and continue for an extended period. 'Real' trends, however, achieve the trend threshold after a period of about five years and usually decline after a further two to three years.

Economic and social developments that have a significantly greater scope, on a global scale, and often much longer duration – perhaps more than decades – are described as megatrends. In general, they characterize a large, powerful, sustained and clear direction of future developments.

MEGATRENDS

Persisting long-term megatrends create particular challenges for logistics managers and result in increasing demands on their network skills. In the context of three studies conducted at the Berlin Institute of Technology, different megatrends with long-term influence on value-adding networks – and thus on logistics – were analysed. In the following sub-sections, key results of the surveys into the megatrends of internationalization, security and ecological sustainability and their implications on logistics systems are considered in more detail.

Megatrend internationalization

The conditions for employment and execution of cross-border economic activities have improved significantly during the past century, and have led to an unprecedented amount of globally exchanged goods and globally dispersed value chains. Liberalization of markets, decreasing transportation costs and huge steps forward in information and communication technologies allow globally interconnected production systems – encouraging companies into a continuing process of internationalization to achieve growth in new markets and gain cost advantages in new locations.

In a rapidly changing environment, time is of major strategic importance for success when companies go global. On the one hand, companies need to manage the specific point in time when they penetrate a foreign market (particularly important in, for example, the current economic downturn), and on the other, the duration of the entire process of entering the foreign market is of decisive importance. In order to keep costs low, utilize assets as quickly as possible and implement business strategies, the internationalization process faces an enormous pressure on time.

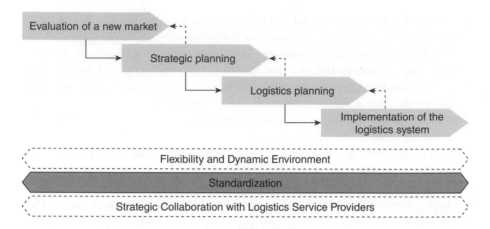

Figure 3.1 Framework of the internationalization process

In 1993 Miller suggested breaking internationalization down into a series of activities that gave access to foreign markets, with a framework that started with 'assessment' and finished with 'implementation'. Generally, all levels of decision making are integrated in such a process, starting with a top management strategic decision, handing over to middle management at a tactical level, and followed by operational tasks at the end. In practice, the internationalization process is more complex than this framework suggests and involves several business functions, and interdependencies are difficult to analyse. However, the simplification allows a structured and more detailed look at the different steps necessary for foreign market entry (as shown in Figure 3.1).

The following findings are based on a study of internationalization of logistics systems[2] that analyses how Chinese and German companies enter foreign markets:

1. *Evaluation of a new market.* This is triggered by the initial strategic idea of starting to work in a specific market or region. The internationalization process begins with comprehensive market analysis where top management evaluates the overall conditions in the target market. If the analysis shows that market entry is feasible and it is expected to meet the respective objectives, this first phase ends with the decision to enter the new market. Chinese and German respondents complete this step in between five and six months on average, meaning that this evaluation of the new market is the longest of all phases.
2. *Strategic planning.* Still at the top management level, in this phase foreign market entry is defined as a project, with a time schedule,

defined milestones, budgets and concrete objectives for different corporate functions. The result of this phase is a framework that will guide the functional divisions of the company in developing their plans of action to achieve the strategic objectives of foreign market entry. Compared with the evaluation of the new market, this phase is much shorter. Chinese respondents calculate less than three months, Germans slightly more than four months.

3. *Logistics planning.* With close cooperation between all relevant functions, inbound, outbound and in-house logistics operations are defined and implementation plans are developed. Relevant topics in logistics planning include the definition of service levels, intended lead times, inventory policy, network structure, capacity calculation, allocation of facilities (such as warehouses and cross-docks), IT integration, decisions about logistics outsourcing, and preparation of tenders. Chinese respondents stated that this phase accounts for nearly two months, German companies need slightly more than three months. This phase has the shortest duration for both Chinese and German companies, which shows the tremendous time pressure under which these complex logistics structures are being planned.

4. *Implementation of the logistics system.* This is where managers find out whether their plans and decisions made in the early phases meet the requirements of the real world. The work in this phase is at an operational level and the organization must have comprehensive problem-solving skills, as unexpected occurrences and developments can raise a lot of unexpected difficulties. Owing to its complexity and the necessity for the success of internationalization, implementing the final logistics system is comparatively time-consuming, with 4.2 months at Chinese and 4.9 months at German companies.

Overall, Chinese companies indicate that the complete internationalization process lasts for approximately 14 months. German companies exceed that, with an average of almost 18 months.

The internationalization process addresses aspects of cross-functional as well as cross-company integration as a top-down process, from the initial idea to enter a foreign market to the closing implementation. The huge numbers of locations, intermediaries and suppliers involved in logistics networks, as well as customers working with different methods, procedures and conditions, always make global logistics a complex task. One proven way of reducing complexity in this area is by standardizing processes. However, since different countries and regions have market-specific conditions and requirements, logisticians need to balance globally standardized procedures with local adjustments to deal with the heterogeneity and complexity of international networks.

For an individual company the range of processes to be standardized differs according to its industry and business models. All kinds of inbound, in-house and outbound processes could be subject to standardization. One might think of boxes and pallets used to transport and store goods, order cycles and replenishment strategies, the application of milk runs and Kanban systems, production scheduling, the design and layout of cross-docks and warehouses, the use of Auto ID technologies etc.

In practice, standardized logistics processes are more or less equally widespread in all three sectors – industry, trade and services. In a study of trends and strategies in logistics,[3] a survey found that a minority of 10 to 15 per cent of companies currently operate without any standardized processes at all. By 2015, this figure will have fallen to between 3 and 8 per cent across all sectors. Across all surveyed companies, the plans for the period up to 2015 indicate a particularly strong trend towards worldwide standardization. According to these findings, the share of industrial companies with worldwide logistics standards will increase from today's figure of 25 per cent to 65 per cent, while the increase in the trading sector will be from 25 per cent today to 50 per cent in 2015. This shows that a high percentage of the surveyed companies have recognized the relevance and potential of globally standardized logistics processes as a means of integrating existing locations (see Figure 3.2).

There are many reasons for the worldwide introduction of standardized processes – one factor that is of key significance in all sectors is the desire to cut costs and reduce complexity. Eighty-five per cent of the surveyed industrial companies and 81 per cent of their trading counterparts name cost reduction as the primary driver of global standards. In addition to reducing costs, 78 to 83 per cent of companies believe that standardized logistics processes can also help to reduce complexity. Across all sectors, the focus of the surveyed companies is on the simplification or standardization of existing structures. In addition to reducing complexity and simplifying interfaces, 84 per cent of industrial companies and 77 per cent of trading companies name supply chain control as a further motive for the standardization of logistics processes (see Figure 3.3).

In the endeavour to maximize the efficiency of logistics processes by standardization, however, each company must decide for itself whether it can employ standardized processes worldwide or to what extent it needs to adapt processes to local conditions. Successful companies often base their internationalization concept on a global strategy that they can adapt to local circumstances as and when needed – in line with the motto 'think global, act local'.

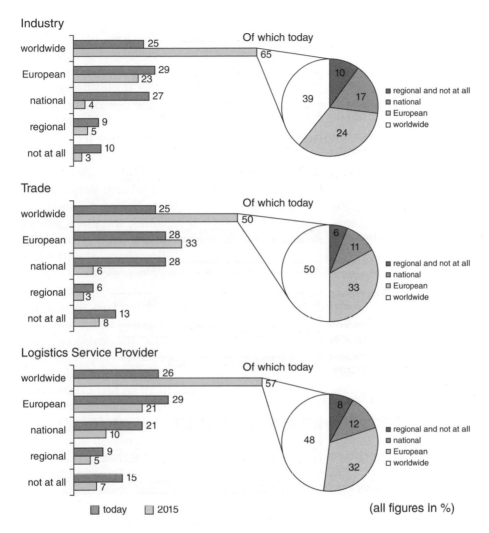

Figure 3.2 Implementation of cross-plant standardization of logistics processes
Source: Straube and Pfohl, 2008, p 97

Megatrend security

Since the number of attacks against vehicles and logistical infrastructure has increased in recent years, a lot of attention has been paid to securing supply chains against terrorism: laws and regulations have been enacted, private initiatives like TAPA[4] have been founded, standards have been established, new technologies have been developed and security

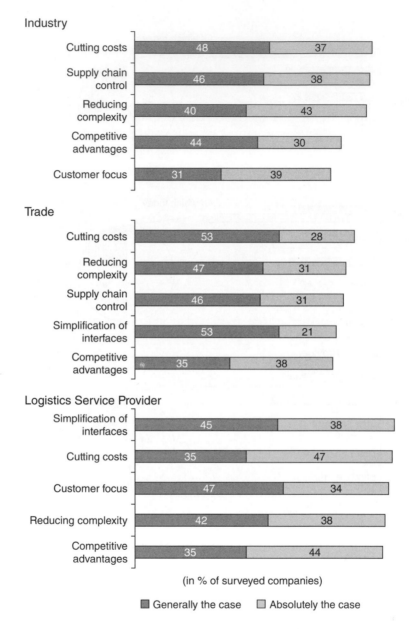

Figure 3.3 Top 5 reasons for the introduction of global standards
Source: Straube and Pfohl, 2008, p 99

management has been improved. Besides terrorism, supply chains have always been confronted with crime. Though many companies still consider supply chain security to be a cumbersome requirement imposed by legislation, other companies recognize that the provision of supply chain security can also be a step towards customer orientation and thus a competitive advantage.

A measured response to the worldwide security and risk situation and the ability to handle risks in an appropriate manner can be key factors in the success of modern companies. These risks include the threats posed by crime and terrorism as well as risks on the procurement or sales front. Risks on the procurement and sales sides can be caused by such things as capacity bottlenecks in the procurement market, transport damage, a lack of transport and storage space or changes in consumer preferences. In addition, companies are also increasingly exposed to the risk of organized crime or terrorism, and this impacts the security situation in the logistics network.

The findings in the Trends and Strategies study on the impact of increasing security requirements and risks in the logistics network on logistics activities show that around one in three respondents across all sectors already feel affected to a high or extremely high degree. The companies saying that these factors have little or very little effect on their logistics activities are still in the majority (between 38 and 43 per cent, depending on sector), but this picture is expected to change in years to come. The percentage of companies that feel affected to a high or extremely high degree will increase by around 20 per cent across all sectors up to the year 2015.

According to our respondents, the main drivers to gear their activities towards the issues of security and risk are the need to improve processes and the expectations of customers. The most important driver for industrial companies is the need to improve processes, while customer expectations are the key factor for the trading sector and logistics service providers. Eighty per cent of service providers name customer expectations in their answer. The third main driver is security regulations, which impact the activities of industrial companies and service providers but play only a secondary role for the trading sector (see Figure 3.4).

While laws, regulations or norms make high demands on companies, there is often a lack of practicable tools, concepts and research findings that would enable companies to increase security and tackle risks under their own steam. Up to one in three surveyed companies lack knowledge in the areas of security (when it comes to choosing safe transport routes and means of transport, for example), shipment tracking, location planning and security management. There is still a great deal of untapped research potential in the field of risk management. There is a lack of practicable tools and concepts, particularly for cross-company supply-chain-wide

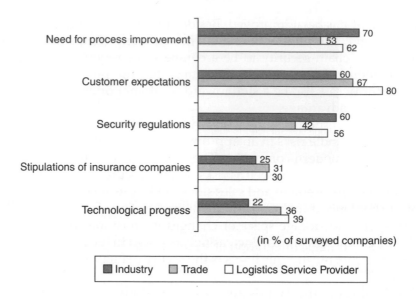

Figure 3.4 Main drivers for implementing security and risk issues
Source: Straube and Pfohl, 2008, p 83

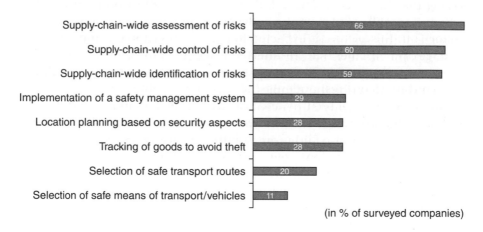

Figure 3.5 Lack of tools and concepts
Source: Straube and Pfohl, 2008, p 85

identification, assessment and control of risks. One of the key challenges in this respect is the assessment of the probability and damaging impact of potential risks in the supply chain (see Figure 3.5).

Alongside the development of suitable tools, successful handling of risks in logistics networks also depends on cooperation between the

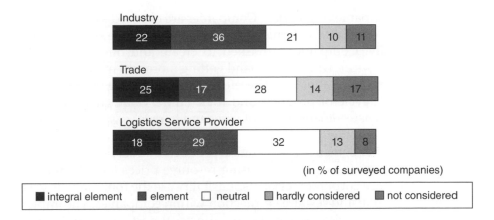

Figure 3.6 Strategic integration of security and risk aspects

Source: Straube and Pfohl, 2008, p 87

companies in a logistics network. The precondition is the kind of mutual trust that ensures a uniform understanding of risks and adequate transparency of processes within the network. This in turn can improve security.

Successful integration of a security and risk management system is only possible if this system is firmly integrated from a strategic and organizational point of view. Security and risk aspects are incorporated in the logistics strategy of many companies. Service providers in particular (58 per cent) describe these topics as part or even an integral part of their logistics strategy. Only 21 per cent say that security and risk play little or no role in their strategy. The integration of security and risk aspects in the logistics strategy is also fairly common in industry (47 per cent) and in the trading sector (42 per cent), even if this is not something the majority of companies do. In industry as well, 21 per cent of companies say that these aspects play little or no role in their logistics strategy, compared to 31 per cent in the trading sector (see Figure 3.6). This underlines the fact that companies recognize the strategic importance of the topic and assign responsibility for this topic to an appropriate organizational level. The entire company is exposed to security threats and risks, and these risks need to be addressed holistically.

Megatrend ecological sustainability

Owing to climate change, increasing environmental destruction and the depletion of natural resources, an enhanced public awareness of protecting the environment and natural resources is noticeable. Thus, the ecological pressure on companies is growing. Companies are exposed to meeting the demand of internal and external stakeholders to operate economically and ecologically. Companies are asked to create and offer sustainable products and services, with this demand getting more and more important owing to different stakeholders. Therefore, the challenging objective is to analyse the life cycle of products and their entire value chain from an environmentally sustainable point of view and to meet customer requirements at the same time.[5]

Rising customer demands for ecological products and services, increasing global regulations (eg CO_2 trade), rising resource prices (eg oil) and the demand for more corporate social responsibility are the four main drivers for environmental and resource protection within companies. The implementation of ecological sustainability affects almost every unit of a company, especially logistics and supply chain management. An essential requirement for logistics, for example, is the reduction of greenhouse gases. It is estimated that today, up to 75 per cent of a company's carbon footprint, ie CO_2 emissions, results from transportation and logistics. Hence, logistics needs to highlight the current need for 'green' solutions.

In the following, the relevance and fields of action for companies for ecological sustainability in logistics will be discussed in more detail. This will convey the potential of optimization and spheres of activity. The results are based on the Global Logistics 2015+ study.[6]

Relevance for companies

Global Logistics 2015+ reveals that environmentally compatible logistics is a relevant issue but has not yet reached the status of a top priority for many companies.[7] The majority of the sample (60 per cent) expect that an absence of green logistics by 2015 may even lead to financially tangible disadvantages. However, interviews revealed that most companies have just begun to put a focus on the greenness of their logistics. The first steps in a green logistics direction were taken (eg reduction in/avoidance of transport and energy) – however, these are rather generic objectives applying only to a particular 'environmental issue'. The majority of the companies have no concrete goals, measures or holistic approaches in order to achieve ecologically sustainable solutions for logistics processes. This is often caused by a shortage of standards, tools and methods, leaving respondents to wait for concrete legal requirements and guidance (for, say, CO_2 emissions). The exact impact of logistics systems on the environment is largely unknown. In the study, 70 per cent of the participants identified a need for tools that measure the overall environmental impact of logistics. Existing tools and methods are sometimes not known or not fully deployable in practice.

Regarding the financing of such projects or green logistics in general, it was determined that in most cases only very limited or no budgets were available. Passing on additional costs to the end customers is not considered a viable option. Only 16 per cent of the respondents believe that their customers display willingness to spend extra money for environmentally compatible products or services.

The status quo and fields of action for ecological sustainability in logistics

Some approaches to implementing environmental compatible logistics systems display remarkable growth in the future. Many companies are planning to implement these approaches by 2015. The fields of growth are:

- *Transportation and packaging.* An environmentally friendly design for transportation and packaging has been regarded as the highest priority for companies in order to achieve green logistics. Considering transportation, an increase of efficiency can be generated in the short term, for example by improving capacity utilization and avoiding empty runs (eg through bundling and route planning wherever possible). Furthermore, 19 per cent of the sample want to utilize intermodal transportation and 44 per cent plan to increase the use of renewable energy sources in their vehicle fleets. The majority of participants aim to realize a twofold benefit, since both higher capacity utilization and a reduction in the level of transport activity lead to a reduction in environmental pollution and also a reduction in costs (see Figure 3.7).

    Companies take various steps towards designing less environmentally harmful packaging. Some companies are specifically applying reusable boxes and containers. However, interviewees did point out that for long-distance transport they need to evaluate whether the ecological and economic effects actually necessitate or even legitimate their use of reusable boxes and containers. Furthermore, the recycling of packaging materials (eg biodegradable materials) was frequently mentioned as a means to increase environmental compatibility.
- *Environmentally friendly sourcing.* Achieving 'greener' business in many cases also includes the involvement of partners. One trend is environmental sourcing, where companies seek to audit their suppliers' greenness or preferably purchase goods certified for their environmental compatibility. Interviewees even stated that they would consider terminating business relationships as a result of inferior environmental compatibility of their suppliers or their products. However, in many cases interviewees would generally be willing to support their suppliers

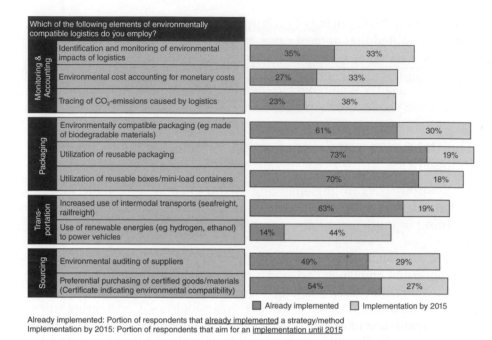

Figure 3.7 Fields of growth for ecologically sustainable logistics
Source: Own illustration according to Straube and Borkowski, 2008, p 55

in the search for solutions in the case of poor results in environmental audits. Ultimately, this reveals another important driver for companies' (and suppliers') environmentally friendly behaviour.

- *Involvement and cooperation with logistics service providers (LSPs)*. LSPs will also play an important role in achieving environmentally compatible logistics. Since companies have almost fully outsourced transportation and major portions of warehousing in many cases, these companies particularly demand LSPs' involvement in their green efforts and require LSPs to ecologically improve their existing logistics services. Forty-five per cent state that they already take LSPs' greenness into consideration upon selection during tenders. This is achieved by demanding certifications and standards (eg ISO, EU emission standards). However, only 23 per cent of the sample are able or willing to spend extra money to employ greener transport. Environmentally friendly transport cannot be established at the expense of the service level since only 12 per cent consider lower service levels (eg longer lead times or less frequent deliveries) acceptable in exchange for more environmentally friendly operations. Thus, LSPs are asked to improve the environmental

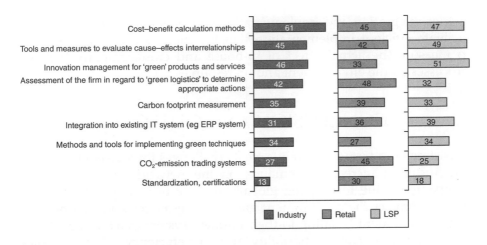

Figure 3.8 Lack of tools and concepts
Source: Straube and Pfohl, 2008, p 69

compatibility of their services while leaving service and cost levels unchanged. By 2015, approximately 45 per cent of the respondents will contract third parties to manage environmental issues. It is still not clearly predictable to what extent LSPs will take over this task, although it is clear that LSPs will consult their customers when designing environmentally compatible logistics on the operational, tactical and strategic level.

- *Measurement and evaluation.* As mentioned earlier, many companies have not yet determined the level of environmental compatibility of their logistics. Thus, identification of drivers, measurement of greenness and evaluation of environmental impact are important steps towards the development of sustainable logistics. By taking into account all activities for achieving environmentally compatible logistics, the measurement and evaluation of environmental impact (eg damage caused to health, damage caused to the environment, CO_2 emissions and monetary costs) will increase most. The Trends and Strategies study intensively analyses the topic of measurement and evaluation. The results underline the fact that there is an absence of suitable tools, concepts and research results across and throughout all three sectors (see Figure 3.8).

It can be observed that there is a lack of strategic concepts that companies can use to determine their own positioning and sensitivity in order to arrive at tailored and effective courses of action. There is a lack of cost–benefit calculations to serve as a basis for these decisions. There is also a lack of integration and implementation concepts and tools that would facilitate efficient implementation. Finally, there is a lack of methods to measure the actual effect of in-house and cross-company logistics processes on the environment and on resources.

CONCLUSION AND OUTLOOK

Persisting long-term megatrends create challenges for logistics managers and result in increasing demands on the network skills of today's companies – due to ongoing globalization, security requirements, the need to protect the environment and spare resources and, last but not least, requirements relating to their business systems such as customer-differentiated reliability, flexibility and cost-efficiency. Many logistics managers need an extended scope of customer-focused responsibility (end-to-end), stronger integration in corporate strategy and organizational structures, better operationalization of logistics goals, more transparency in the area of logistics costs and a stronger focus on innovative cross-company projects.

At present, many companies still focus their efforts on internal processes and operational goals. But the picture is different in different companies and also varies from sector to sector. The majority of companies have still not implemented holistic responsibility concepts for the customer-to-customer process, and this is something that will require major effort. The trading sector has been successful with its end-to-end implementation concepts based on the idea of reverse integration and has therefore made more progress in some areas than many industrial companies.

The analyses in these studies show that very few surveyed companies have already attained a high level of logistics network maturity. When formulating their logistics goals, companies react to global challenges by prioritizing service-level-oriented logistics goals, which in some areas take precedence over cost goals. This applies above all to global and fragmented logistics networks with high outsourcing levels and qualities.

In future, cooperation in global networks will increasingly depend on how successful the various players are in identifying the key central trends and then integrating the resulting tasks in their value systems, strategies and operational logistics systems. The 'best' companies strategically integrate their logistics activities in the overall business system. They have recognized the benefits of logistics and can measure these benefits. This means they are able to create a higher end-to-end scope of responsibility and to successfully complete strategic projects. As a result, they already achieve provable cost advantages by implementing successful outsourcing projects in a globalized corporate environment with the emphasis on sustainable solutions.

In doing so, they succeed in arriving at a holistic assessment of risks and opportunities throughout the entire network (end-to-end) and coordinating these risks and opportunities with their network partners, and this is ultimately what enables them to develop a focused network strategy. This strategy is based on, among other things, frequent use of horizontal cooperation models and a standardized network-wide assessment procedure for their suppliers and service providers.

Moreover, the 'best' are increasingly using supra-regional and cross-border benchmarking systems on a regular basis – primarily to identify network-wide optimization potential. We assume that benchmarking in this area is not designed solely to allow comparisons but also serves as a management concept. This would mean that it would be justified to claim that the 'best' review and compare their logistics performance and skills on a regular basis. They use the resulting insights to identify best practices geared towards further optimization and adaptation – and then implement these practices globally.

Notes

1   Cf. Straube and Pfohl (2008), p 6
2   Cf. Straube *et al* (2008). In the survey, 70 Chinese and 50 German companies from industry and retail were interviewed.
3   Cf. Straube and Pfohl (2008). In the survey, 1,300 executives from logistics and supply chain management across Europe, the United States and China were interviewed.
4   The Transported Asset Protection Association (TAPA) is a unique forum that unites global manufacturers, logistics providers, freight carriers, law enforcement agencies and other stakeholders with the common aim of reducing losses from international supply chains.
5   Cf. Beamon (1999), p 341
6   Cf. Straube and Borkowski (2008). In the survey, 111 executives from logistics and supply chain management from leading companies were interviewed. Additionally, 19 interviews were conducted with selected participants to validate the findings.
7   Flexibility and robustness had the highest priority for the participants in the survey.

References

Beamon, BM (1999) Designing the green supply chain, *Logistics Information Management*, **12** (4), pp 332–42

Miller, MM (1993) Executive insights: a road map for creating profitable operations in foreign markets – a case study, *Journal of International Marketing*, **1** (4), pp 91–102

Straube, F and Borkowski, S (2008) *Global Logistics 2015+: How the world's leading companies turn their logistics flexible, green and global and how this affects logistics service providers*, Universitätsverlag der TU Berlin

Straube, F and Pfohl, H-C (2008) *Trends und Strategien in der Logistik – Globale Netzwerke im Wandel*, Bremen

Straube, F, Ma, S and Bohn, M (2008) *Internationalization of Logistics Systems: How Chinese and German companies enter foreign markets*, Springer, Berlin

4

Incentives and the strategic management of suppliers

Glyn Watson, Chris Lonsdale and Joe Sanderson,
University of Birmingham

As far as the modern discipline of microeconomics is concerned, incentives play a central role in supplier management. Indeed, arguably they play the central role. It is incentives (in the form of gains from trade) that bring buyers and suppliers together in the first place, and it is incentives that govern the nature of that relationship thereafter. Incentives determine the decision to outsource, the choice of trading partner and the depth of trading relationship, as well as the terms of trade. Without incentives there would be no suppliers and there would be no supply management.

This is hardly a controversial assertion; today's microeconomics rests upon it. However, when surveying the existing literature on the subject it becomes clear that literature is not so much wrong as incomplete. This is because the preponderance of what has been written treats the firm as though it were a black box. Profit optimization is assumed to be axiomatic, with both parties striving to maximize the returns to their respective shareholders. Because this is the case, activities within the firm are held to be of second-order importance.

However, such a belief sits uncomfortably with the everyday experience of supply managers. A supply manager is acutely aware that his or her choices are not made in a vacuum. They are highly political in that they have an impact, not only on the supplier, but on other actors within the firm. Some choices leave supply managers pushing at an open door, in that they find a receptive audience among internal stakeholders. Other choices are more controversial, though. They unsettle a status quo to which a stakeholder has become accustomed, or finds profitable. Where such is the case, supply managers can count on finding themselves opposed. Where such a stakeholder is powerful, he or she is able to exercise a veto over what is being proposed.

This chapter seeks to describe the role played by incentives in supply management. Using mainstream analysis, it covers the traditional literature on interorganizational relationships. However, it also examines the politics of supply management, and particularly the potential influence of powerful internal actors on the supply management process.

COLLABORATION VS COMPETITION AND THE ROLE OF INCENTIVES IN THE EXCHANGE PROCESS

All exchange involves elements of both cooperation and competition. Assuming that the parties concerned have voluntarily agreed to the deal, the very act of signing a contract is a cooperative activity. The vendor (or seller) is getting something that it wants – cash – while the buyer is getting something it wants – the products and services supplied by the vendor. However, the cooperative aspects of an exchange can (and frequently do) go beyond this. Buyers and sellers can actively work together to streamline the contracting process and/or adapt/develop the vendor's products and services so that they more closely match the requirements of the buyer. The creation of such value-adding relationships has today become a staple of supply chain management.

Buyers and sellers are also in competition, however. While both sides gain from a trade (else why trade in the first instance), it is not necessary for both sides to gain equally for a trade to take place. For the buyer, the aim is to get value for money from a deal. If it is a rational agent, this means maximum value for money. Every time it is able to negotiate the contract price down a notch, the value for money that is obtained increases. Of course, for the vendor, passing value to its customers means smaller profits. Economists refer to the contested ground that exists between the two parties to a trade as the surplus value. Surplus value is the difference between the value that the customer places on the vendor's products (ie the customer's utility function) and the supplier's costs of production. That portion of the contested ground that passes to

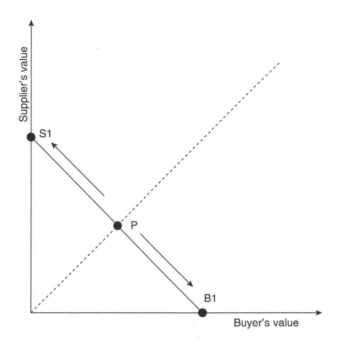

Figure 4.1　Conflict and the exchange process

the customer is said to be the consumer surplus, while that which is retained by the vendor is the producer surplus. This competitive element is represented in Figure 4.1, where the potential returns (or surplus value) are assumed to be fixed (B1–S1). However, the proportion of the returns that falls to the buyer increases the closer the contract price moves towards the x-axis. Conversely, the returns to the buyer increase the closer the contract price moves towards the y-axis. Where the contract price falls equidistant between B1 and S1, the gains from trade are shared equally (point P). Typically this is referred to in the literature as a win–win. Figure 4.2 depicts the value-adding nature of some relationships. Here, the surplus value is not fixed, but as a result of cooperation it increases from B1–S1 to B2–S2.

However, even when buyers and sellers increase the cooperative element of an exchange by actively working together to add value to the relationship, the competitive element to it remains, ie cooperative relationships can be adversarial or non-adversarial. This is because the fruits of the cooperation (in the form of either lower production costs for the vendor or a higher valuation of the vendor's products on the part of the customer) have to be divided up. If, for example, the effect of collaboration is to reduce the supplier's costs by £100 a unit, there would be

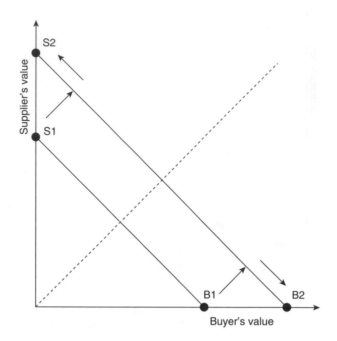

Figure 4.2 Cooperation and the exchange process

an issue about whether the vendor should pass all of the savings on to the customer or whether it should retain some of them in the form of higher profits. Alternatively, if the supplier invests £100 in developing its products and as a result increases the value to the customer by £200, should the vendor raise its prices by £100 to cover just the cost of the investment, or by the full £200?

Figure 4.3 illustrates this dual dimension to the exchange process. In Figure 4.3 the two parties start the relationship at point P1, which sits above the point where the dotted line (which runs 45° from the origin) bisects the line of surplus value. Ex ante, therefore, while the association operated to the advantage of both parties, it benefited the vendor more than it did the buyer. Ex post, after the contract price has shifted to point P2, this is still true. The diagram clearly shows that the gains from collaboration have been mutual. This is because point P2 sits both above and to the right of point P1 (indicated by the shaded triangle). And whenever a new contract price moves to the right of the original settlement it indicates a gain to the buyer; whenever it moves above the original settlement point, the vendor has gained also. This is what economists refer to as a Pareto improvement. However, while both parties have gained from the collaborative process, they have not gained equally. The vendor is

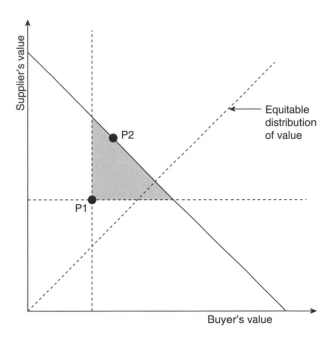

Figure 4.3   Cooperation and conflict in the exchange process: supplier-dominated supplier development

still, relatively speaking, the better off (because the contract price sits above the dotted diagonal line, which indicates an equitable settlement).

Whether a relationship is predominantly adversarial or has a significant cooperative component, what determines who wins out in this competitive process are the incentive structures that underpin the exchange relationship. Take, for example, the vendor that finds itself in a highly competitive market where its many customers are free to pick and choose where they buy their goods and services. Such a context forces the vendor into a Dutch auction in which it is forced constantly to drop its prices to buy its customer's business. In such a situation, the surplus value is bound to pass to the consumer (ie towards the x-axis). Compare that to a situation in which a particular customer has invested heavily in the vendor's technologies, even building the value proposition that it offers its own customers around the technologies of a particular supplier. This happened in the case of the PC market where PC manufacturers fell over themselves to advertise the fact that their machines had 'Intel inside'. In the end, it became impossible for PC manufacturers to compete unless they were able to make this boast. Unfortunately, this had the effect of handing enormous leverage over to Intel and as a result the surplus value passed from the consumer to the producer (ie towards the y-axis).

Consequently, much of supply management is reduced to game between poachers and gamekeepers in which the vendor assumes the role of the poacher (trying to 'steal' its customers' scarce financial resources), while the procurement manager assumes the role of the gamekeeper, in trying to stop them. What follows is a cat and mouse game in which, through a combination of guile and the development of distinctive capabilities, the vendor attempts to close markets, while the buyer's procurement manager responds in kind with a range of counter-strategies, designed to stop its vendors by keeping its supply markets contested. To the victor go the spoils. Power (formally defined as the ability of one party to adversely affect the interests of another) and the pursuit of power are at the heart of the exchange process (Lukes, 1974; Cox, Sanderson and Watson, 2000; Cox et al, 2002).

To some, it might appear that the competitive elements of an exchange have been overstated. While it is true that some people in life are maximizers (ie they are always looking for the highest possible return from a deal), critics would argue that most people are in fact happy just to 'satisfice' (ie obtain a settlement that provides them with a deal that they can live with). If two people cooperate on a venture, then generally speaking those people are happy to split the proceeds. This may or may not be true; it is hard to say. What is true, however, is that such an approach is suboptimal and imprudent. That satisficing is suboptimal should be self-evident. The fact that it is also imprudent needs further elaboration.

The issue of prudence arises in a number of contexts. First, it puts the profitability and even the survival of a firm at risk. The reason that firms come into business in the first instance is to make a return for shareholders. While it is true, as a number of resource-based writers have observed, that markets are often heterogeneous (ie they are capable of supporting laggards as well as world beaters), it is not true that markets are infinitely forgiving of the weak (Peteraf, 1993). Firms that fall too far behind the competitive frontier are on borrowed time. Firms that forget about the competitive elements of an exchange, however, risk seeing their costs rise and falling behind the competitive frontier.

The second problem with cooperation and trust is that it demonstrates an unwarranted confidence in the capacity/willingness of others to reciprocate. Many firms that acquire leverage are happy to use it. Even those who do not possess a structural advantage may attempt to use guile instead, where they think it will pay off for them. Furthermore, denials that this is not true cannot be taken at face value (Williamson, 1985). The thing about people is that very few of them are honest all of the time. One only has to reflect on one's own experience to see that this is true.

According to business economists, economic agents are not simply self-interested but they pursue this self-interest with guile – not all of the time, but sufficiently often that opportunism is a fact of commercial life. What permits the existence of opportunism is two things: a lack of honesty (obviously); and a lack of transparency between buyers and sellers. Economists distinguish between public and private information (Molhow, 1997). Information is regarded as public if it involves something that is widely known. Information is regarded as private when access to it is restricted. When 'restriction' means that one side in an exchange knows something that the other side does not, then an information asymmetry is said to exist. It is information asymmetry that permits dishonesty to pay.

Business opportunism exists in a number of forms but for buyers the three guises in which it is most common are adverse selection, moral hazard and hold-up. Adverse selection is ex ante opportunism or mis-representation that arises prior to the signing of a contract. Shorthand definitions of the concept might revolve around buying a 'lemon' or being sold a 'turkey'. The scope for adverse selection varies but is more common under some circumstances than others. Commentators often distinguish between search, experience and credence goods. Search goods are products that allow buyers to make systematic comparisons prior to a purchase. They are normally tangible products like chairs, pens or iron ingots. Experience goods, by contrast, are products that can only be evaluated subsequent to purchase. Typically, they include services like cinemas or restaurants. However, the category can also include tangible products like cars or records. The final category of good is the credence good. Credence goods defy easy evaluation, even after consumption. They include intangible services such as advertising, consultancy or medical services. What makes evaluation so hard usually comes down to a difficulty with attributing blame or success. For example, a piece of professional advice might have been responsible for a commercial disaster. However, the blame might lie with some other concomitant factor. The point is that where pre-contractual evaluation of a product is difficult – either because evaluation is inherently difficult or because the buyer lacks the resources or expertise to undertake it – the buyer is open to the risk of adverse selection. Experience goods and credence goods, by definition, are difficult to evaluate prior to purchase.

If adverse selection involves being suckered before a contract is signed, moral hazard and hold-up involve being suckered once a party has signed on the dotted line. Moral hazard is concerned with shortfalls in effort. For example, prior to an agreement, a consultancy company might promise to dedicate its best staff to the task of servicing the client and set its costs accordingly. Unbeknown to the client, however, once the contract has been secured, the work is passed down to junior colleagues whose time is charged out at inflated rates. Alternatively, moral hazard may involve charging a client for materials that were never used or which were used but which came from another job and which had been paid for by another client.

Hold-up occurs as a result of an extended association with a supplier, where the terms of the association cannot be fully specified in advance and where the association requires one of the parties to incur significant sunk and/or switching costs. As, with time, the full requirements of the relationship are revealed, this combination of factors allows the non-dependent party to renegotiate the terms of the deal in ways that are most favourable to it. According to some observers (Klein, 1980), it is the incompleteness of the original agreement that gives rise to the need for subsequent renegotiation. However, for Williamson it is the existence of high sunk and switching costs, in combination with the initial uncertainty, which is the source of the problem. It is this that can support blatantly opportunistic behaviour in which the non-dependent party is even able to renege on promises that are covered by a legal agreement. The calculation here is that any benefit that can be obtained through legal redress will be insufficient to compensate for the damage to, or loss of, the relationship. The dominant party is in a position to leverage the weaker party up until the point where it is more profitable for the weaker party to exit from the relationship than to continue to be extorted. Economists refer to the return enjoyed by the dominant party as a quasi-rent.

This is illustrated in Figure 4.4, where both parties start with equal power and an initial settlement point P1. As a result of the dedicated investments made in support of the relationship, the surplus value increases from B1–S1 to B2–S2. Based on the initial agreement, the buyer has an expectation that the final contract price will locate somewhere around point P2, and that the distribution of benefits in the relationship will remain equitable. In effect the relationship will deliver a win–win. However, in this case it is the buyer, rather than the supplier, who has made all of the dedicated investments. Based on the supplier's calculation of the buyer's sunk and switching costs, this allows the supplier to push the actual contract price to P3. This leaves the buyer worse off than it had been at the start of the relationship. However, it is still more efficient for the buyer to agree to the contract price than it is for it to write off the sunk and switching costs. Only if the supplier attempts to push the buyer beyond the threshold that marks the buyer's next-best option does it make sense for the buyer to exit from the relationship.

Regardless of whether Williamson is right and hold-up is the product of strategic behaviour, or Klein is right and it is the product of the need to recalibrate the relationship as future contingencies become known, the relationship still needs to be renegotiated. This renegotiation, though it can deliver gains for both sides, is still a competitive process.

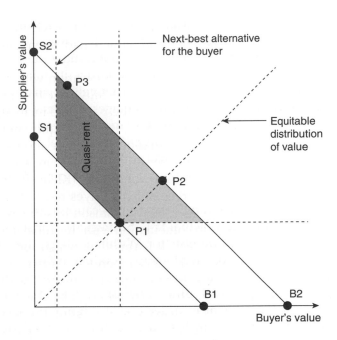

Figure 4.4 Sunk and switching costs, and the problem of hold-up

INCENTIVIZATION AND THE QUESTION OF MAKE VS BUY

Nowhere are the issues of competition between buyers and sellers more acute than with respect to outsourcing. This is evidenced by the fact that so many outsourced contracts go wrong. One survey found that in only 5 per cent of cases did outsourcing prove to be an unqualified success (details of this survey are reported in Lonsdale and Cox, 1998). More often than not, respondents indicated that it was something of a curate's egg (that is, good in parts). Thirty-nine per cent of respondents in the survey said that their outsourced contracts were simultaneously moderately successful and moderately unsuccessful. Of course, this may have something to do with the way in which the contracts were managed. (The issue of contractual mismanagement will be discussed in the next section.) Such is the scale of disappointment, however, that it suggests that something deeper than simply poor contracting is at work.

On the face of it, the decision to outsource should not be particularly problematic. It should involve a simple cost comparison between the expenses associated with undertaking the activity in-house as opposed to the expenses associated with contracting it out. For example, the size of the firm's requirement might be insufficient to cover the fixed costs associated with production in an efficient fashion. Under these conditions, sourcing externally, from a firm that can amortize its fixed costs more efficiently, might make eminent sense. Alternatively, a particular activity might be suffering from a lack of effective managerial oversight. Managerial time within the firm is a scarce resource and most of it tends to be devoted to the firm's key activities. Residual activities tend to get overlooked and production suffers as a result. It is this thinking that in effect underpins much of the core competence writing. If your firm can't do something well, find another firm that can.

Outsourcing tends to go wrong, however, because it exposes the firm to either a strategic or a contractual risk. Strategic risk arises if the firm outsources its competitive differentiator. Within strategy, there are three types of differentiation: cost leadership, product differentiation and niche production (Porter, 1980). In each case the firm is attempting to achieve the same thing through differentiation, ie break the relationship between cost, price and profit in order that it might earn an economic rent or sustained producer surplus. In a competitive marketplace, the consumer's ability to pick and choose between alternative vendors drives the firm's prices down towards the marginal cost of production. This is the last thing a firm wants.

In the case of cost leadership, the firm is attempting to earn a rent by developing a uniquely efficient production process that is difficult for its competitors to imitate through the creation of ex post barriers to entry. So long as the firm is able to stave off competitive imitation it can afford to drop its prices below those of its competitors and still make a higher return. In the case of product differentiation, by contrast, the firm is attempting to develop a superior utility proposition for the customer. The idea here is that when people comparison-shop and realize that the firm's products are better than those of its competitors, they will be prepared to pay a premium for the product that offers the higher utility. Again, its ability to sustain its producer surplus and turn it into a rent is contingent upon its capacity to hinder or retard competitive imitation. Finally, niche production also seeks to target customer's utility. This it achieves, however, not by creating relatively superior products but by servicing segments of a marketplace that nobody else is particularly interested in.

Because being able to differentiate competitively is so valuable to the firm (and indeed it is what strategy is all about), firms must be able to protect those resources and capabilities that generate the differentiation in the first place. However, if the firm outsources such a resource or capability then the odds are that it will end up paying to its supplier the rent that it should be earning for itself.

Outsourcing can also expose the firm to significant contractual risk (moral hazard and hold-up). Again, this involves the surplus value passing to the vendor, rather than being retained by the consumer. Sustaining the performance of a vendor depends upon a firm's ability to monitor or motivate it. Monitoring becomes more difficult after a competence has been outsourced because either the staff that used to manage the activity move onto the supplier's payroll, or else they are lost from the equation altogether. Once the organization lacks the resource, or at least resource that is sufficiently qualified to exercise proper oversight, the supplier starts to renege on its commitments.

Avoiding the risks of hold-up in an outsourced relationship involves maintaining motivational incentive. Such motivation might take the form of a carrot (bonuses for good performance) or a stick (the cancellation of the contract if the performance is poor). But in order for the incentive structure to work, the threat of sanctions as a last resort must be credible. This means being able to monitor the supplier to see if it is complying with the terms of the deal; and having the ability to punish the supplier (by invoking penalties or by threatening exit), if it is not. Imagine a myopic and doddery old teacher trying to keep discipline in a playground if his head teacher has told him that even if he catches one of the children misbehaving, he is not allowed to threaten him or her with punishment. Under such circumstances the children in his charge would run wild. So it is with suppliers.

The tasks that the firm has to perform, therefore, concern being able to spot those transactions for which there is significant scope for opportunism and being able to craft safeguards against the risk. Where contractual safeguards cannot properly be introduced, then the firm would probably be better to retain the competence within the organization, rather than to outsource it.

Hold-up is always a problem with outsourced contracts because effective monitoring is always an issue. However, sometimes the risks are particularly acute. Contracting that takes place in a highly volatile or uncertain environment is difficult because it raises the issue of renegotiation. Buyers attempt to draft contracts in as complete a fashion as possible, but when an environment is particularly volatile, specifying all the terms of an agreement in advance is likely to prove next to impossible. This in itself need not present a difficulty unless the firm becomes locked into its outsourced provider. If this happens, the supplier may choose to renegotiate on terms that benefit it, rather than its customer (Williamson, 1985).

As was indicated in the preceding section, contractual lock-in occurs if the contract requires the buyer to make some form of highly specialized investment in the relationship. The investment might take the form of time. An organization that has spent months negotiating and implementing an outsourced relationship might be reluctant to write off all of this hard work – especially if re-sourcing means repeating the effort with no greater chance of success next time around. Alternatively, firms might have made substantial and non-fungible investments in specialized training or equipment (otherwise known as asset-specific investments – Williamson, 1985). Less creditably, though, firms are often reluctant to call time on a poorly performing supplier if the managers who negotiated the contract have a significant reputational investment in the deal. Calling a halt to the affair means admitting that they got it wrong, and nobody likes doing that. Whatever the form of the lock-in, the effect is the same: the firm loses its capacity to impose costs on the vendor and thus its ability to impose discipline.

Of course, just because an outsourced contract presents the firm with a risk, it does not follow that the risk cannot be managed and that outsourcing should not take place. One strategy often pursued by firms involves unbundling a contract. This means separating out those elements that pose a risk from those that do not. The highly risky elements are retained in-house and only the less risky elements are outsourced. The supplier may even be asked to post a bond or share the costs of the dedicated investments, as a sign of its good faith (ie to show that its word of honour and commitment to the relationship are credible).

INCENTIVIZATION AND THE RELATIONSHIP MANAGEMENT CHOICE

Outsourcing requires the firm to understand what it is that allows it to leverage its customers (in the case of strategic outsourcing) and what it is that allows its 'potential' suppliers to exploit it (in the case of both strategic and tactical outsourcing). Effective relationship management is about reversing things by understanding what it is that allows the firm to control and leverage its suppliers. The question is to what end? This is where we are required to reintroduce the subject of surplus value.

The first decision that the firm must ask itself is whether the relationship should include a value-added element. Many commentators would argue yes, citing the benefits that often flow from extending the cooperative elements of a trade. Lean thinking, for example, highlights the seven supply chain wastes that often plague buyer–supplier relationships. These relate to overproduction (1), unnecessary inventory (2), waiting (3), motion (4), transportation (5), defects (6) and inappropriate processing (7) (for a discussion of these see Hines et al, 2000). Yet, just because extended cooperation might potentially generate additional value it doesn't mean that it will or that the buyer will be the main beneficiary if it does. Four factors play a part in determining the buyer's calculation about whether cooperation is worthwhile: the upfront investment, the potential pay-off, power and risk. Creating a value-adding relationship requires an investment, even if only in terms of the time and managerial effort that it involves. The first thing that the firm must ensure is that the expected payback matches the upfront investment. No firm is going to spend a lot of time developing its supplier of toilet rolls. The improvement for the buyer is likely to be miniscule compared to the effort.

What complicates the calculation is that both the investment and return may be hard to determine ex ante. Take defence contractors. Suppliers of defence equipment work closely with their customers (governments) to ensure that the weapons they develop are the ones that the customer wants/needs. The industry, however, is notorious for delays in introducing new equipment and cost overruns. In a number of instances the additional cost to which the customer ends up committing itself runs into the £billions. When the equipment finally arrives, it may be too late to be useful. It may not even work properly. Consequently, there is the issue of which party takes the risk and which party obtains the reward. This is a question of power. A simple example will illustrate the nature of the calculation the buyer faces.

Take two firms: a buyer (A) and its supplier (B). B proposes to A that an upfront investment of £50 is capable of yielding cost savings of £200. In other words, the additional surplus value that has been created through cooperation comes to £150. If A exercises leverage over B it will probably think that cooperating is a good idea. As it has the power it will probably insist that B takes all of the upfront risk, agreeing to cover B's costs only if the initiative pays off. This is a no-lose situation for A. If, however, A and B are interdependent then the calculation becomes more complex. B will probably insist that A shares both the investment and the reward. This means that A must invest £25 (half the £50 cost) to get a payback of £100 (half the £200 cost savings). This leaves it with a net gain of £75 (£100 savings – the £25 costs). Once again cooperating makes sense – although the pay-off for the buyer is smaller than in the first example. What if the costs are fixed but the gains are far from certain, however. Say, for example, there was only a 25 per cent chance of a successful outcome. Under these circumstances the firm would be investing £25 to get a 25% × £100 return. The cost–benefit calculation here is finely balanced (£25 cost – £25 return = zero). Change the parameters again (eg increase the upfront investment by £1) and the initiative may cease to make commercial sense. This is why power is so important to all relationships: it affects the pay-off structures of buyers and sellers and thus over-determines the management of the relationship. It decides which side takes most of the risks and which side extracts most of the rewards. Furthermore, the same calculation pertains whether the firm is thinking in a dyadic or a wider supply chain context.

INCENTIVES AND THE ROLE OF CONTRACT

The second set of supplier management issues facing supply managers concerns the management of the chosen vendor. Supply management involves two issues: relationship management and contracting. Relationship management concerns how the buyer and seller are going to interact on a day-to-day basis. Is the association between the two essentially going to be an arm's-length one, or is something closer going to be called for? If the firm has opted to pursue a value-adding relationship them presumably close interaction is required. The contracting parties will need to trade information, mutually adapt their processes etc, so that the maximum value-adding potential is achieved. At the same time, relationship management will also involve managing the tensions that exist between the two. Some forms of cooperation, for example, might be deemed neutral in the sense that they add value to the relationship without disturbing the commercial balance within it. Other forms of cooperation, however, are far from neutral. For example, if the buyer calls for the supplier to open its books, then the buyer is acquiring a considerable advantage over its supplier in that it now knows just how much money the supplier is making from the deal. Both buyers and sellers, therefore, tend to want to manage the relationship so that while it adds value it doesn't tip the balance of power the wrong way. The same goes for performance measurement. Performance measurement may be a way of monitoring how quickly things are improving – or if they are not improving, where and why this is the case. However, performance measurement is also a mechanism of control and both sides tend to be aware of this.

In contrast to relationship management, which tends to contain a value-adding element as well as a controlling element, contracts are primarily about control. They are about specifying, in a legally binding way, the manner in which buyers and suppliers are to work together, ie who is responsible for doing what. They are also about specifying (again in a legally binding way) the outputs of the relationship: what the supplier is expected to deliver, what the buyer is expected to pay, and which party owns the rights to any exploitable technologies or processes that might emerge from the association.

Conventional contracts take two main forms: tight and flexible (Williamson, 1985). The shift from tight to flexible contracts tends to occur as the risk within the relationship increases. Risk, in this context, has a very specific meaning. It refers to events that can be foreseen but that have a probability of occurring of less than one but greater than zero. Where the probability is one or zero (ie the event is certain), this means that an element to a deal is can be specified (or ignored) with total confidence. This allows the parties to use a tight contract. For example, if an organization requires laptops for a hundred employees, it is relatively easy for it to specify when it wants the machines, what it will pay and what level of after-sales support it will need.

By contrast, where there is a lack of clarity surrounding particular aspects of the deal, but where the lack of clarity falls within clearly defined limits (ie where the probability is between one and zero), the parties may seek to include a flexible element to the contract to take account of this ambiguity. This allows the requirement/reward relationship to be adjusted in a predictable way. For example, an organization requiring the development of a new piece of software may know what is needed but may not know how long it will take to develop the new product. Because the organization is aware, however, that the main variable driving cost will be the staff-hours required to develop the software, the terms of the contract are set out so as to reflect the range of potential effort levels.

However, some events are genuinely uncertain in the sense that they were not, or could not have been, anticipated prior to reaching the original agreement. Such events may range from occasional but devastating acts of God (or man) to the more mundane. For example, many IT agreements are entered into before the requirement has been properly worked out. Under such circumstances it is simply not possible to draft a contract flexible enough to take account of all future possibilities. In the place of contracts, therefore, firms must use relational agreements. The purpose of such agreements is to provide a structured framework within which the terms of a deal can be renegotiated as the future becomes clear.

Although a buyer–supplier relationship may largely consist of one of these control mechanisms, on occasion it can contain elements of all three. For example, short-term, arm's-length relationships tend to call for tight contracts but may include a subsidiary element. Longer-term arm's-length relationships tend to require the flexible element to increase. Long-term cooperative relationships (whether they are adversarial or non-adversarial) tend to call for all three.

Of course, while contracts aim to serve as instruments of control, whether in fact they succeed in this function depends on the ex post power balance. As we saw in our discussions on outsourcing and contractual risk, if the buyer loses his or her power then the contract may not be worth the paper it is written on. As the political philosopher Thomas Hobbes once put it, 'contracts without the sword are but empty breath'. In the case of either a tight or flexible contract the threat of the courts is only credible if they can be accessed at relatively low cost and if the plaintiff believes that it has a good chance of winning. Where fault is ambiguous or where an agreement has been poorly drafted, then the use of a contract as an incentive mechanism will start to break down. The reluctance to use this mechanism may then be further eroded by the fear that if the plaintiff fails to make an effective case, then it will also be saddled with the costs. In addition to this, the plaintiff may also have to manage a disintegrating relationship while a replacement is found – assuming that one can be found in a timely manner.

In the case of relational agreements, where there may be no contract or at least where the terms of the contract do not cover the issues in question, the courts may not be an option at all. Neither might be the termination of the agreement. This is because the incidence of significant sunk and switching costs in arrangements that are likely to require a relational agreement tends to be quite high. This is why observers like Williamson (1985) generally recommend that parties look to mechanisms like the posting of hostages, which can be forfeited should the relationship collapse, as a way of maintaining some control. And, if such arrangements cannot be agreed upon, they would advise that either the organization look for a different vendor or else it should consider the possibility of vertical integration.

INCENTIVES AND THE IMPACT OF INTERNAL POLITICS

While all of the proceeding discussions are fundamental to the process of the supply management, they are not in themselves complete. This is because so far the firm has been treated as a black box. However, this is not an accurate representation of either the buyer or the supplier. Each is a complex political entity, comprised of different functional actors, each with differing expectations regarding how the other party can and should be managed. Unless the internal politics of the firm are properly aligned to the external opportunities, then the ability to manage the other party effectively may be lost.

However, for the buying organization, creating this effective internal alignment is easier said than done. Operationally, the key to effective supply management is usually effective demand management, but as often as not a supply manager will experience considerable difficulty in getting the managers in other functions to recognize this point. In order to source effectively it is essential that buying organizations develop appropriate specifications, avoid unnecessary (last-minute) changes to specification, create regular patterns of demand and ensure that as little buying as possible takes place outside of the organization's commercial rules.

Most importantly, however, it is essential that organizations do not unnecessarily fragment spend, thereby spreading their demand across an artificially large number of suppliers. The reason for this is twofold. First, it raises transaction costs – substantially in some instances. Second, it reduces the potential leverage that the organization has over its suppliers. And, as has already been indicated: generally speaking, the weaker the leverage, the poorer the deals.

Of course, a certain level of fragmentation will always arise. For one thing, different business units within an organization often have very different missions and as a consequence have very different supply requirements. Additionally, when attempting to consolidate demand, organizations are often confronted by legacy issues. Standardizing demand may offer only a false economy if it is accompanied by significant write-off costs. Finally, organizations have to balance the short-term gains that may arise from obtaining volume deals with the long-term risk that they may become overly dependent on a particular supplier. Over time this dependence may translate into higher prices and poorer service. Together, these factors combine to create what the authors have described elsewhere as a 'natural level of fragmentation' (Lonsdale and Watson, 2005). This natural level can be defined as the point at which any further consolidation results in a 'net reduction in organizational performance/ welfare, notwithstanding any commercial gains that might have accrued from the consolidation initiative' (p 161). Where exactly this point lies will vary by commodity, organization and time.

Furthermore, where that point lies will often be one of the major areas of dispute between supply managers and their internal clients. This is because issues of consolidation are as much political issues as they are technical ones. There are a number of reasons why an internal client may not recognize that there are benefits to be obtained from consolidation. First, there is the issue of functional culture. Managers from different departments are usually functional specialists. Their specialisms may be largely commercial (as in the case of sales or purchasing), or largely operational (as in the case of human resource management (HRM) or production). Alongside the specialized knowledge that resides in a department there is often also a strong functional culture. This culture reflects the training of staff but it also reflects the management priorities of particular departments. For example, because a production manager's performance is measured in terms of faults or downtime, he or she is likely to be particularly sensitive to anything that might spoil or interrupt output. Such sensitivity may be justified, if what is being proposed poses a real threat to operational sustainability. For example, it would be ridiculous for an oil company to attempt to save a couple of thousand pounds on its spend on industrial valves if the downside risk was several hundred thousand pounds in lost production if the new and untried products failed. However, a natural sensitivity can easily become an unnatural over-sensitivity. The same production manager may refuse to participate in an initiative that will save sixty thousand pounds because there is an infinitesimal chance that the new product might fail.

Second, there is the principal–agent problem. Principal–agent problems arise because managers and indeed all employees have divided loyalties. For example, managers have a loyalty to the organization that pays their wages. For many commentators, this loyalty constitutes (or should constitute) the manager's primary loyalty. In practice, however, managers also develop loyalties for those around them, and particularly departmental colleagues. And less creditably, managers also have loyalties to their own interests (Milgrom and Roberts, 1992). Where firm and department/personal priorities conflict, it is often the firm's priorities that are sacrificed.

This is significant from the perspective of a consolidation programme because although such a programme is intended to benefit the organization as a whole, it does not necessarily follow that consolidation will benefit all departments equally (or at all), or that the initiative will be without cost (or indeed that these costs will be evenly distributed). It is relatively easy for a manager to sign up to a consolidation programme if the supplier that stands to get most of the organization's business is the one that he or she is already using and the price that is being offered represents an improvement. It is less clear, however, that a manager would be enthusiastic if the new deal is more expensive for him or her, or if it involves the termination of a relationship that is particularly valued.

Regardless of whether the dissent arises because managers have failed to understand the advantages of the initiative, or because they understand the advantages for the organization but are anxious to avoid the costs to their department (or them personally), such dissent is likely to make implementation problematic. Faced with such opposition, organizations have one of four options. Option one involves taking the path of least resistance and doing nothing. Options two, three and four all require the organization to confront the problem. Option two involves persuasion: demonstrating to the manager concerned that any fears are exaggerated or unfounded and setting them against the very obvious benefits. This may or may not work. However, it is most likely to work where a hostile manager has misunderstood the issues involved. It is less likely to work when a manager understands the issues and realizes that the initiative is not in his or her particular interest. Under these circumstances, the supply manager may pursue option three: coercion. Coercion involves the threat of sanctions or the use of the organization's authority structures to override the opposition of the hostile party. The limitation of this strategy, however, is that the procurement function often sits towards the bottom of the organization's hierarchy and the procurement manager lacks the clout to make credible threats. Furthermore, more senior colleagues may prove reluctant to intercede on the procurement manager's behalf if it involves confronting one of the organization's more powerful constituencies. Option four, therefore, is bribery. Bribery involves compensating a manager for the costs of participation. It is perhaps not surprising if a manager does not want to get involved in a consolidation programme if all of the benefits flow to the centre. However, if some of the benefits can be passed back to the manager, then the initiative may appear to be more worthwhile.

CONCLUSION

Exchange takes place in the first instance because it is mutually profitable. Closer forms of cooperation occur because they can increase this level of profitability. However, mutually profitable exchange is not the same as equally profitable exchange. Buyers and sellers are competitors as well as collaborators. Consequently it is important for supply chain managers to understand the following things: first, they must understand when it is not sensible to exchange (that is, when exchange imposes unacceptable levels of strategic and contractual risk). Second, they must also understand (when it is sensible to exchange) how to craft the incentive structures that will maximize the return to their organizations. Obviously, such structures need to cover relationships between buyer and supplier. However, they are also needed to regulate relationships within the organization. This is because poor demand management can have significant knock-on effects. Consequently, managers within an organization need to be encouraged (through the threat of sanction or the promise of reward) to engage in activities designed to maintain the organization's control over its external environment At root, therefore, the study and practice of supply chain management is the study of managerial and contractual incentives.

References

Cox, A, Sanderson, J and Watson, G (2000) *Power Regimes*, Earlsgate Press, Boston, UK

Cox, A *et al* (2002) *Supply Chains, Markets and Power*, Routledge, London

Hines, P *et al* (2000) *Value Stream Management*, Pearson, Harlow

Klein, B (1980) Transaction cost determinants of 'unfair' contractual arrangements, *The American Economic Review*, **70** (2), 356–62

Lonsdale, C and Cox, A (1998) *Outsourcing: A business guide to risk management tools and techniques*, Earlsgate Press, Boston, UK

Lonsdale, C and Watson, G (2005) The internal client relationship, demand management and value for money: a conceptual model, *Journal of Purchasing and Supply Management*, **11**, pp 159–71

Lukes, S (1974) *Power: A radical view*, Macmillan, London

Milgrom, P and Roberts, J (1992) *Economics, Organization and Management*, Prentice-Hall, Englewood Cliffs, NJ

Molhow, I (1997) *The Economics of Information*, Blackwell, Oxford

Peteraf, M (1993) The cornerstones of competitive advantage: a resource-based view, *Strategic Management Journal*, **14**, pp 79–91

Porter, M (1980) *Competitive Strategy*, Free Press, New York

Williamson, O (1985) *The Economic Institutions of Capitalism*, Free Press, New York

5

Time compression in the supply chain

Adrian Beesley, DHL Supply Chain

This chapter explores the 'time compression' approach to business process improvement in the supply chain. The concept and strategic relevance of this approach were first published in the West in the early 1990s; however, it is an approach that still offers good potential and a fresh approach to achieving competitiveness through re-engineering. The rate of adoption of 'time compression' has been slow and part of the reason for this is that the approach requires the total commitment of the whole business, from the top of the organization downwards. Coupled with this is the fact that change within any organization has always been challenging, particularly when it involves making difficult decisions in one department or function to benefit another for the good of the whole company or even supply chain. Supply chain objectives and their relation to time compression implementation strategies will be touched on, coupled with explanations of achievable benefits and case study examples.

Over 200 years ago, Benjamin Franklin stated that 'Time is Money', and this was reiterated in 1990 by Stalk and Hout who claimed that 'time is the last exploitable resource'. Today 'time' is still largely ignored by many companies owing to enduring approaches that create inertia in organizational structures and associated business processes. Managers have always used time to manage their operations but control has usually been limited to a segment, or business function, within the supply chain. For example, in the past, 'time' has been used for 'work study' and human performance measurement, but this approach is based on the use of past observations in relation to operations usually associated with a long-established and outdated business processes. Moreover, this approach, and even some modern-day approaches, focus purely on the value-adding elements of business process that often account for only 5 per cent (sometimes referred to as the business process velocity) of total process time. This emphasis on just the value-add time tends to be focused around making people work faster, often with a risk to quality, safety and ultimately livelihoods as competitiveness starts to become an issue. There is also another problematical dimension to these approaches in that the time-based implications of individual actions recognized only one side of a 'trade-off' that may have holistic implications in a much broader supply chain context. Examples include companies that manage capacity and cost through applications and frameworks such as traditional accounting, functional budgeting, manufacturing resource planning (MRPII) and even enterprise resource planning (ERP). The resultant scope of thinking is usually constrained by not recognizing how time, stock, resource and service interrelate with each other along the supply chain. Using 'time' as a measure creates a deeper understanding of the total holistic business process, therefore providing scope for optimization and a pragmatic approach to change. The use of time in this context is directly linked with competitiveness, and this is what is meant by the 'time compression' approach.

TIME COMPRESSION AND COMPETITION

Wormack, Jones and Roos's landmark work within the automotive sector in 1990 pointed out that competition had become more aggressive and customers more demanding, so there was a constant need for a new source of competitiveness. In 1991 Riech went further and demonstrated the general applicability of this statement in a global context across many industrial sectors. Global competitive forces around the world are placing increasing pressures on markets and supply chains. Demand for increased service, product performance and variety across supply chains that extend across the globe create new requirements and challenges.

The time compression approach is one route to addressing these demands and improving the design, balance and flexibility of the supply chain. If this approach is combined with a focus on customers that operate in markets that are time-sensitive, then a further dimension is added. Stalk and Hout (1990) make the comment that 'the world is moving to

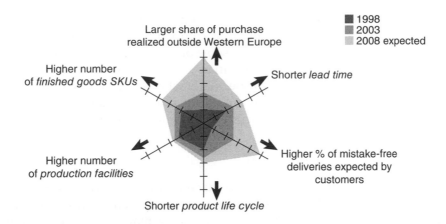

Figure 5.1 Complexity factors relative change (2003 = 100)

increased variety with better levels of service and faster levels of innovation. For suppliers that operate and service these sectors, time based competition is of significant advantage'.

A survey conducted by the European Logistics Association in 2004 identified factors that are increasing the complexity of supply chains; see Figure 5.1. This highlights the current and continuing trend to source product outside of traditional supply markets, and this is coupled with the concerns and demand for mistake-free deliveries. Despite the presence of these two significant factors, the increase in stock-keeping units (SKUs) will continue, as will demand for shorter lead times.

These results have today manifested themselves, with cycle times being a key consideration for most companies in the West. It is interesting, however, to note that the more holistic approach offered by time compression remains an opportunity for many companies. This, for example, is borne out by the content of numerous industrial requests for quotation (RFQs) directed to third-party logistics providers over the past decade. The majority of these tend to focus on cost reduction, with often little or no consideration for the attainment of holistic supply chain benefits.

The question is why some of the major corporations seem to ignore or do not directly engage with this approach. The answer may lie in the fact that the use of time compression to some extent relies on viewing the supply chain as a business process that can be designed and managed, ie the original concept of supply chain management (SCM). Some commentators such as Lamming (2002) consider that the idea of managing the supply chain as a holistic entity using approaches such as SCM is totally impractical. He considers SCM to be a flawed concept because it has been around since 1982 and industry is still having difficulty with implementing and mastering this area of potential competitiveness. This may well explain, or support, the reason why some of the more insular approaches to business improvement still dominate company key objectives. This debate will no doubt continue irrespective of whether SCM or, say, network management is the approach for the future. Opportunities, however, for time compression still exist and this will be explored further.

What is time compression?

The key aspect for the use of 'time' is that it is not necessarily about being faster or the fastest. Quality is paramount to competitiveness and substituting, say, quality for speed is not the primary objective. A time compression approach focuses on how companies use time to deliver a sustainable fast response to customer needs, through business processes that are organized around a strategic time-based focus. The concept is about strengthening the holistic supply chain structure to achieve time-based objectives, with tactical decisions being made at the correct level to enable the speed of response.

The term time compression was originally introduced by New in 1992, and in its most basic form relates to the reduction of the time consumed by business processes through the elimination of non-value-adding process time. Value-add processes are defined as entities that transform inputs into outputs that are of value to the customer and that they are willing to pay for (or negate their costs) and involve no correction or rework, ie right first time. Some processes may be identified as producing very little added value and this may highlight the need to totally re-engineer them. This can take advantage of a number of possible strategies detailed below.

One of the reasons why the approach is important relates to the levels of time compression that can be achieved across business processes. Within, for example, a typical UK manufacturing company at least 95 per cent of the process time is accounted as non-value-adding. This well-established statistic was supported in the UK by the TCP (University of Warwick's Time Compression Programme) in 1995 and in the United States by Barker in 1994. Consultants in 2004 (SUCCESS, 2004) confirm that these sorts of value-add statistics still hold true, making the approach powerful as well as relevant in today's business environment.

If this statistic is viewed in the context of a typical supply chain, as little as 0.01 per cent of time can add value. However, as New (1992) demonstrated, all of these percentages require qualification on two counts. First, a large proportion of the non-value-adding time is due to product queuing, so the value-adding percentage is a function of how much is being pushed through the supply chain at a particular point in time. Even if a particular supply chain is grossly inefficient, but had only one order during a particular period, the actual value-adding time would be high because of minimal queuing. A second consideration is that inventory should add value and it is, therefore, usually included in the overall value-adding percentage. Consequently a view has to be taken on how much of the inventory element of the pipeline – usually measured in days or hours of throughput cover – is actually adding value. The amount of value added by inventory is intrinsically linked to the process cycle times, as well as demand throughput levels and predictability.

The statistics do, however, show the enormity of the opportunities for companies and their associated supply chains – and they differ significantly from any perceived opportunity that might be available from, say, a cost-based approach.

Time compression can be achieved using any one or a combination of seven strategies identified by Carter, Melnyk and Handfield (1994) and these can be applied from company level through to a total supply chain. These are summarized below:

- simplification, removing process complexity that has accumulated over time;
- integration, improving information flows and linkages to create enhanced operability and visibility;
- standardization, using generic best practice processes, standardized components and modules and information protocols;
- concurrent working, moving from sequential to parallel working by using, for example, teams and other forms of process integration;
- variance control, monitoring processes and detecting problems at an early stage so that corrective action can be taken to avoid problems with quality and waste;
- automation, applied to improve the effectiveness and efficiency of entities and activities within the supply chain process;
- resource planning, allocating resources in line with SCM best practice. For example, plan by investigating bottleneck activities and consider use of multi-skilled workforces to provide resource flexibility.

These strategies should ideally be utilized in the sequence they appear above. However, depending on any particular supply chain or company situation, various stages and combinations may be more pragmatically deployed to account for changes that are already, or about to be put, in place. Through the use of these strategies, time compression can directly achieve increases in value-add time and help to contribute to objectives associated with fundamental principles of SCM and best practice. Putting

Table 5.1 SCM principles relating to time

	Nature of the principle	Useful attributes of a time compression approach
The principle of end-user focus	Long-term supply chain profitability is dependent on the end (ultimate) user being satisfied. This acts as the focus for all supply chain design, development and process engineering.	Time compression requires that the end user is identified as the principal anchor point. This provides the focus for all time-based parameter measurement across the supply chain.
The principle of horizontal boundary definition	Different end-user needs are more competitively satisfied by channels (horizontally defined routes or workflow) designed and engineered ideally across the supply chain from a logistics service perspective.	Time defines the principal characteristics of the logistically distinct channels and service needs. The time compression approach provides a good diagnostic and basis for redesign.
The principle of vertical boundary definition	Boundaries of ownership and control (dividing the chain vertically) should be positioned to suit the needs of the end user according to best practice and make/buy theory.	The consumption of non-value time highlights where ownership and general boundary issues exist and require adjustment.
The principle of inventory positioning	The positioning, levels and characteristics of inventory are best determined in a total supply chain context to suit end-user needs in line with stock and postponement theory.	Time and cost provide a good deterministic framework with cycle time as a fundamental driver of stock positioning, levels and service. 'Value add stock' is a time-based diagnostic.
The principle of control over demand dynamics	Understanding and levels of control over demand dynamics are best achieved by having a holistic supply chain perspective. The principal basis is through information integration and the use of best practice relationship management.	Time measures the problem and time compression tackles the root causes of demand dynamics.
The principle of cooperation and coordination	The attainment of the above principles requires cooperation and coordination between supply chain participants. For this to work effectively each SC participant must have self-defined and motivating objectives based on trust and some common business aspirations.	Time provides a common and trustworthy metric across the supply chain that highlights the opportunities and issues.

aside the debate surrounding the merits of SCM, a brief description of the nature of the key SCM principles and how they relate to time is detailed in Table 5.1. It can be argued that these principles hold true irrespective of whether a company is operating using a holistic approach to SCM or a more focused and less total 'system'-based approach to process re-engineering.

THE TIME COMPRESSION APPROACH – COMPETITIVE ADVANTAGE

The time compression approach can be applied at two levels: first, as a holistic approach in the context of, for example, the above principles, and second, as a competitive market focus. The former could be regarded as an internal time focus of the key supply chain processes that lie on, or close to, the critical path of the business process. The latter element is the supply chain's external time that is of direct value to the customer. Both are interdependent and therefore have outcomes that are strategically significant.

When examining business strategy from first principles, reference is made to Ohmae's (1965) strategic model. He states that competitiveness relates to three basic elements: the customer, the competition, and the company that is under scrutiny. There must be differentiation between the elements of value and cost if competitiveness is to emerge. A time compression approach addresses these two sources of differentiation in a specific way. The first objective must be the elimination of non-value activity – that is, waste – and thereby maximize the value created in the supply chain. The removal of non-value activity in turn gives rise to a cost advantage, hence forming the basis of cost differentiation. Tersine and Hummingbird (1995) state that 'managing time is the mirror image of managing quality, cost, innovation and productivity. Reducing wasted time automatically improves the other measures of performance in a multiplier fashion'. If, however, companies go for the reverse and apply cost reduction initiatives without reference to the time-based implications, additional costs may be incurred elsewhere in the supply chain. An example relating to the inventory positioning principle can be used to demonstrate this point. At the outset of a cost reduction initiative it could be proved that upgrading a warehousing management system (WMS) will deliver cost advantages. It may, for example, help to reduce product storage and retrieval times, and drive cost reductions associated with resource utilization. However, a time-based examination of the holistic business process may lead to considerations about whether the particular segment of the supply chain in question should operate on a 'just in time' or a 'make to order' basis (Beesley, 1996). This total supply chain perspective may remove or displace the stock point and hence the requirement for a WMS at this point. In addition, if process times are compressed in other parts of the supply chain, the economic structure of the supply system may change the appropriate locations for inventory stock points, and the short-term cost savings associated with the proposed warehouse system could be negated by a new inventory regime. If the new WMS is still established, its associated payback demands may impose an inappropriate constraint preventing future supply chain optimization. This will have ramifications in terms of cost as well as service levels, flexibility and agility.

THE TIME COMPRESSION APPROACH – COST ADVANTAGE

Cost reduction will generally occur as a direct result of the removal or compression of non-value-added time. This time compression can result in a number of cost savings associated with the removal of fixed and variable overheads (such as rent and management), direct costs (such as labour and materials) and working capital. Other cost savings will depend on the nature of the compression, perhaps minimizing risk in the decision process by making relevant information available earlier in the process. The reduction, or even removal, of a rework activity can result from process change such as compression of information queues. These improvements can also have ramifications downstream and upstream of the chain by reducing or removing expediting activities that are in place to cope with ongoing inadequacies.

The cost implications of compressing time are extensive and complex but rarely absent. This is why the prescribed approach is to focus on time, which directly affects the service a supply chain can offer, without the complications of having to identify every cost 'trade-off'. The cost-based focus has been encouraged in the past by the use of performance measures linking profit margins with cost. With the 'time compression' approach there may be a requirement to determine cost values associated with the processes to assist with evaluation and project prioritization. Generally, the time-based implications of any proposal are easy to comprehend and quantify, because the length of time consumed by processes is typically a proportional representation of the costs (New, 1992).

The SUCCESS programme, a joint university and industry-led initiative, developed a tool kit called the Supply Chain Time and Cost Mapping

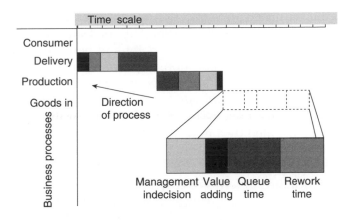

Figure 5.2 Time-based process mapping – value-add analysis

(SCTCM). This usefully combines time-based process mapping (Beesley, 1997) with process cost analysis. The former highlights opportunities using value-add analysis (see the example in Figure 5.2), and the latter translates and attributes functional costs to processes. SCTCM has the benefit of being able to see how time, value-add and cost interrelate with each other along the supply chain. This can be useful for prioritizing projects, analysis and gaining buy-in to the time compression approach. This, however, needs to be carefully weighed against the issue of collecting vast quantities of cost-based data at the risk of prolonging total project duration. It may also be a particular issue when the cooperation of process owners and operators is required for the project because it can then be perceived as a cost-cutting exercise. As a consequence, using these individuals to help with data collection, analysis and solution design may become more challenging. SCTCM is, however, a positive recent development, which keeps time compression on the re-engineering agenda through the use of a rigorous project tool set and application process. The link to commerce's acute focus on cost provides the approach with the added credibility and robustness that is often required.

Time-based process mapping – value-add analysis

The time compression approach – quality advantage

The achievement of time compression requires a quality-based approach. This can be viewed from two perspectives of quality. First, time compression demands that product quality is to a specification that matches

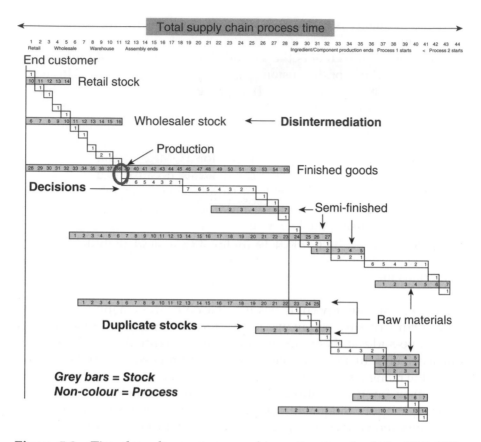

Figure 5.3 Time-based process map of an entire supply chain. This UK example shows the key processes that move material out of the ground and maps the processes that evolve the material into something that fulfils customer demand. Value time is not displayed in this view; however, value analysis revealed that the aspects noted in bold are key issues. The longest process time in this example was the decision-making process, which consumed 14 days and is therefore the largest element of the finished goods supply lead time. In contrast, the overall production time of just a few minutes is the shortest element

customer needs and more specifically end-user needs. Anything less will obviously have strategic market implications, such as a loss of customers and goodwill. This will consume unnecessary time in the sales, marketing and manufacturing process, which will have to rectify or replace the product or customers. An investigation of these time-wasting activities can, therefore, highlight possible root causes of problems that may be founded in quality issues. Time, therefore, provides the focus for quality improvement.

The above complements the second dimension of quality where it is not just important for the customer but also for the company. This is the total quality management (TQM) approach (Oakland and Beardmore, 1995), which also focuses on waste elimination. One key issue with TQM programmes is that they have been known to lose impetus because of a lack of focus. Mallinger (1993) and Glover (1993) identify the need for a holistic approach to provide a focus for TQM to operate effectively. A time compression approach provides this because it uses a simple measure that is visible to the total supply chain and not just a small isolated segment. It can thus link and integrate all of the elements of a TQM approach using the key metric of 'time'. An example of this might be a focus on the time taken to make critical decisions that in effect constrain an order or product batch being processed. Typically sales and operations meetings tasked with matching demand and production may represent this process constraint, as illustrated in the TBPM shown in Figure 5.3. By implication, the lapse times of these meetings sit on the critical path of any supply chain process. The majority of this time is non-value-add and therefore provides a key focus for addressing the total quality of all activities that interplay with the process. Examples will in-clude the major quality-related aspects, from systems to produce accurate and timely information through to the more routine but easily under-estimated aspects such as people attending meetings on time, effective communications and proper prioritization of tasks and activities. The non-value activity, particularly the low-profile issues, may not be generally recorded from a cost perspective but the delay on the critical path can be measured in terms of inventory cover and customer lead time and is therefore high visible.

THE TIME COMPRESSION APPROACH – TECHNOLOGY ADVANTAGE

Technology should not be applied purely for reasons associated with what is on offer or mimicking the competition. Its application must take account of the individual circumstances of the business and its customer needs, and then ensure a competitive differentiation. A focus on the time-based impact of the application of technology will help steer a company to this goal. Examples of technologies that can achieve time compression are numerous and some of the more notable developments (Barker and Helms, 1992) include: computer numerically controlled (CNC) machines, robotics, computers in manufacturing (CIM) and logistics-related examples such as the WMS application mentioned earlier. All of these reduce time for individual activities, but the time-based impact must be considered holistically in order to check that the technology is appropriate for the supply chain. A key perspective is that many automated systems cannot cope with high levels of demand variation, largely because the technology is designed against very exacting functional specifications. A time compression approach provides the focus for the application of technology when the seven strategies identified by Carter *et al* are addressed in a carefully considered sequence. This usually considers the low- or non-technology strategy solution before moving to state-of-the-art automated solutions, such as computerized material handling and control or the various forms of ERP. This approach will ensure that the application of technology is strategically significant as well as delivering tactical productivity gains.

THE TIME COMPRESSION APPROACH – CUSTOMER FOCUS

Different customer and ultimate end-user needs are satisfied by channels that are capable of delivering different types of service. Different product and market sectors have different service needs. The most appropriate way to meet these needs is through channels that are specifically designed to have distinct logistical capabilities. The alternative is to push everything through the same channel – but the result will be that some customers will be over-served while others are underserved. This will have an adverse effect on costs, customer goodwill and ultimately sustainable profitability. This is all linked with the principle of horizontal boundary definition and is important in channel construction because of the significant impact it can have on the customer.

One of the key impacts of the requirement for distinct logistics channels is the need to align them to different types of market and product segment. Figure 5.4 illustrates a simplified form of segmentation into four generic supply categories for differing product and market types (adapted from FhG ISI, 1993). The horizontal axis represents levels of demand certainty, with the vertical axis showing levels of product complexity. Different product types fit into one of the quadrants according to the certainty and complexity criteria.

The chart shows that products that have a volatile demand pattern and low constructional complexity will require flexible supply operations to minimize risk. An agile approach is required so that the business process

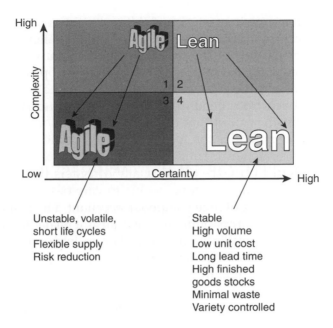

Figure 5.4 Generic supply strategies
Source: adapted from FhG ISI, 1993

can respond rapidly to new customer requirements in a market that is populated by 'fast follower' competitors enabled by low product complexity. Conversely, products that have more stable and predictable demand are usually in more cost-focused supply situations demanding lower unit costs through tighter management control and probable large economies of scale.

There are therefore two basic supply concepts, one where a business process must be agile, for example a high fashion garment supply chain, and one lean, where a typical example would be commodity-based products such as industrial chemicals. It must be recognized that a range of different products lie between these extremes and may therefore require a mix of both approaches. For example, quadrant 1 would be represented by super-value goods such as the manufacture of aircraft. These are highly complex items sold into markets with some uncertainty and influenced by fluctuating business cycles and therefore require process agility. Some lean approaches will, however, be required to underpin the longer-horizon investments in a supply market that has the time to evolve and apply competitive pressure. Quadrant 2 is the converse of 1 in that it is characterized by fast-moving consumer goods (FMCG)-type products, which generally sell in more consistent market demand conditions, giving rise to high competition and the need for a lean cost focus. This, however, is mixed with some need for agility in areas linked with product development and innovation.

The various stages of development and evolution of product in terms of its life cycle may cause it to move across segments. The latest FMCG LCD TV has moved from quadrant 1 to quadrant 2 and is progressing towards quadrant 4.

BENEFITS OF TIME COMPRESSION

There are two categories of time compression benefit. The first is internal time, which has indirect impact on the customer as it relates to the internal consumption of time within a company. The second is external time, which relates to all aspects of time that have direct impact upon the customer, such as lead time from a stock or decoupling point such as a production facility. The net effect of internal time improvements has ramifications on external time-based benefits through cost and service interrelationships.

Internal time benefits in most manufacturing facilities, such as cycle time reductions, give work-in-progress reductions and productivity increases. Stalk and Hout (1990) claim empirically that for every halving of cycle times and doubling of work in process turns, productivity increases by 20 to 70 per cent. A halving of manufacturing lead time using the same number of people reduces costs by 50 per cent. These changes are reflected in the return on assets where increases of 80 per cent are possible. Then 45 per cent less cash is required to grow the company at an equable rate.

Generally, the longer the elapsed time in the supply chain, the greater the commercial risk associated with under- or over-forecasting demand. This results in the use of speculation stock for future customer needs (Mather, 1992). If, for example, a fashion-associated product has to be ordered from the Far East nine months in advance, then the risk of forecasting error is high. Consequently, the costs associated with potential markdowns are high where significantly large stocks of inventory are held, and in the converse situation where minimal or under-stocking occurs then the opportunity cost of lost sales and goodwill is substantial. The key point for time compression is that if lead times (cycle times) are compressed, not only is cycle stock (pipeline inventory) reduced, but the period over which forecasting has to be performed reduces – and the shorter the period, the better the forecast accuracy. The better the forecast accuracy, the less demand variance will exist and the less buffer or safety stock is required. Less overall demand for inventory means that less has to be produced and supply processes can respond more promptly. Again, therefore, lead times compress and a virtuous time compression cycle comes into existence.

The internal benefits provide scope to assist the external benefits of a time compression approach. The primary aspect to consider is the consequence of compressing customer lead times and the opportunity to increase business turnover and possibly prices. Stalk and Hout infer that customers of time-based suppliers are willing to pay more for their products for both subjective and economic reasons:

- The customer needs less stock (cycle and buffer stock).
- The customer makes decisions to purchase nearer the time of need, therefore reducing risk.
- Reduction of cancelled/changed orders, with less time available and less need to change.
- Increase in the velocity of cash flow.

The factors influencing risk have an implication on market share. By being faster and more reliable than the competition, market share can be increased. A time-compressed supplier can use its flexible delivery system to supply increased variety to the customer in the form of increased style and/or technological sophistication. If this is delivered with a response advantage, the time-compressed supplier will attract the most profitable customers. Conversely, competitors will be forced to service the customers that are prepared to wait and, as a consequence, be prepared to pay less for the product. Generally, time-compressed suppliers appear to grow at three to four times the rate of their competitors and three times faster than overall demand with twice the level of profitability. When the slower competitor companies do decide to become time based they must do so from the disadvantaged position of having to incur the costs of regaining market share without securing the full benefits.

Experience from TCP has shown that the general price and market share advantage must be considered in the context of the local market and the logistical characteristics of product being supplied. For example, in the UK during the 90s, as the spectre of cheaper overseas sources became a reality, time compression enabled companies such as H&R Johnson to optimize its business processes. This enabled it to retain market share against cheap foreign imports of ceramic tile products rather than gaining a specific price advantage. Some price advantage could, however, be applied in time-sensitive market segments such as high-fashion products where process time from design concept to full volume provided a sustainable strategic differentiator over distant competitors.

Demand acquisition approaches such as customer relationship management (CRM) help predict, define and place new customer demands on supplying companies within short time spans. The need to respond to this level of rapidly communicated customer transparency has become the new competitive frontier. Companies that do not adjust their business processes fast enough will quickly lose ground to the competition. Agility coupled with lean is key, with a focus on the use of time compression as an enabler of process delivery and reinvention.

EXAMPLES OF THE APPLICATION OF TIME COMPRESSION

Many companies in the United States, Japan and Europe use a time compression approach either as an open policy or as something philosophically buried within the strategic mix (Stalk and Webber, 1993). Table 5.2 illustrates the nature of, and results from, a number of TCP projects.

Table 5.2 Results from a sample of TCP projects

Company	Scope of the project	Compression achieved	Strategic significance of the improvement
H&R Johnson	Customer lead times	Two weeks to two days	To counter competitive import products and retain a strategic segment of the market
Massey Ferguson	Process time	Reduced by 20%	To reduce cost of inventory by compressing cycle times via a manufacturing cell
British Airways	Warehouse link removed	Two days' compression	To maximize on aircraft flying hours, reduce inventory costs and increase asset utilization by moving into a contract market
Fairey Hydraulics	Component arrears	50% reduction	Retain market share and reduce inventory costs
GKN Hardy Spicer	Inbound logistics	Reduced by 85%	Reduce raw material and operating costs to maintain competitiveness
CV Knitwear	Time to develop product	Reduced by 50%	To meet the customer's time-based requirement for an increased number of ranges each year. Customer retained

Time compression of a global supply chain

The following case study has been compiled from a number of projects to demonstrate a diverse range of applications within one example. Use of this hybrid hypothetical example has also enabled demonstration of some world-class solution examples while maintaining confidentiality.

The case study demonstrates the application of a combination of time compression strategies focused on the attainment of a number of the supply chain principles in a global context. The principles addressed are underlined and the various strategies are denoted in italics. The example takes one of the big Western retailers and an aspect of its global supply chain involved with sourcing product from a major low-cost manufacturing nation.

Two categories of product will be considered, defined by their market and product segmentation relating to the four generic supply strategies above. The first is a product group that has stable demand but a low margin, due in part to intense competition. This might be, for example, wall fixings such as screws and nails, and would require a lean supply chain concept capitalizing on the stable product demand, thereby underpinning a low-cost solution. In contrast, a fashion product category such as women's skirts has less stable demand, with more scope to attain higher margins as competition from exact product replicas or substitutes is more limited within the initial short sales launch time frame. To cope with the higher demand variability and volatility, the fashion product supply chain must have the ability to react to change via fast product replenishment or product reinvention. The supply chain has to be agile rather than lean, with emphasis on risk mitigation via resource deployment rather than a pure cost minimization approach.

This form of product categorization enables constructive supply chain design (or re-engineering) based on the *end-user focus* which in these examples is highlighted by the need for different levels of flexibility and cost attainment. These 'end-user' demands translate into logistical requirements which can be met by specific logistic *(horizontal) channel* design specifications. One key aspect of the design specification of any channel is the *inventory positioning* and this will depend on supply and demand variability coupled with lead times. These factors will give rise to appropriate types or forms of inventory being held in specific quantities at strategic locations within the channel. An example for the agile channel might include the need for inventory to be held close to the retailer but in semi-finished form, thereby postponing final product assembly, at a location a short distance, and therefore with a short period of risk exposure, from the market. Products designed using *standardized* components and modules lend themselves well to postponement.

The majority of supply chains are under the ownership of different legal entities, such as companies, and also under the influence of different organizations, such as departments and employees. These entities legally and organizationally interact with each other and create areas of focus and specialization along the supply chain at the same time as creating constraints and check points (eg for quality or *variance control*) at the various interfaces (*vertical boundaries*). The optimal operation of any channel is strongly influenced by the position of these vertical boundaries and the influence that they exert on the supply chain. These boundaries must therefore be designed and negotiated into the channel in line with the application of concepts such as make/buy decision theory, best practice outsourcing and the idea of organizational process design. In our two-channel example the question of who should own the inventory is one key aspect of this issue. Often the weakest channel partner is left with the cost of ownership; however, in the agile or lean supply chain the suppliers may, for example, own the inventory in the retail store. This might be for good logical reasons of control and focus in a retail environment that has to merchandise and replenish thousands of other diverse product lines.

Ownership of either the inventory, process or the company entity is a major influence, hence the focus on conflict resolution in supply chains with aspirations to use partnership and empowerment approaches. At a more generic level some form of *cooperation and coordination* will always be required between the various forms of interface along the supply chain. System-based exchange of information and data has transformed the way supply chains can operate and has expanded the scope of what can be achieved between the interfaces. For example, systems (generically a form of *automation*) allow for the rapid transfer of data globally along supply chains. For practical purposes this is usually instantaneous (*concurrent working*) and *integrated* in that interconnecting process links are available, compatible and can respond. In our agile channel example, retail sales information can be made available to the supplier on the other side of the world. They are motivated and can respond accordingly and for example be in a position to authorize and generate replenishment orders on behalf of the retailer. This form of linkage alleviates the effects of *demand dynamics* where time delays in the supply of information along the chain creates uncertainty, causing suppliers to mitigate against risk using standby resources and processes that are non-value-adding and result in unnecessary costs.

The final aspect of this example considers the inbound flow of materials to support the manufacturing operations. There is a natural tendency to focus on the parts of the supply chain that directly affect customers to the exclusion of the inbound supply chain. Vendor management initiatives and carefully considered inventory ownership policies often provide the desired focus on this sometimes neglected area. However, scope often exists to investigate and map the entire inbound supply chain and consolidate into appropriate *horizontal channels* and to *simplify* the types of flows using a unified approach for handling raw materials that have logistically distinct characteristics. In the example of fixings, supply of metal rods, chemicals and other materials all arrived at the factory via a range of different channels – some via direct delivery via a carrier network, others supplied in bulk to the factory warehouse, some supplied from a vendor regional warehouse or a combination of all three types of supply via a range of providers. An equal level of complexity and variety existed to support the range of information flows and communications. Typically these supply arrangements and associated communication complexities arise for historical reasons and establish themselves over a period of time.

The inbound supply chain operated and sustained manufacturing but no one could identify the logistical cost of the operation as this was hidden within the procurement cost. Further to this, the complexity of all the channels made service level agreements difficult to maintain and manage, giving rise to safety stocks and non-value-add cost. The inbound supply chain was mapped from a time, cost and value-add perspective. Horizontal channels of supply were identified and a neutral third-party logistics provider was given responsibility for implementation and delivery. This provided ownership, the ability to consolidate flows and a new focus on the factory as a customer of the logistics service and not just the product. *Resource* allocation in terms of inventory, transport, warehouse and IT capacity was designed into the solution on the basis of balancing service and cost, rather than using a just-in-case mentality driven by pure procurement and sometimes emotionally perceived needs.

TIME COMPRESSION AND THE FUTURE

At the time when the author was working on the Time Compression Programme, no significant tool existed to assist with the production of time-based process maps. Excel spreadsheets help to a limited extent but are not automated or tailored sufficiently to use in a seminar environment. Typically seminars are the appropriate way to engage users and obtain buy-in to any diagnosis, change plan or potential solution.

Since the TCP disbanded, software tools have come a long way and the following wish list of support tool features is now a reality:

- Discovery of process:
  - Simple process flows with automatic translation into a TBPM.
  - Cross-reference every element contained in above into a relational database.
  - Every aspect of process, including time, cost and resource levels, embedded within one map.
- Realization, improvement and deployment of process:
  - Ability to perform and enable what-if, impact analysis and re-engineering.
  - Provision of logical links to objectives, customer value propositions, organizational structures, functions, regulatory structures, quality conformance regimes, supporting documents, software applications etc.
  - Software requirements definition, testing and implementation.
- Continuous improvement of process:
  - Enable change via effective communication and user engagement.
  - Support ongoing operations and continuous improvement.
- Governance of change:
  - Version control all of the above between users and various versions, scenarios and variances of the process so that incremental improvements can be rolled out over time.
  - Notification provided to all stakeholders when changes affect their role.

One software application that exists and provides most of the above and which is being further developed to support time compress re-engineering is Nimbus Control (Figure 5.5) (Gotts, 2007). The potential that this tool offers for assisting business improvement in general is immense. It is therefore anticipated that time compression, alongside a range of complementary business initiatives driven by the use of tools such as Control, will become more widespread in the near future.

CONCLUSION

Time, as a measure, has been established as being strategically significant for contemporary business. The scale of time compression that is possible in most businesses is very significant because non-value-add time in most processes is at least 95 per cent. The impact of commercial benefit is wide and includes increased market share, price, productivity and innovation together with reduced levels of commercial risk.

Time compression has been established as a mechanism for addressing most of the aspects of business strategy and overarches the key objectives

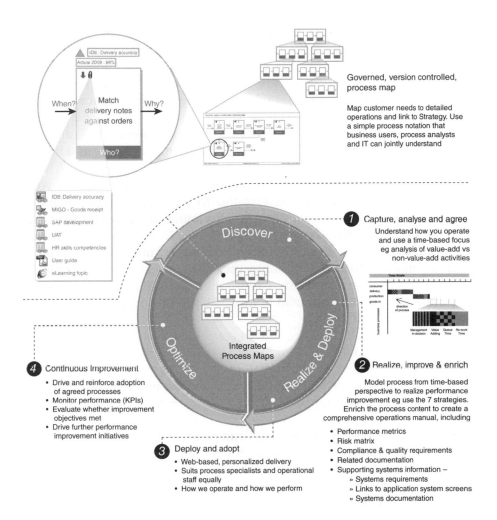

Figure 5.5 Nimbus Control
Source: www.nimbuspartners.com

associated with in-company logistics and managing the broader supply chain. Six principles aligned with the latter have been identified and linked to the idea of the time-based approach. To identify and achieve the time compression objectives, some tools such as time-based process mapping have been noted and coupled with a strategic re-engineering framework.

The approach supports a new source of competitiveness for time-sensitive markets and, as a focusing criterion, it enables one company or supply chain to be compared with another in terms of the internal and external benefits of time. This can provide the impetus for change and an improvement plan. Even the end user or the internal supply chain customer not operating in a time-sensitive market would find it difficult to argue that a benefit could not be acquired from the application of time compression. The approach does, however, require a top-down commitment and for full impact a lead organization within a supply chain needs to drive the initiative. This can become a challenge where trust is an issue and there is the need for an unbiased hand to guide, arbitrate and have a stake in the process.

Looking towards the future, companies must blend leanness with agility in order to be able to respond to at least two possible key challenges. The first is ensure that supply chains are designed, operated and evolved to meet and drive end-user needs. The second is to manage the supply chain in a dynamic commercial environment that is making network management rather than supply chain management a challenging reality. The time compression approach's simplicity and transparency across company and functional boundaries provide a good platform for meeting these challenges.

References

Barker, B and Helms, MM (1992) Production and operations restructuring: using time based strategies, *Industrial Management and Data Systems*, **92** (6), pp 3–7

Barker, RC (1994) The design of lean manufacturing systems using time-based analysis, *International Journal of Operations and Production Management*, **14**, pp 86–96

Beesley, A (1996) Time compression in the supply chain, *Industrial Management & Data Systems*, **96** (2), pp 12–16

Beesley, A (1997) Time compression in the supply chain, *Logistics Information Management*, **10** (6), pp 300–05

Carter, CR, Melnyk, PL and Handfield, SA (1994) *Identifying Sources of Cycle Time Reduction*, Quorum, Westport, CT

Christopher, M (1992) *Logistics and Supply Chain Management*, Pitman, London

Cooper, J (1994) Cranfield University, European Survey, unpublished work

European Logistics Association/A.T. Kearney (2004) *Excellence in Logistics*, ELA, Brussels

FhG ISI (Fraunhofer-Institut Fur Systemtechnik und Innovationsforschung) (1993) *Factory for the Future*, FhG ISI, Karlsruhe, Germany

Glover, J (1993) Achieving the organizational change necessary for successful TQM, *International Journal of Quality & Reliability Management*, **10** (6), pp 47–64

Gotts, I (2007) *Common Approach, Uncommon Results: How adoption delivers the results you deserve*, Ideas-Warehouse [online] www.ideas-warehouse. com (accessed 8 February 2010)

Indevo/PIMS Research (1991) *Identification and Quantification of Potentials from Reduced Lead-Times for the 'Lean Enterprise' Concept*, PIMS Associates GmbH, Cologne

Inman, A (1992) Time-based competition: challenges for industrial purchasing, *Production and Inventory Management Journal*, March/April

Lamming, R (2002) Lecture to Thames Valley Supply Chain Network Group

Mallinger, M (1993) Ambush along the TQM trail, *Journal of Organizational Change Management*, **6** (4), pp 30–42

Mather, H (1992) Design for logistics, *Production and Inventory Management Journal*, **33** (1), pp 7–9

New, CN (1992) *The Use of Throughput Efficiency as a Key Performance Measure for the New Manufacturing Era*, Cranfield School of Management, BPICS Conference

Oakland, JS and Beardmore, D (1995) Best practice customer service, *Total Quality Management*, **6** (2), pp 135–48

Ohmae, K (1965) *The Mind of the Strategist*, Penguin, Harmondsworth

Reich, RB (1991) *The Work of Nations*, Simon and Schuster, New York

Stalk, G and Hout, TM (1990) *Competing Against Time*, Free Press, New York

Stalk, G and Webber, AM (1993) Japan's dark side of time, *Harvard Business Review*, July–August

SUCCESS The route to, project managers' handbook (2004) Cranfield University, The University of Warwick

TCP (1995) The Time Compression Programme Conference, 'Profit from Time Compression', Delegate pack, Birmingham International Convention Centre

Tersine, RJ and Hummingbird, EA (1995) Lead-time reduction: The search for competitive advantage, *International Journal of Operations and Production Management*, **15** (2), pp 36–53

Womack, JP, Jones, DT and Roos, D (1990) *The Machine that Changed the World*, Maxwell Macmillan, New York

6

Building more agile supply chains

Remko van Hoek, COFELY

INTRODUCTION

There is no shortage of strategic opportunities for using supply chains and supply chain capabilities to achieve competitiveness and to achieve faster, more profitable company growth. There is a shortage of companies that achieve full potential and develop and leverage all needed supply chain capabilities. For almost a decade now, the benefit of creating a more agile and responsive supply chain has been widely accepted. Recently, however, the head of the supply chain of a major European manufacturer told me: 'We have realized the need to become more agile for years and have tried several things but do you have any suggestions for how we can actually accomplish higher levels of agility?'

The point is clear: there has been a more or less clear vision of the benefits of creating an agile supply chain going back to Harrison, Christopher and van Hoek (1999), defining it in terms of responsiveness to markets based upon the dimensions of market sensitivity, virtual integration, process integration and network integration (as shown in Figure 6.1). This vision has been widely cited and reinforced since, as a key competitive ambition and supply chain best practice aspiration (eg Christopher, 2004; Lee, 2004). However, there has been a shortage of studies and cases of companies

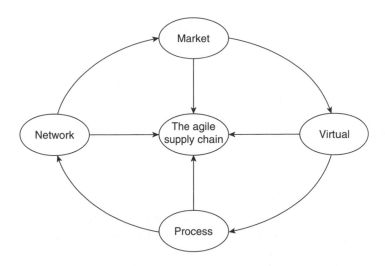

Figure 6.1   Theoretical framework for creating the agile supply chain

actually turning the vision or ambition into reality, let alone tools that they use to do so – and the theoretical argument in the above-referenced pieces are not sufficiently helpful in that respect.

So we now know that the market turbulence of the 1990s was only a start, and that continuing uncertainty makes the responsiveness that comes from agile supply chains a more valuable consideration than ever before. The key word here is 'consideration'. If there is one rule in supply chain management, it is that 'there is no universal solution to all operating circumstances'. So the key questions for this chapter become: (1) where to implement agile capabilities, or 'which operating environments most favour an agile supply chain?', and (2) how to approach implementation of agile capabilities.

The first part of this chapter introduces contingencies or operating factors that help answer the first question. It incorporates these factors into a more comprehensive description that shows when a supply chain should focus on agility, leanness and other options. The second part will introduce four pitfalls that companies commonly find themselves in and through which – despite good intentions and efforts to improve agility and responsiveness – they achieve anything but that. Instead they under-perform by driving practice away from the agile vision and generating cost of complexity with little value return.

OPERATING CIRCUMSTANCES
REQUIRING AGILITY

Factors previously introduced include demand volatility, product variety, forecastability and 'fashion-type' short life cycles and fast delivery. Van Hoek and Harrison (2001) introduced demand and supply characteristics as dimensions impacting the relevance of agile versus alternative approaches (Figure 6.2).

The relevance of factoring in demand and supply characteristics lies in the notion that creating the agile supply chain is about linking supply capabilities to demand requirements. In this respect, demand and supply 'characteristics' may be too general a term. There is an underlying dynamic between the two dimensions: supply abilities are to be created in response to demand requirements. Then one may think of the two dimensions as 'demand' indicating the viability of agility, and 'supply' indicating the feasibility of agility.

Responding to demand with a short lead time is a relevant feature of responsiveness to demand – but it also is a relatively basic one. It certainly does not capture a comprehensive set of responsiveness enhancers. When considering relevant agile capabilities, additional operating contingencies should be included. The remainder of this section will discuss demand and supply contingencies to be included in the categorization for operating environments.

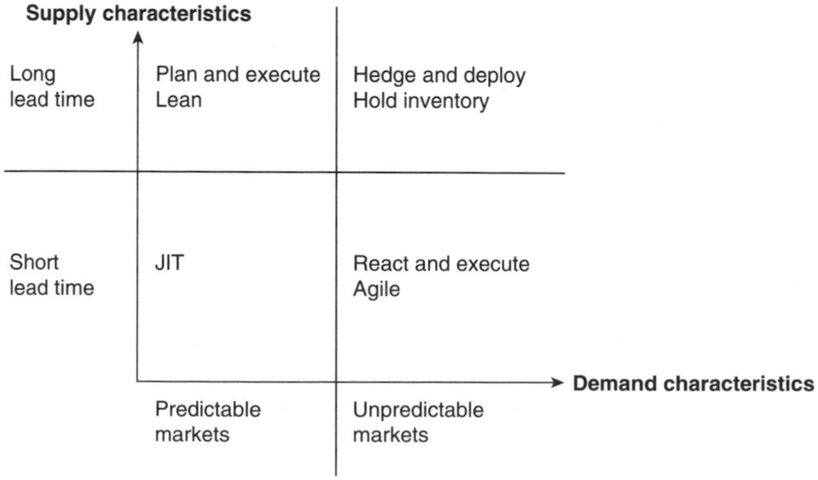

Supply characteristics		
Long lead time	Plan and execute Lean	Hedge and deploy Hold inventory
Short lead time	JIT	React and execute Agile
	Predictable markets	Unpredictable markets

Demand characteristics

Figure 6.2 Leanness and agility under demand and supply

Demand contingencies

Returning to lead times, the length of response time is predominantly a relative measure; when developing a cross-industry categorization for operating environments the absolute length in weeks, days or hours may be less relevant than the relative length. Lead-time tolerance is often the most relevant factor, as it captures any leeway that supply chains have in responding to demand. It also incorporates the fact that reliability of delivery may be more important than absolute lead time. A lead-time tolerance, therefore, contains both a speed and a reliability element.

'Forecastability' of demand is a better measure than predictions of market conditions because it is more closely linked to supply chain management capabilities. Market conditions are generally very difficult to predict at the detailed level (of individual stock-keeping units (SKUs), for example), but that does not mean that companies cannot forecast demand relatively accurately. More importantly from the contingency point of view is the fact that forecastability includes a supply chain management requirement of aligning mid- to longer-term capacity decisions to demand, rather than the hard-to-predict market conditions. Of course, one might argue that an ultimately responsive system removes the need to forecast, but this is more of a theoretical perspective than a realistic one. Irrespective of the supply chain's responsiveness to actual orders, companies still have to forecast for mid- to longer-term factors, including advanced orders to suppliers, long cycle-time production processes and capacity-building plans.

Demand for a product is rarely stable, but contains spikes and valleys. It is traditionally difficult to accommodate this variance in demand across a given time period, because every supply chain has a limited capacity and other constraints, such as maximum order volumes or limits on the availability of expensive slack capacity. However, there are two underlying features here: the difference between peak and valley of demand, and the frequency with which up- and downswings occur.

For the latter, a standard seasonal pattern may have just one peak (in the summer for garden furniture, for example), whereas the fashion industry may have a minimum of six or eight seasons. Retail promotions may have peaks every other week. These seasonal swings in demand may be significant, with peak demands often accounting for 60 to 70 per cent of total demand.

Figure 6.3 shows an operationalization of the above three demand contingencies – lead-time tolerance, forecastability and variance in volume.

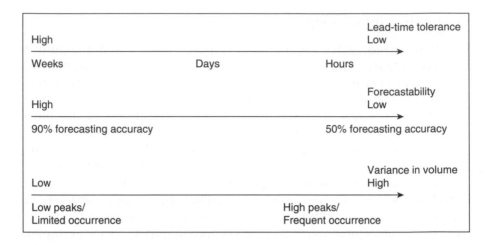

Figure 6.3 Demand contingencies impacting the viability of an agile supply chain

Supply contingencies

What are key supply contingencies that impact the feasibility of creating an agile supply chain? It is in this area that most gaps in current knowledge exist, as most of the publications on agile supply chains focus on the relevance of the approach itself in modern markets. Given the strength of this argument in favour of agility, and its importance in the current uncertain economic landscape, it is time to move beyond this basic view and consider the four layers (at least) of supply contingencies – or requirements for an agile supply chain.

'Postponement' has been widely identified as a mechanism that can support the creation of responsive supply. Delaying inventory allocation in the supply chain creates hedging options for responding to demand. This logistics postponement (delaying time and place functionality decisions) is helpful in the distribution segment of the supply chain but ultimately offers only partial responsiveness. It still assumes that stocks of finished goods build in anticipation of unknown demand, with all the risks of stock-outs still largely in place. Stock-outs generally have a very high cost in agile environments. It is for this reason that 'form postponement' is used – to delay the specification of final form and function of products until the last moment. Many companies do this by delaying packaging, labelling, adding documentation or product peripherals. Extending postponement into manufacturing, assembly, module manufacturing etc may help create the greater flexibility required for agility.

Associated with the need for form and function customization is the manufacturing and engineering principle of 'design variance' across products and product lines. In order to achieve levels of customization beyond the appearance of products, designs may have to vary beyond packaging – even beyond modules and into components and more basic features of design. This creates obvious design, manufacturing, sourcing and inventory complexities, which have to be dealt with in agile operating environments. This contingency also shows how creating an agile supply chain requires more than revising logistics and distribution management – it can have an impact all the way back to product design. The impact on suppliers and trading partners is discussed in the next contingency.

'Supply chain partner modularity' specifies the extent to which individual companies participating in the creation of an agile supply chain will have to align operations through the redesign of management practices and interfaces for the flow of goods and information. Some examples may help clarify this. Traditional sourcing and contract logistics has a buy–sell approach that suggests interfaces limited to a transactional level; just-in-time (JIT) sourcing has more extensive interfaces with sharing of demand data and alignment of operations. Integrated contract manufacturing, in which a third party controls the majority of build and make operations, extends the interface beyond aligned supply into integrated form and functionality creation. Fourth-party logistics is similar to this, with a third party taking over the organization and coordination of the entire flow of goods, information and management for the entire logistics function, and based around tightly structured interfaces. These approaches lead to a modular supply chain in which boundaries between partners are blurred and players are all orchestrated around real demand and service to the end customer.

It is important to note here that this contingency is not limited to upstream suppliers, but also involves the downstream trading partners between the company and end customer. This is traditionally a hard set of interfaces – compared with upstream suppliers who are paid for their supply efforts, giving companies an obvious lever in the structuring of these interfaces. The implication of agile reasoning, however, is that downstream partners and direct customers can also encourage alignment around this approach. Then channel interfaces should be structured around end-customer demand contingencies. Service to the end customer gives the key to this; it is an objective that all supply chain players share and where there is significant unification in purpose and objectives.

This brings us to a final contingency, which is the 'supply chain scope'. In order to completely meet the standards demanded for customization, modularity and partner integration, the scale or scope of supply chain involvement may be significant. It goes far beyond traditional views,

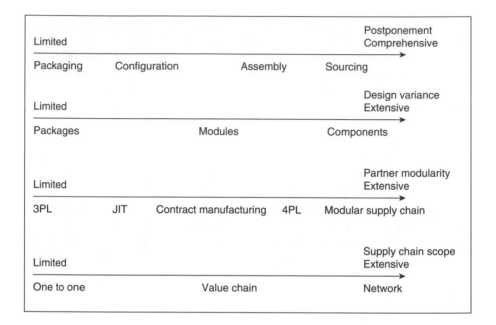

Figure 6.4 Supply contingencies impacting the feasibility of an agile supply chain

and develops one-to-one interfaces that extend into a 'value chain'. A value chain is a sequence of one-to-one interfaces leading up to a customer, while a supply chain has many-to-many interfaces and inter-connections, which must be dynamically rearranged around key processes and players in response to real demand. A network approach is far more appropriate here.

Figure 6.4 shows an operationalization of the above four supply contingencies – postponement, design variance, partner modularity and supply chain scope.

THE CATEGORIZATION FOR OPERATING ENVIRONMENTS

Figure 6.5 shows a categorization for operating environments based on the contingency factors introduced in the previous section. In the categorization a number of alternative approaches to agility are mentioned. The first consideration is to distinguish A, B, C products – based on Pareto analysis. Here A products (accounting for 80 per cent of volume and

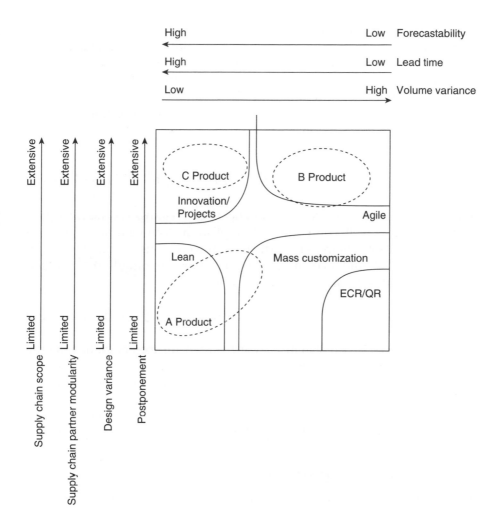

Figure 6.5   Categorization of operating environments

20 per cent of orders) are more standardized, and the greater forecastability, lower volume variance and less customization make them more suited to lean approaches. B products are more variable and more suited to agility.

Efficient customer response (ECR) and Quick Response are generally better in environments where demand requirements particularly impact delivery and distribution, but have less effect on upstream operations. Mass customization is generally better in environments with modest to significantly challenging demand that can be met with medium postponement and customization.

Agility is positioned near project environments. This is the right place from a supply contingency point of view, but is not so good from a demand contingency perspective. For example, in environments of innovation and single projects, lead-time leeway is often significantly bigger.

With contingencies and operating environments considered, the question that remains is: how to avoid pitfalls in implementing agility? This is the focus of the next section.

MITIGATING THE MINEFIELD OF PITFALLS

Figure 6.6 conceptualizes the 'minefield' of creating the agile supply chain. If all goes well, companies accomplish the four central dimensions of the agile supply chain as introduced in the previous section. However, lacking practical guidance and experience, there are pitfalls at every step of the way and companies can be found to be:

1. not actually responding to the customer as opposed to creating market sensitivity;
2. not coordinating governance, which allows for too much or too little responsiveness as opposed to virtual integration;
3. proliferating product in meaningless and valueless areas due to failures in process integration; and
4. despite a coming focus on service, not actually measuring that, leading to failed network integration.

Poor response to customers

It is common practice for companies to measure customer service in multiple ways. Customer satisfaction is the most widely used measure. However, there are several challenges with customer satisfaction measurement and surveys:

- Averages scores hide extremes at the end (problems and excellence).
- What opinions and strategies are behind subjective measures?
- Who is speaking? There are many different voices within the customer organization.
- What is the value of individual responses averaged out (innovators, key accounts, marginal accounts)?
- A lack of clear implications for service (what does a 3.75 mean in comparison to a 3.95 score?).

In response to these challenges, companies like GE, Honeywell and the Ford Motor Company have developed voice of the customer (VOC)

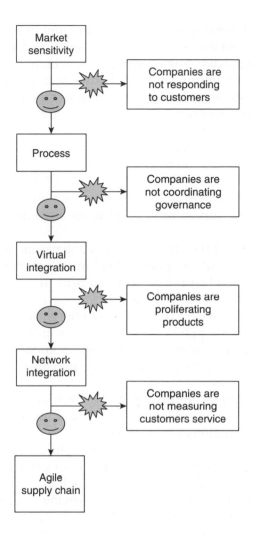

Figure 6.6 The 'minefield' of creating the agile supply chain

processes. These aim to go beyond customer satisfaction measurement by crafting a more comprehensive exchange with selected customers.

Typical features of this exchange include:

- Senior manager to senior manager meetings to avoid leaving the exchange to revenue-pressured situations, to signify commitment and to elevate the conversation.
- Expansion of the interaction to an ongoing exchange to drive beyond measurement at points in time only and establish sustained improvement and alignment.

- Involving additional functions, including logistics and engineering, and multiple contacts on the customer side in order to broaden the exchange into a bidirectional learning and alignment opportunity.
- Establishing joint improvement initiatives to turn the exchange into more than a listening exercise, including so-called 'at the customer – for the customer' teams.

The key distinctions between voice of the customer processes and customer satisfaction measurement are:

- It is based upon conversation, not surveys, which helps capture the story behind the survey scores and learn more about what actually drives scores.
- It is not the task of the customer service department but often starts with a senior executive sponsor talking to a customer peer and is followed by cross-functional work groups at a management and execution level working together on improving responsiveness and process alignment where that matters to the customer.
- It is ongoing, not a point measurement, as initial conversations are followed up with reviews of process improvements.
- It is customer centric as opposed to measuring average market performance scores.
- It captures multiple inputs from the customer, not just a single respondent; this is important because there are many voices of the customer and it matters who is talking.
- It is linked to action, with project teams deployed 'at the customer, for the customer'; hence the outcomes of the review are not internalized but used as a basis for customer-focused action.
- It actually improves customer relations owing to improved learning about the customer, relationship development and resource investments to address service issues, and improvement opportunities.

Overall, voice of the customer leads to much better market sensitivity as opposed to running the risk of misguided interpretation, or limited channels for capturing market input.

Governance does not support virtual integration

Agility requires the ability to be able to respond to local market requirements and opportunities. But this does not mean that companies should not aim at leveraging skills and capabilities across the regions in which they operate – let alone avoiding reinventing the wheel across parts of the organization. Local responsiveness and global efficiency need to be integrated into a network organization that is a virtually integrated entity, despite operating in multiple locations and regions.

One way in which I coped with this pitfall at Nuon (a €6bn European utility) when I worked there in the procurement organization was to use account plans with internal stakeholders and customers to balance business needs and local considerations with global category opportunities. The account plan was a simple one-page template used to capture priorities in collaborating with the business, ensuring alignment between procurement and internal customers and stakeholders without being able to control those business unit peers directly. Effectively this account planning was used as a practical way to achieve virtual integration.

Around the annual business planning cycle, procurement would discuss with the business unit its main priorities for the coming year and how procurement could help achieve those. Main areas for joint focus and projects or collaborative initiatives between procurement and the business unit would be captured, including key performance indicators (KPIs) to measure success. During the year the plan would then be revisited in a discussion between procurement and the business unit's management team to evaluate results so far and progress in the collaboration. Using account planning proved an effective way to keep governance simple yet practical and work oriented.

Meaningless product proliferation

A particular area of concern when it comes to process integration is product proliferation. Owing to process misalignment between several parts of the supply chain, companies often end up proliferating products, driven by internal misalignment rather than market driven. How this often happens is that R&D wants to innovate and expand product ranges, sales wants to create more opportunities to sell, while supply chain and operations want to avoid margin reductions from cost of complexity in operations. A lack of process integration leads to uncontrolled efforts disconnected from market opportunity.

New products are created, hoping that this will aid in growing the business by offering more revenue opportunities. In theory this improves the ability to respond to customer demand. In reality, however, companies typically get a lot of product proliferation wrong and end up creating too many products that do not sell, adding cost and needless complexity into their supply chain.

One company found that the bottom 25 per cent of products generated less than 1 per cent of revenue and were actually unprofitable, reducing the company's overall profit. Another company saw its SKU count double in two years, with SKU growth far outpacing revenue growth, resulting in a reduction of volumes per product and return on investment in designing and marketing products – while mushrooming the cost of warehousing. While all of this is happening the supply chain is left holding the bag, with the business not really owning any responsibility for SKU management. One warehouse manager of this company said: 'When I meet people from the business I ask them how many SKUs they have in the warehouse. They never get it right and always underestimate.'

To summarize, common flags for product proliferation include:

1. growth of SKU count outpacing revenue growth;
2. SKUs that do not meet revenue and volume thresholds for generating return on design, marketing and shipping them;
3. SKU management is not distributed across the business and there is no accountability for, or even transparency of, SKU proliferation in the business.

Additional complexity flags can be found in the warehouse and sales, including:

- Warehouse flags:
  - ongoing order and shipment size reduction;
  - a constant need for more stock-locations in the warehouse;
  - nightshifts and rush shipments outside seasonal peaks.
- Sales flags:
  - a catalogue that is as thick as the Yellow Pages, running the risk of confusing customers;
  - more products than any sales person could every carry in the boot of a car;
  - special SKUs are being added based upon special (key-)customer requests, events or market opportunities but they may not be removed after the event.

Faced with a lot of the bad consequences of SKU proliferation outlined above, Company A, a consumer products company, has reduced SKU count by 30 per cent during the past three years while growing the company and adding new products, breaking away from flag 1. It did so by actively managing to avoid flags 2 and 3. The company initiated an SKU management effort – introduced by the CEO – with a mandate that 50 per cent of SKUs that do not meet revenue thresholds will be cut each quarter. The reason for the target being 50 per cent and not 100 per cent is that new products are being developed in the market that might not yet have come to flourish fully, there are products that do not perform steadily every quarter (because of seasonality, for example), and it leaves the business some autonomy in making cut decisions. Key to this approach is that it establishes SKU management as an ongoing discipline. A lot of companies do one-off efforts but a manager from Company A says: 'Without sustaining the management focus SKU count is likely to creep back up in no time. You cannot expect behaviour to just change without ongoing focus and accountability.'

In order to accomplish this accountability, SKU count has been elevated to one of the measures on the global dashboard that is reviewed monthly by the senior executive team. Additionally, a so-called 'glide-path' has been established. This is a set of SKU reduction targets on a timeline. In addition to sustaining the focus on – and accountability for – SKU reduction, incorporating the SKU count on the dashboard also removes decisions from the execution level. The supply chain team has dedicated a person to the SKU effort and this person creates transparency to the business about its SKU count, flags them when they are not on the glide-path and offers help in reducing the SKU count. Because senior management owns the outcomes of the effort at the dashboard level the supply chain team is positioned as aiding the business rather than being the bad guys. Furthermore, it removes discussion about the effort from the execution level. According to the senior supply chain executive, this is important because otherwise, 'you end up with emotion involved at this level resulting in endless discussion instead of focused action'.

Incorrect measurement that focuses responsiveness wrongly

All companies include customer service in some form in their performance measurement system. However, almost all operationalize this measurement internally, leading to responsiveness that is misguided and focused wrongly – not being directly and fully on customers. In particularly, most companies measure delivery service in one or multiple ways based upon their internal definition of success. Typically the measures focus on how reliably and fast the company delivered against the timetable it put forward. This misses the point, as this timetable might not be aligned with the customers' needs. So companies are not tracking responsiveness to customer need at all. The better way is to ask customers for their desired delivery window and measure execution against that customer-defined measure of success. General Electric realized this when it presented high delivery reliability scores from its own measurement to customers and received a negative reaction. In short, customers reacted that performance was not at all good according to their own measurement, which considered the time when they needed deliveries to take place.

GE changed its measurement set towards what it call Span measurement. Span stands for the range of delivery around customer requested due dates. Essentially, the company now measures, across all deliveries globally, how close it was to the delivery date the customer requested when ordering. In its plastics business the company brought Span down from 30 days to just a few days – meaning that every customer can depend upon GE delivering any product, anywhere in the world, when they ask for it, with a maximum variation of a few days.

Experience from GE suggests the value of several actions to improve measurement for agility:

- Share measurement dashboards with customers, and aim to measure your performance using the measures that customers use to measure your company.
- Do not measure against your own measures of success, but ask the customer what defines success.
- Hold all parts of the supply chain accountable against the customer-defined measure of success, so that there is no escape from market sensitivity.

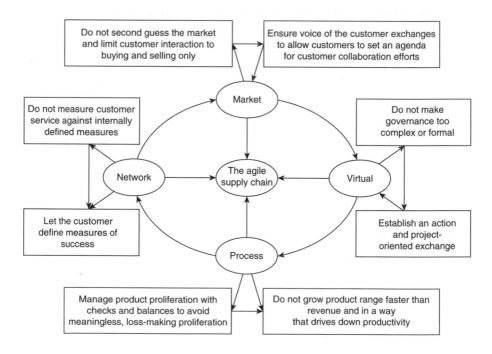

Figure 6.7 Enhanced agile supply chain theoretical framework

Enhancing the vision of agility

This chapter has offered practical findings from aspiring practitioners, several years of research and dozens of case studies. As valuable a starting point as the theory surrounding the vision of creating an agile supply chain is, it is still only vision-centred. The experiences and cases presented in this chapter show where the vision can be supplemented, thereby enhancing the theoretical framework presented in Figure 6.1. Figure 6.7 captures the particular axioms identified and visually displays the enhanced agile supply chain theoretical framework.

CONCLUSION AND REFLECTIONS

This chapter has attempted to offer additional insight into the questions of where and how to consider developing agile capabilities in the supply chain. The identification of operating environments that favour – or disfavour – agile supply chains gives a more realistic chance of successful implementation. Avoiding the implementation pitfalls will further increase the likelihood of success.

As one of the authors of the original agile supply chain vision, I would like to apologize to the head of supply chain referenced at the start of this chapter – I hope that this contribution will be more helpful and make up for the shortcomings of the original vision.

References

Christopher, M (2004) Supply chains: a marketing perspective, in *Understanding Supply Chains*, ed S New and R Westbrook, pp 69–108, Oxford University Press, Oxford

Harrison, A, Christopher, MC and van Hoek, RI (1999) *Creating the Agile Supply Chain*, Institute of Transport and Logistics, Corby

Lee, H (2004) The Triple-A supply chain, *Harvard Business Review*, October

Van Hoek, R and Harrison, A (2001) Editorial Special Issue on Creating the Agile Supply Chain, *International Journal of Physical Distribution and Logistics Management*, **31** (4), pp 231–34

7

Using marketing and services strategies for logistics customer service

David Grant, University of Hull

The customer is the immediate jewel of our souls. Him we flatter, him we feast, compliment, vote for, and will not contradict. (Ralph Waldo Emerson)

INTRODUCTION

The term 'logistics' comes from militaristic roots and is not readily associated with the non-tangible notion of 'customer service'. And yet, customer service represents the output of a firm's business logistics system and the physical distribution or 'place' component of its marketing mix. Thus, customer service is the interface between logistics activities and the demand creation process of marketing, and measures how well a logistics system functions in creating time and place utility for customers (Pisharodi and Langley, 1990).

Initially, physical distribution or logistics and marketing were linked; early writings in marketing related to distributive trade practices due to the increasing significance of 'middlemen' who were performing more functions between producers and consumers (Weld, 1915). Middleman specialization included activities still prevalent today, such as assembling, storing, risk bearing, financing, rearranging, selling and transporting. Such activities provide place and time utility, ie products in the right place through movement and at the right time through availability. Conversely, manufacturing provides form utility of goods through making tangible products from raw materials, while other marketing activities such as credit and quantity discounts provide possession utility. The operative instrument for such middlemen is the channel of distribution.

A disintegration or segregation of physical distribution from the other three marketing mix variables of product, price and promotion began in the 1950s with the introduction of the marketing concept. Physical distribution activities were reduced to only physical supply and distribution functions and the notion of physical distribution customer service was misplaced (Bartels, 1982).

However, a move to reintegrate physical distribution and marketing began in the 1970s when writers argued they belonged together in terms of theoretical progress and applications owing to their strong historical linkages and conceptual developments. Such a rediscovery stemmed from the need to focus on customers in a changing environment (Sharman, 1984) and the realization that firms that did so would obtain additional business and profits from leveraging their distribution operations (Shapiro, 1984).

Further, customers have become more sophisticated and demanding during the past 30 years and their expectations of suppliers' abilities to meet their needs have subsequently increased. Accordingly, many suppliers, retailers and service organizations have striven to improve logistics customer service processes to establish or maintain a competitive advantage. Desired outcomes are satisfied customers, increased customer loyalty, repeat and increased purchases, and improved corporate financial performance (Daugherty, Stank and Ellinger, 1998).

But what exactly is customer service, particularly in a logistics or supply chain context? Johns (1999) noted there are 30 definitions for the word 'service' in the dictionary; thus the concept of service in a business context may be elusive or confusing. Service can mean an industry or organization (eg government services), an outcome that has different perspectives for both service provider and customer (eg on-time delivery), product support (eg after-sales service) or an act or process (Johns, 1999).

La Londe and Zinszer initiated a refocus on logistics customer service with their major study, *Customer Service: Meaning and measurement*, published in 1976. Their definition of logistics customer service was presented as:

a process which takes place between buyer, seller and third party. The process results in a value added to the product or service exchanged. ... the value added is also shared, in that each of the parties to the transaction or contract is better off at the completion of the transaction than they were before the transaction took place. Thus, in a process view: Customer service is a process for providing significant value-added benefits to the supply chain in a cost effective way. (1976, p 15)

The notion of process suggests that logistics activities are more like services than goods. There are distinct differences between services and goods within the marketing mix category of product and Hoffman and Bateson describe the four important characteristics that distinguish services from goods as:

intangibility as services cannot be seen, smelt, felt, tasted or otherwise sensed similar to goods; inseparability of production and consumption as most services involve the customer in the production function; heterogeneity or inconsistency of the service from the perspective of the service delivery and customer experience; and perishability of the service if it is not consumed at the moment in time it takes place, ie the service cannot be inventoried. (1997, p 43)

Primary logistics activities include transportation, warehousing, inventory management and order processing, and usually do not physically transform or affect goods. Logistics activities can certainly be heterogeneous, eg order cycle time variability and consistency, and are also intangible eg the storage or delivery of a good, and perishable, eg a lorry leaving on its delivery route.

What is less clear is how inseparable logistics activities are as regards the customer. The customer is involved in the ordering and receiving stages but is relatively passive throughout the provision of the logistics activities, provided the variability is within accepted bounds.

Nevertheless, logistics activities generally encompass characteristics and classification of services, ie benefits received by a customer such as time, place and possession utilities are provided by way of a service or enhanced product offering from logistics activities rather than from attributes of a basic product.

Products and prices are relatively easy for competitors to duplicate. Promotional efforts also can be matched by competitors, with the possible exception of a well-trained and motivated sales force. A satisfactory service encounter, or favourable complaint resolution, is one important way that a firm can really distinguish itself in the eyes of the customer. Logistics can therefore play a key role in contributing to a firm's competitive advantage by providing excellent customer service.

Thus, application of logistics customer service would be well served by the use of evaluation and analysis concepts and tools from the services marketing area. However, theories and techniques in the marketing discipline have been slow in finding application in logistics research, notwithstanding calls for reintegration with logistics (Harris and Stock,

1985) and calls for other interdisciplinary applications in logistics (Stock, 1997).

The foregoing raises practical questions regarding logistics customer service and its application within firms. For example, what is the state of play in logistics customer service today? What are important elements of logistics customer service? And how can firms establish appropriate customer service strategies and policies? These issues are explored in the following sections.

LOGISTICS CUSTOMER SERVICE TODAY

Firms attempt to meet various shareholder/stakeholder requirements in the ordinary course of their business. Profitability, calculated from sales revenue (or turnover) minus expenses, is one of those requirements and is by no means assured for those firms that do not consider both factors carefully. Without profits, shareholder capital and retained profits will erode and bankruptcy might result.

Logistics costs such as inventory, warehousing, transportation and information/order processing comprise a firm's expenditure on customer service. Further, the objective for the firm is to maximize profits and minimize total logistics costs over the long term, while maintaining or increasing customer service levels. Such an objective might be considered a 'mission impossible' and firms must carefully choose among the various trade-offs to satisfy customers' needs and maximize profits while minimizing total costs and not wasting scarce marketing-mix resources. Thus, there is a necessity to evaluate trade-offs between determining/providing additional customer service features sought by customers and the costs incurred to do so.

However, customer service levels may be higher than a customer would set them and firms should 'banish the costly misconception that all customers seek or need improved service' (Sabath, 1978, p 26). However, choosing when to meet and when to exceed customer expectations is a key factor. Not all service features are equally important to each customer, and most customers will accept a relatively wide range of performance in any given service dimension (Markham and Aurik, 1993).

Further, most firms in the supply chain do not sell exclusively to end users. Instead, they sell to other intermediaries who in turn may or may not sell to the final customer. For this reason, it may be difficult for these firms to assess the impact of customer service failures, such as stock-outs, on end users. For example, an out-of-stock situation at a manufacturer's warehouse does not necessarily mean an out-of-stock product at the retail level. However, the impact of stock-outs on the customer's behaviour is important.

Recent research has found that an average out-of-stock rate for fast-moving consumer goods retailers across the world is 8.3 per cent, or an average on-shelf availability of 91.7 per cent. Consumer responses to stock-outs were: buy the item at another store (31 per cent), substitute a different brand (26 per cent), substitute the same brand (19 per cent), delay their purchase until the item became available (15 per cent) and do not purchase any item (9 per cent). Thus, 55 per cent of consumers will not purchase an item at the retail store while 50 per cent of consumers will substitute or not purchase the manufacturer's item (Corsten and Gruen, 2003).

One way to establish a desirable customer service level at the retail level is to take into account such consumer responses to stock-outs. When a manufacturer is aware of the implications of stock-outs at the retail level, it can make adjustments in order cycle times, fill rates, transportation options, and other strategies that will result in higher levels of product availability in retail stores.

These observations reinforce the notion that firms must adopt a customer-oriented view and seek out customer needs. Firms also have to ask customers the right questions to ensure that important and relevant criteria are captured. For example, one food manufacturer maintained a 98 per cent service level, which necessitated large inventories in many warehouse locations. However, this practice often resulted in shipping dated merchandise and customers therefore perceived this practice as evidence of low quality and poor service (Sabath, 1978).

Quality in logistics means meeting agreed-to customer requirements and expectations (Byrne, 1992). Suppliers need to develop and deliver service offerings more quickly in the light of the many changes to distribution that have emerged, such as technological advances of efficient consumer response and just-in-time delivery. However, the notion of pleasing the customer at every turn regardless of cost has undergone a re-evaluation such that suppliers or shippers are now attempting to accommodate customers while optimizing the supply chain.

This tactic requires suppliers to negotiate with the customer and possibly cost-share with other actors in the supply chain (Richardson, 1998). Such negotiations may be difficult to implement as there is little evidence that logisticians and suppliers have developed sufficient customer interest in logistics activities (Blanding, 1992). This may be indicative of suppliers not properly determining customer needs when they establish customer service policies and trade-offs.

Despite 30 years of research and application of logistics customer service, this attitude still appears to be the case. Van Hoek, in Chapter 6 of this book, examines barriers to establishing an agile supply chain and argues that many firms are not considering the customer's point of view, nor are

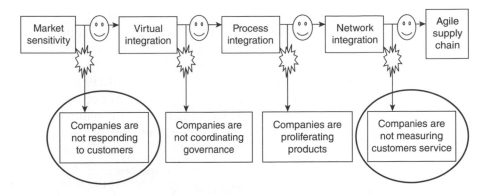

Figure 7.1 Pitfalls in logistics customer service
Source: adapted from van Hoek, 2009

they measuring customer service in a meaningful way. Figure 7.1 presents these 'pitfalls' relative to flows in an agile supply chain.

The foregoing suggests that a customer's product and service needs, and their subsequent supplier selection criteria for logistics services, extend beyond usual business-to-business criteria such as product quality, technical competence and competitive prices. Customer evaluation of logistics suppliers may include a number of intangible factors related to the service being provided as the customer seeks added value or utility from it.

An example is whether customer service representatives are on call 24 hours a day. A firm must therefore have the ability to recognize and respond to customer needs if it is to have any chance of satisfying them and achieving the benefits of loyalty and profitability. But to do that it must initially determine what the customers' needs are, both from its own perspective and from that of the customers. The next section discusses possible elements of logistics customer service.

ELEMENTS OF LOGISTICS CUSTOMER SERVICE

A first step in understanding a customer's service requirements or needs is to audit existing customer service policies (Christopher, 2005). This will allow the firm to see what they presently offer and determine how important employees believe these logistics customer service elements are to customers. Difference industrial sectors will, of course, have different emphases regarding such elements; however, the basic groupings should be similar.

La Londe and Zinszer (1976) proposed that logistics customer service contains three distinct constructs: pre-transaction, transaction and post-

Construct	Variable name
Pre-order (Pre-transaction)	Availability Appropriate OCT Consistent OCT
Order service and quality (Transaction)	Accurate invoices On-time delivery Complete orders Products arrive undamaged Accurate orders Consistent product quality Products arrive to specification
Relationship service (Post-transaction)	After-sales support Delivery time Helpful CSRs Customized services
Relationship quality (Post-transaction)	Trust Commitment Integrity
Global satisfaction (The outcome . . .)	Overall supplier quality Feelings towards suppliers Future purchase intentions

Figure 7.2 Elements of logistics customer service and relationships
Source: Grant, 2004, p 191

transaction, which reflect the temporal nature of a service experience. La Londe and Zinszer's work was conducted 30 years ago and a more recent study (Grant, 2004) from the customer's perspective, as opposed to the supplier's perspective, found similar constructs of logistics customer service. However, Grant's work found that the post-transaction construct also includes elements of relationships; his entire set of variables related to the three constructs is shown in Figure 7.2.

Firms can use this list of elements to develop their own customer service features; this list is by no means exhaustive but does provide an appropriate starting point for firms to develop logistics customer service strategies. Firms will likely have to add or delete some elements to service their own sectoral and local requirements.

These two studies also confirm that firms should categorize customer service elements into dimensions related to pre-transaction, transaction and post-transaction events when facilitating operations design and customer service planning. This categorization will enable firms to determine critical events in their service and allow them to monitor and follow up on service failures, as will be discussed in the next section.

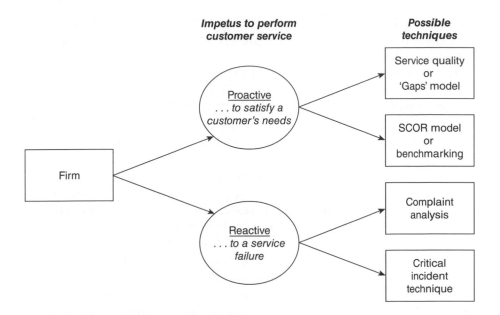

Figure 7.3   Customer service strategy process

STRATEGIES FOR LOGISTICS CUSTOMER SERVICE

The impetus to develop a logistics customer service strategy can be either proactive, reactive or a combination of both. A proactive impetus follows from a firm's desire to satisfy its customers' needs, while a reactive impetus results from a service failure. Figure 7.3 illustrates this dichotomy and presents possible customer service techniques related to each impetus.

Reactive techniques

Understanding and obtaining information about customer requirements necessitates an exchange of information between customers and firms. Complaint analysis is one such exchange, concerning perceived customer dissatisfaction resulting from a customer service experience or critical incident.

Complaints derive from a 'moment of truth' between supplier and customer that is considered a critical incident. Critical incidents are defined in psychology as 'any observable human activity that is sufficiently complete in itself to permit inferences and predictions to be made about the person performing the act. To be critical, an incident must occur in a situation where the purpose or intent of the act seems fairly clear to the observer and where its consequences are sufficiently definite to leave little doubt concerning the effects' (Flanagan, 1954, p 327). Thus, a critical incident is a moment of truth that becomes representative in the mind of a customer (Lewis, 1993).

The critical incident technique (CIT) was developed as a process to investigate human behaviour and facilitate its practical usefulness for solving practical problems (Flanagan, 1954). CIT procedures consist of collecting and analysing qualitative data to investigate and understand facts behind an incident or series of incidents. Some uses of CIT applicable to business include training, equipment design, operating procedures, and measurement of performance criteria or proficiency.

Complaint handling is significantly associated with both trust and commitment (Tax, Brown and Chandrashekaran, 1998). These concepts are important for supplier–customer relationship development. Complaint analysis thus has a role as part of a post-transaction process but is not a complete form of information for firms when used in isolation.

Such information does not provide an understanding about what customer service features actually provide customer satisfaction. Thus, while it 'might be an effective way to fix yesterday's problems' it is 'a poor way to determine today's (or tomorrow's) customer requirements' (Markham and Aurik, 1993, p 55).

Complaint analysis has also been called a defensive strategy since its focus is directed at aggressively protecting existing customers rather than searching for new ones (Lapidus and Schibrowsky, 1994). Therefore, firms using only complaint analysis or CIT techniques might find it difficult to determine current and future success factors and establish a competitive advantage.

Proactive techniques

It is important that a firm establish customer service policies that are based on customer requirements and that are supportive of the overall marketing strategy. What is the point of manufacturing a great product, pricing it competitively and promoting it well, if it is not readily available to the consumer? At the same time, customer service policies should be cost-efficient, contributing favourably to the firm's overall profitability. A proactive customer service strategy allows a firm to consider all these factors.

One popular method for setting customer service levels is to benchmark a competitor's customer service performance. One major question is what to benchmark, and the Supply Chain Council's supply chain operations reference (SCOR) model provides a framework to analyse internal processes – plan, source, make, deliver and return (Christopher, 2005).

There are several issues about the effectiveness of benchmarking, for example it may promote imitation rather than innovation, best practice operators may refuse to participate in any benchmarking exercise, it focuses on particular activities and thus there is a failure to allow for inter-activity trade-offs, and there is difficulty in finding well-matched comparators (Santhouse, 1999).

Further, while it may be interesting to see what the competition is doing, this information has limited usefulness. In terms of what the customer requires, how does the firm know if the competition is focusing on the right customer service elements? Therefore, competitive benchmarking alone is insufficient. Competitive benchmarking should be performed in conjunction with customer surveys that measure the importance of various customer service elements.

Opportunities to close differences between customer requirements and the firm's performance can be identified and the firm can then target primary customers of competitors and protect its own key accounts from potential competitor inroads. The service quality model developed from the services marketing discipline and presented in the next sub-section enables a firm to identify such differences and follows the call to use more interdisciplinary techniques in logistics customer service.

The service quality model

Customers evaluate services differently from goods owing to their different characteristics. One popular method to investigate such evaluations is the service quality or 'gaps' model (Parasuraman, Zeithaml and Berry, 1985). Customers develop *a priori* expectations of a service based on several criteria such as previous experience, word-of-mouth recommendations, or advertising and communication by the service provider.

Once customers 'experience' a service they compare their perceptions of that experience to their expectations. If their perceptions meet or exceed their expectations they are satisfied; conversely, if perceptions do not meet expectations they are dissatisfied. The difference between expectations and perceptions forms the major 'gap' that is of interest to firms.

Figure 7.4 presents this model and includes the customer's and firm's positions. The expectations and perceptions 'gap' is affected by four other 'gaps' related to the firm's customer service and service quality activities which are for the most part invisible to the customer.

First, the firm must understand the customer's expectations for the service. Gap 1 is the discrepancy between consumer expectations and the firm's perception of these expectations. Second, the firm must then turn the customer's expectations into tangible service specifications. Gap 2 is the discrepancy between the firm's perceptions of consumer expectations and the firm's establishment of service quality specifications.

Third, the firm must actually provide the service according to those specifications. Gap 3 is the discrepancy between the firm's establishment

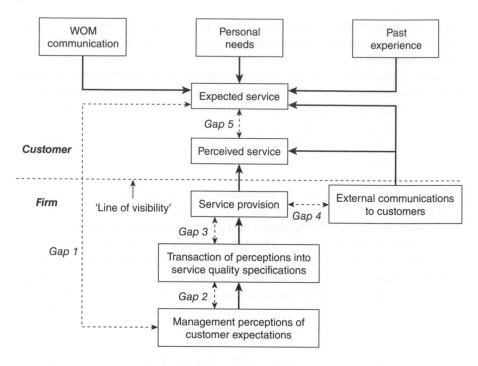

Figure 7.4 Service quality or 'gaps' model
Source: adapted from Parasurman *et al*, 1985, p 44

of service quality specifications and its actual service provision. Last, the firm must communicate its intentions and actions to the customer. Gap 4 is the discrepancy between the firm's actual service provision and external communications about the service to customers.

Gap 5 is associated with a customer's expectations for a service experience compared with its perceptions of the actual event, and is the sum of the four gaps associated with the firm, ie Gap 5 = (Gap 1 + Gap 2 + Gap 3 + Gap 4). The firm must minimize or eliminate each discrepancy or gap that it has control over in order to minimize or eliminate the customer's discrepancy or gap related to the service experience. Using the service quality model forces a firm to examine what customer service and service quality they provide to customers in a customer-centric framework.

AN EXAMPLE FROM ONLINE RETAILING

During the past decade the internet has created a retail and consumer revolution by providing a new, convenient channel for shopping. The online retail market is growing rapidly and now covers a large assortment of products and services. Throughout this period, retailers have had to ensure that they offer consumers appropriate customer service and a pleasant online shopping experience, including the order fulfilment process.

The responsibility of many physical aspects of the fulfilment process, which previously lay with the consumer in-store and beyond, is now taken on by the retailer. This final extension to the usual definitions of logistics management from 'point of origin to point of consumption' is referred to as the 'last mile' process and means that greater complexity now attaches to a retailer's distribution system. This has major implications for a retailer as the efficient management of distribution and fulfilment in the 'last mile' can reduce costs, enhance profitability and thus provide competitive advantage.

Online retailing of physical products accounts for two-thirds of total online sales in the UK (Internet Measurement Research Group, 2008). These online purchases involve the handling and transferring of physical products, ie packing, picking, dispatching, delivering, collecting and re-turning. Further, a product purchased online or 'virtually' cannot be used by the consumer until it is delivered to him or her at the right place, at the right time, in the right quantities and in the right condition.

Thus, from a consumers' perspective, fulfilment is generally considered to be of the utmost importance and a crucial attribute affecting their judgement of service quality and satisfaction. Further, fulfilment has been identified as a main challenge facing internet retailers and a major barrier preventing consumers from purchasing online (Burt and Sparks, 2003).

Xing and Grant (2006) developed an electronic physical distribution service quality (e-PDSQ) framework from the consumer's perspective that addresses the foregoing issues facing retailers who sell on the internet. The framework consists of four constructs – availability, timeliness, con-dition and return, and related variables – as shown in Table 7.1.

Table 7.1   E-PDSQ framework constructs and variables

Constructs	Variables
Timeliness (T)	Choice of delivery date; Choice of delivery time slot; Deliver on the first date arranged; Deliver within specified time slot; Can deliver quickly
Availability (A)	Confirmation of availability; Substitute or alternative offer; Order tracking and tracing system; Waiting time in case of out-of-stock situation
Condition (C)	Order accuracy; Order completeness; Order damage in-transit
Return (R)	Ease of return and return channels options; Promptness of collection; Promptness of replacement

Source: Xing and Grant, 2006, p 285

This e-PDSQ framework was empirically tested in a survey of online consumers in Edinburgh, Scotland and confirmed the framework's appropriateness. Price was the most important online purchasing criterion, which suggests it is the principal motivator in the online market and that the market is getting more price-transparent with consumers who are becoming more price-sensitive.

The five variables most important to consumers in an online delivery context were: order condition, reflecting its role in demonstrating a retailer's reliability; order accuracy, considered important for repeat business; order confirmation, which demonstrates consumers' unwillingness to wait and their intolerance with stock-outs; and easy return and prompt replacement, which reflect consumers' concerns over product returns.

The Xing and Grant study provided a parsimonious set of e-PDSQ variables and constructs for retailers to use to design and operate their online offerings, based on the Parasuraman *et al*'s (1985) service quality model, and thus demonstrates how firms can adapt and use models and ideas from other disciplines to provide effective customer service in a logistics context.

SUMMARY

Customer service is a necessary requirement in logistics activities and is affected by various environmental factors shaping today's marketplace. Logistics customer service has its roots in the marketing discipline and logisticians can use and learn from marketing techniques and methodologies to investigate customer service.

A strategy for logistics customer service requires a basic trade-off between costs incurred and enhanced profit received. Each industrial sector will also have its own unique needs and issues that further complicate such considerations. However, while the importance of individual customer service elements varies among firms, there is a common set of elements presented above that should provide a useful starting point for most firms.

A global perspective focuses on seeking common market demands worldwide rather than cutting up world markets and treating them as separate entities with very different product needs. However, different parts of the world have different customer service needs such as information availability, order completeness, and expected lead times. Local infrastructure, communications and time differences may make it impossible to achieve high levels of customer service. Also, management styles in different global markets may be different from those prevalent in the firm's 'home' environment.

Although customer service may represent the best opportunity for a firm to achieve a sustainable competitive advantage, many firms still do not implement logistics customer service strategies, or do so by simply duplicating those implemented by competitors. The service quality framework discussed above can be used by firms to collect and analyse customer information, determine what is really important to customers, and thus enhance their customer service initiatives. Globally, customer services provided by the firm should match local customer needs and expectations to the greatest degree possible. A successful output of such customer service considerations will be a satisfied customer, which should lead to increased profitability for the firm.

References

Bartels, R (1982) Marketing and distribution are not separate, *International Journal of Physical Distribution & Materials Management*, **12** (3), pp 3–10

Blanding, W (1992) Customer service logistics, in *Logistics: The strategic issues*, ed M Christopher, pp 179–93, Chapman and Hall, London

Burt, S and Sparks, L (2003) E-commerce and the retail process: a review, *Journal of Retailing and Consumer Service*, **10**, pp 275–86

Byrne, PM (1992) Global logistics: improve the customer service cycle, *Transportation & Distribution*, **33** (June), pp 66–67

Christopher, M (2005) *Logistics and Supply Chain Management: Creating value-adding networks*, 3rd edn, FT Prentice Hall, London

Corsten, D and Gruen, T (2003) Desperately seeking shelf availability: an examination of the extent, the causes, and the efforts to address retail out-of-stocks, *International Journal of Retail and Distribution Management*, **31** (12), pp 605–17

Daugherty, PJ, Stank, TP and Ellinger, AE (1998) Leveraging logistics/ distribution capabilities: the effect of logistics service on market share, *Journal of Business Logistics*, **19** (2), pp 35–51

Flanagan, JC (1954) The critical incident technique, *Psychological Bulletin*, **51** (July), pp 327–58

Grant, DB (2004) UK and US management styles in logistics: different strokes for different folks? *The International Journal of Logistics: Research and Applications*, **7** (3), pp 181–87

Harris, WD and Stock, JR (1985) Marketing and distribution: coming back together at last! in *Distribution Research and Education: Today and tomorrow*, ed MC Cooper and JR Grabner, pp 48–67, Ohio State University, Columbus, OH

Hoffman, KD and Bateson, JEG (1997) *Essentials of Services Marketing*, Dryden, Orlando, FL

Internet Measurement Research Group [accessed November 2008] 10% of retail sales now online [Online] http://www.imrg.org

Johns, N (1999) What is this thing called service? *European Journal of Marketing*, 33 (9/10), pp 958–73

LaLonde, BJ and Zinszer, PH (1976) *Customer Service: Meaning and measurement*, National Council of Physical Distribution Management, Chicago

Lapidus, RS and Schibrowsky, JA (1994) Aggregate complaint analysis: a procedure for developing customer service satisfaction, *Journal of Services Marketing*, 8 (4), pp 50–60

Lewis, BR (1993) Service quality measurement, *Marketing Intelligence & Planning*, 11 (4), pp 4–12

Markham, WJ and Aurik, JC (1993) Shape up & ship out, *Journal of European Business*, 4 (5), pp 54–57

Parasuraman, A, Zeithaml, VA and Berry, LL (1985) A conceptual model of service quality and its implications for future research, *Journal of Marketing*, 49 (Fall), pp 41–50

Pisharodi, RM and Langley, CJ, Jr (1990) A perceptual process model of customer service based on cybernetic/control theory, *Journal of Business Logistics*, 11 (1), 26–48

Richardson, HL (1998) Must you meet all customer demands? *Transportation & Distribution*, 39 (June), pp 55–99

Sabath, RE (1978) How much service do customers really want? *Business Horizons*, 21 (2), pp 26–32

Santhouse, D (1999) Benchmarking, in *Global Logistics and Distribution Planning: Strategies for management*, ed D Waters, pp 193–202, Kogan Page, London

Shapiro, RD (1984) Get leverage from logistics, *Harvard Business Review*, 62 (May–June), pp 119–27

Sharman, G (1984) The rediscovery of logistics, *Harvard Business Review*, 62 (September–October), pp 71–79

Stock, JR (1997) Applying theories from other disciplines to logistics, *International Journal of Physical Distribution & Logistics Management*, 27 (9/10), pp 515–39

Tax, SS, Brown, SW and Chandrashekaran, M (1998) Customer evaluations of service complaint experiences: implications for relationship marketing, *Journal of Marketing*, 62 (April), pp 60–76

Weld, LDH (1915) Market distribution, *The American Economic Review*, 5 (1), pp 125–39

Xing, Y and Grant, DB (2006) Developing a framework for measuring physical distribution service quality of multi-channel and 'pure player' internet retailers, *International Journal of Retail & Distribution Management*, 34 (4/5), pp 278–89

8

People powering contemporary supply chains

John Gattorna,
Macquarie Graduate School of Management

OPENING COMMENTS

In some ways a lot of progress has been made in the supply chain field (including logistics) over the past decade since the dawn of the internet. The concept of linking enterprises together to facilitate the smooth flow of products, services, information and finances came alive once we had access to the omnipresent capabilities of the internet as a communications medium, and the related burst of software development. The convergence of these two fields of activity allowed us to break away from the constraints of flawed organization designs and poor IT connectivity, and in the process 'operationalize' the concept of supply chain management, at last!

But in achieving this surge of progress in the past decade we failed to grasp the fundamental reality that what really drives supply chains is people and their behaviour – not technology, or infrastructure, or assets, or anything else – those are just enablers at best and bit players at worst. Even the supposedly best organizations in the world have missed this fundamental issue, although the likes of Dell and Nokia are now moving quickly to readdress this oversight.

THE PEOPLE THAT DRIVE CONTEMPORARY SUPPLY CHAINS

First and foremost, it is customers that drive supply chains. Whether as a single consumer or a complex corporate customer, these are the people that set the die through the way they prefer to buy particular products and/or services. And by the way, those in the so-called service industries take note – everything I say in this chapter applies to you equally as much as to those with tangible products to sell.

Customers are in effect the 'head of the dog' and as such they should be wagging the tail (suppliers). But unfortunately, over the past two decades of easy business and easy money, suppliers have been allowed to design their logistics systems and infrastructure to suit their own purposes, rather than heeding signals coming from customers. So we got the 'one-size-fits-all' mindset, because this seemed to indicate a way of managing the marketplace with just one value proposition – easy if you can make it work. And work it seemed to, up until recent volatile times, and we found out that customers were different after all!

Unfortunately, many companies have persisted with the 'one-size-fits-all' mentality right up to the current time, in the mistaken belief that things will get better. Wrong. Things can only get worse if this policy is pursued, because the number of exceptions will increase exponentially, and so will the corresponding cost-to-serve! Time to rethink and reset your supply chains.

There is only one way to tackle the increasingly complex operating environment today, and that is to go back and re-engage with customers, and let this experience guide and inform you as to how to design and manage contemporary supply chains. Meet the complexity at source, and not in some artificially protected internal environment. This was the challenge I and other researchers set ourselves two decades ago – to find a new business model that would work no matter how dynamic the market was. And we found it, and labelled it – dynamic alignment.

DYNAMIC ALIGNMENT CONTROL

The great thing about this business model is that it is not a logistics or even supply chain model – it is a multidisciplinary business model. By going back to the fundamentals of how firms work, we found a way of linking the customer with the firm across a bridge of 'strategy'. Here is how it works.

From research and empirical observation we found that firms that performed well on a sustainable basis seemed to have superior alignment

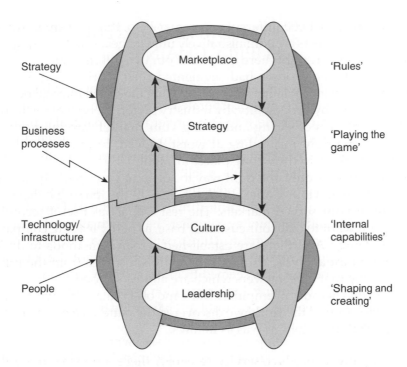

Figure 8.1 Elements of the 'dynamic alignment' framework
Source: adapted from Figure 1.2 in Gattorna, 2006, p 16

between the following four elements: customers; strategy; internal cultural capability; and leadership style. I have depicted this configuration in Figure 8.1.

Furthermore, the firms that seemed to perform best, in all industries, seemed to be those where the leadership of those enterprises had a deep understanding and empathy for their marketplace and the customers within. It seemed that if these two fundamentals were in place, the appropriate strategies followed, as did the shaping of the appropriate internal cultures necessary to propel those strategies into the marketplace. The trick is to have in place a management team that really does understand the marketplace. This is the clear and inexorable precondition for success.

But as we have already hinted, any marketplace you want to consider will have differences within it – people (customers) are just not the same. They look different and are different. The question is: how different? And are useful approximations possible on some bases?

So the big question we set out to answer in the early 1990s was: if we can't treat the marketplace as if all customers are the same, just how many different groupings or customer segments are needed to gain an adequate 'fit'? Is it 100? Is it 1,000 different segments? If so, then we are in trouble because such numbers are administratively unmanageable in the workplace.

The solution was right there in front of our eyes all the time.

Traditionally, enterprises had segmented their markets in just about every way possible, but almost always invoking their own internal perspectives, eg by size; by profitability; by industry sector; by type of institution. All these methods of slicing and dicing your markets are interesting at best, and downright misleading at worst. Indeed, to put it bluntly, we have been looking in the wrong places all along!

In truth, there is only one right way to segment your marketplace, and that is along behavioural lines. Look for clues to the 'buying behaviours' that exist in your served markets. The rest will act as useful secondary filters if you want to cull your customer base, as many leading companies are now doing.[1] And there are established research methods to do just this, eg conjoint analysis, although there are short-cuts from the full-on methodology that give answers which are almost as good.

So, over two decades of empirical work and observation in a wide variety of industries around the world we discovered the patterns we were looking for, and what these told us was as follows:

1. For any given product/service category, there are never more than three or four dominant buying behaviours, which together account for up to 80 per cent of that market.[2]
2. Here comes the dynamic bit – customers will change their dominant buying behaviour if the situation they find themselves in is such that they have no other choice; witness what is currently happening in markets all over the world due to the impact of the global financial crisis (GFC).

So this was the answer we had been seeking, and it was an encouraging answer because it meant that any enterprise could get up to an 80 per cent fit to its market with three, or possibly four (at most) different value propositions – a very manageable number. Quite a few enterprises around the world are busily doing just this as we speak!

FINDING THE BEHAVIOURAL METRIC – KEY TO UNRAVELLING THE PUZZLE

The key to unravelling this puzzle lay in finding a metric that could describe what went on at all four levels of the dynamic alignment model – market, strategy, internal culture and leadership style. Three of these four have a common factor – human behaviour, and the fourth (strategy) can easily be described in the selected metric.

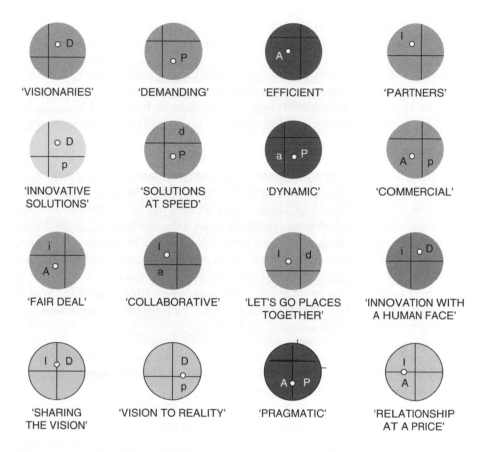

Figure 8.2 The 16 possible behavioural segments/logics
Source: Gattorna, 2006

Through our research into the work of Carl Jung[3] and Icak Adizes[4] we found the coding system that was to lead us towards the answer mentioned above – not one but three or four different behavioural patterns at most would provide an adequate fit to most if not all markets. This coding system, which we labelled P-A-D-I, is the DNA of business enterprises driven by human beings.[5]

Based on this work and our own observations, we came to the conclusion that there were up to 16 variants of human behaviour as depicted in Figure 8.2, but never more than three or four of these were evident in any market at any one time.

We have observed all 16 behaviours at different times and labelled these for ease of communication, but the most common buying behaviours were undoubtedly the four described in Figure 8.3.

You must identify the dominant buying behaviours
evident in your marketplace – normally 3 or 4 at most

Collaborative	Efficient	Dynamic (QR)	Innovative Solutions
Close working relationships for mutual gain	Consistent low-cost response to largely predictable demands	Rapid response to unpredictable supply and demand conditions	Supplier-led development and delivery of new ideas
Ia	A	Pa	Dp
• Mostly predictable • Regular delivery • Mature or augmented products • Primary source of supply • Trusting relationship • Teamwork/partnership • Information sharing • Joint development • Forgiving • Price not an issue	• Predictable demand within contract • Regular delivery • Efficiency low-cost focus • Multiple sources of supply • Little sharing of information • More adversarial • Standard processes • Power imposed • Transactional • Very price sensitive	• Unpredictable demand • Commodity relationship • Time priority/urgency • Opportunity focus • Ad hoc source of supply • Low loyalty, impersonal • Fewer processes • Outcome oriented • Commercial deals based on pragmatism • Price aware	• Very unpredictable demand • Higher risk • Flexible delivery response • Innovation focus • Rapid change • Individual decision making • Solutions oriented • Management of IP • Incentives/ego • No price sensitivity

Figure 8.3 Four most common dominant buying behaviours
Source: adapted from Figure 2.2 in Gattorna, 2006, p 41

NOW THE HEAD OF THE DOG IS BACK IN CONTROL

Just as Gary Barter,[6] the golf pro I go to for lessons, is always saying that 'the left arm drives the company', the same principle applies to business; the customer drives the enterprise, often in ways that it doesn't fully appreciate.

Now that we had established that four behavioural segments largely describe many of the product/service markets being served, it was a short step in logic to recognize that this in effect meant the existence of up to four different supply chain configurations. I have described these four generic supply chain types in Figures 8.4 and 8.5. Variations around these four do occur, but it is rare.

So, designing supply chains becomes relatively easy. All you have to do is 'reverse engineer' back from an understanding of the behavioural segments in your market. You may even choose not to service all four – that is a judgement call you can make.

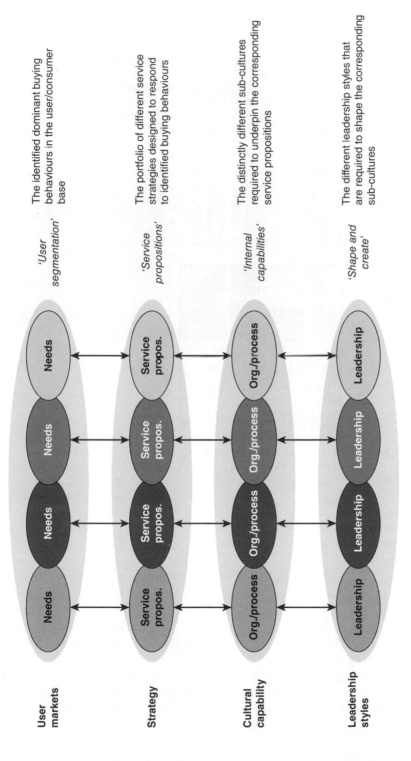

User markets

'User segmentation'

The identified dominant buying behaviours in the user/consumer base

Strategy

'Service propositions'

The portfolio of different service strategies designed to respond to identified buying behaviours

Cultural capability

'Internal capabilities'

The distinctly different sub-cultures required to underpin the corresponding service propositions

Leadership styles

'Shape and create'

The different leadership styles that are required to shape the corresponding sub-cultures

Figure 8.4 'Multiple supply chain alignment' on the customer side
Source: adapted from Figure 2.1 in Gattorna, 2006, p 40

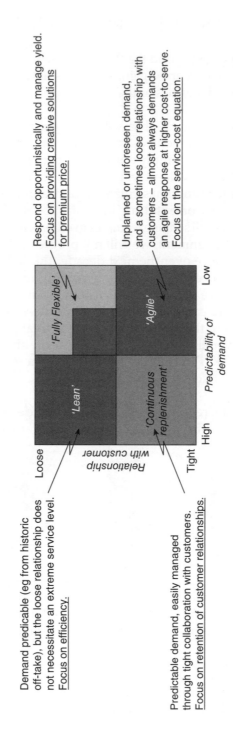

Respond opportunistically and manage yield. Focus on providing creative solutions for premium price.

Unplanned or unforeseen demand, and a sometimes loose relationship with customers – almost always demands an agile response at higher cost-to-serve. Focus on the service-cost equation.

Demand predicable (eg from historic off-take), but the loose relationship does not necessitate an extreme service level. Focus on efficiency.

Predictable demand, easily managed through tight collaboration with customers. Focus on retention of customer relationships.

Figure 8.5 Four generic supply chain types
Source: adapted from Figure 2.3 in Gattorna, 2006, p 43

BUT THE 'FORCES OF DARKNESS ARE LURKING'

So far, so good – until we get beyond the design phase to implementation, and we hit the next big snag. People again, and this is not an issue confined to those people working in logistics or the wider supply chain. It involves all the people in the business.

What we found from empirical observation is that 40–60 per cent of best-laid plans were not implemented, and the reason was not anything to do with competitors. It was simply a matter of people in the rump of the enterprise saying 'No', they don't want to do this or that as requested. This is the internal people factor that so many organizations do not understand how to deal with, or worse still, are in denial about.

In my view, unless and until senior executives in enterprises come to grips with this impediment to alignment, we will not progress much further in pursuit of peak performance over the next decade; this issue simply has to be addressed and resolved, just as we are coming to terms with the external influence of people in the form of customers and suppliers.

Listed below are the 12 capability levers that we need to understand and work with in shaping the types of sub-cultures that are required in the enterprise at any given time and situation. We know about all of them individually, but the trick is in the way we combine them into different recipes to address different change requirements:

- organization structure, reporting relationships, and decision rights;
- positioning people in the organization according to their natural strengths;
- job design;
- processes;
- IT systems;
- methods of internal communication;
- training and development initiatives;
- key performance indicators (KPIs)/performance metrics;
- corresponding incentive schemes or motivators;
- planning systems;
- recruitment from external sources with both the required technical skills and appropriate mindset to support planned initiatives;
- role modelling; and leadership style of the top management team.

The four generic supply chains discovered

Now we have all the ingredients, it remains to describe how these all come together in each of the four generic supply chain configurations. This is best done diagrammatically as depicted in Figures 8.6, 8.7, 8.8 and 8.9.

Figure 8.6 Continuous replenishment supply chain configuration: demand side

MARKET SEGMENT   **'EFFICIENT'**   REQUIRE RELENTLESS FOCUS ON COST AND EFFICIENCY

FULFILMENT STRATEGY   **VALUE PROPOSITION**   **STRATEGIES**

- Seek economies of scale
- Low cost production and distribution
- Forecast demand; mature products; predictable lead times

INTERNAL CULTURAL CAPABILITY   **CULTURAL LEVERS**   *'HIERARCHICAL'* **SUB-CULTURE**

1. OD
2. People positioning
3. Processes
4. IT/Systems
5. KPIs
6. Incentives
7. Job design
8. Internal coms.
9. T & D
10. Role modelling
11. Recruitment

- Organize clusters around core processes
- Ensure bias towards personnel with 'S' in their MBTI profile
- Standard processes; emphasis on cost
- Replace legacy systems with ERP system
- DIFOTEF; forecast accuracy; productivity ratios
- Conformance to policies
- Centralized control – rules and regulations apply
- Regular; structured on 'need to know' basis
- Emphasis on analysis and measurement
- Managers with ISTJ (A) MBTI profile are ideal
- Recruit players with deep analytical skills

LEADERSHIP   **12. LEADERSHIP STYLE**   **TRADITIONAL**

- Leads by procedure; precedent
- Implements only proven business practices
- Cost controller; efficiency focus
- Uses information to control
- Seeks stability
- Is risk averse

Figure 8.7   Lean supply chain configuration: demand side

MARKET SEGMENT

'DYNAMIC'

RESPONSE REQUIRED TO UNPLANNED OR UNFORESEEN DEMAND

FULFILMENT STRATEGY

VALUE PROPOSITION

STRATEGIES

- Fast decision making
- Fast delivery
- Rapid response in unpredictable conditions

INTERNAL CULTURAL CAPABILITY

CULTURAL LEVERS

1. OD
2. People positioning
3. Processes
4. IT/Systems
5. KPIs
6. Incentives
7. Job design
8. Internal coms.
9. T & D
10. Role modelling
11. Recruitment

'RATIONAL' SUB-CULTURE

- 'Clusters' designed for speed and focused on specific sub-segments
- Ensure bias towards personnel with 'N' in their MBTI profile
- Process short-cuts; fast response; postponement techniques
- Software applications: SCP; APS; Network models
- Absolute speed of response
- Achieve targets; cash and in-kind bonuses
- Authority/Autonomy established by clear and published limits
- Formal; regular; action-orientated
- Problem solving; resource allocation and management
- Managers with ENTJ (P) MBTI profile are ideal
- Recruit personnel who are results-driven

LEADERSHIP

12. LEADERSHIP STYLE

COMPANY BARON

- Leads by objectives (MBO)
- Embraces change
- Goes for growth
- Focuses on what's important
- Analytical; fact-based negotiations

Figure 8.8 Agile supply chain configuration: demand side

MARKET SEGMENT — CREATIVE SOLUTIONS REQUIRED, VERY FAST

FULFILMENT STRATEGY — 'INNOVATIVE SOLUTIONS'

STRATEGIES

- Meet unplanned/unplannable demand
- Innovative solutions, delivered fast

VALUE PROPOSITION

INTERNAL CULTURAL CAPABILITY

CULTURAL LEVERS

1. OD
2. People positioning
3. Processes
4. IT/Systems
5. KPIs
6. Incentives
7. Job design
8. Internal coms.
9. T & D
10. Role modelling
11. Recruitment

ENTREPRENEURIAL

- Small multidisciplinary 'cluster', usually on standby, but can be full-time
- Ensure bias towards personnel with 'P' in their MBTI profile
- No standard processes; use local initiative at the time
- Low systems requirements; event management applications
- Emphasis on finding creative solutions, very fast
- Reward individualism and risk-taking behaviour
- Autonomy through empowerment
- Spontaneous and informal
- Lateral thinking; brainstorming
- Managers with ENFP (D) MBTI profile are ideal
- Recruit enterprising, resourceful personnel

LEADERSHIP

12. LEADERSHIP STYLE

VISIONARY

- Leads by inspiration; is authentic
- Informal
- Decisive
- Cares about ideas
- Values innovation

Figure 8.9 Fully flexible supply chain configuration: demand side

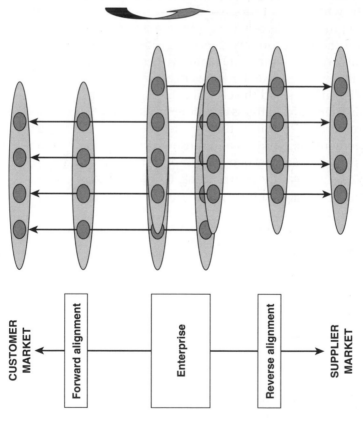

Figure 8.10 Supply side alignment, the mirror image of the customer side
Source: adapted from Figure 3.5.2 in Gattorna, 2003

The different leadership style required for each type of supply chain configuration is also depicted in the same set of diagrams.

The supply-side as a mirror image

But there is more. On the supply-side of our enterprises there is a stakeholder that has largely been ignored in the past – suppliers. They have gone about their business, seemingly in isolation, unconnected to the supply chain as we know it. Those days are also gone as enlightened enterprises move to reconnect their procurement functions and suppliers on the back end of the enterprise to the rest of the business. The silos are gone and working together in multi-functional clusters is the way forward to improved performance. Figure 8.10 is a schematic that depicts how the two sides of the business, forward and reverse, are connected.

Indeed, the whole area of supply-side sourcing is coming back into focus once again as the world reels from the impact of the financial services meltdown on the real economy. Since the start of the new millennium, multinational corporations in particular have been pursuing global sourcing strategies in the relentless search for lower-cost sources of inputs to manufacturing. This in turn has had the effect of '… making supply chains longer and more fragmented, and this is exposing firms to greater costs and risks'.[7] The same research also found that most firms were still largely basing their procurement decisions on a minimum price approach rather than a more sophisticated 'total cost of ownership'.[8] Finally, the same global trade appears to be significantly contributing to the emission of greenhouse gases because of the added transportation legs involved, and this flies in the face of efforts to reduce such emissions. Maybe we will see a change back to regional and local sourcing as a result of this new factor that is concerning the community at large. Indeed, from our own work we see a clear trend towards a sub-segment, within the overall 'Collaborative' segment, that appears to be very empathetic towards the environment, and will punish suppliers along the supply chain who do not take appropriate measures to minimize their carbon footprint.

SUPPLY-SIDE ALIGNMENT

Like demand-side alignment, supply-side alignment is multidimensional, and takes its lead from the market side. However, it seems that many of the activities practised on the supply side (strategic sourcing; global sourcing; spend analyses; etc) have been taking place in a relative vacuum, with little direct reference to demand-side customer buying patterns. Even worse, assumptions are too often made inside the procurement side of the business about the assumed 'selling behaviour' of suppliers, and this leads directly to inappropriate procurement strategies. For example, Brazil's largest meat processor was endeavouring to gain a larger share of the live cattle herd for slaughter, and the conventional wisdom inside the firm was that all ranchers (suppliers) are sensitive to the price they are paid, and will move to the buyer who offers a few more dollars per head. When a behavioural segmentation of sellers was undertaken, the results were quite the opposite. Over three-quarters of the ranchers were found to be inclined towards some element of relationship with the buyer, and open to a service package involving different combinations of technical assistance; training and development; credit; and other non-price factors. As a result, the buying company was able to adjust its procurement strategies to reflect these underlying buying preferences and thereby better align with the supply market.

HYBRID SUPPLY CHAINS

In the end, the most common situation in industry is that different combinations of demand-side and supply-side supply chain elements occur. It is rare to see a pure 'lean' or pure 'agile' supply chain all the way through. This then brings into focus the question of organization structure, which we will have to leave for another day. Suffice to say that our recommendation is that enterprises embrace a multidisciplinary 'cluster' design as depicted in Figure 8.11.

As depicted, the individual clusters are designed around the characteristics in both the customer and supplier segments, in a pure sense. However, where there is a mix of different elements, say lean on the supply side and agile on the demand side, then the corresponding clusters will work in a coordinated way to get the desired alignment at both ends. This is the innovative new aspect in supply chain management, which has the potential to lift performance by a quantum.

REVERSE LOGISTICS

Finally, to round things off we must mention 'reverse logistics' where the customer becomes the supplier and again we must embrace 'alignment' principles for best results. We will handle this topic by studying the different reverse paths that it is possible for a product to take.[9]

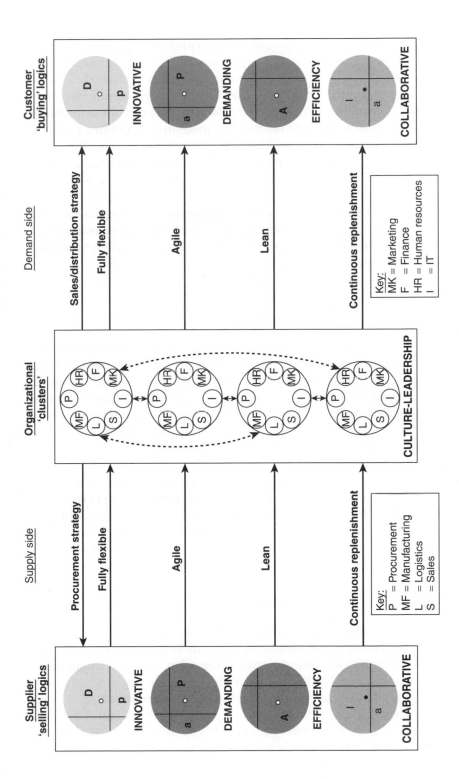

Figure 8.11 A new and dynamic business model for supply chains of the future
Source: Gattorna, 2009, Figure 9.6, p 143

The continuous replenishment return path – where relationships are the key driver

Bessemer is an Australian company that has made and distributed premium quality aluminium cookware for 40 years. It offers customers a 40 per cent discount on a new product with a trade-in of an existing product. Many of its customers are loyal devotees of its product and this very attractive incentive keeps them repurchasing. As the items have a longer than normal life cycle, however, the repurchase period may be 8–10 years after the original sale.

On many dimensions this is a very savvy approach. Returns constitute a third of the total aluminium used in production. At a cost per tonne, at the time of writing, of over USD 2,000 and as recycled product requires considerably less processing, the economics are very attractive. The offer also enhances the 'premium' brand image by providing an additional benefit, and positions Bessemer as a responsible manager across the full life cycle of the product.

The return path is supported by the extensive national network used for forward movements, and the complexity is minimized because the returned item is introduced into the return path when it is exchanged for the new item. When each depot reaches an economic transfer quantity (usually a pallet), the items are dispatched, mostly with the vehicle delivering new stock. The quantities returned, after many years of this operation, are quite predictable.

This is a classic example of leveraging a loyal customer base appropriately and developing a stable and cost-effective return operation around that relationship. The continuous replenishment return path will often be built on dependencies. In this case the manufacturing operation is highly dependent on the returns as inputs, and the marketing arm is dependent on the incentive to maintain and build an ongoing relationship with customers. Stable patterns also lend themselves to fine-tuning based around analytics, and in this case the variability of supply would be a key element in the analysis.

The lean return path – where cost is the key driver

Where items are expected to have no reclaimable value, or for regular and stable recycling of low-value inputs, the key driver is usually cost, and the emphasis is on routine patterns with minimal need for management intervention.

The household waste recycling process, where paper, glass, steel and aluminium are removed on a regular weekly/fortnightly basis and directed through a predictable separation process, should be designed around the reliability and rigour of a lean path.

The agile return path – where time is the key driver

Where there is an opportunity for resale, time usually needs to be the key driver in the returns process. Studies undertaken on the Hewlett-Packard Equipment Management and Remarketing (EMR) operation[10] found that laptops being refurbished for resale in secondary markets could take over four months through the various phases of staging and processing before being made available for sale. Obviously the recovery value of computer equipment deteriorates rapidly and time lost is value lost in these markets. One source of delay in this process was the use of the same manufacturer for refurbishment as for original equipment production. Inevitably new production was given a higher priority. A complicating factor in this market was also management's perception that they needed to limit sales of refurbished items to hold the price of new laptops up. Analysis as part of this study, however, found that the markets for each were different and there was little substance to this concern.

Time-sensitive returns should be treated as a value stream, not a waste stream. The priority is to manage lead times, avoid bottlenecks and support the operation with a flexible organization structure geared around identifying and quickly capturing market opportunities.

The fully flexible return path – where it's all about risk

Whereas the fully flexible supply chain features rarely in the forward supply chain, in the reverse supply chain it is a feature of every major manufacturer's armoury – but hopefully only in their contingency plans. A fully flexible path requires fast, dynamic and creative responses to unforeseen situations. For most companies this means recall programmes, natural disasters or other, similarly high-risk, situations.

The recall programme is an important reverse logistics situation. It requires detailed contingency planning with specialized arrangements, and capacity commitments from logistics providers that can be turned on immediately they are needed. Despite all the planning, however, when the situation arises it will inevitably also require creative and fast decisions responding to the particulars of the situation. Reputational risk is so high in these situations that cost cannot be a consideration, just as holding or paying for spare capacity can often be justified as a risk minimization strategy.

LAST WORD

I hope that the impression that this chapter leaves you with is that there is an enormous upside available if the customer-centric dynamic alignment business model is adopted in full. It applies first at the customer end, but then naturally influences what we do inside the enterprise and backwards to our supply base, and it also guides and informs us as we try to design a sustainable reverse logistics process for our products and services.

Notes

1 Linfox, an Australian-based 3PL that serves 11 Asian markets, has culled its customer base over the past three years by 40 per cent, and at the same time doubled revenue and doubled profits.
2 See chapter 2 in Gattorna (2006), pp 38–39 for more details.
3 See Adler, Fordham and Read (1971).
4 Adizes (1979)
5 See also Gattorna (2006), pp 16–24 for a more detailed explanation.
6 Gary Barter is an award-winning teaching golf pro based at the Australian Golf Club, Sydney.
7 Christopher (2007), p 3
8 Christopher (2007), p 3
9 I am indebted to my colleague Deborah Ellis for her input to this section.
10 Guide, Muyldermans and Van Wassenhove (2005), pp 281–93

References

Adizes, I (1979) *How to Solve the Mismanagement Crisis*, 1st printing, Dow-Jones-Irwin, Homewood, II; 5th printing (1985), Adizes Institute, Santa Monica, CA

Adler, G, Fordham, M and Read, H (eds) (1971) *The Collected Works of C G Jung, Volume 6; Psychological Types*, trans RFC Hull, Bollinger Series 20, Princeton University Press, Ewing, NJ

Christopher, M (2007) *Global Sourcing and Logistics*, Research Report by Martin Christopher *et al*, Cranfield School of Management, May

Gattorna, J (2006) *Living Supply Chains*, FT Prentice Hall, Harlow

Gattorna, J (2009) *Dynamic Supply Chain Alignment*, Gower, Farnham

Guide, Jr, VDR, Muyldermans, L and Van Wassenhove, LN (2005) Hewlett-Packard Company unlocks the value potential from time-sensitive returns, *Interfaces*, July–August, **35**, pp 281–93

9

Creating shareholder value through supply chain management

Heimo Losbichler, University of Applied
Sciences Upper Austria
Farzad Mahmoodi, Clarkson University

INTRODUCTION

Intense global competition, short product life cycles and the need to create shareholder value have resulted in significant interest in supply chain management over the past decade. More recently, the force and speed of the global downturn have further reinforced the importance of supply chain excellence as a key to unfreeze cash, reduce operating cost and meet rapidly changing customer demand. Against a backdrop of economic uncertainty and rising supply chain risk, it is more critical than ever to select the supply chain initiatives that create the most shareholder value.

This chapter describes the link between supply chain management and shareholder value creation. We first define economic value added (EVA) as the primary financial metric, and conduct an analysis of four companies that are generally perceived to be supply chain leaders. Then we link supply chain management to shareholder value and propose a comprehensive five-step framework to identify supply chain initiatives that create the most shareholder value by utilizing EVA. Finally, we describe the difficulties and pitfalls of creating shareholder value along the entire supply chain.

FINANCIAL PERFORMANCE AND ITS DRIVERS

The goal of a corporation and its top executives is generally to maximize the long-term financial performance of the company and its value to shareholders. Financial performance and shareholder value are measured by utilizing a variety of metrics at different levels. In today's global equity markets, companies are expected to generate competitive returns for the investors. For publicly traded companies, the total return to shareholders (TSR) is measured by the increase in stock price plus the dividends paid. It is the external financial performance of a company and a very critical view of shareholder value (fuelled by stock option programmes) that can easily distort management's focus towards short-term strategies, which might be rewarded on the stock market but often turn out as a burden, in the long term. Even Jack Welch, the former CEO of General Electric who is regarded as the father of the shareholder value movement, said amid the consequences of the economic crisis that he never meant to suggest that boosting a company's share price should be the main goal of the top executives (*Financial Times*, 2009).

In fact, shareholders can only increase their individual wealth from an increase in stock price and dividends they actually receive. Nevertheless, TSR is an inappropriate metric because it is not always clear what drives a company's stock price. However, in the long run, stock price is driven by company profits or cash flows. Therefore, we refer to shareholder value in this chapter from the perspective of the internal financial performance of a company. Even from this internal perspective shareholder value goes by many names. Over the years two basic concepts related to either discounted cash flow or economic profit, such as EVA, have been established to measure shareholder value. Despite the ongoing debate about which metric is superior for explaining the value of a firm (O'Byrne, 1996; Anderson, Bey and Weaver, 2005), in practice EVA is the metric that most executives value.

The key performance metric: EVA

EVA is defined as the residual wealth, calculated by subtracting from revenues the total cost of doing business (ie operating costs, taxes and cost of capital). EVA is a comprehensive measure that enables managers to determine whether they are earning an adequate return (Stewart, 1991). While accounting profits measure profits earned, EVA defines the difference between that value and what should have been earned in other investments of similar risk. If EVA is positive, the operational business can cover total costs, including the cost of all the capital employed (ie equities and liabilities). Thus, if the company is earning a higher return than other investments of similar risk, investors should be attracted, the stock price should increase and shareholder value is created. However, if EVA is negative, value is being destroyed and the company faces the flight of capital and a lower stock price.

As illustrated in Figure 9.1, EVA is a measure of net operating profit after taxes, less cost of all capital employed. EVA is also the spread between a company's return on capital employed (ROCE) and the weighted average cost of capital (WACC), multiplied by the capital employed (CE).

The key point is that value is created only when revenues exceed all costs, including cost of capital. In other words, ROCE has to exceed WACC. Management guru Peter Drucker described EVA as: 'There is no profit unless you earn the cost of capital. Alfred Marshall said that in 1896, Peter Drucker said that in 1954 and in 1973, and now EVA has systematized this idea, thank God' (Drucker, 1998).

Drivers of financial performance

The key point in creating shareholder value is that ROCE has to exceed WACC. In other words, the return on the capital that is required for doing business has to be higher than the interest rate we have to pay for the capital to lenders and shareholders. Thus, the return of capital employed (ROCE) is EVA's major driver and ROCE itself can easily be mapped to its basic drivers: revenues, costs and capital employed (assets). Note that it is better to break down capital employed into fixed assets and working capital. This allows the analysis of the trade-offs between lower inventory and higher equipment efficiency. As a result, ROCE and EVA have four basic value drivers, all of which can be impacted by supply chain management initiatives:

- higher revenues measured by revenue growth;
- lower cost measured by profit margin;
- lower fixed assets measured by fixed asset utilization; and
- lower working capital measured by cash-to-cash (C2C) cycle time.

The C2C cycle time is a composite metric describing the average days required to turn a dollar invested in raw material into a dollar collected

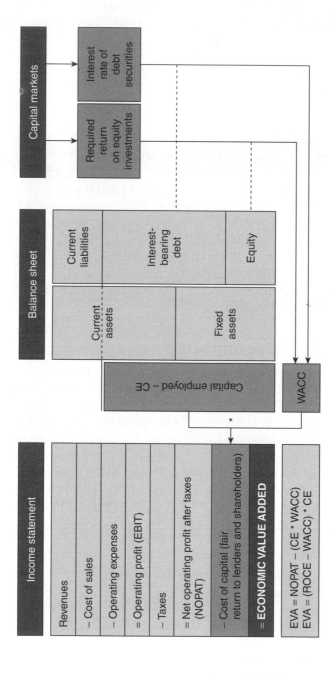

Figure 9.1 Calculating EVA

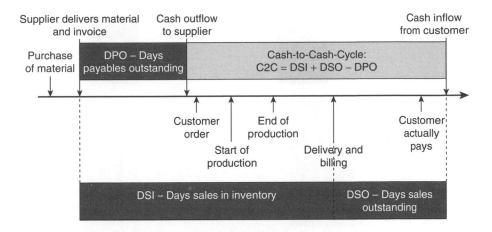

Figure 9.2 Cash-to-cash cycle time calculation

from a customer. The C2C cycle time is equal to days sales in inventory (DSI), plus days sales outstanding (DSO), minus days payables outstanding (DPO), as illustrated in Figure 9.2.

Figure 9.3 illustrates the basis link between supply chain management and shareholder value: supply chain initiatives can affect all four value drivers of a company's internal financial performance measured by EVA. This financial performance enables companies to pay dividends to shareholders and it drives companies' stock price, in the long term. Thus, supply chain management can create shareholder value.

Note that EVA is a comprehensive metric that accounts for the trade-offs between income statement and balance sheet. Supply chain decisions often simultaneously affect more than one driver of financial performance. In fact, they involve trade-offs between revenues, costs and assets. For instance, lower unit costs as a result of offshoring can be offset by higher in-transit costs, an increase in the lead time and higher inventory carrying costs due to increased safety stock requirements. It may be the case that the source with the lowest unit cost does not have the highest impact on shareholder value (Ferreira and Prokopets, 2009). Utilizing EVA can help managers make better decisions and extract greater value from supply chain initiatives.

LINKING SUPPLY CHAIN MANAGEMENT AND FINANCIAL PERFORMANCE

There is empirical evidence that high-performing supply chains have a major influence on companies' internal and external financial performance. Singhal and Hendricks (2002) and D'Avanzo, Von Lewinski and Van

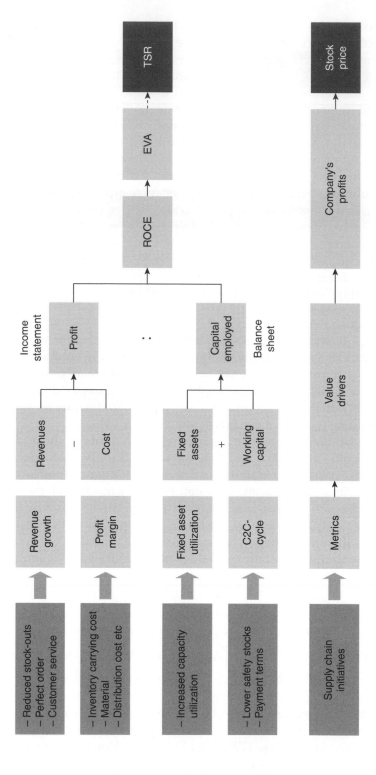

Figure 9.3 Link between supply chain management and shareholder value

Wassenhove (2003) analysed the impact of supply chain management on companies' stock price performance. Singhal and Hendricks (2002) demonstrated a direct link between supply chain performance and company stock prices. They also showed that companies that announced a glitch in supply chain performance (defined as a disruption in the matching of supply and demand) suffered an average decline of 18.5 per cent in stock price starting two quarters before and ending two quarters after the glitch. D'Avanzo *et al* (2003) showed a direct link between successful supply chain initiatives and financial performance, as measured by market capitalization. They also demonstrated that the growth rates of market capitalization are 7 to 26 per cent higher in companies with excellent supply chain management compared to the average company.

Furthermore, many studies have analysed the impact of supply chain management on the internal financial performance of a company for both large-scale studies and individual case studies. For instance, Deloitte (2003) demonstrated that only 7 per cent of manufacturers are effectively managing their supply chain, but they are 73 per cent more profitable than other manufacturers.

According to a recent McKinsey study (Constantine, Ruwadi and Wine, 2009), companies with high-performing supply chains enjoy lower distribution and logistics costs, better customer service and better inventory performance than ordinary performers. This study, which is based on in-depth interviews with more than 60 company operations executives across Europe and North America, assessed the performance of companies in more than 50 aspects of supply chain management, including business processes, corporate culture, network configurations, organizational structures, supporting infrastructure, and the capabilities of personnel. They conclude that six broad practices have significant impacts on customer service, inventory, and distribution/logistics costs:

- linking supply chain strategy to corporate strategy;
- segmenting the supply chain to master the product/service complexity that matters most;
- tailoring the supply chain network to optimize service, cost and risk goals;
- using lean tools to optimize supply chain from end to end;
- creating integrated sales and operations planning processes; and
- finding top talent, and holding people accountable.

Interestingly, among the practices that they did not find to be critical is formal IT systems (beyond basic enterprise resource planning), indicating that strong processes cannot be easily replaced by sophisticated IT systems.

Fisher (1997) distinguishes between functional and innovative products and proposes a different type of supply chain for each category. While the functional products are characterized by slow clockspeeds, low product variety, predictable demands and low profit margins, the innovative products are characterized by fast clockspeeds, high product variety, unpredictable demands and high profit margins. Fisher (1997) promotes an efficient supply chain with a focus on minimizing total landed cost for functional products. On the other hand, for innovative products he promotes a responsive supply chain with a focus on agility and flexibility.

Lee (2004) extended Fisher's ideas further by claiming that the best supply chains aren't just fast and cost-effective, but agile and adaptable, and they ensure that all their companies' interests stay aligned. He claims that companies whose supply chains are primarily focused on efficiency do not gain a sustainable competitive advantage over their rivals. According to Lee (2004), top-performing supply chains possess three qualities:

- agility (ie respond to short-term changes in demand and supply quickly and handle external disruptions smoothly);
- adaptability (ie adjust supply chain's design to meet structural shifts in markets);
- alignment (ie create incentives to align the interests of all the firms in the supply network so that companies optimize the chain's performance when they maximize their interests).

Major challenges in supply chain integration

According to Grey et al (2003), supply chain initiatives such as vendor management inventory, postponement and risk pooling can have a significant impact on all four drivers of financial performance. However, the benefits of such initiatives are notoriously difficult to quantify owing to supply chain integration issues, resulting in supply chain misalignments. Major challenges in supply chain integration include:

- Many supply-chain-related expenses cut across organizational units; the practice of grouping expenses into natural accounts such as salaries, rent, utilities and depreciation fails to identify or assign operational responsibility. In addition, the budgeting process generally lacks systems perspective by viewing requirements in any specific activity on a unit-cost basis, resulting in efficiency in one area without full appreciation of the impact on other areas.
- Traditional accounting practice fails to assign appropriate inventory carrying costs by primarily focusing on the cost of capital (ie understate

the carrying costs by not including insurance, taxes, obsolescence, damage, spoilage, shrinkage, overhead etc).

- The two largest individual supply chain expenses (ie transportation and inventory) are generally reported in a manner that obscures their importance and are not meaningful to other senior executives. For example, utilizing metrics such as transportation costs per mile, or warehouse picking costs per unit, versus more systemic and comprehensive supply chain metrics that relate supply chain activities to the overall financial objectives of the organization.

As a result, companies focus on what they can see and measure rather than what is relatively invisible and hard to measure. For example, since lost revenue does not appear on the income statement, companies tend to focus on supply chain solutions that are slow and cheap rather than fast and more expensive.

What supply chain leaders do in practice

In this section we describe the supply chain characteristics, practices and strategies pursued by four companies that are generally perceived to be supply chain leaders in their respective industries: Zara, Dell, Wal-Mart and Nokia.

The unique supply chain management practices of Spanish garments retailer Zara has enabled it to gain competitive advantage over other global fashion retailers. Zara is the largest and most profitable arm of the retail conglomerate, Inditex. By 2005 Inditex had emerged as one of the world's fastest-growing makers of fashion clothing, with over 2,000 stores and promising to double that number by 2011 (Anderson and Lovejoy, 2007). Zara brings a large variety of high-fashion apparels to the market very quickly, based on customer feedback at a relatively reasonable price by utilizing a responsive supply chain. Zara's vertically integrated and aligned supply chain enables it to place the latest designs in any store across the world in two to three weeks. The company produces about 12,000 fashionable designs a year in a limited quantity, with new designs appearing in the stores twice a week. Such small and frequent shipments have kept inventories fresh and scarce, compelling customers to visit the store frequently in search of what's new and to buy now, because it will be gone tomorrow (Anderson and Lovejoy, 2007).

Empowered store managers provide headquarters with real customer feedback via Zara's effective in-house IT system. Constant information exchange occurs throughout every part of Zara's supply chain, mitigating the so-called bullwhip effect (Ferdows, Lewis and Machuca, 2004). Its quick turnaround on merchandise helps generate cash, which eliminates the need for significant debt. Potential bottlenecks are avoided because Zara is vertically integrated. For short lead times, 60 per cent of the manufacturing processes are outsourced in countries close to the Zara headquarters, and the postponement strategy is utilized effectively. Finally, Zara maintains a strong relationship with its contractors and suppliers, viewing them as part of the company (Anderson and Lovejoy, 2007).

Dell provides a large variety of customized products (with highly uncertain demand) at a reasonable price by utilizing a responsive supply chain. Dell spearheaded a process in which a 'back-end' intranet links its material planners directly to supplier inventories, to share a wide variety of real-time information regarding its customers and its own assembly plants. Dell immediately shares incoming order information with its suppliers, who deliver to Dell plants from supplier-owned warehouses located near the plants in less than 90 minutes after receiving a replenishment order (Mayersohn, 2001). The suppliers also use this information to improve the accuracy of their forecasts, because of long delivery lead times of some of their parts from second- and third-tier suppliers. From the time a customer order is received at Dell's plant, a personal computer can be shipped in less than four hours, and the computer can be in customer's possession the next day.

Wal-Mart, the largest retailer in the world, is believed to be one of the best supply chain operators of all time. Many analysts attribute Wal-Mart's leadership status in the retail industry and its phenomenal growth to its pursuit of a hybrid supply chain management strategy that focuses on both efficiency and responsiveness. The company has been able to offer a large variety of products at the lowest cost. Two major factors have contributed to this success: efficient and responsive distribution and transportation systems (resulting in reduced logistics costs and lead time), and its computerized inventory system, which has shortened replenishment cycles and speeded up the checking-out time and recording of transactions, as well as minimizing inventory carrying and stock-out cost. Furthermore, Wal-Mart has been able to reduce its purchasing costs by procuring directly from manufacturers, bypassing all intermediaries, as well as utilizing its enormous purchasing power to obtain more favourable terms from its suppliers. Finally, Wal-Mart has utilized sophisticated technology and information systems to track sales and merchandise in its facilities, and to communicate effectively both internally and with its supply chain partners across the globe. The benefits of such supply chain practices include lower costs, reduced lead times, higher inventory turnover, increased warehouse space, reduced safety stocks, better customer service and better working capital utilization.

In the mobile phone industry, supply chain responsiveness is considered a basic competitive requirement, as the industry had been characterized by frequent market changes and varying customer requirements (Collin and Lorenzin, 2006). Nokia has been successful in building a responsive supply chain by developing an agile operations strategy and in-built process capabilities to respond to short-term changes in demand or supply quickly. Nokia has invested heavily, building distribution systems and networks of retailers in fast-growing and developing countries (Ewing, 2007). Nokia's remarkable line-up of about 100 models is just one of many reasons why more than one out of every three handsets in the world is Nokia's. Perhaps most impressive is that Nokia has managed the shift to low-cost phones while maintaining healthy profit margins. This has been accomplished by utilizing efficient supply chain and manufacturing systems. Nokia has also kept costs and complexity under control by taking advantage of standardization and component commonality among devices, as well as designing phones that have fewer parts than competing models. Such hybrid supply chain practices, with simultaneous focus on responsiveness and efficiency, pushed Nokia to the top spot in AMR Research's 2007 annual survey of top supply chain operators.

There are clear trade-offs between possessing a responsive and an efficient supply chain. Agile supply chains create shareholder value by primarily increasing revenue growth and shortening C2C cycle time. Efficient supply chains, in contrast, create shareholder value by increasing a company's profit margin and fixed asset utilization. It is critical to view supply chain management as a powerful tool to pull all the financial levers at the beginning.

FRAMEWORK TO IDENTIFY INITIATIVES THAT CREATE THE MOST SHAREHOLDER VALUE

A framework is required to support supply chain managers to create value and achieve supply chain excellence. While the SCOR model advocates a set of supply chain performance indicators as a combination of reliability, cost, responsiveness, and asset measures, it does not guide managers to identify the supply chain initiatives that create the most shareholder value. We propose a five-step framework, which spans from identifying value gaps to defining the business case for selecting specific supply chain initiatives, as depicted in Figure 9.4.

Step 1: Identify value gaps

At the beginning, management attention needs to be directed to the areas where value creation is high. Therefore the first step is to conduct a

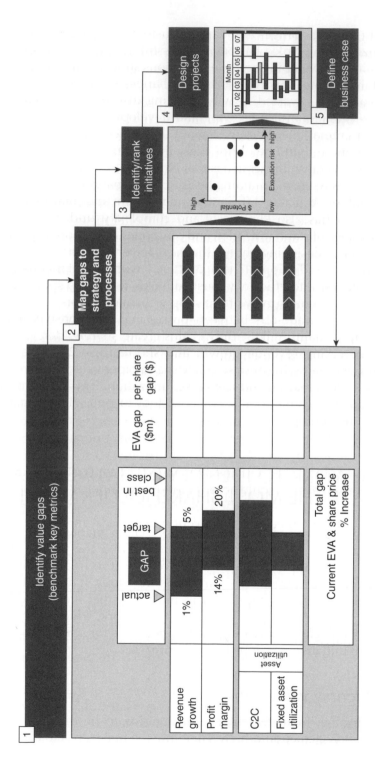

Figure 9.4 Proposed framework to create value and achieve supply chain excellence

high-level financial performance gap analysis. The four value drivers – revenue growth, profit margin, fixed asset utilization and cash-to-cash cycle time – should be benchmarked with a peer group. Value gaps can be identified and targets can be set. For example, if a company's revenue growth rate is 1 per cent per year while its peer group is experiencing a 5 per cent growth rate per year (and the best in class is growing by 8 per cent), then the gap of this value driver (compared to the peer group) is 4 per cent. Subsequently, the improvement in ROCE and EVA (ie EVA gap) can be calculated by applying 4 per cent additional growth to the company's current growth rate (see step 1 in Figure 9.4). The gaps can be converted into ROCE, EVA or stock price gaps. The size of these gaps helps to identify those supply chain drivers that offer the greatest leverage on shareholder value and ensure that managers consider only the supply chain initiatives that can create the most value.

We have already analysed the financial leverage of all four value drivers for the supply chain leaders. The financial impacts we present rely on numerous assumptions. For instance, which liability accounts are deducted from current assets to determine working capital? This task is critical, as it has a significant impact on the outcome and requires accounting expertise. A detailed presentation of the balance sheets and description of these assumptions would go beyond the scope of this chapter.

Figure 9.5 illustrates the impact of the four value drivers on ROCE for both Wal-Mart and Zara. Cost reduction provides by far the highest leverage to improve financial performance. For Wal-Mart, a 5 per cent reduction of total operating cost (cost of sales plus operating expenses) would boost ROCE by about 14.3 per cent (from 14.3 to 28.6 per cent), assuming everything else remains unchanged. In contrast, a 5 per cent reduction of fixed assets would account for only a minor ROCE improvement of 0.7 per cent. Note that these figures rely on certain assumptions. For instance, we assumed an 80 per cent variable cost model for determining the impact of revenue growth. If we compare Wal-Mart and Zara we can see that, for Zara, increasing the fixed asset utilization is more attractive than revenue growth. This is not the case for Wal-Mart because of its hybrid strategy. Finally, Figure 9.5 illustrates the limited potential of working capital improvements for Wal-Mart and Zara because they have optimized working capital over many years. Wal-Mart's cash-to-cash cycle time equals 8.2 days while Zara already has a negative cash-to-cash cycle time of – 19.5 days (numbers and Figure 9.5 are based on the 2008 annual reports).

Determining EVA-gaps and analysing the leverage of the value drivers at the beginning guarantees that managers consider only supply chain initiatives that can create the most value. Interested readers are referred to Timme and Williams-Timme (2000) for further details.

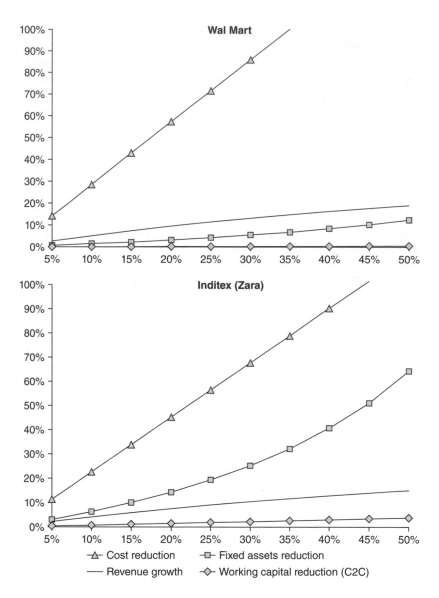

Figure 9.5 The impact of the four value drivers on ROCE for Wal-Mart and Zara

Step 2: Map gaps to supply chain processes

In the second step, the identified gaps have to be mapped to the company's strategy and its supply chain processes. For instance, if the company desires shorter cash-to-cash cycle time and its unique selling proposition is short delivery times, the company may carry a significant amount of inventory, resulting in a higher cash-to-cash cycle time. Upon comparison of the company's cash-to-cash cycle time with its peer group in step 1, the company will realize that its cash-to-cash cycle time is longer. Subsequently, in step 2, the company is required to justify this choice rather than blindly reducing inventory and potentially losing customers. However, if the value gap is simply due to supply chain inefficiencies, then the company should address root causes and make process improvements.

Step 3: Identify and select supply chain management tools

The goal of this step is to identify and select appropriate supply chain initiatives that can improve the identified business processes and close the value gap. An EVA impact matrix, categorizing supply chain initiatives based on their level of execution risk and their corresponding financial leverage (ie EVA improvement), such as the one depicted in Figure 9.6, can help evaluate the estimated EVA improvement and its difficulty of implementation. This would offer a systematic framework to unveil and rank supply chain initiatives according to their attractiveness in terms of financial leverage and likelihood of success. Note that at this stage it is not necessary to quantify the financial impact precisely.

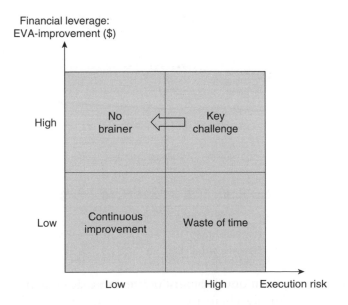

Figure 9.6   Financial leverage versus execution risk matrix

To be successful, it is important to distinguish between the potential financial leverage and the difficulty of achieving the expected improvements. For instance, in Figure 9.5 the great leverage of cost reductions is illustrated. If Zara was able to reduce total cost by 50 per cent it could boost ROCE from 46.2 per cent to an amazing 155.0 per cent. But how likely is such an improvement? Most companies' supply chain initiatives are typically designed to reduce stock-outs, lead times, purchase prices, transportation costs, warehousing costs, inventory carrying costs and fixed costs, as well as increasing service levels. Despite all these efforts, according to a recent study (Losbichler and Rothboeck, 2008) the majority of European companies were not able to make improvements in the four value drivers from 1995 to 2004, as illustrated in Figure 9.7. Note that while the scale for profit margin and revenue growth is on the y-axis on the right-hand side, the scale for cash-to-cash cycle time and fixed asset utilization is on the y-axis on the left hand side. Also, note that the profit margins and fixed asset utilization of the European companies have remained fairly flat and their revenue growth has been inconsistent, while their cash-to-cash cycle time has improved only slightly. Thus, European companies have not been able to improve their financial performance, in the period 1995–2004.

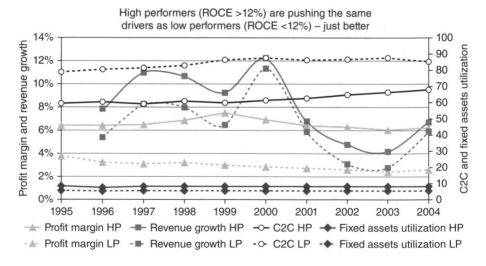

Figure 9.7　Long-term development of the value drivers in Europe (1995–2004)

Step 4: Design projects

This phase transforms the alternatives for optimizing the supply chain into specific projects. For each project, the scope, targets and resources should be defined. These project plans are needed to develop the business case, as discussed in step 5.

Step 5: Define the business case

For each individual project a business case has to be developed to determine the value created. Therefore, the impact on the four financial value drivers (ie growth, profitability, fixed asset utilization and cash-to-cash cycle time) must be determined. Because of the complex nature of supply chain initiatives (ie they typically impact several corporate functions), managers should be aware that developing the business case for each project independently can lead to double counting of benefits or ignoring synergies. Business cases should be determined for the portfolio of initiatives (Grey *et al*, 2003). Clearly, using scenarios created in interdisciplinary teams can be very helpful. Then, the potential value created for each project and required investment is evaluated to determine which projects should be accepted and rank the accepted projects. Finally, the EVA improvement as a result of the business case should be compared with the identified EVA gap.

DIFFICULTIES IN IMPROVING SUPPLY CHAIN FINANCIAL PERFORMANCE

While only a few executives question the relevance of supply chain management as a tool to improve a company's financial performance, many remain critical about its ability to achieve major improvements across the entire supply chain. This may seem to be a paradox, but it's the nature of supply chain management that is diminishing the power beyond a firm's border. Many supply chain management efforts to improve the financial performance in one area of the supply chain will actually be offset by a decline in other downstream or upstream areas. For example, lower purchase prices will reduce the buyer's cost, but will also lower the supplier's revenues. Lowering working capital by shortening the cash-to-cash cycle time through longer payment terms to suppliers will be correspondingly offset by the increase in the supplier's cash-to-cash cycle time. In such a scenario, the supply chain cash-to-cash cycle time will not change at all, as illustrated in Figure 9.8.

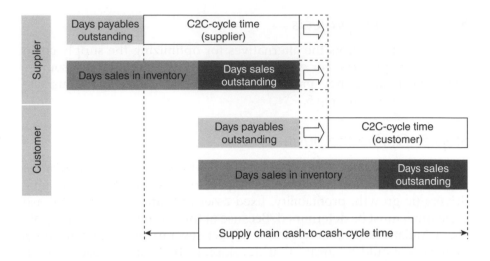

Figure 9.8   Company's C2C cycle time versus supply chain
C2C cycle time

Good intentions can produce bad results, as improvements in one area of the supply chain may be offset by the decline in other areas. In fact, improvements in one area can actually lower the overall financial performance of the supply chain. Consider a company that shifts raw material inventory to its supplier in order to relieve its balance sheet. This shift would reduce its working capital and its associated capital carrying cost. If suppliers have higher cost of capital than the company does, total supply chain carrying cost will actually increase. Someone in the supply chain will have to absorb these higher costs. Depending on the company's bargaining power, it is fairly common to shift working capital to suppliers. A well-known company wrote in its annual report: 'at the same time we have succeeded in increasing the level of our payables through renegotiating contracts with key suppliers, to ensure a gradual and sustainable reduction in our trade working capital requirements. This accounted for over 85% of our working capital reduction.'

To unfold the power of supply chain management companies have to be aware of the supply chain initiatives' impact across the supply chain, and differentiate between 'win–win' and 'win–lose' initiatives. While win–lose initiatives usually involve shifting or 'claiming' financial performance, win–win initiatives involve 'gaining' financial performance for the different parties in the supply chain, as illustrated in Figure 9.9. Increasing liquidity by lowering inventory based on increased synchronization and visibility, and making cost savings by perfectly aligning business processes, are examples of win–win initiatives.

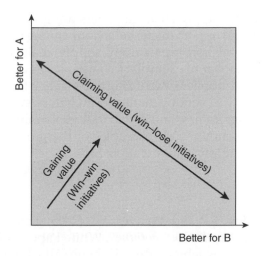

Figure 9.9   Win–win versus win–lose initiatives

IMPROVING THE FINANCIAL PERFORMANCE ACROSS THE SUPPLY CHAIN

As indicated earlier, to take full advantage of supply chain management companies need to consider supply chain initiatives' financial impact across the entire supply chain, resulting in win–win scenarios. This would require overcoming supply chain integration issues discussed in the section above on major challenges in supply chain integration. Possible strategies to overcome these challenges and to better align the supply chain include:

- Activity-based costing – tracing the costs of activities performed and then relating them to specific product or customer segment that generate revenue. This is certainly easier said than done, as identifying the activities, related expenses and the drivers of expenses is very tedious and time-consuming.
- Utilizing comprehensive supply chain metrics such as cash-to-cash cycle time or supply chain days of supply. Note that such metrics are impacted by multiple functional areas (eg logistics, marketing, procurement, manufacturing etc), resulting in a systems perspective.

As supply chains have become more extended in recent years, coordination and information sharing among supply chain members to improve system efficiency have become more common. Such collaborative relationships among supply chain members are gradually replacing the more self-serving and opportunistic behaviour among the firms. Although such collaborative relationships among supply chain members are not commonplace, a number of exemplary companies have begun to practise them with their best suppliers. According to Davis and Spekman (2004), the increased popularity of vendor-managed inventory systems, continuous replenishment programmes, and collaborative planning, forecasting and replenishment programmes are examples of the growing acceptance of such collaborative supply chain relationships.

References

Anderson, AM, Bey, RP and Weaver, SC (2005) *Economic Value Added Adjustments: Much to do about nothing?*, White Paper, Lehigh University [Online] http://www.lehigh.edu/~incbeug/Attachments/Anderson%20EVA%204-7-05.pdf

Anderson, K and Lovejoy, J (2007) The speeding bullet: Zara's apparel supply chain, TechExchange.com, March

Collin, J and Lorenzin, D (2006) Plan for supply chain agility at Nokia, *International Journal of Physical Distribution & Logistics Management*, **36** (6), pp 418–30

Constantine, B, Ruwadi, B and Wine, J (2009) Management practices that drive supply chain success, *The McKinsey Quarterly*, February

D'Avanzo, R, Von Lewinski, H and Van Wassenhove, L (2003) The link between supply chain and financial performance, *Supply Chain Management Review*, **7** (11–12), pp 40–47

Davis, E and Spekman, R (2004) *The Extended Enterprise: Gaining competitive advantage through collaborative supply chains*, Prentice Hall, Upper Saddle River, NJ

Deloitte (2003) Powering profits and growth through value chain synchronization [Online] www.deloitte.com/dtt/cda/doc/content/DTT_DR_TAL_May2005Web.pdf, accessed 8 June 2009

Ewing, J (2007) Why Nokia is leaving Moto in the dust, *Business Week*, 30 July

Ferdows, K, Lewis, M and Machuca, J (2004) Rapid-fire fulfillment, *Harvard Business Review*, November, pp 104–10

Ferreira, J and Prokopets, L (2009) Does offshoring still make sense?, *Supply Chain Management Review*, **13** (Jan/Feb), pp 20–27

Financial Times (2009) Welch denounces corporate obsessions, 12 March

Fisher, ML (1997) What is the right supply chain for your product?*Harvard Business Review*, March–April, pp 105–16

FORTUNE Magazine (1998) Peter Drucker takes the long view. The original management guru shares his vision of the future with FORTUNE's

Brent Schlender, 28 September [Online] http://money.cnn.com/magazines/fortune/fortune_archive/1998/09/28/248706/index.htm, accessed 8 June 2009

Gopal, G and McMillian, E (2005) Synchronization: a cure for bad data, *Supply Chain Management Review*, **9** (4), pp 58–62

Grey, W *et al* (2003) Beyond ROI, *Supply Chain Management Review*, **7** (3), pp 20–27

Lee, H (2004) The Triple-A supply chain, *Harvard Business Review*, October, pp 1–10

Losbichler, H and Rothboeck, M (2008) Der C2C-Cycle als Werttreiber in Supply Chain Management, *ZfCM – Zeitschrift fuer Controlling and Management*, **52** (1), pp 47–57

Mayersohn, N (2001) Dell's killer app: keeping close to the customer, *Customer Goods Technology*, **2** (7), pp 1–3

O'Byrne, SF (1996) EVA and market value, *Journal of Applied Corporate Finance*, **9** (1), pp 116–125

Singhal, V and Hendricks, K (2002) How supply chain glitches torpedo shareholder value, *Supply Chain Management Review*, **6** (1), pp 18–24

Stewart, BG (1991) *The Quest for Value*, HarperCollins, New York

Timme, S and Williams-Timme, C (2000) The financial–SCM connection, *Supply Chain Management Review*, **4** (2), pp 32–43

10

Outsourcing: the result of global supply chains?

Stephen Rinsler, Bisham Consulting

BACKGROUND

There can be no doubt that outsourcing has become big business. From the early beginnings in the mid- to late 1970s many companies have travelled the outsourcing road, and as technology and accessibility to shared electronic data have increased, so has the range of services offered by outsourcing companies.

In the past few years the government has openly encouraged outsourcing, and private finance initiative (PFI) and other deals have spawned. Not all the outsourcing arrangements in the private or the public sectors have been successful. There is a steady but small stream of processes being 'taken back in-house' and there have been some high-profile failures in the press.

We will explore why outsourcing takes place and how to avoid some of the pitfalls that undoubtedly can occur. We have tried to place outsourcing in the context of the more recent moves to source manufacture from overseas, particularly the Far East.

The drive for lower process costs and better margins has driven the outsourcing of product manufacture, often from the Far East. It is possible that this form of outsourcing has peaked given the increasing emphasis on carbon footprints and the more pragmatic reason, that of difficulties in managing sourcing over much extended supply chains. The risks involved have often been mitigated by raising stocks and suffering reduced market flexibility.

DEFINITION

Outsourcing describes the deliberate movement of a series of connected business processes to a third party who manages them on behalf of the company. The classic processes were IT, warehousing and distribution, facilities management, and payroll, and to these can now be added: call centres, manufacturing, web-development, home shopping, credit cards, and even merchandising and design. In these movements the commercial risk and assets are usually passed to the outsourcing company.

However, not all companies refer to the process of business process management transfer as outsourcing; for some, they are just buying a service or a series of products. In this case the transfer of assets is unlikely.

The definition of outsourcing does not imply abdication of responsibility.

Examples

Some retailers over the years became very vertically integrated. They would manufacture their own goods, own and run their stores, own and run their warehousing and distribution to store services, and some even ran their own store loyalty schemes: Co-op stamps.

Now, many retailers outsource all their manufacturing, they do not own and run their stores, they have outsourced their warehousing and distribution, a bank runs their store cards, and some have outsourced their design, packaging design and merchandising by franchising their floor space to design or cosmetic houses and niche labels.

For others, including manufacturing companies, warehousing and distribution are outsourced and even those who run outsourcing services often outsource their accounts and IT functions.

REASONS FOR OUTSOURCING

You may have heard these reasons:

- We do not have the management expertise.
- We need to jump the learning curve.

- We want to move fast.
- The area requires major re-engineering.
- We do not have the management resources.
- We pay too much to do it ourselves.
- It is not core.
- The business is going through major change, and we need to make more areas variable cost.
- We need to focus our resources for training, investment, time etc.

However, some of the strategic reasons above are overshadowed by the personal objectives of the management involved; some like to follow a trend and therefore outsourcing is encouraged; some, when joining a company where that department has been outsourced, start the process of re-integration to enlarge their role.

These reasons for outsourcing can therefore be structured into five groups:

- financial;
- technology;
- managerial;
- resource management;
- personal.

Financial reasons for outsourcing

Although companies now have to declare in their statutory accounts and to many stock exchanges the value of assets leased and the methodology used by their businesses to access their markets, it is still the case that some companies have limited access to investment funds and see the need to leave the raising of cash to their outsourcing partners. Sometimes the outsourcing provider can borrow at a better rate than the company since their operation has a lower risk through better focus; sometimes the additional borrowing costs are worth the flexibility.

Flexibility of use of resources is also an important factor; if the company's use of the resources can be pooled with others, creating better scale and better marginal costs, then using an outsourcer ensures some independence of management of those resources and releases the company from having to manage the other users of the facilities.

Another facet of outsourcing in the past five years has been the pensions factor. While many larger companies have seen their pension deficits soar, the companies to whom they outsource often do not have final salary benefit schemes. Thus outsourcing crystallizes the deficit at the point of transfer, but it only does so for those people who transfer under TUPE (Transfer of Undertakings (Protection of Employment) Regulations) arrangements. There is constant churn and while those people who did transfer can freeze their pensions, new people do not create the same pension deficit as they join defined benefit schemes based on personal pensions. Thus the deficit will decline with time and the actuaries can take that into account at the point of the company sale or merger.

Technology

Technology half-lives have fallen dramatically over the past 20 years and the predictions are that they will fall faster still. Competitive edge comes from the rapid integration of new technologies into the company (if they are relevant). Consider the board looking at the choice of investing in the skills necessary to sell to its clients or the skills needed to operate the latest technology in its delivery vans or the warehouse. If resources need to be rationed, is it better to concentrate on the sales skills and the sales systems?

Many manufacturers maintain their own machinery completely. Current technology comes often in 'black boxes' that are replaced on failure and the skills of the supplier used to renew them. Major UK utility companies have agreed the outsourcing of their maintenance since the engineering companies have better skills, the latest training and the latest diagnostics; the company acts as the voice of the consumer in this instance.

Health and safety legislation and the tighter requirements of the insurance industry are leading to some companies outsourcing operations because specialization of knowledge and service leads to lower risk and costs.

In addition, the role of IT and the necessity for robust, integrated systems have moved business in two directions: one where they purchase integrated systems and outsource the systems analysis and implementation to IT consultancies; or one where they supplement their IT support staff with analysts and programmers, often through a consultancy to whom they delegate the resource provision to create the company's own software.

Resource management

One facet of the management of a company never changes: one forecasts resource requirements and the forecasts are never right; one allows for risk, and resource investment is therefore either too high or too low.

By focusing on your core resource business areas you can probably match investment and requirements more closely than in your other business areas. In the periphery areas, either you have to apply the same focus as the core areas to manage your resources or you will not optimize those areas. Given that many of these areas are likely not to use your core skills, the likelihood of optimizing them well and achieving good service levels and costs is lower than outsourcing them to a specialist.

Furthermore, the outsourcing company can act as an independent manager for your resources, should you wish to pool your resources with others and spread the fixed costs.

Management skills

The point has been made in the other sections that businesses should concentrate their management skills and training resources in those areas in which they can make a real difference to the profitability of their company or they should find partners to help them. Remember that you own the vision and strategy; that is part of the management and entrepreneurial skills you need to run a successful business. Maximizing your selling and procurement skills, ensuring you have the right products and services to sell to your clients, ensuring pricing provides the cash return you need for investment and paying for services bought should be the management skills you provide.

However, if outsourcing is the answer then there are important new skills to develop, namely the skills of choosing your partners and managing them.

Personal

It is rare for managers to have totally altruistic motives when deciding to in-source (take back an outsourcing contract) or to outsource a series of business processes. Unless there are clear strategic reasons for a change to be made, bringing back processes can often be to enlarge their role, just as pushing for outsourcing can be to ensure a job move.

In the past, strange decisions have been made: for example, a major retailer started to backload goods that were delivered by manufacturers to reduce costs by raising the utilization of their fleet. Then it was found that their primary movements from regional distribution centre (RDC) to store were being delayed as the fleet was not returning to regular times because both the extra running and the pickups compounded to increase the round trip time variability. The fleet was enlarged to cope with that. It is probably not known whether the final cost model was more or less expensive than the original model.

The question that was not asked was whether the fleet was required in the first place.

Current relevance

Given the pace of globalization, it is inevitable that outsourcing will take place. It is not usually sensible for manufacturers to set up their own manufacturing plants in the Far East. Some have, particularly if the products can be sold for internal consumption in the country of manufacture as well as for exports, but in the main, retailers or manufacturers are taking only part of the output of a Far East plant and therefore manufacture, distribution to the port and customs clearance tend to be outsourced. It is not always economic to have one's own management in place in China or Taiwan or Indonesia etc. There are specialist skills in arranging consolidated shipments from a port and the use of freight forwarders to ensure the shipping is booked and the goods are customs cleared in the UK is very normal.

These extended supply chains have risks like any other supply chain but we will discuss the amplification of the risks later.

However, the rise of concerns about the carbon footprint of extended supply chains and the move to reduce shipping carbon emissions will inevitably raise questions about Far East manufacture. The volatility of sterling against the US dollar, the higher price of fuel oil, the political uncertainty of some locations and the realities of managing over long distances and many time zones are causing a return to European manufacturing for some companies.

HOW DIFFERENT IS THE PUBLIC SECTOR FROM THE PRIVATE SECTOR WITH REGARD TO OUTSOURCING?

There are some fundamental differences between the public and private sectors: public businesses are about cost containment rather than long-term profit sustainability; public finances do not differentiate between capital expenditure and costs easily and therefore to remove all expenditure from the public borrowing figures is often the driver. Investments to reduce costs are far easier in the private sector where a return over time can be benchmarked against the internal rate of return for that company.

Now the pensions factor is the same for the public and private sectors, with the additional facet that members of the civil service retire at 60 while many in the private sector do not. If the new owning company does not have a final salary scheme then the pensions cost declines with time as the people who replace the original transferees, who leave or retire, join the new pension arrangements.

It is probably the experience of government trying to build its own systems that has led to the level of IT and business process outsourcing that is currently being progressed. Government wishes to distance itself from the day-to-day management of projects and is trying to move the risk of overrun expenditure to its contractors. Politically that is understandable, but as we will see later, it is crucial that organizations outsourcing business processes continue to keep a close eye on the efficiency of any interfaces and the delivery of the strategy.

The other major difference is that of the stakeholder community. The private sector includes customers, employees, shareholders, regulatory bodies and suppliers (for many, the local community should also be included and the press often is included in this category); the public sector has customers, employees, regulatory bodies and suppliers but also parliament, ministers, voters, the civil service, and a much closer media scrutiny.

THE PITFALLS IN OUTSOURCING

Given the outsourcing arrangements are about two companies joining together to provide a service or a range of products then the pitfalls become fairly easy to list when one views the arrangements dispassionately from the outside as a third party. They are in the main caused by differences in strategy, objectives, culture and, at a basic level, how the two sets of management who have to liaise with each other on a daily basis work together, trust and respect each other.

However, from the start, success comes from how well any tender document was detailed, how well the tasks were described and how open the client management were about their ongoing strategy and the reasons for outsourcing. Any hiding of real facts at this stage and the contract is likely to end in considerable difficulties.

Similarly, any over-expectations raised by the outsourcing company, particularly in terms of timing, complexity and the level of cost savings the client might enjoy, will also ensure that the contract flounders quite early in its life.

Major initial questions that must be addressed

The board, and it has to be at that level for major outsourcing arrangements, must review the following questions with care. They are designed to highlight the strategic changes needed to accept outsourcing:

- What are the company's current strengths, weaknesses, opportunities and threats (SWOT)?

- Does outsourcing resolve some of the weaknesses and threats and open up opportunities to build 'new' or consolidate our current strengths?
- What should our partner look like?
- What will we be depending on them for?
- Who should drive the outsourcing project at board level, who should be the 'project manager'?

With these questions answered honestly, the job of writing the tenders and evaluating the outsourcing companies' responses will be that much easier.

Once outsourcing has been agreed as part of the strategy, the major questions to be answered by the client company to avert the outsourcing pitfalls are:

- What is our current strategy and what strategic changes are we looking for?
- What are the boundaries to our outsourcing?
- How will we evaluate the tenders?
- How will success and failure be judged in the contract itself?
- How will we remunerate and reward them?
- How will we link the organizations?
- How can we reduce internal frictions and the feelings that they are just another supplier?

Strategy and the changes we need?

Outsourcing is about dovetailing other companies' expertise and focus into your company to improve competitiveness and customer service.

You must keep control of the strategy – you cannot outsource that; however, your outsourcing partner will also have a strategy and the marrying of the strategies is an important part of the early meetings between the companies and should form part of the selection process.

Partners with diverging strategies cannot work together for long and outsourcing cannot be a two-minute wonder; the time period for an outsourcing contract should reflect the life of the underlying assets supporting the contract and the time and effort required to tender, renegotiate and implement a new contract.

The outputs from the strategy that your stakeholders – customers, shareholders, employees etc – can see need to be defined. For example, customer service levels, return on investment etc. These should be discussed with your outsourcing partner only if their input to your business processes has an effect on these outputs.

What are the boundaries to outsourcing?

There needs to be a board process that challenges the added value that in-house processes provide to the overall success of the company. This is part of the input into the company SWOT analysis. The in-house picture then needs to be compared with that provided by outsourcing some of the business processes. The changes to the SWOT analysis need to be tracked. Of importance is the threats or risks that change between the two pictures and these must be analysed carefully. Risks in global supply chains are discussed a little later.

How will success and failure be judged?

Many outsourcing arrangements start without clarity on this question; the key performance indicators (KPIs) have not been agreed, the measurement methodology is not clear and reporting arrangements have not been defined. This does not allow the two partners to have the same vision of the operation and the lack of clarity will inhibit either side learning how to improve the services etc. In many ways, if the first question on strategy has not been answered then it is likely that this one will remain cloudy.

The indicators of success and failure and the rewards and redress required need to be fully laid out in the contract before the operation starts. The KPIs (for a warehouse operation) can cover: customer service measured in customer terms, budget performance (savings), damages, stock losses, accident rates, productivity measures etc.

So when looking at the remuneration of the partner, bonuses for beating customer service targets and a sharing of the budget savings are a good way of incentivizing the partnership. Sharing the losses, with penalties for poor customer service, is another powerful way of ensuring the correct behaviours.

Tender process

The tender process is a chapter in its own right, but what is important strategically for successful outsourcing is that there is sufficient detail in the tender about the current operations, a clear statement of the key performance requirements and a strategic vision, which is shared with the prospective partners. Without the detail, without a clear pro-forma of the response required, it will be difficult to evaluate the various replies. Honesty will provide better answers and honesty will build better relationships; both are needed if the operation is to be successful over time.

Company linkage and reducing internal friction

Outsourcing of a number of business processes implies that those outsourced need to communicate, to link with the rest of the company's business processes. Thus not only are there data linkages that need to be forged, but the management and administration of the two companies need to be joined as well.

A lot of time and care must be taken to ensure a high degree of efficiency about the interfaces; slow, inefficient interfaces will cost money, increase friction between the two groups and in the end result in poorer customer service and lost sales. Thus, a good strategic board will ensure that teams are built across the interface; the outsourcing company must not be held at complete arm's length such that face-to-face meetings are not accepted as part of the contract's life. The managers working the interfaces must be compatible; they must work together and respect each other. Attempts must be made to ease any cultural differences.

That does not mean that both sides should not challenge each other. No challenge, no creativity and an operation that will slowly fossilize; but challenge must be constructive. The internal assassins to the process of outsourcing must be dealt with.

Summary

In summary, most of the pitfalls experienced by companies outsourcing are down to:

- not being open about strategy or other market or business factors that are germane to the evaluation of the business the outsourcer will perform as they build their bid;
- a failure to gain the buy-in of the company management during the tender process;
- being unconstructive during the life of the contract;
- the contractor not assigning the right people with the right skills and competences to the contract.

Outsourcing can only work with the active cooperation of both sides.

GLOBAL SUPPLY CHAINS AND THE OUTSOURCING RISKS

Global supply chains, somehow, have brought the promise of better margins and both retailers and manufacturers have rushed to move the source of manufacture and some services to Eastern Europe, India and the Pacific rim, including China.

While manufacturing costs have undoubtedly fallen, not all commodities have fallen as well: shipping costs, for example, have risen as the laws of supply and demand have remained true.

It should be noted that the new extended supply chain hides a number of potential risks that, if not properly accounted for, could have a severe effect on your profits. Boards need to have identified and evaluated the costs of these risks in order to judge the real business case for overseas sourcing. The fact that some companies are now considering sourcing from countries that are geographically closer to the UK means that the balance may be shifting away from much-extended supply chains.

What are these important risks? They fall into the following four groups:

- supply chain risks;
- management risks;
- financial risks;
- political risks.

Supply chain risks

These arise through the new geography that is a backdrop to the outsourcing arrangements. The factory is no longer in the UK or nearby in Europe. Many of the problems are the same as the original supply chain but the risk of not resolving the issues increases with distance and the language and culture divide. The problems of quality, of specifying exactly what you want after the first proofing runs, of tying the supplier into your business are good examples.

You now have lower costs because you have agreed a single long-run production slot with your supplier but the slot is usually not very flexible. Thus changes to quantity and timing are much harder to arrange. Under-order stock, ask for a smaller, more expensive additional run to be slotted into the production schedule and you may have to have the quantity sent by air-freight in order for it to be on the shop-floor in time for the sales period. Realizing this additional cost, you may feel forced to over-order stock deliberately at the start. Many retailers now have higher stocks than they used to have; that requires larger warehouses and results in lower warehouse productivity. Then the sales forecasts, the merchandising forecasts are not met: clearing unnecessary stock through the sales channel generally requires heavy discounting, which means a reduction in profits.

Then there is the quality of goods on arrival; having been packaged, often badly, in the container, you now have an extensive new operation of finishing, steaming, and sometimes pricing etc that has to be done in the UK to make the merchandise look shop-ready. Who pays for the stock as it resides in customs awaiting clearance?

Your extended supply chain is forcing you to make decisions on fabrics, design and colours earlier and earlier in the process. There is the real risk that the product range needs to be specified before you have sold this year's same-period merchandise, raising the risk of getting it wrong.

Many of the above are judgemental risks that supply chain or merchandising managers have to take, but then there are the physical, environmental risks in the supply chain: hurricanes, earthquakes and typhoons all play a part in the equatorial climate and geography; they are risks that must be quantified and sourcing strategies and contingencies should take the results into account.

Management risks

The longer the supply chain, the greater the number of nodes, the greater management time that is required to achieve a smooth result. This resource will be more than the company currently has and even if functions are outsourced there will be the need to coordinate the outsourcing partnerships.

The greatest concern in this area for most retailers is quality. It can be difficult to oversee the accreditation and auditing of suppliers and manage proofing runs over a long distance. Once product is agreed, production schedules have to be monitored, which requires time, personnel and particular skill sets.

Outsourcing requires regular contact between the various parties to make it work. The question to bear in mind is: has the cost of the additional merchandising and quality management been taken into account?

Outsourcing is not about abdication; you still need to control the strategy, you need to spend time integrating the outsourced service and you need to ensure that customer service is provided at the level you require. The more central the activity is to the heart of the company, the more time that is required to really ensure that the outsourced operation is integrated. How the organizations are linked is one of the keys to the success of outsourcing.

The other management risks are that you did not define what the strategic changes that you are looking for are and you may not have shared them with the prospective partner. You may not have decided how success and failure will be judged and therefore not decided whether any form of gain share is appropriate to the contract.

Another risk that requires to be dealt with is the risk of poor internal communication about the potential to outsource and, once the contract is implemented, communicating the successes.

Financial risks

Your suppliers like hard currency, quite often US dollars, and thus a significant proportion of your costs will be exposed to the fluctuations of that currency. If the dollar strengthens and your margins decrease as you are connected to UK price competition, you are forced to try to reduce the purchase price, which may result in reduced product quality and greater finishing costs.

It is possible to hedge the dollars by buying in advance, but there is a cost to these transactions. As an alternative, you might buy product in pounds sterling, but if there is currency movement against the supplier, they must in the long run recover lost margin or refuse to do business with you, resulting in time and expenditure accrediting a new supplier.

Shipping costs increase markedly as routes become more popular, resulting in a reduction of your margins. If the price of oil increases, so will your shipping surcharges. Were these potential costs taken into account in the budget?

Your extended supply chain requires you to offset the supply risk by receiving the stock earlier, and because the stock is produced in one run, shipping costs can be minimized by shipping the whole quantity together. But this will result in extra warehousing and financing costs. What must also be taken into account is the cost of the additional write-down of unsold stock. You will require financial information systems that allow all the various costs to be posted against each product in the range so the real margin can be reviewed.

Political risks

These are very hard to assess but we have had some examples recently: EU trade quotas, instability in some countries, your suppliers having very different working conditions compared to European plants. These risks can directly affect your ability to trade or can become consumer relations issues that affect your brand.

Risk analysis

The risk analysis required is a detailed review of each step in the extended supply chain, starting with ranging and supplier selection and following the course of the product and information flows through the supply chain. At each stage the possible failures (the risks) to the process need to be understood and assessed. The classic quadrant:

High value:	High value:
Low impact	High impact
Low value:	Low value:
High impact	Low impact

needs to be populated. Once done, contingency plans, a necessity for at least the high-value/high-impact risks, need to be detailed and agreed. These could include sourcing alternative suppliers and holding additional stocks, starting the next season early, putting in place better systems and management controls etc.

Risk analysis should also cover the contingency requirements should it be decided, or be necessary, to take the outsourcing back in-house or move the management of the processes to a new company.

SUMMARY

The benefits from overseas, global sourcing need careful analysis both before starting the transfer and at regular intervals thereafter. The analysis requires the whole cost of acquisition of each product to be determined to allow comparison with other countries, including the UK. What is most important is that the analysis must be conducted dispassionately and that the interests of consumers and shareholders remain the most important consideration.

'Getting it wrong' is not hard – losing control of the strategy is all too easy; outsourcing requires continual effort to harness the outsourcer but such management resource is at a very different level from running the whole operation oneself. A company that harnesses the skills and re-sources of an outsourcing company and provides products and services at a lower cost and higher added value than its competitors as a result of letting experts run some of its operations will be more profitable than its competitors and quite possibly more flexible.

11

Risk in the supply chain

Lars Stemmler, BLG Consult GmbH

INTRODUCTION

Risk management is an established tool in the financial environment of the business world. The same holds true for logistics and the concept of supply chain management. The increased level of integration and cooperation along supply chains leads to new risk categories. Risk management might help in the understanding of the key risk drivers of supply chains and enable the partners to optimize their internal risk management system – at least developing an understanding of supply chain risks.

This chapter suggests an expansion of risk management into the scope of the supply chain. The objective is to provide arguments to actively pursue risk management as a planning tool. The chapter is written from the perspective of a non-financial firm such as a logistics service provider. This will highlight also the practical perspective of risk management.

RISK MANAGEMENT AND THE SUPPLY CHAIN – A NEW PERCEPTION!

The identification, assessment and control of risks are inherent in managing commercial undertakings. Risk management was developed in the financial services industry before it spread to other sectors. However, in many companies risk management is just considered a legal obligation following the introduction of the Sarbanes–Oxley Act in the United States. The statutory requirement to establish a formal risk management system also took hold in Europe. For example, the German commercial code stipulates the development of a reconnaissance system in order to identify risks that threaten the existence of the company at an early stage.

The perspective of such a system is principally financial. Concerned shareholders and an equally anxious public domain drove the introduction of risk management. Owing to the perceived character of risk management as a statutory obligation for companies, it is in many cases associated with additional non-value-adding costs to the enterprise. The task of managing risks constituted just another source of costs – an opportunity for planning was clearly missed.

However, a number of companies have realized the potential of risk management to improve planning processes and help to mitigate potential and actual sources of risk. It is not just banks that actively pursue risk management. Companies of other sectors are increasingly becoming aware of the potential added value of an integrated risk management. The fate of Ericsson is just one example:

> The effect on Ericsson, a Swedish mobile-phone company, of a fire in a New Mexico chip-making plant belonging to the Dutch firm Philips, has become a legend. The fire, in March 2000, started by a bolt of lightning, lasted less than 10 minutes but it caused havoc to the super-clean environment that chip-making requires. Ericsson, unable to find an alternative source of supply, went on to report a loss of over USD 2 billion in its mobile-phone division that year, a loss that left it as an also-ran in an industry where it had once been a leader. (*The Economist*, 2005)

The Ericsson example highlights a necessary shift in perception regarding risk management. This shift is driven by logistics; the case comfortably sets out the framework for this new perception of risk management:

- The logistics function provides a clear competitive advantage to a company regardless of which strategy it pursues. With either of Porter's (1980) strategies of cost leadership or differentiation, logistics helps to fulfil the company's objectives and to deliver added value to the customer. The example of Ericsson's disrupted supply chain is clearly the tip of the iceberg, and the quality problems of Robert Bosch AG, a major supplier to a German car manufacturer, in 2004 are just another example.
- Supply chain management aims at integrating partners along the supply chain, reducing interfaces and smoothing the flow of material,

information and finance. However, the higher the level of integration, the higher the probability of dependency on single partners. In addition, global sourcing adds a further dimension of uncertainty in terms of long transport legs, unstable political environments and different levels of commitment to quality and reliability.

● A closely knit international supply chain results in complex processes of coordinating and administering the partners along the chain. Different levels of accountability of staff and partners have to be taken into account. The focus of risk management necessarily shifts from an enterprise-only to a supply chain perspective.

These developments clearly have an impact on the scope and functionality of a company-focused risk management system. However, the concept of risk management can be actively employed along a supply chain. It enables all partners contributing to a supply chain to limit adverse risks to the chain. For this objective to be achieved, risk management along the supply chain has to address the following issues:

● all three flows – material, information and finance – along a supply chain and its associated processes;
● the boundaries of the system, which have to be pushed beyond the organization to cover the full length of the chain;
● the challenge to cover not only the strategic but also the operational level, turning the risk management system from a statutory reporting function into a planning function.

Figure 11.1 illustrates the scope of risk management in a supply chain management context.

OBJECTIVE AND PROCESS OF RISK MANAGEMENT

What do we associate with the term 'risk'? Risk denotes the chance of danger, loss or injury. In a commercial environment the chance of a good bargain must also be summarized under the term. Risk is to be differentiated from the term 'uncertainty'. Whereas risk assumes that the probabilities of the possible results of an event are known, this is not the case with uncertainty. Hence, risk is measurable uncertainty.

Risk management includes activities to identify, analyse and assess, and communicate, as well as control, risks (Müller, 2003). In an ideal case, risk management is directly assigned to the top management, providing

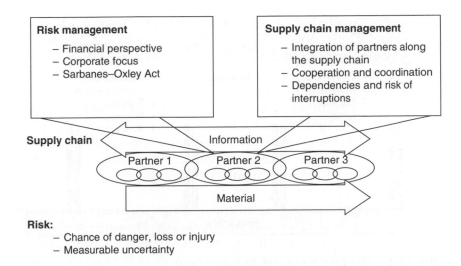

Figure 11.1 Risk management in the supply chain – a new perception

continuous support to ensure the company's ability to survive in the marketplace (Burger and Buchhart, 2002). Risk management is governed by the internal risk policy, making the enterprise in extreme cases either a risk taker or a risk avoider.

The risk management process describes systematically the framework and methods from initially identifying the risks to finally controlling them (Holzbaur, 2001). The first activity is to identify and describe all actual and future sources of risk – at this stage of the argumentation – to the company (see Figure 11.2). In a second step the risks are assessed. When determining the exposure of a company, risks are characterized through the quantification of the probability of the occurrence and the extent of the potential damage or gain. The risk exposure can be illustrated by means of a risk map or risk portfolio, leading to a segmentation of risks into commonly three categories. Category A risks represent risks that have a potentially disastrous impact on the company, in terms of both high probability of occurrence and high damage potential (with only adverse risks normally included in the analysis). On the basis of this analysis, appropriate measures can be taken in order to control risks. Measures are taken in accordance with the stipulations of the risk management policy. A feedback loop is obligatory to ensure the effectiveness of the measures.

In theory, the risk management process looks consistent and straight-forward. However, practical experience shows that not only does the

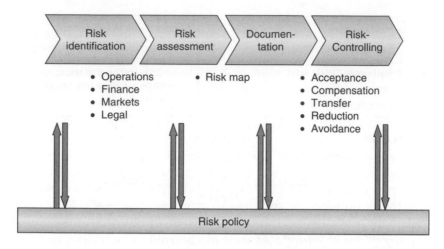

Figure 11.2 The process of risk management

quantification pose considerable problems to line managers but also the identification of risks in the first place poses an almost insurmountable challenge for line managers. The quantification, estimating both probabilities of occurrence and the monetary level of impact, is limited through the lack of data of past experiences of similar events in other companies. Further, the identification of risks is often subject to managers' reluctance to admit the existence of risks in their fields of responsibility: admitting to the presence of risks is considered a sign of weakness. But the effort should be made to come up with a meaningful risk portfolio.

FROM AN ENTERPRISE PERSPECTIVE TO THE SUPPLY CHAIN PERSPECTIVE

Having outlined the risk management process, let us now focus on how to incorporate the requirements of a sophisticated supply chain management into risk management, and answer the question of what benefits are produced for whom.

Ensuring supply chain integrity

Supply chain management can be described as a holistic management approach to integrating and coordinating the material, information and financial flows along a supply chain (Handfield and Nichols, 1999). Further, this includes the management of the interfaces between the partners involved in this chain, particularly from an information management and technology point of view (Schary and Skjøtt-Larsen, 2001).

A supply chain is basically a sequence of processes – however, the processes are owned and managed by different legal entities. This requires inter-organizational cooperation. Conflicting interests due to the legal and economic independence of the supply chain partners need to be aligned to a single supply chain objective. If successful, the competitive advantage of these partners increases considerably.

There are a number of implications of supply chain management on risk management. As already said, risk management is an important tool in ensuring the economic integrity of an organization. This holds particularly true if the boundaries of the organization are clearly set, for example by means of arm's-length transactions. In a supply chain management environment these boundaries become blurred, which does not mean that they no longer exist legally, but operations-wise it becomes very difficult to identify the separating line between the two companies. Just consider employees of a logistics provider doing packaging work on the premises of the shipper. The implications on the risk management system are obvious – the scope of traditional risk management is to be extended to integrate a supply chain. At the same time, having to ensure process quality, risk management evolves into logistics.

Parallel to an expansion of the scope of managing a supply chain, risk management has to grow in responsibility as well (see Figure 11.3). The

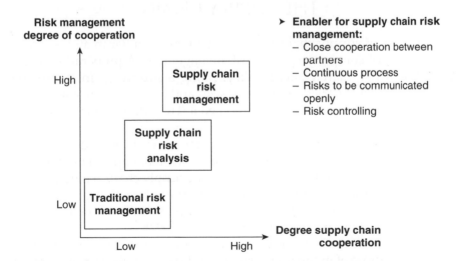

Figure 11.3 Supply chain integration to be supported by risk management
Source: Kajüter, 2003

higher the degree of integration along a supply chain is, the larger the required scope of risk management becomes. And the concept of supply chain risk management is raised.

Martin Christopher (2002) suggests defining supply chain risk management as 'the integration and management of risks within the supply chain and risks external to it through a co-ordinated approach amongst supply chain members to reduce supply chain vulnerability as a whole'. The vulnerability of the chain stems from external and internal risks to it. The objectives of supply chain risk management are clearly laid out by Kajüter (2003). He sees risk management in the supply chain as 'a collaborative and structured approach to risk management, embedded in the planning and control processes of the supply chain, to handle risks that might adversely affect the achievement of the supply chain goals'.

Practitioners can agree to these definitions and clarifications, and they will clearly see the need for an inter-organizational management of risks. As with organizational or company-specific risk management, identifying the relevant risks is the first task to master in the process of supply chain risk management. It is here that the first challenges are encountered. The following section focuses on developing a framework for risk identification and assessment along a supply chain.

RISK ASSESSMENT AND CONTROL ALONG THE SUPPLY CHAIN

The process of supply chain risk management is similar in all respects to the process of company-specific risk management. A preparatory step is to define a risk management policy. Along a supply chain, companies with different industry backgrounds, sizes and ownership structures have to work together to achieve a common goal. Their differing interests have to be merged in a consistent risk management policy.

Having clarified how much risk the partners are prepared to take, the identification of supply chain risks is the next step. Figure 11.4 illustrates the two different types of risks inherent to a supply chain: exogenous and endogenous risks. The former result from the interaction of the supply chain with its environment, whereas the latter stem from the interaction of the supply chain partners (Chapman et al, 2002).

The endogenous risks can be divided into the categories of organizational risks (those of individual partners) and specific risks from integrating, coordinating and cooperating along the supply chain. Company-specific risks are adequately described in traditional risk management maps. Specific supply chain risks can now be identified, for example risks from

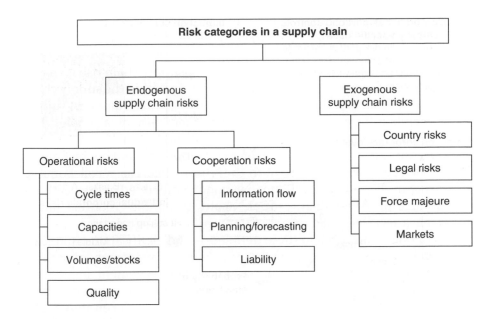

Figure 11.4   Risk categories' identification into supply-chain-specific risks

the sharing of information on integrated platforms (integration), risks of a high level of interdependence among the partners (cooperation) and risks stemming from interwoven processes (coordination).

The prime objective of supply chain risk management is to identify those risks posing a major threat to the supply chain. A measurement tool is needed here to help transfer (existing) company-specific risk maps into a supply chain risk map and to integrate the supply-chain-specific plus the endogenous risks. How this can be done is illustrated in Figure 11.5. The company-specific risk portfolios form the basis for an ABC classification of these risks, ideally after an inter-organizational risk-controlling process. The ABC classification leads to a two-dimensional matrix showing the probability of the risk-relevant event and the net impact (after company-specific risk management) of this event (level of damage in monetary terms). The product of the two gives the expected value of the risk.

Following this step, managers have to decide which of these risks have what implication on the supply chain. Each risk in the ABC classification is assigned a high-, medium- or low-impact category, leading to the supply chain risk map. Into this map the supply-chain-specific risks as well as the endogenous risks are integrated. The latter two categories are evaluated using an expected value. Regarding the impact on the partners along the supply chain an aggregated figure for possible damages has to be found.

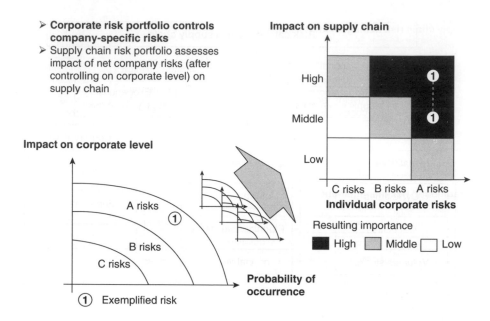

Figure 11.5 Supply chain risk assessment

As with traditional risk management, the phase of risk controlling concludes the overall process of risk management. Accepting the risk and avoiding it are the poles between which risk controlling takes place. Avoiding the risk might mean doing no business at all (see Figure 11.6). Accepting the risk means in the last instance simply living with it. In between there is an array of measures to control risks. These measures can be summarized under the categories of risk compensation, risk transfer and risk reduction.

The ability to reduce business risks is to be preferred over other measures. On a supply chain level, risk reduction includes a particular focus on interfaces. Risk transfer – although comparatively easy to achieve in traditional risk management, for example by means of buying insurance – is by definition a difficult approach for a supply chain, as we are obliged to look not at individual companies but at the whole chain. Risk compensation along a supply chain – on a company level achieved through provisions or hedging – manifests itself in rules governing cooperation between the partners. One partner is obviously not prepared to compensate another one monetarily. However, compensation can be initiated through behaviour. Partners might agree on defined actions to be taken on a mutual basis.

Risk compensation in terms of mutual rules is to be delimited from risk transfer measures, for example outsourcing or vendor-managed inventory

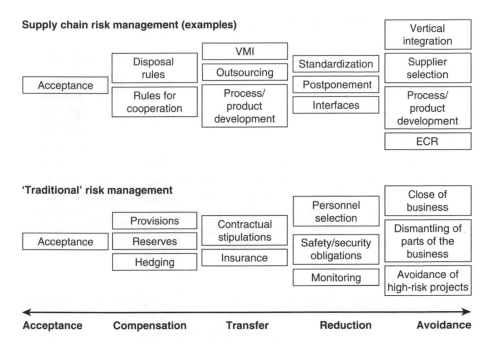

Figure 11.6 Risk controlling between avoidance and acceptance
Source: Indefurth, 2002

(VMI). The latter measures feature a far more institutionalized contractual basis. Whereas in rules-based risk compensation schemes each partner takes risks (close to risk acceptance), transferring risks among the partners means selecting those partners that are willing to take a risk from another. In a supply chain perspective this only contributes to an indirect reduction of risks, as the risk is transferred to the partner that can manage it better than the other.

What becomes apparent when discussing risk controlling is that risk management does not mean simply reacting to emergencies along the supply chain but pursuing an active approach anticipating supply chain risks. Having looked into the toolbox of risk controlling it becomes further apparent that deciding on suitable measures is a complex task in terms of decision making and implementation among the partners – even assuming that there is a consistent risk policy in place.

The latter issue is worth exploring in some more detail, bearing in mind that we would like to pursue a practitioner's view in this chapter. The following section sheds some light on obstacles to profound supply chain risk management.

IMPLEMENTATION IN PRACTICE

Obstacles to implementation

The necessity and the theoretical framework of supply chain risk management sound convincing. Parallel to the development of supply chain management, which introduces a high degree of integration, cooperation and coordination among supply chain partners, the company-specific risk management systems have to keep up, and need to expand from the traditional financial perspective into logistics – as well as focusing on supply chain risks. No doubt, there are specific supply chain risks to be addressed. However, implementing risk management that focuses on the supply chain might end in a 'prisoner's dilemma'. Let us look at the most commonly observed obstacles to implementing risk management on a company level:

- *Risk identification.* Risks are collated in a risk map and subsequently reported to top management. Hence, at middle management level or in operating units of an organization, managers tend to hide risks by simply denying their existence.
- *Risk identification is not done through neutral eyes.* External help is expensive, so that risk identification is carried out internally, resulting in a different perception of certain risks. For example, if carried out by accounting staff, operational risks are either not understood or are considered more severe compared to financial risks (zur Horst and Leisten, 2002).
- *Required quantification lacks understanding.* A basic requirement of sound risk management is to quantify the potential loss or damage and to estimate the probability of occurrence. If a process fails, the company loses sales in the amount of the damaged lot size. What if a customer deems this company as no longer reliable and holds back future orders? Regarding the probabilities, estimating the failure rate seems simple, but what about political risks?

Assuredly, any risk management system should be implemented under the auspices of the company's auditors. However, obstacles multiply with a supply chain perspective:

- *Admitting the risks.* Drawing a supply chain risk map implies that any risk with a potential impact on the complete chain needs to be disclosed by its 'owner'. You run into a problem here if there is a dominant player along the chain, for example a manufacturer in the automobile industry. A supplier or logistics provider cannot simply admit that there is a risk. On the contrary, there is a strong tendency towards risk transfer from the manufacturer to the partner up and down the chain (Kendall, 1998).

- *Putting effort into risk management.* How much effort are companies prepared to put into a concept that potentially is a risk in itself, ie the risk of being blacklisted as a result of disclosing risks?
- *Relying on the risk map.* Bearing in mind the hidden risks as discussed here, can each partner rely on the input of other partners, or does risk controlling become mere 'risk engineering'?

An option for avoiding these issues is to use a 'bottom-up' approach, rather than the traditional 'top-down'.

Bottom-up instead of top-down

Risk management must provide tangible benefits to managers, particularly on an operational level. Coming back to our initial example of Ericsson, simply insisting on an answer to the question of what ensures business contingency is too broad an approach. Unfortunately, risk management – in the traditional sense – is a 'top-down' management tool imposed by regulation and law. Trying the opposite way and going 'bottom-up' might be part of a solution.

Admittedly it is far more cumbersome, as a bottom-up approach starts with a process model of the supply chain. This is where the supply chain operations reference (SCOR) model might be useful. Alternatively, many companies already have quality managers in place and process charts to hand, which include detailed descriptions that are amended by the stochastic information (see Figure 11.7). Simulating the processes under different, risk-oriented parameters and putting the know-how of security managers into the simulation results in a robust picture of a risk map. The focus is first of all operational: how well do our processes and those of the supply chain work?

More strategic issues come in when looking at the materials flows and the stock levels at the links and nodes of the supply chain. These links and nodes can also be modelled as processes and subsequently simulated, bearing in mind different performance and cost levels. By aggregating those processes, a company – and then a supply chain – risk map emerges.

CONCLUSIONS

The concept of supply chain management brings additional risks to the supply chain, which – in accordance with the objective of SCM of increasing

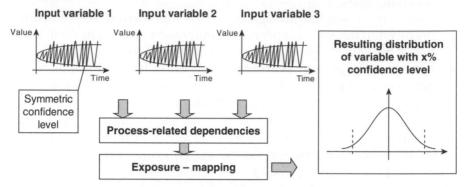

Figure 11.7　Random walks with 'at-risk' models
Source: Wiedemann and Hager, 2003

the level of integration and coordination among the supply chain partners – should be addressed jointly. Those risks include the endogenous risks of a supply chain, such as operational and cooperation risks. A supply chain risk portfolio is suggested to initiate the risk management process along the supply chain, leading to a toolbox of risk-controlling measures on a strategic and operational level.

This is the opportunity for risk management to expand from the financial and corporate perspectives respectively into the field of logistics and inter-organizational cooperation. However, easy as it sounds, problems that have to be addressed include:

- the challenge of turning risk management from a mere statutory obligation into a planning tool;
- the identification of hidden risks and overcoming dominant players in the supply chain;
- the quantification of probabilities and damage levels;
- the pursuance of a bottom-up approach for supply chain risk management to avoid the overload of top management as in the case of a top-down approach.

An elegant, but complex, task might be to simulate (parts of) the supply chain by means of stochastic modelling in order to support the risk mapping and to evaluate the influence of variations in different risk parameters.

Despite the efforts needed, supply chain partners should develop a sound understanding of how well the processes along their chain work and what the key risk drivers in the structure are.

References

Burger, A and Buchhart, H (2002) *Risiko-Controlling* [Risk controlling], Oldenbourg, Munich

Chapman, P *et al* (2002) Identifying and managing supply chain vulnerability, *Journal of the Institute of Logistics and Transport*, **4** (4), May, pp 59–64

Christopher, M (2002) Supply chain vulnerability, Executive Report, Cranfield University, Cranfield

The Economist (2005) 29 October, p 71

Handfield, RB and Nichols, EL (1999) *Introduction to Supply Chain Management*, Pearson, Upper Saddle River, NJ

Holzbaur, U-D (2001) *Management*, Kiehl, Ludwigshafen

Inderfurth, K (2002) Risikomanagement in der Supply Chain [Risk management in the supply chain], in *Wissenschaftssymposium Logistik der BVL*, ed Bundesvereinigung Logistik, Tagungsband, Munich

Kajüter, P (2003) Risk management in supply chains, in *Strategy and Organization in Supply Chains*, ed SA Seuring *et al*, Springer-Verlag, Heidelberg

Kendall, R (1998) *Risk Management for Executives*, FT Prentice Hall, London

Müller, S (2003) *Management-Rechnungswesen: Ausgestaltung des externen und internen Rechnungswesens unter Konvergenzgesichtspunkten* [Management accounting: developing a convergent management accounting system], Gabler, Wiesbaden

Porter, ME (1980) *Competitive Strategy*, Free Press, New York

Schary, PB and Skjøtt-Larsen, T (2001) *Managing the Global Supply Chain*, 2nd edn, Copenhagen Business School Press, Copenhagen

Wiedemann, A and Hager, P (2003) Messung finanzieller risiken mit cash-flow-at-risk/earnings-at-risk-verfahren, ccfb, Eitorf

zur Horst, A-D and Leisten, R (2002) Supply Chain Controlling: Vertrauen ist gut – Controlling ist noch besser! [Supply chain controlling], in *Forum Forschung 2002/2003*, GMU Duisburg, Duisburg

12

Supply chain vulnerability, risk and resilience

Helen Peck, Cranfield University

INTRODUCTION

Few areas of management interest have risen to prominence in recent years as rapidly as supply chain vulnerability. In only a handful of years the subject has been transformed from a truth that dare not speak its name to one of the most fashionable disciplines of the decade. This chapter looks first at the factors and events behind the rise of the field. Next it tackles the thorny issues of supply chain definitions and dissonance within supply chain management, before moving on to see how they pan out when competing concepts of risk and risk management come into play. How, when and why the different concepts from risk management fit with some elements of the supply chains but not others are explained, positioning each within a multi-level framework, based on a simple exploded model of a supply chain. It provides a holistic overview of supply chain vulnerability, and explains why supply chain resilience is perhaps a more appropriate concept in this context. In conclusion the chapter draws on earlier writings in open systems theory to explain why supply chains should be viewed as open societal systems as well as engineered processes.

SUPPLY CHAIN VULNERABILITY: AN IDEA WHOSE TIME HAD COME

At the dawn of the new century, industry and policy makers waited to see whether efforts to contain the Y2K 'millennium bug' had been successful. Happily for most organizations, the year 2000 arrived without a hitch. Y2K made everyone aware of how IT-dependent our societies had become, but its legacy was to leave managers sceptical about the need to spend scarce time and resources warding off supply chain disruptions that might never occur. In government the event was viewed differently. Business continuity planning (BCP) had successfully averted an economic meltdown.

The UK fared less well the following September when a small number of protestors managed to blockade oil refineries, causing chaos at the petrol pumps and serious economic disruption. The outbreak of foot-and-mouth disease in the national livestock herd only months later sent government searching for ways to improve the national resilience to all manner of disruptive challenges. Few realize that it was these events – together with BSE (mad cow disease) in the 1990s – and not terrorism that prompted a major review of UK emergency planning doctrine and sowed the seeds of the Civil Contingencies Act (2004). It was because these events were so different from the 'sudden onset' emergencies – bombing accidents or natural disasters – that national emergency planners had hitherto focused upon that such a revision was deemed necessary. For a start, these were not site-specific as a bombing might be. They had many sites or none at all. Moreover, these crises tended to build slowly at first (often almost unnoticed at a national level) and then escalate quickly, causing enormous economic damage and social disquiet. In each instance it was industry and government, not the emergency services, that found themselves in the unfamiliar role of first responders. These creeping crises were remarkable in one other respect – they represented *systemic supply chain disruptions*, hinting that there might be a dark side to the ever-increasing efficiency of contemporary supply chains. Nevertheless, the whole notion of supply chain vulnerability remained deeply unfashionable until 11 September 2001.

The international terrorist attacks on New York and Washington marked the beginning of a change in attitude towards the whole notion of supply chain vulnerability. In general terms the attacks put a supercharger behind the business continuity industry, and all aspects of security management. It is now widely recognized that the terrorist attacks did not themselves cause any significant disruption to global supply chains or even North American industry. But the reaction of the US authorities did.

The closure of US borders and grounding of transatlantic flights caused massive disruptions following an outpouring of press articles (mainly in the United States) highlighting the terrorist threat and the frailty of international supply chains.

Post-9/11, new security measures were hurriedly introduced at US borders, ports and airports, affecting inbound cargos to the United States. The new measures – including the Container Security Initiative (CSI) and Customs–Trade Partnership (C–TPAT) – employed principles and approaches borrowed from the application of total quality management in manufacturing supply chains. They demanded much more rigorous and earlier electronic presentation of manifests, as well as documentation and validation of security policies and procedures from the companies involved. Compliant companies could then, it was suggested, become approved 'known shippers', thereby ensuring speedier customs clearance. Inevitably, the measures slowed down 'abnormal' shipments or those coming in from non-approved shippers. Moreover, the programme required all inbound shipments to the United States to be vetted at designated approved overseas ports, thereby displacing much of the cost of compliance and subsequent congestion to the ports and airports of departure. Around the world, national or supranational customs authorities adopted similar mindsets and soon tabled rafts of similar measures.

Meanwhile, back in the 'business as usual' world of corporate profitability, the Enron Corporation, once held up as a model of best-practice corporate risk management, wobbled and collapsed, taking international auditors Arthur Andersen with it. Another North American giant, WorldCom, quickly followed. In Europe, Dutch retailer Royal Ahold and Italian dairy conglomerate Parmalat Finanziara did the same.

Financial markets, like supply chains, rely on confidence. In a bid to protect shareholders – and ultimately the well-being of the financial markets – regulators hurried to bring in their own more rigorous reporting requirements. The international banking community had faced the same stark realities only a few years earlier, when the unchecked activities of 'rogue trader' Nick Leeson led to the collapse of London-based Barings Bank, threatening irreparable damage to Singapore's reputation as a financial centre. These scandals highlighted the need for more diligent corporate governance in general and the appetite for measures to monitor, manage and control operational risk (ie internal threats to organizational well-being) in particular. The Basel Accords in International Banking (1998, 2004) and the introduction in the United States of the Sarbanes–Oxley Act (2002) formalized the requirements.

Sarbanes–Oxley (SOX), mentioned in the previous chapter, has been a particularly potent force in raising the profile of all aspects of corporate risk management. It focused minds more directly than ever before by making jail sentences a realistic possibility for negligent chief executives. It did so by removing the opportunity to claim ignorance of wrongdoing as a defence. SOX demanded disclosure of all potential risks to corporate well-being, including those that might once have been considered beyond the legal boundaries of the firm. Section 401 demands that organizations declare all 'material off-balance sheet transactions' including 'contingent obligations' and 'interests transferred to an unconsolidated entity'. These clauses encompass some inter-organizational risk sharing and risk transfer activities. For example, fixed-volume shipping service contracts are guarantee contracts; VMI and outsourcing agreements – sometimes used to hedge risk and place retained assets off-balance sheet – must also be declared. SOX also requires that providers of outsourced services (including logistics service suppliers) must be able to demonstrate the existence of appropriate internal process controls. Finally, it demands that consideration be given to other possible externally induced disruptions. Externally induced disruptions include disruptions to transport and communications. SOX was rolled out in successive waves, beginning with US quoted companies, but later extending to their US-based suppliers, and then to those in other countries in 2003.

All of the factors described so far have raised the profile of supply-chain-related risk and vulnerabilities, and attitudes have changed dramatically in just a handful of years. Being concerned with matters of supply chain vulnerability has become the epitome of good corporate governance and the socially responsible thing to do. Clearly, supply chain managers should be part of those discussions, but it is also important to recognize that managers from many disciplines now need to have a clear understanding of what supply chains are and how they fit in with their own responsibilities and risk management concerns.

SUPPLY CHAIN RISK MANAGEMENT: A RECIPE FOR CONFUSION

The term 'supply chain' lingers on despite the near-universal recognition that supply chains are not simply linear processes. They are in fact complex systems of interlocking networks. Beyond that, there is no commonly agreed definition of 'supply chain'. Several different definitions are given within this book, and for the purpose of this chapter two are included here. Both emerged in the late 1990s. Aitken (1998) proposed: 'a network of connected and interdependent organizations, mutually and co-operatively working together to control, manage and improve the flow of material and information from suppliers to end users'. Shortly afterwards, Christopher (1998) adopted a value-based variation on the theme, defining a supply chain as 'the network of organisations that are linked through upstream and downstream relationships in the different processes and activities that produce value in the form of products and services in the hands of the ultimate customer'.

Thus supply chains comprise flows of materials, goods and information (including money), which pass within and between organizations, linked by a range of tangible and intangible facilitators, including relationships, processes, activities, and integrated information systems. They are also linked by physical distribution networks, and the national/international communications and transport infrastructures. In their totality, supply chains link organizations, industries and economies.

Notwithstanding the different interpretations of what constitutes a supply chain, understanding supply chain vulnerability is complicated by two other distinct problems. The first is confusion over the scope of supply chain management. The second (which deserves a volume in its own right) is the nature of 'risk'.

The confusion surrounding the scope of supply chain management is well documented, not least its ambivalent relationship with logistics (Larson and Halldorsson, 2004). The term 'supply chain management' (SCM) first appeared in the early 1980s when Oliver and Webber (1992) used it to describe an amalgamation and relabelling of established functions – notably 'logistics' (integrated transport, warehousing and distribution) and manufacturing-based 'operations management' (elements of purchasing, order and inventory management, production planning and control as well as customer service). Though the title was new, many of the fundamental assumptions, such as the sharing of information – to allow the substitution of information for inventory – and systems integration across organizational boundaries, had been around for decades (Forrester 1958, 1969; La Londe, 1984).

The SCM agenda has unquestionably broadened in recent times to include aspects of marketing, new product development, order management and payment (Cooper *et al*, 1997). According to Stock and Lambert (2001), it had become 'the integration of key business processes, from end user through original suppliers that provides products, services and information that add value for customers'. Christopher (1998) adopts a more relational value-adding perspective, when he describes SCM as 'the management of upstream and downstream relationships with suppliers and customers to deliver superior customer value at less cost to the supply chain as a whole'. However, closer examination shows that these and other writers are actually conceptualizing SCM in several different ways, eg as a management philosophy, the implementation of a management philosophy, or a set of management processes (Mentzner *et al*, 2001). In short, SCM is used to describe at least two quite different concepts. One is the functional scope of SCM, encompassing the tactical management of those elements of logistics and the many other supply chain processes, across functions and between businesses. The other is a philosophy demanding strategic-level recognition of the need for coordination and collaboration throughout the supply chain, which must be present across three or more adjacent firms.

For the practitioner, academic arguments about the nature of supply chains or scope of supply chain management are probably viewed as just that – academic. In the real world, functional legacies and assumptions remain and resurface regularly in writings on the subject. In much of that literature, 'risk' is simply the commercial consequence of failure to implement functional best practice, be it in purchasing, materials management or manufacturing process controls. However, if supply chain management is indeed the interdisciplinary, inter-organizational, globe-spanning concern it purports to be, then these characteristics should be recognized and reflected in both our understanding of supply chain vulnerability and our approaches to risk management.

Given that supply chains comprise many different elements, and supply chain management embraces many different functions, it is perhaps useful first to ask the question 'What is it that is vulnerable, ie at risk?' Is it the performance of a process or specific activities, or the well-being of an organization, a trading relationship or the wider networks as a whole? Or is it the vulnerability of one or more of these to some external malevolent force that should be the focus of our consideration? In fact, supply chain vulnerability takes in all of these. What seems to muddy the water is when concepts of risk and risk management come into the equation.

RISK: THE GREAT DIVIDE

The starting point for many discussions of risk is in classical decision theory (Borge, 2001). Here risk is a measure of the possible upside and downside of a single rational and quantifiable (financial) decision. In a seminal paper on managerial perceptions of risk and risk taking, March and Shapira (1987) define risk – from a decision theory perspective – as 'variation in the distribution of possible outcomes, their likelihoods and their subjective values'. However, they go on to observe that this interpretation has been under attack for many years, particularly by those studying financial markets. The problem is that research has shown that it does not reflect how managers see risk, nor does it reflect their behaviours or the social norms that influence them (MacCrimmon and Wehrung, 1986; Shapira, 1986). Studies show that managers adopt and apply only selected elements of the total risk equation. They pay little attention to uncertainty surrounding positive outcomes, viewing risk in terms of dangers or hazards with potentially negative outcomes. Moreover, it is the scale of the likely losses associated with plausible outcomes, rather than the range of possible outcomes, that focuses managerial minds. Underlying March and Shapira's (1987) observations about dissonance between how people are supposed to behave and how they do behave is a wider debate on the nature of risk that has been gathering momentum for over 20 years.

In 1983, scientists and engineers of the Royal Society in London produced a report that presented risk as 'the probability that a particular adverse event occurs during a stated period of time, or results from a particular challenge. As a probability in the sense of statistical theory, risk obeys all formal laws of combining probabilities'. The report reflected the prevailing international orthodoxy of the time and was widely accepted as a definitive document in the field. It made a clear distinction between 'objective risk', as determined by experts applying quantitative scientific means, and 'perceived risk' – the imprecise and unreliable perceptions of the laity. This 'objective' position, combined with the Society's definition of 'detriment' as 'the numerical measure of harm or loss associated with an adverse event', reflects the compound measure of risk widely encountered within the engineering, health and safety literature.

In 1992, the Royal Society revisited the subject of risk, this time inviting a group of social scientists – psychologists, anthropologists, sociologists, geographers and economists – to add their expert opinions. Only the economists supported the earlier stance of their colleagues from the physical sciences. The other social scientists took an opposing position, arguing that objective and perceived risk are in practice inseparable, particularly where people are involved. They argued that risk is not a discrete or objective phenomenon, but an interactive culturally determined one that is inherently resistant to objective measurement. The essential problem is that people modify their behaviour and thereby their likely exposure to risk in response to subjective perceptions of that risk, subtly balancing perceived costs and benefits. Writers such as Adams (1996), therefore, contend that these unquantified or unquantifiable changes in exposure invariably defeat all attempts to measure risk outside the casino, where odds can be mechanically controlled. The outcome of the Royal Society's 1992 study was discord within the Society and a descent into 'uncertainty' within the risk management discipline.

Risk and uncertainty are terms that in practice are often used interchangeably, but back in the 1920s Knight (1921) made a helpful distinction: 'If you don't know for sure what will happen, but you know the odds, that's risk and if you don't even know the odds, that's uncertainty.' Uncertainty is, according to Knight, 'the realm of judgement'. Nevertheless, as Adams (1996) points out, 'Virtually all the formal treatments of risk and uncertainty in game theory, operations research, economics and management science require that the odds be known, that numbers be attachable to the probabilities and magnitudes of possible outcomes'. In these disciplines, risk management still strives to identify, quantify, control and where possible eliminate specific narrowly defined risks. Similarly, most of the tools, techniques and concepts used for identifying, evaluating and estimating risk remain rooted in the thinking of scientific management. Consequently they fail to consider that failures and accidents may be emergent properties arising from the wider system as a whole (White, 1995). Even in enterprise risk management, it is clear to some that risk management models have failed to keep pace with the realities of our networked world. They have failed to account for operational interdependencies between firms brought about by the trend to outsource and the reality of supply chain networks, thereby underestimating the range and severity of risks faced by a company (Starr, Newfrock and Delurey, 2003).

Why this all matters from a practical supply chain risk management perspective is that, if supply chains are seen only from a business process engineering and control perspective, then a selective (downside only) version of a variance-based view of risk sits quite well. However, if we also accept that supply chains involve relationships that link organizations sharing a common philosophy and purpose, then there is an equally persuasive argument that supply chains should be viewed as open interactive societal systems. Organizations are, whether we like it or not, socially constructed, managed and populated by people, imbued with all the fallibility of human nature and its good common sense. Moreover, if we also accept that these may be global supply chains, then those culturally determined perceptions of risk could vary greatly from one country to another. Along the way the forces of nature can easily demonstrate just how far removed from the controlled environment of the casino this all might be.

SUPPLY CHAIN RESILIENCE: A HOLISTIC VIEW

Mindful of the need for more holistic approaches to risk management, this section looks not only at risks in terms of specific vulnerabilities and hazards, but at what that means for the resilience of the supply chain as an integrated system. In this context, the term 'resilience' refers to the ability of the system to return to its original (or desired) state after being disturbed. However, keeping our feet in the real world, it is important to remember that no one person manages a whole supply chain. Many

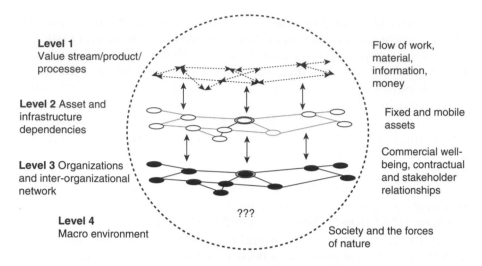

Figure 12.1 A supply chain as an interactive system

people are responsible for the management of activities, functions, processes or other aspects of these complex dynamic networks. Each will be viewing supply chain risk through the lens of his or her own performance measures. The upshot is that, in practice, supply chain risk management is likely to be a patchwork of sometimes complementary, but often conflicting or competing, efforts. Figure 12.1 shows a supply chain broken down into its component parts, hopefully without losing the sense of dynamic interaction. Looking at supply chains in this way enables the inclusion of many different functional and hierarchical perspectives and their respective interpretations of risk, as well as an opportunity to position some of the management tools and techniques currently available.

Process engineering and inventory management

Level 1 in Figure 12.1 concentrates on a process engineering or inventory management perspective. It focuses on what is being carried – work and information flows – and process design within and between organizations. This perspective underlies lean operations and the 'end-to-end' perspective required for the 'agile' supply chain, where reliable, responsive processes and inventory management concerns remain central themes. Risk management is largely about improved visibility (of demand and inventory), velocity (to reduce the likelihood of obsolescence and optimize asset utilization) and control. If processes are tightly monitored and controlled, then non-conformance to plan can be quickly detected. Risk reduction tools are often borrowed from total quality management. Related process improvement and control methodologies such as Six Sigma are also favoured by some, as are automated event management systems, which readily alert managers to deviations from plan and minimize human intervention.

In the ideal world of scientific management, mastery of process control methodologies would facilitate the identification, management and elimination of risk. Unfortunately, we do not live in an ideal world, so Levels 2, 3 and 4 of the model bring in a host of other factors that regularly intervene.

Assets and infrastructure dependencies

Level 2 considers the fixed and mobile assets used to source, produce or carry the goods and information flows addressed at Level 1. When viewed at this level, nodes in the networks may be farms, factories, distribution centres, commercial retail outlets, or public service delivery points such as schools or hospitals. Alternatively, they may be facilities housing IT servers and call centres. Links in the network are the transport and communications infrastructure, ie roads, railways, flight paths and sea lanes, pipelines and grids, plus mobile assets – boat, trains, trucks and planes. The transport and communications networks have their own nodes too – ports, airports, satellites etc.

Well-known asset-based approaches to risk management, developed in insurance, are appropriate and commonly used in this context. They tend to define risk as the probability of a given event multiplied by the severity (negative impact) should it occur. They draw on plentiful historical data to provide some indication of the likelihood of fire, flood and many other eventualities affecting the insured asset. In a wider vein it is helpful to explore the impact on operations of the loss of links or nodes in the production/distribution and infrastructure networks, through network modelling.

Mitigating the impacts of potential disruptions to nodes and links is where business continuity planning (BCP) has a place. As a discipline, BCP is gradually moving beyond asset-based approaches to risk management, to a wider remit of maintaining 'mission critical activities'. In practice, though, efforts are still first and foremost concerned with safeguarding against the loss of IT systems, or loss of a particular facility, whether that be due to accident, attack or natural disasters. However, more often than not, disruptions at this level are not the result of catastrophic failures caused by the phenomena that have exercised generations of actuaries. The disruptions are just as likely to be the results of poorly managed IT upgrades or physical network reconfigurations (Peck *et al*, 2003). Planned site closures, relocations or indiscriminate outsourcing of activities are often to blame. Nevertheless, it is worth noting that cross-sector surveys undertaken in recent years suggest that loss of key skills is actually a more frequent problem than either loss of site or loss of IT systems (Peck and Jüttner, 2002).

Level 2 is the territory of unglamorous 'trucks and sheds' logistics – an early candidate for outsourcing in most manufacturing and retail organizations. Within Europe, manufacturing has migrated eastwards. Globally, it has headed for China, which means that for much of the world the transport element of supply chain management and the associated resource requirements are increasing. HGV driver shortages are a familiar problem to companies in the UK, while shortages of shipping capacity from the Far East at certain times of the year have been causing problems for some retailers in Western Europe.

In terms of monitoring mobile assets, we see radio frequency identification (RFID) used in consignment tracking systems. Of course, technological solutions need appropriately trained people, though this simple fact is often overlooked. RFID was used to some extent during the 2003 invasion of Iraq – but nobody informed front-line troops, who had no idea what the tags were or what should be done with them when they reached their destination. As a result, many were simply unclipped and thrown into buckets. The people part of the equation was also overlooked in the C–TPAT and CSI anti-terrorism initiatives. Automated solutions seemed to offer a way forward, but insufficient customs personnel were available to undertake the necessary validation checks to admit those applying to be 'known shippers' on to the programme. Thus the measures are regarded by many as increasing the difficulties faced by organizations already struggling to keep pace with a dramatic increase in volumes of global shipments.

Organizations and inter-organizational networks

Level 3 looks at supply chain risk at the strategic level of organizations and the inter-organizational network. These are the organizations that own or manage the assets and infrastructure that make or carry the goods and information flows. At this level, risk is likely to be perceived as the financial consequences of an event or decision for an organization – particularly its impact on budget or shareholders. This is where strategic management concerns and corporate governance requirements really kick in. It is also where conflicts of interest in risk management become most evident.

From a purely supply chain management perspective, risk at this level is the downside financial consequences of a specific event. The loss of a sole supplier or customer is the most obvious danger here. The trading relationships that link organizations and power dependencies between them should also be watched carefully. Low margins are likely to encourage consolidation within the industry, changing power balances and reversing dependencies. They also herald network reconfigurations and the associated disruptions described at Level 2. Partnering, dual sourcing and outsourcing are likely to be put forward as risk management solutions, backed up by contractual obligations. However, anecdotal evidence abounds to suggest that in times of shortage contractual guarantees become unreliable, with suppliers diverting scarce resources to their largest customers, regardless of contractual requirements. Indeed software is now available that allows companies to divert supplies automatically to service their most valuable accounts.

Best-practice strategic management and corporate governance tend to see things a little differently. Here risk retains the upside as well as the downside connotations of decision theory. Strategic management is likely to encourage 'big bets' to maintain competitive advantage. High-risk big bets are likely to be offset by a requirement for lower risk taking in non-core activities. This line of logic encourages strategists and corporate risk managers (few of whom have operational supply chain management experience) to attempt to transfer risks associated with non-core activities off-balance sheet to suppliers. One pitfall associated with this reasoning is that the definition of what is, and is not, a core capability may be too narrowly drawn, with key elements of supply chain management falling by the wayside. Outsourcing and contractual means are nevertheless seen as legitimate methods employed to reduce exposure to financial risk. The option is even more tempting if short-term cost saving can be realized. However, when liability for risk management is transferred in this way, the operational consequences of failure remain.

The industrial relations battle between the Swiss-based, North American-owned airline catering company Gate Gourmet and its UK workforce in the summer of 2005 illustrated the point. The Gate Gourmet dispute was a landmark case in that it marked the return of secondary industrial action, not seen in the UK for decades. It also illustrates why supply chains should also be viewed as interactive social systems. Gate Gourmet was sole supplier of in-flight catering services to British Airways (BA). The staff had been BA workers until a cost reduction programme prompted the airline to outsource the activity. The move had been financially beneficial to BA, which, in a competitive environment, had continued to pursue further cost reductions through its supply chain. A dispute involving catering staff did not, on the face of it, represent a significant threat to BA, as the airline could operate its core business without in-flight meals. However, when around 670 BA ground staff – many with family ties to sacked catering workers – decided to walk out in sympathy, the consequences for BA were unavoidable. The four-day strike halted BA flights out of Heathrow, costing an estimated £40 million in cancelled flights, and additional costs of food and accommodation for 70,000 stranded passengers.

The macro environment

The fourth and final level of analysis is the macro environment, within which the assets and infrastructure are positioned and organizations do business. The PEST (political, economic, social and technological) analysis of environmental changes, used in strategic management, is useful here. Sometimes environmental and legal/regulatory changes are included in the basic analysis or given separate treatment. Socio-political factors – such as action by pressure groups (eg environmentalists or fuel protestors) or supposedly unrelated industrial disputes – should be picked up by routine 'horizon scanning' using specialist or general media sources, allowing measures to be put in place to mitigate the impact. Geo-political factors (eg war) should not come as a surprise, but the extent to which they can influence demand for all manner of goods and services should not be underestimated. The 2003 invasion of Iraq coincided with a drop in business confidence, leading to a drop in advertising and a marked reduction in demand for high-quality paper – with the reverse impact on oil prices.

Far from our controlled casino environment, there are also the forces of nature – metrological, geological and pathological – to contend with. Most are likely to be far beyond the control of supply chain managers, so risk avoidance and contingency planning are appropriate courses of action. However, one category of pathogens – ie contaminants and diseases – is worth particular attention here. Whether it is BSE, foot-and-mouth, avian flu, or the computer viruses that mimic them, what makes pathological factors so dangerous is that they are mobile. They have the ability to hitch a ride with the flows of goods and information that supply chain managers speed around the globe. Once inside the system, they have the potential to bring it down from within. The creeping crises referred to at the beginning of this chapter are all Level 4 disruptions – but it would be wrong to regard them only as external threats to the supply chain. Their potency as disruptive challenges is a reflection of our interconnected, interdependent societies and the efficiency of our supply chains.

SUPPLY CHAINS AND WICKED PROBLEMS

Having run through the levels of the model, examining the perspectives and risk management methods prevalent at each, it is important to reiterate the fact that managers at every level see risk first and foremost through the lens of their own performance measures. The snag here is that efforts to optimize performance (and thereby reduce risk) in one dimension will often have unexpected and undesirable consequences for others. While this notion may sit uncomfortably with objective approaches to risk management and prevailing wisdom in supply chain management, it comes as no surprise to some complex systems thinkers. That is because supply chain risk is technically a 'wicked problem'.

The term was coined in the early 1970s by Rittel and Webber (1973), whose paper on 'Dilemmas in a general theory of planning' is not an obvious source of enlightenment for those charged with the management of supply chain risk. Nevertheless, their contribution was to produce a lucid explanation of why societal problems are inherently different from the problems that scientists and some engineers tackle. Scientists and engineers tend to deal with discrete, identifiable problems, where the desired outcome is known, providing clarity of mission and an easily recognizable desired end state. But Rittel and Webber argued that the assumption of discrete problems did not reflect the reality of societal dilemmas – including most public policy issues. These are complex 'wicked problems'. Societal problems invariably encompass the interests of multiple stakeholders who rarely share a single definitive common goal. The absence of a definitive common interest means that the clarity of mission is also absent, and there is unlikely to be a definitive universal solution. Personal interests and value sets invariably come into play. Moreover, once implemented, any solution will probably generate consequences elsewhere in the system, often over an extended period of time. The term 'wicked' is not used in the sense that something is ethically deplorable, but in the sense that it is vicious, displaying the characteristics of a vicious circle. Moreover, attempts to solve wicked problems are quite likely to result in malignant side-effects.

It is clear that some threats to supply chains (eg Y2K) do fall into the discrete problem category, but there are many other problems facing managers of supply chain risk that do not – including creeping crises and counter-terrorism. Given the nature of wicked problems, searching for a one-time definitive optimal solution is not the way forward. Instead Rittel and Webber (1973) observed it is better to ask the right questions about the consequences of actions, within the context of multiple frameworks, recognizing social processes as the links tying open systems into larger interconnected networks of systems. This chapter concurs with that advice, and has put forward just such a framework, addressing supply chain vulnerability at many levels and risk from multiple perspectives – but all within the context of an integrated supply chain system.

Engineering perspectives do have a well-deserved place in that framework, as does lean thinking and least-cost efficiency, but the notion that everyone can minimize risk (however that is construed) and optimize performance simultaneously is far from realistic. Compromises do have to be made. Resilience requires redundancy or slack in terms of time, capacity and capability within and preferably throughout the system, which means that suboptimal efficiency for someone is inevitable. In the ideal world of collaborative supply chain management, all parties should be willing and able to share the risks – benefits and cost burdens – for the greater good of all. In practice, human nature and short-term financial pressures give a distinct possibility that, instead of everyone carrying slack, no one will carry it. All will be hoping that just over their network horizon someone else will be doing the right thing or that market forces can be relied upon to ensure that resources will always be there, ready and waiting, just in case they are needed. They might be but, in an emergency, would you be willing to bet on it?

References

Adams, J (1996) *Risk*, Routledge, London

Aitken, J (1998) Supply chain integration within the context of a supplier association, PhD thesis, Cranfield University, Cranfield

Borge, D (2001) *The Book of Risk*, John Wiley & Sons, New York

Christopher, M (1998) *Logistics and Supply Chain Management: Strategies for reducing costs and improving services*, Pitman Publishing, London

Cooper, MC *et al* (1997) Supply chain management: more than a new name for logistics, *International Journal of Logistics Management*, **8** (1), pp 1–13

Forrester, JW (1958) Industrial dynamics: a major breakthrough for decision makers, *Harvard Business Review*, **38**, July–August, pp 37–66

Forrester, JW (1969) *Principles of Systems*, Wright Allen Press, Cambridge, MA

Knight, F (1921) *Risk, Uncertainty and Profit*, Harper & Row, New York

La Londe, BJ (1984) A recognition of logistics systems in the 80s: strategies and challenges, *Journal of Business Logistics*, **4** (1), pp 1–11

Larson, PD and Halldorsson, A (2004) Logistics versus supply chain management: an international survey, *International Journal of Logistics: Research and applications*, **7** (1), pp 17–31

MacCrimmon, KR and Wehrung, DA (1986) *Taking Risks: The management of uncertainty*, Free Press, New York

March, JG and Shapira, Z (1987) Managerial perspectives on risk and risk taking, *Management Science*, **33** (11), pp 1404–18

Mentzner, JT *et al* (2001) *Supply Chain Management*, Sage, Thousand Oaks, CA

Oliver, RK and Webber, MD (1992) Supply chain management: logistics catches up with strategy, in *Logistics: The strategic issues*, ed M Christopher, Chapman & Hall, London

Peck, H and Jüttner, U (2002) Risk management in the supply chain, *Logistics and Transport Focus*, **4** (11), December, pp 17–22

Peck, H et al (2003) Supply chain resilience, Final report on behalf of the Department for Transport, Cranfield University, Cranfield

Rittel, HWJ and Webber, MM (1973) Dilemmas in a general theory of planning, *Policy Sciences*, **4**, pp 155–69

Royal Society (1983) *Risk Assessment: A study group report*, Royal Society, London

Royal Society (1992) *Risk: Analysis, perception and management*, 2nd edn, Royal Society, London

Shapira, Z (1986) Risk in managerial decision making, Unpublished manuscript, Hebrew University, cited in JG March and Z Shapira (1987) Managerial perspectives on risk and risk taking, *Management Science*, **33** (11), pp 1404–18

Starr, R, Newfrock, J and Delurey, M (2003) Enterprise resilience: managing risk in the networked economy, Booz, Allen and Hamilton, McLean, VA

Stock, JR and Lambert, DM (2001) *Strategic Logistics Management*, 4th edn, McGraw-Hill, Boston, MA

White, D (1995) Applications of systems thinking to risk management: a review of the literature, *Management Decision*, **33** (10), pp 35–45

13

Information systems and information technologies for supply chain management

Xinping Shi and Simon Chan,
Hong Kong Baptist University

INTRODUCTION

Data, information and knowledge are critical assets to the performance of logistics and supply chain management (SCM), because they provide the basis upon which management can plan logistics operations, organize logistics and supply chain (SC) processes, coordinate and communicate with business partners, conduct functional logistics activities, and perform managerial control of the physical flow of goods, information exchange and sharing among SC partners.

Information systems (IS) are the effective and efficient means to manage those critical assets, and to provide sustainable competitive advantages. As far as SCM is concerned, information technology (IT) consists of telecommunications, networking and data processing technologies – and is narrowly regarded here as the technological tools used to develop IS, capture or collect data, perform data analysis for generating meaningful information, and exchange and share this information with SC partners.

IT is clearly an important enabler for the achievement of SCM effectiveness and efficiency (Bowersox, Closs and Cooper, 2007; Simchi-Levi, Kaminsky and Simchi-Levi, 2003).

In this chapter, we explore the functionality of IS/IT in SCM and discuss its evolution and adoption.

FUNCTIONALITY OF IS/IT IN SCM

Efficiency-oriented IS/IT

From an information management perspective, IS/IT is conventionally utilized in the application of efficiency-oriented SCM to increase productivity and reduce operational costs. Specifically, it is used to:

- capture and collect data on each product and service in a specific logistics activity, such as purchasing, to provide accurate, reliable and real-time raw facts;
- store collected data in a specific IS in predetermined categories and formats, such as a customer database management system;
- analyse stored data to generate meaningful information for management decision making in response to SCM events, and to evaluate SCM performance in cost reduction and productivity enhancement;
- collaborate and communicate with SC partners, in order to reduce information time-lag and misunderstandings, and to make the data resources available and visible to all SC partners;
- standardize logistics operations and data retrieval procedures, and develop generalized and rigorous information management policies, regulations and control measures; and
- apply transaction cost theory to SCM to gain economies of scale and implement low-cost strategies.

Effectiveness-oriented IS/IT

Today, IS/IT is widely applied in the area of effectiveness-oriented SCM to enhance competitive advantage, add value and globalize operations. In particular, IS/IT is deployed to:

- enhance core competence and positioning of a focal SC organization through designing and controlling the sharing and flow of information;
- re-engineer SC operations and eliminate duplicated facilities or activities, for example vendor managed inventory (VMI) instead of physical warehouses;

- manage marketing, customer, product and service knowledge or expertise developed (accumulated) in SCM, and share this with suppliers and partners, for example collaborative planning, forecasting and replenishment (CPFR);
- manage partner and customer relationships through resource-based and relational views, to stabilize SC structure and enhance relations with adjacent upstream and downstream partners; and
- deploy SC resources and capabilities to compete with other SCs at worldwide level, and through international sourcing and offshore manufacturing.

There are two main driving forces for organizations to invest in IS/IT, develop technological advantages in SCM and push the development of IS/IT applications: changes in the business environment and technological advancement. Changes in the business environment demand growing capacity for data and information management in SCM, thus continuously pulling organizational IS/IT investment. Technological evolution supplies the tools and systems to facilitate and satisfy the demands of data and information processing and transmission, and delivers innovative technology such as wireless technology and radio frequency identification (RFID).

IS/IT development for SCM

The development and application of IS/IT in SCM can be divided into four main levels:

1. IS/IT in logistics functional areas – transaction support system. Here, IS/IT is typically used for applications such as bar coding technology in point-of-sale (POS) systems, order process and inventory management, warehouse management systems (WMS), transportation management systems (TMS) etc.
2. IS/IT for controlling information flows in integrated logistics operations across functional areas in an organization – intranet system, such as enterprise resources planning (ERP), groupware system and distribution requirement planning (DRP).
3. IS/IT used for information exchange and sharing between organizations – extranet system. The system is a structured and standard communication system, used to exchange logistics information among SC partners in certain transactions, such as ordering and trading information. Two of the most widely adopted extranet systems are electronic data interchange (EDI) and CPFR.
4. SCM system, or inter-organizational information system (IOS) – internet or network system for SC partners to exchange information, coordinate

SC and logistics activities. Compared with an extranet system, an internet system is much more flexible and powerful in information distribution and conducting logistics transactions. Typical applications are electronic banking, electronic portal, electronic procurement and customer relationship management (CRM).

The difference between intranets, extranets and internets lies in who is allowed to access and use them. An intranet is intended only for internal members of an organization; an extranet is used by those who perform predefined logistics activities and transactions between two or more organizations. Internet systems allow anyone to access and use the system functions available and facilitate SCM information sharing.

Level 1: Transaction support IS/IT

At this level, IS/IT is mainly used as an efficient tool for supporting logistics operations, and the main concerns are whether IS/IT can provide reliable, accurate and real-time operation data and information to support core logistics activities. From an IS perspective, a database management system is the core technique. From an IT perspective, bar coding and scanning is the core technology to capture real-time sales data and convert it into information through POS, and then to produce receipts for customers – and to track stock-keeping units to provide accurate inventory status information and facilitate inventory replenishment. WMS help to maximize the turnover of warehouse space, utilization of equipment and productivity of labour, and to minimize the movement of goods, store time, and the lead time in responding to shipment and distribution scheduling.

Through data and information processing, TMS provides transportation planning, freight payment auditing, carrier selection and performance monitoring. It also performs administrative tasks, reviewing transportation bills and management–carrier relationships. Together, these transaction support systems support SCM to execute low-cost strategies and provide better customer services. However, they provide regional-optimal solutions in processing logistics data and information, they are often not integrated with other IS in an organization and may not be aligned with overall organizational objectives, and may be incompatible with SC partners' IS/IT when information exchange is required.

Level 2: Integrated organizational IS/IT

Integrated organizational IS/IT provides intranet systems that facilitate data, information and communication within an organization, among widely dispersed logistics departments and locations. For example, an intranet system is used to share order processing, inventory and shipping status, and customer credit and accounting information within a firm. The characteristics of intranet systems are that they standardize organization-wide data and information structure and format, integrate isolated trans-actional support systems and allow data and information sharing.

ERP is the most widely deployed intranet system. It integrates logistics transaction modules with common, standard and consistent databases or data warehouses – and provides multiple interfaces to logistics functional users. It digitalizes logistics operational procedures, regulations, organ-izational policies and industrial standards into an integrated system, and also contains some advanced managerial support functions such as data mining, decision support and executive report functions. Essentially, ERP uses the local area network and client–server technologies to implement an organization-wide information and communication framework, and to integrate functional logistics IS such as WMS and POS.

Level 3: Information sharing and exchange IS/IT

Extranet system is designed to control and coordinate the flow of logistics data and information for sharing with SC partners. The system creates an effective and formal communication channel between the SC focal organization and its upstream suppliers and downstream customers, and the information flow is structured in standard business documents with standard formats. With a resource-based view, organizations in an SC become more interdependent when one organization accesses information owned by other organizations and when uncertainty affects the supply of resources. When the business environment changes and shifts power downstream in the SC, those organizations with richer information about markets and customers gain an advantage over other SC partners.

EDI is the most widely deployed extranet system for inter-firm infor-mation exchange. LaLonde and Cooper (1989) have addressed EDI as one of the most important changes to affect SCM, and 'it is the glue that binds long-term relationship, and plays an important coordinating role in managing the interfaces between firms as business process go beyond the boundaries of the firm' (Mentzer, 2001). The main benefits of using EDI are: upstream SC partners can access timely and accurate information from markets and customers, and incorporate this into planning and scheduling; downstream SC partners can provide better customer services, responding to market changes and customer demands; all SC partners can reduce paperwork and enjoy quality communication. Other benefits derived from deployment of EDI are increased productivity, cost saving, accurate billing, and improved tracking and expenditure.

CPFR is also an extranet system developed for sharing logistics management processes with suppliers, and it enhances VMI and continuous replenishment by incorporating joint forecasting. SC partners exchange information related to past sales trends and scheduled promotions, forecast future market development and customer behaviour, and even share opinions and suggestions. The system contributes to SC partners by focusing on their core business values and benefiting from each other. Like EDI, CPFR can also improve SC efficiency, increase sales and timely responsiveness to markets and customers, and reduce fixed assets investment and inventory costs.

Level 4: Internet-based SCM systems

The internet is becoming the most useful business communication and information exchange system. It will eventually replace EDI because all information flows performed by EDI can be carried out through the internet, with low access costs and consistent transfer standards. Furthermore, it can synchronize information from all SC participants – including worldwide customers. Perhaps the most outstanding feature of the internet is that it changes information exchange from one-to-one to one-to-many and many-to-many. Then traditional business partnerships can be changed into an SC organization with many alternative SC partners simultaneously, the stability and trust of conventional SC relationships become unstable, and the development of virtual relationships challenges all existing theories and empirical findings.

Organizations increasingly use advanced IS/IT for manipulating information flows in SCM. However, current IS/IT may not reflect real organizational needs for timely information control, information quality and visibility, reduced information costs, and excellent service. The roles of IS/IT in SCM have changed dramatically in the past few decades – and will continue to change with IT advancement in the future. This raises a series of strategic issues.

STRATEGIC ISSUES OF IS/IT IN SCM

SCM and IS/IT address information flow from different perspectives. SCM focuses on developing tightly integrated relationships with suppliers and customers; IS/IT focuses on the technology for developing a comprehensive system or sophisticated platform, often regardless of context. Users, organizations and IS managers are often overwhelmed by media hype and are unsure how – if at all – to migrate from their existing SCM real processes to digitalized or virtual SCM operations. We discuss this movement from the perspective of three stakeholders – SC users, SC focal organization and IS/IT managers.

Users' perspective

Users are the SCM operators, who are concerned about the processes, relationships with SC partners and the costs of using IS/IT for daily operations. Some strategic issues are:

- Does IS/IT fit organizational SCM strategies and core competence?
- Is IS/IT adoption compatible with current philosophies and practices?
- What changes in business process and SC structure will take place?
- How will existing suppliers and relationships be affected by the new IS/IT?
- What costs will be incurred during and after IS/IT adoption?

Just-in-time manufacturing and efficient consumer response in retailing have brought significant changes to SC practices. SCM attempts to achieve cycle time reduction and faster inventory turnover by establishing tight linkages with suppliers – and to move from a pure efficiency orientation to greater coordination and integration of business processes in functional areas, including product design and development, market research, production planning etc. A high level of trust and extensive information sharing are required for successful implementation of these initiatives. But a focus on individual transactions and price reductions achieved by using IS/IT may be inconsistent with the SC philosophies of trust and long-term relationships, so IS/IT may jeopardize an organization's existing relationships with its long-term suppliers. Since the adoption of new IS/IT takes significant effort and time, organizations should check that there is alignment with current SCM strategies. A worst-case scenario is that the introduction of IS/IT is inconsistent and creates confusion among suppliers. Change management, both internal and external, is critical as there are many instances of good IS/IT not producing the desired results due to faulty implementation. For example, Nike had a major problem with production/distribution after introducing an advanced production planning system. They found later that their problem was not the software, but the quality of data input to the system.

Focal organization perspective

Some strategic issues faced by the SC focal organization are:

- Shall we build our own IS/IT or jointly develop IS/IT with SC partners?
- What strategic approach shall we take to developing IS/IT for all SC partners?
- How does the proposed IS/IT impact on our current SC operations?
- What will happen to existing long-term and arm's-length relationships with key customers?
- Will the adoption of IS/IT consolidate our leading SC position and enhance the competitiveness of our products?

A critical SCM decision is how to develop and introduce IS/IT, and still maintain trustworthy, long-term relationships with key SC partners. While long-term relationships and contracts provide stability, they reduce the flexibility of exploring alternative markets, the possibility of faster growth, or increasing profits in some markets. The focal organization needs clear objectives and strategic planning, collaboration with other SC partners to share the risks and benefits, and a careful analysis of the impacts of new IS/IT.

IS/IT managers' perspective

Some strategic issues confronting IS/IT managers are:

- How do we migrate from dyadic EDI platforms to the advanced SCM systems?
- How do we integrate our ERP or other functional systems with SCM systems?
- What internal and external IT infrastructure has to be developed with our suppliers/users?
- What are the system and data compatibility issues in interacting with non-standardized systems?

Naturally, IS/IT managers pay more attention than others to technological issues in the development of new IS/IT, because there are usually internal legacy systems that work with EDI middleware to communicate with their trading partners. EDI provides a standardized data format for two computers to communicate automatically without any manual intervention. This brings a high level of transaction efficiency, but it is not very useful for communication of unstructured information, or for evaluation and negotiation processes. Migration to new IS/IT may require interacting with different web applications and non-standardized data formats that may create problems with organizational intranet systems. For example, getting demand forecast information from multiple customers and incorporating it into intranet systems would require visiting customers' websites individually, retrieving information, checking their data formats and re-entering them in internal systems. This may be a step backward in technology for retailers unless interfaces are developed to retrieve information automatically from websites and store it in intranet systems.

An integrated SCM system that links all the SC partners may be the ultimate solution for IS/IT managers. While communication incompatibilities are relatively easy to overcome through XML and related technologies, data incompatibilities are harder to handle. Unless there is a significant benefit in moving from existing EDI-based systems to an SCM system, IS/IT managers will be reluctant to migrate.

IS/IT ADOPTION FOR SCM

The strategic importance of IS/IT in SCM means that its introduction needs careful planning with SC partners to guarantee successful implementation. Four theories – resource-based view, relational views, transaction cost theory, resource dependence theory – provide theoretical foundations for IS/IT adoption in SCM. Here, adoption is defined as the development of the 'first' successful IS/IT using a new information-process technology in organizational processes or products.

Resource-based view and transaction cost theory

An organization is a bundle of assets (resources) and capabilities, and the firm's competitive advantage is derived from the possession of unique strategic resources and capabilities. These resources are: value, rareness, imperfect imitability and unsubstitutability (Barney, 1991; Wernerfelt, 1984). In this vein, IS/IT adoption is a strategic investment in the organization's capability of utilizing information resources – and leverages the value of information to increase the firm's competitive advantages. Studies show that IT is deployed to develop organizational IS, to manipulate organizational information and for operational effectiveness (Mata, Fuerst and Barney, 1995; Santhanam and Hartono, 2003).

Transaction cost theory mainly focuses on the market governance structures of supplying relationships (Williamson, 1985, 1991). The core concept is that in a perfect market, a firm will optimize its supply of materials from specialized suppliers (or make its own). Firms engage in repeated and contract-based transactions with suppliers. In cases where the resources or products are highly supplier specific, time specific, and complex in nature, this is an appropriate approach. The transaction costs of managing the relationships and interactions with the suppliers – including searching, negotiating and monitoring execution of the transactions – are high. By reducing the transaction costs, IS/IT – especially SCM systems – allows a high level of coordination and increases the value of coordinated resources through economies of scale, vertical integration or virtual hierarchies (Clemons and Row, 1991; Johnston and Lawrence, 1988; Holland, 1995).

The resource-based view and transaction cost theory provide a sound foundation for SCM systems. According to these theories, adoption and diffusion of IS/IT can optimize a firm's internal and arm's-length market resources, and integrate vertical business operations with the firm's suppliers at lower transaction costs and higher efficiency. However, the theories focus on organizational resource utilization rather than inter-organizational relations (IOR), and more on inter-firm coordination rather than SC partners' cooperation and resource sharing. Thus, vertical integration or a virtual hierarchy is a focal-firm-specific, economic-oriented and contract-based relationship; and the relationship may suffer from long-term instability when economic and market mechanisms change (Dyer, 1997; Premkumar and Ramamurthy, 1995).

Relational view and resource dependence theory

A relational view offers a theoretical understanding of the sources of interorganizational competitive advantage from interorganizational alliances – SC partnerships or IOR (Dyer and Singh, 1998; Oliver, 1990). The relational view asserts that SC competitive advantage comes from: 1) the relation-specific assets of IOR; 2) substantial knowledge exchange routines, joint learning and partner-specific absorptive capabilities; 3) the synergistic effect of complementary and distinctive resources and capabilities among SC partners; and 4) the ability to employ informal self-enforcement relationship governance mechanisms (Dyer and Singh, 1998; Kanter, 1994; Zhara and George, 2002).

In line with social exchange theory authors (Benson, 1975; Blau, 1964; Emerson, 1962), Pfeffer and Salancik (1978) postulated a resource dependence theory, where resource dependence is based on an organization's ability to 1) control resources needed by other firms and 2) reduce their dependence on others for resources. That is, an organization must gain control over resources that are critical to its operations, and must reduce the uncertainty in acquisition of these resources.

Much research on resource dependence has been conducted (Gaski and Nevin, 1985; Oliver, 1990; Provan and Skinner, 1989). Organizational power – a firm's capacity to control, the actual act of control, and the impact of an organization's perception of dependence on its partners – has been intensively studied to reveal its influence on IOR. In addition, analysis of four dimensions – goal compatibility, domain consensus, evaluation of accomplishment, and norms of exchange – has made significant contributions to understanding the environmental influence of IOR. It has been found that a favourable transaction climate results in more cooperation and better information flows and decision making (Reve and Stern, 1986; Williamson, 1975).

Compared with the resource-based view and transaction cost theory, the relational view and resource dependence theory pay much attention to external resources and collaboration. The relational view focuses on a fair investment of relation-specific assets, and on the development and governance of routines for collaboration; resource dependence theory concentrates on asymmetric resource distribution in social and political settings, and how a powerful organization can employ the dependency of others to accomplish its objectives. Therefore, the relational view is trust-based, and resource dependence theory is power-based.

Using power, position and role differences, a focal organization in SC may exercise its coercive influence to control scarce and strategic resources, such as privileged information, knowledge and expertise, technology competence etc. The organization may force its dependent SC partners to adopt innovative IS/IT, such as SCM systems, that serve mainly its own interests (Pfeffer and Salancik, 1978). Evidence of coercive isomorphism has been found in EDI adoption cases (Hart and Saunders, 1997; Webster, 1995). Wal-Mart is a typical example of resource dependence theory, in the way it mandates its top 100 suppliers to use RFID labels. Suppliers who cannot satisfy this mandatory requirement endanger their business transactions and relations with Wal-Mart.

Strategic framework of IS/IT adoption in SCM

Based on these theoretical foundations for IS/IT adoption, we have developed a strategic framework (Figure 13.1) to specify strategies for IS/IT adoption.

Within the framework, the horizontal dimension – technology orientation – refers to organizational and inter-organizational technology capabilities, and the ability to develop products, services and operation processes that contribute to SC competitiveness. Facing an innovative IS/IT, the focal SC organization has two broad options: proactive and reactive. With a proactive approach an organization holds a positive attitude towards IS/IT, is motivated by IS/IT adoption opportunities, devotes resources to understanding and evaluating them, and is willing

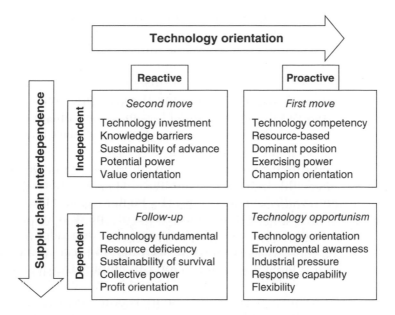

Figure 13.1 Strategic framerork of IS/IT adoption in SCM context

to initiate IS/IT adoption. On the other hand, with a reactive approach an organization shows less interest in new IS/IT, holds back from the system or technology, carefully investigates the implications and impacts of a new system or technology, does tentative trials of IS/IT, closely monitors trends in IS/IT among SC partners and industries, and controls the timing of IS/IT adoption.

Vertical dimension–supply chain interdependence refers to IOR in an SC context, and it reflects the relational view of mutual influence, exchange, interactions, knowledge and information sharing, coordination, cooperation and integration (Dyer and Singh, 1998; Hart and Estrin, 1991; Oliver, 1990). Interdependence has two positions. One is independent, suggesting that an organization has a powerful position in an SC network, more decision-making discretion and a strong influence on other SC partners, the firm's resources and operations are independent of its SC partners, and SC partners are heavily dependent on the organization. The other is dependent, suggesting that an organization in an SC network has limited resources, influence, ability to change SC structure and process, decision making, and bargaining for privileged information and favourable treatment. And there are potential substitute firms in the marketplace, competing to join the SC network with the dominant firm and replace dependent organizations.

The framework shows that there are four strategies for focal organizations to adopt.

First-move strategy

This is an aggressive and self-motivated strategy driven by intrinsic organizational demand for advancement, privilege and advantages over SC partners. A firm using this strategy clearly recognizes the benefits of IS/IT and initiates changes for the firm and SC as a whole. Through adopting IS/IT, the firm can further consolidate its SC position and enhance its influence. However, this strategy is expensive, and needs high technology competence and resources; it also presents a higher risk and lower measurable return of investment than other strategies. Further, deployment of this strategy may require the firm to exercise its power to force any unwilling SC partners to accept and use IS/IT accordingly. (Otherwise, IS/IT is adopted only in the focal organizational, with substantially reduced benefits.)

Dos Santos and Peffers (1995) found that banks that pursued the first-move strategy with ATM machines were able to increase market share and income – with the gains remaining over the long term. This empirically justifies a first-move strategy for capable firms that can lead technological change. Another attractive feature of this strategy for the SC-dominant firm is that successful IS/IT adoption will build competitive barriers, and define the rules and norms of the game in its own SC.

Second-move strategy

This is a conservative strategy, and is driven by the focal organization's management style and policies – and stakeholders' interests rather than potential opportunities from the adoption of IS/IT. A firm deploying this strategy has organizational resources, technology capability, SC position and influence – but it may regard IS/IT adoption as an investment, with evaluation focusing on the return on investment and risk management. The firm may strive to be a competent technology user, but not a pioneer of IS/IT or SCM systems – because its core values and assets may not be derived from technological innovation. When facing innovative IS/IT change, the firm may have knowledge barriers, and will hold back and take a 'wait and see' attitude.

The advantages of this strategy lie in its value orientation – and its rationale is in transaction cost theory. A firm does not invest resources in uncertain projects without obviously added value. Only when the investment environment is favourable, the IS/IT is approaching maturity and the value-add from investment in IS/IT is achievable and accountable will the firm take a positive view of IS/IT adoption. So it mainly uses IS/IT to enhance operational efficiency and cost-effectiveness – but cannot fully utilize the strategic benefits of IC/IT. The disadvantage of the strategy is obvious, as delayed adoption of IS/IT cannot give technology leadership and the firm cannot establish competitiveness based on a SCM system.

Follow-up strategy

This is a passive strategy for SC partners who do not have an initiative for active IS/IT adoption. It is adopted by organizations with limited resources, small-scale operations and little influence on their SC partners. For firms taking this strategy, the theoretical foundations are transaction cost theory and resource dependence theory – and their business transactions are largely dependent on the dominant organization in the SC network. These firms generally adopt some almost outdated IS/IT to support their business operations, to connect with the dominant firm and to process essential business information – with EDI adoption in small businesses being a typical example. These firms may regard investment in new IS/IT as a waste, or at least a luxury – and they hardly achieve technology competency, using technology to satisfy leading business partners' requirements and business procedure.

Technology opportunism strategy

This is defined as a sense-and-respond capability for proactive IS/IT adoption, responding to new opportunities in ways that do not violate principles of fairness (Srinivasan, Lilien and Rangaswamy, 2002). There are two components of technology opportunism: technology sensing and technology response. Sensing is a firm's ability to scan internal and external innovation, acquire knowledge about and understand new technology – and then provide innovative products and services derived from utilizing or deploying the technology. Response is an organization's willingness and ability to respond to new technologies, to re-engineer its business strategy, and explore opportunities (Miles and Snow, 1978).

A firm using a technology opportunism strategy strongly believes that new IS/IT can create a substantial opportunity, so it proactively scans technological opportunities and seeks to capitalize on them. The firm is not restricted to traditional principles and experience, but understands, analyses and utilizes new IS/IT technology for developing innovative products and services. It is a strategy for ambitious and strongly self-motivated firms. The firm may be small or dependent on the dominant firm in an SC context, but it wants to be powerful by using IS/IT. It may actively cooperate with the dominant SC firm to adopt IS/IT, and create unique value for the firm itself and its SC partners. Microsoft's growth experience in the 1980s is an excellent example of a firm taking a technology opportunism strategy and successfully changing its position in the operating systems and software industry.

This strategy is particularly useful for small firms and requires flexibility in the managerial mindset and operations, and technological competence. Top management direct the firm, while operational flexibility and efficiency speed up organizational change. Of course, this strategy needs a risk-taker mentality, but the benefits of success are far great than the costs of failure.

Table 13.1 summaries the four strategies in 12 strategy evaluation scales, which measure an organization's strategic readiness for IS/IT adoption. The scales cover organizational, inter-organizational and technological

Table 13.1   Factors for strategic evaluation of IS/IT adoption

	First move	Second move	Following up	Technology opportunism
Organization size	Large	Large	Medium/Small	Small
Strategic importance of IS/IT adoption	Very much	Unclear	Not necessary	Ultimate
Leadership motivation of IS/IT adoption	High	Moderate	Low	Very much
Organization readiness of IS/IT adoption	High	Holdback	No	High
Pressure of SC competition of IS/IT adoption	Medium	Medium	Low	High
Pressure of SC partners of IS/IT adoption	Low	Low	High	Medium
Perceived SC needs of IS/IT adoption	Strongest	Strong	Neutral	Strongest
Relation of IS/IT adoption to SC core business	High	Medium	Unclear	High
Firm's mandatory power over SC partners	Strong	Moderate	None	Occasional
Perceived technology radicalness of IS/IT	Acceptable	High	Hardly acceptable	Appreciated
Propensity to IS/IT adoption risks	Risk taking	Avoiding	Risk averting	Aggressive risk taking
Technological slack for IS/IT initiation	Sufficient	Adequate	Lack	Specializing in RFID

issues, and suggest theory deployment in strategy selection for IS/IT. The scales can also be used as a checklist to help an organization make strategy choices, and evaluate whether it is ready to take a proactive strategy.

IS/IT UTILIZATION IN SCM

The utilization of IS/IT in SCM can have an effect on performance, but how can an organization make sure that IS/IT is fully utilized? We suggest the following considerations for fulfilling organizational and SC performance requirements:

1. It is reasonable to have a detailed understanding of customer and supplier requirements, as well as all SC partners' concerns. IS/IT adoption should be flexible and adaptable, depending on specific needs and how these needs are satisfied. Performance criteria for IS/IT adoption and utilization include regular reviews of the usage of SC partners.
2. IS/IT advancement has been moving away from logistics functional areas towards a process and SC orientation. Emphasis on the latter ensures more meaningful measurement of relevant processes and more timely and accurate process feedback and coordination.
3. To grasp IS/IT adoption opportunities it is vital to integrate the knowledge of logistics managers, IS/IT managers and knowledgeable SC partners. Logistics managers need to know more IS/IT – and information specialists must develop greater insight into SCM.
4. Financial resources are needed to ensure a smooth IS/IT implementation. Employees' cooperation and use of systems are also critical.
5. Managerial experience and expertise in managing SC relationships and IS/IT adoption also play a critical role in the implementation of SCM systems – and if management keeps a proactive attitude, encourage organizational learning and work together with SC partners, then SCM system adoption among all partners is close to success.

SUMMARY

In this chapter, we show how IS/IT can make significant contributions to efficient and effective SCM. We discuss the development of IS/IT at four levels, reflecting the advancement of IT and the involvement of IS/IT in SCM. IS/IT development and adoption in SCM is complicated, and organizations have to take many strategic factors into account. Facing such a tough challenge, we provide a literature review of IS/IT adoption, and reveal the theories underpinning IS/IT adoption. We provide theoretical guidance – a framework of strategy adoption – and identity the conditions and resources for organizations to initiate IS/IT adoption.

Effective SCM requires SC partners to collaboratively develop a plan for coordinating the flows of goods and services, with timely information to ensure that these are delivered at the right time, to the right place and at the right price. IS/IT plays an important role in achieving SCM objectives. To fully utilize IS/IT potential, organizations need an effective strategy that fits the organizational resources and relationships with SC partners – and they need to work together with SC partners to share the risk and costs of IS/IT development, and to enjoy the benefits derived from SCM systems.

References

Barney, J (1991) Firm resources and sustained competitive advantage, *Journal of Management*, **17** (1), pp 99–120

Benson, JK (1975) The interorganizational network as a political economy, *Administrative Science Quarterly*, **20** (2), pp 229–49

Blau, PM (1964) *Exchange and Power in Social Life*, Wiley, New York

Bowersox, D, Closs, DJ and Cooper, MB (2007) *Supply Chain Logistics Management*, 2nd edn, McGraw-Hill International, New York

Clemons, E and Row, M (1991) Sustainable IT advantage: the role of structural differences, *MIS Quarterly*, **15** (3), pp 275–92

Dos Santos, BL and Peffers, K (1995) Rewards to investors in innovative information technology applications: first movers and early followers in ATMs, *Organization Sciences*, **6** (3), pp 241–59

Dyer, JH (1997) Effective interfirm collaboration: how firms minimize transaction costs and maximize transaction value, *Strategic Management Journal*, **18** (7), pp 535–56

Dyer, JH and Singh, H (1998) The relational view: cooperative strategy and sources of interorganizational competitive advantage, *Academy of Management Review*, **23** (4), 660–79

Emerson, RM (1962) Power dependence relations, *American Sociological Review*, **27** (1), pp 31–41

Gaski, JF and Nevin, JR (1985) The differential effects of exercised and unexercised power source in a marketing channel, *Journal of Marketing*, **22** (2), pp 130–42

Hart, P and Estrin, D (1991) Interorganizational networks, computer integration, and shifts in interdependence: the case of the semiconductor industry, *ACM Transactions on Information Systems*, **9** (4), 370–417

Hart, P and Saunders, C (1997) Power and trust: critical factors in the adoption and use of electronic data interchange, *Organizational Science*, **8** (1), pp 83–103

Holland, CP (1995) Cooperative supply chain management: the impact of interorganizational information systems, *Journal of Strategic Information Systems*, **4** (2), pp 117–33

Johnston, R and Lawrence, PR (1988) Beyond vertical integration – rise of the value-adding partnership, *Harvard Business Review*, **66** (4), 94–101

Kanter, RM (1994) Collaborative advantage: the art of alliance, *Harvard Business Review*, **72** (4), pp 96–108

LaLonde, BJ (1997) Supply chain management: myth or reality? *Supply Chain Management Review*, **1** (Spring), pp 6–7

LaLonde, BJ and Cooper, MC (1989) *Partnerships in Providing Customer Service: A third party perspective*, The Council of Logistics Management, Oak Brook, IL

Mata, FJ, Fuerst, WL and Barney, JB (1995) Information technology and sustained competitive advantage: a resource-based analysis, *MIS Quarterly*, **19** (4), pp 487–506

Mentzer, JT (2001) *Supply Chain Management*, Sage, Thousand Oaks, CA

Miles, RE and Snow, CC (1978) *Organizational Strategy, Structure and Process*, McGraw-Hill, New York

Oliver, C (1990) Determinants of interorganizational relationships: integration and future directions, *Academy of Management Review*, **15** (2), 241–65

Pfeffer, J and Salancik, G (1978) *External Control of Organizations: A resource dependence perspective*, Harper and Row, New York

Provan, KG and Skinner, S (1989) Interorganizational dependence and control as predictors of opportunism in dealer–supplier relations, *Academy of Management Journal*, **32** (1), 202–12

Premkumar, GP and Ramamurthy, K (1995) The role of interorganizational and organizational factors on the decision mode for adoption of interorganizational systems, *Decision Sciences*, **26** (3), 303–36

Reve, T and Stern, LW (1986) The relationship between interorganizational form, transaction climate, and economic performance in vertical interfirm dyads, in *Marketing Channels – Relationships and Performance*, ed L Pellgrini and S Raddy, Lexington Books, Lexington, MA

Santhanam, R and Hartono, E (2003) Issues in linking information technology capability to firm performance, *MIS Quarterly*, **27** (1), pp 125–53

Simchi-Levi, D, Kaminsky, P and Simchi-Levi, E (2003) *Design and Managing the Supply Chain: Concepts, strategies and case studies*, 2nd edn, McGraw-Hill, New York

Srinivasan, R, Lilien, GL and Rangaswamy, A (2002) Technological opportunism and radical technology adoption: an application to e-business, *Journal of Marketing*, **66** (3), pp 47–60

Webster, J (1995) Networks of collaboration or conflict? Electronic data interchange and power in the supply chain, *Journal of Strategic Information Systems*, **4** (1), pp 31–42

Wernerfelt, B (1984) A resource based view of the firm, *Strategic Management Journal*, **5** (2), pp 171–80

Williamson, OE (1975) *Markets and Hierarchies: Analysis and antitrust implications: A study in the economics of internal organization*, Free Press, New York

Williamson, OE (1985) *The Economic Institutions of Capitalism*, Free Press, New York

Williamson, OE (1991) Comparative economic organization: the analysis of discrete structural alternatives, *Administrative Science Quarterly*, **36** (2), pp 269–96

Zhara, S and George, G (2002) Absorptive capability: a review, reconceptualization and extension, *Academy of Management Review*, **27** (2), pp 185–203

14

Improving management of supply chains by information technology

Heikki Holma, Seinäjoki University of
Applied Sciences
Jari Salo, Helsinki School of Economics

INTRODUCTION

Supply chain management (SCM) literature is eclectic in nature and draws insights from different but overlapping areas of research (Storey *et al*, 2006; Stock, 1997). Along similar lines, Croom, Romano and Giannakis (2000) describe how 11 different subject literatures – including purchasing, logistics, marketing and organizational behaviour – have contributed to the supply chain domain. Despite attempts to map the terrain (eg Giannakis and Croom, 2004; Mills, Schmitz and Frizelle, 2004), the field remains disparate (Storey *et al*, 2006). The multidisciplinary approach gives a strong theoretical base but also some degree of fragmentation. In practice this means that SCM and uses of information technology (IT) in management of supply chains and networks are addressed in information systems journals and operation research journals as well as SCM-specific journals.

The term 'supply chain management' first appeared in the literature in 1982 (Keith and Webber via Christopher, 1992). Usually, the beginning of modern SCM is located to the mid-1980s (Houlihan, 1985; Jones and Riley, 1985). In the 1980s just-in-time (JIT) philosophy was popular, as were attempts to adjust production to meet demand. Gradually it was realized that SCM is something other than just an efficient physical supply of goods. Viewing the supply chain as a social system became more popular in the 1990s, as did studying a move from arm's-length relationships to alliances and partnerships (eg Bensaou, 1999). Studying IT was accompanied by studying information sharing. Electronic commerce was monitored as a potential way to reduce trading cost. For instance, Mason-Jones and Towill (1999) argued how important it is to encourage marketplace information to move through the supply chain.

Characteristic of the current decade is the shift of focus from supply chain management to demand chain management (DCM) (eg de Treville, Shapiro and Hameri, 2004). It is argued that the change of terminology from SCM to DCM better describes the change of managerial thinking from efficient supply to meeting the needs of the customer (Vollmann, Cordon and Heikkilä, 2000). The research has shifted from efficiency to satisfying the needs of the customer for service. The change of thinking to the markets, marketing and demand end of the supply chain is also revealed by Jüttner, Christopher and Baker (2007). They suggest that integrating marketing and SCM attempts to build a new business model aimed at creating value in the marketplace and combining the strengths of marketing and supply chain competencies (Lapide, 2006; Cecere, 2006). In the IS field, a focus on SCM has been shown with efficient consumer response (Kurnia and Johnston, 2003), use of SCM information systems like i2 (Tarn, Yen and Beaumont, 2002), use of extranets to manage suppliers (Vlosky, Fontenot and Blalock, 2000) and, recently, the use of radio frequency identification (RFID) systems and other mobile systems (Wu et al, 2005; Salo, 2009). The change is described in Table 14.1.

Christopher (1998) sees the following aspects as important in future supply chains, which may be also virtual ones: the use of shared information that enables cross-functional, horizontal management should become a reality. Information shared between partners in the supply chain is even more important, making possible a responsive flow of products from one end of the pipeline to the other. Virtual enterprises or supply chains will be more common, and in fact they can be seen as a series of relationships between partners based on value-added exchange of information (Christopher, 1998). We express Christopher's themes for managing supply chains successfully: responsiveness, reliability and relationships. Assumptions about the 'the paradigm shift' to partnering and strategies of cooperation are also very familiar in marketing, especially among the Industrial Marketing and Purchasing (IMP) Group.

Table 14.1 Shift from shallow to broader focus

Paradigm shift	Leading to	Skills required
From functions to processes	Integral management of materials and goods flow	Cross-functional management and planning skills
From products to customers	Focus on markets and the creation of customer value	Ability to define, measure and manage service requirements by market segment, ie perfect order achievement
From revenue to performance	Focus on the key performance drivers of profit	Understanding of the 'costs-to-serve' and time-based performance indicators
From inventory to information	Demand-based replenishment and quick response systems	Information systems and information technology
From transactions to relationships	Supply chain partnership	Relationship management and win–win orientation

Source: Christopher, 1998

COORDINATION OF SUPPLY CHAINS WITH INFORMATION TECHNOLOGY

Coordination of different social networks and relationships has become more vital. Relational factors associated with the critical links between suppliers, manufacturers and customers are emphasized as firms strive for more efficient ways to work in supply chains or networks (McGrath and Sparks, 2005). This development stems from firms focusing on their core competencies and outsourcing less important functions. Consequently, this tendency has accompanied partnership and network thinking. There are still some barriers to overcome. According to Günther, Grote and Thees (2006), improving interaction and collaborative planning are the real challenges in today's world of partnership thinking. Tight cooperation can be seen as a perilous idea, as partners still want to preserve their independence. Thus the challenge is mainly a challenge of coordination (eg Fawcett and Magnan, 2002).

Coordination can be seen as an essential part of integration, where the other important elements are cooperation and collaboration (eg Spekman, Kamauff and Myhr, 1998; Christiaanse and Kumar, 2000; Lee and Whang, 2001). According to Spekman *et al* (1998), cooperation is seen as a threshold level of interaction. Coordination is a level of integration 'whereby both specified workflow and information is exchanged in a manner that permits

JIT systems, electronic data interchange (EDI), and other mechanisms that attempt to make many of the traditional linkages between and among trading parties seamless'. Collaboration can be seen as the highest level of integration, which requires partners to have high level of trust, commitment and information sharing as well as a shared common vision of the future. The antecedent for successful IT adoption and usage in the supply chain is trust between the channel parties. If trust and the seeking of common interests in IT investments exist, a fruitful basis for effective IT usage is established (Cripps, Salo and Standing, 2009).

Although deep collaborative attitudes may not have been adopted in many industrial sectors, a certain level of coordination among the players involved in the supply chain is needed to ensure the effectiveness, efficiency, growth and long-term survival of the chain (Stern, El-Ansary and Brown, 1989). The viability of the total chain or network does not allow for too much independent and sub-optimizing behaviour on the part of individual channel participants. On the other hand, the capability of business partners to have access to shared information on a timely basis is critical for improving their performance (Lee and Whang, 2001). In particular, information flow about real demand is vital. This means that firms in distribution networks should cooperate in developing an inter-organizational system (IOS) in order to minimize sub-optimization and make a high degree of chain or network coordination possible. In fact this requirement has been realized in various supply chain management systems (SCMS), which firms have developed in order to improve coordination of the flow of goods and information across intra- and inter-organizational boundaries (Davenport and Brooks, 2004).

Lee and Whang (2001) express how important it is to develop coordination and interaction among business partners by using IT. Information sharing, planning synchronization, workflow coordination and new business models are the escalating degrees of coordination culminating in whole new ways of conducting business. For example, adopting e-business approaches to coordination promises improvements in efficiency, effectiveness, service and consistency in business. IT and its benefits are an important topic, as companies are beginning to make more use of the possibilities of the internet.

Argyres (1999) and Orlikowski (2000) also provide insights into how IT facilitates coordination and cooperation. Argyres' case of aircraft designing process shows how crucial the information system is to coordination. The system helped to create social conventions that supported designers in coordinating their activities. The social conventions further limited the need for hierarchical authority to promote coordination. Orlikowski (2000) discusses technologies-in-practice. These practices reinforce social structures and these structures become firm prescriptions for social actions or routines. If shared by others, these routines make actions within a community of users more predictable (Günther *et al*, 2006).

However, a lack of glue connecting member organizations (Gadde and Håkansson, 2001) and poor coordination of the distributed autonomy are common problems in supply networks. Also, poor IT skills, complicated information-rich processes and lack of trust have been identified as major sources of problems in IT adoption in relationships (Cripps *et al*, 2009). Nevertheless, IT enables organizations to decrease costs and increase capabilities as well as affecting interorganizational coordination structures (den Hengst and Sol, 2002).

Attempting better coordination may lead to new business models. Lapide (2007) argues that the finest goal of any supply chain organization is to match supply and demand optimally over time. In fact the concept of demand chain management has widely been discussed as a new business model (eg Lapide, 2007; Cecere, 2006). Selen and Soliman (2002) have defined DCM as 'practices aimed at managing and coordinating the whole demand chain, starting from the end customer and working backward to raw material supplier'. Jüttner *et al* (2007) discuss the concept and its connections with marketing in detail. Coordination as part of integration can be argued to be crucial in the main elements of DCM: integrating demand and supply processes, managing digital integration, managing the cross-functional relationship between marketing and supply functions and configuring the value system. According to Langabeer and Rose (2002), DCM helps to advance the coordination of many demand-driven activities. Lapide (2006) describes how new strategies require coordinated decision making among supply chain, marketing, sales and customer service organizations.

According to Cecere (2006), the focus of firms is moving from planning, implementing and controlling operations in order to meet customer demand, to sensing demand, shaping a market response and driving profitable and reliable supply. As supply chain technologies have been developed more for demand and supply matching than for sense and response, this means quite a big transition in the supply chain market. Table 14.2 depicts different types of IT application that can be used to coordinate supply chains. Each has unique impacts on supply chains and when used in combination the changes are even more radical. Figure 14.1 outlines IT applications' relation to and influence on supply chain coordination.

Research methodology

We have undertaken a research project to see how IT can enhance coordination of activities within supply chains, with a qualitative twin-case study.

Table 14.2 IT-based systems for creating and integrating stable IT structures in supply chains

Information-technology-based system	Purpose	Source of information
Electronic data interchange (EDI)	Standard protocols are used to share information among participating companies through computer-to-computer exchange of electronic documents relating to purchasing, selling, shipping, receiving, inventory control, financial, and other activities.	Stern and Kaufmann (1985)
Electronic data interchange over secured internet (I-EDI)	Similar to EDI but over a secured internet connection. Usually cheaper and has higher scalability than EDI. Identical to web-based EDI.	Angeles (2000), Garcia-Dastuge and Lambert (2003)
Extranet	An extranet is usually built to communicate and exchange information with customers, suppliers, and other important third parties. In a technical sense, an extranet is formed when an organization permits outsiders to access their internal TCP/IP networks like the intranet. It is often less costly than the previous tools. Can be used to deliver more information-rich material than EDI.	Radosevich (1997), Vlosky et al (2000)
First generation enterprise resource planning (ERP1) system	Total automation of the procurement process, from the point where an employee places an order, through the internal approval process, and right to eventual fulfilment with the help of different software modules. May include human resource management, payroll activities and other financial documentation modules.	Motwani et al (2002)
Second generation enterprise resource planning (ERP2) system	Similar to ERP1 but extended beyond one organization to include inter-organizational parties. Provides a tool for managers to visualize inter-organizational processes. In practice it is hard to differentiate between first- and second-generation systems.	Gardiner, Hanna and LaTour (2002)
Enterprise application integration (EAI)	Used as an enabler application between applications that are otherwise incompatible. Achieves application integration through four layers: connectivity, transportation, translation and process automation.	Whiting (2003), Linthicum (2000)

Source: modified from Salo, 2006

Information-technology-based system	Purpose	Source of information
Web services	Can be used universally to standardize communication between applications in order to connect systems, business partners, and customers cost-effectively through the World Wide Web. Enables easier and faster integration with trading partners. Usually less expensive than EAI but only suitable for small organizations.	Curbera *et al* (2002), Chen, Chen and Shao (2003)
ERP adapters	Some ERP software houses provide adapters that enable integration between their ERP system and competitors' ERP systems. Provides real-time information retrieval and update.	Stoer *et al* (2003)
Supply chain management system (SCM)	Usually used to manage information and material flows between a manufacturer and a retailer. Retailing industry-specific solutions are labelled efficient consumer response (ECR) solutions.	Lancioni, Smith and Oliva (2000)
Mobile technologies (WLAN, PDA, RFID, M-CRM)	Can be used to mobilize various activities, including sales force automation (SFA), order pickups and other information and transaction flows between business parties. Warehouse and logistic processes are made less costly and more accurate. M-CRM encompasses customer relationship management via handheld devices such as a mobile or hybrid phone.	Aungst and Wilson (2005) Salo (2009)
Intelligent agents	Intelligent agents can interpret information and identify events based on some logical rule. Based on this, the individuals who have access to the system can make more accurate decisions regarding, for example, production, calls for bids, and logistic services. Limited access could be given to customers so that they could see eg in which phase of production their order is. May be used to coordinate business information in business networks.	Liu, Turban and Matthew (2000)

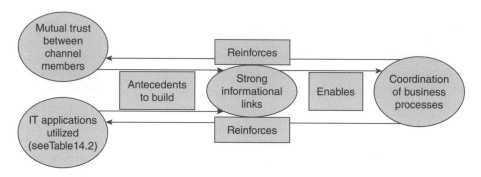

Figure 14.1 IT applications, supply chain elements and informational links fostering coordination

The cases studied are in the wood and steel industries, partly because they have a long tradition of using new technologies (Juslin and Hansen, 2002). The authors conducted in-depth interviews at multiple organizational levels within these industries (Arksey and Knight, 1999). Qualitative data analysis was used to group the material into themes and analyse it (Miles and Huberman, 1984). The authors also used documents, minutes of meetings, industry reports and plant visits to triangulate the respondents' answers in order to validate the research results (Yin, 1989).

Case study: sawmill industry

Considerable changes, such as shorter distribution channels, outsourced shipping operations, general rationalization and adoption of modern IT tools, have characterized the immediate past of our target industry, as well as the development of all traditional industries. Internal coordination, the first SCM development area of the company, was later accompanied by coordination of the supply chains and integration of business processes. Customer relationship management and working in networks dominated many discussions.

The facilities and cheapness of the internet compared to EDI systems have dramatically increased the use of IT applications. The adoption of e-business applications has correlated with company size. Large companies have adopted e-business tools more extensively but internet applications have increased in small and medium-sized enterprises (SMEs). The most commonly used internet business applications are customer contacts, basic web publishing, marketing, vendor contacts and price enquiries.

First steps towards the internet era at sawmills

In the sawmill, use of the internet along with open mail systems arrived in the mid-1990s. The first mobile phones came to the mill in 1990. The mobile phone improved communication significantly and saved time. In the late 1990s e-mail replaced telex and fax but it was just a tool like any other. The advantage of e-mail was that it required no special modifications like EDI. Transferring messages between organizations by means of EDI was discussed in theory but never came into everyday use. At that time the company considered EDI standards and systems too bureaucratic and expensive. However, in the late 1980s an experiment having same features as a modern extranet was carried out with a foreign importer. Specifications and invoices were just transferred as bits. This type of data transfer could have made the relationship between the sawmill and the importer stronger, but unfortunately the arrangements in the supply chain stopped this experiment.

Further steps

Internal coordination and integration stems from the late 1970s in our case company. Progress was made gradually. By using new IT tools stock management is better coordinated. When the batch of sawn wood comes out of the process, the system gives it a number. The system asks where the packet should be taken and gives it a bar code. The code is registered in the information system. This system automatically updates the information if the packet is moved or shipped. From the managerial point of view the system is as follows: the process system sends data regarding when the products will be finished to a higher-level system and in the shipment phase it provides shipping documents and invoicing material.

Internal integration was put into practice between departments and controlled many functions, including procurement. But external integration with customers' systems never happened at our case sawmill in the way that it has been realized in the best practice companies or was already utilized in more developed industries.

Modern information tools help to monitor economic development. Production and sales could be seen on a computer screen just by pressing one button. Moreover, responsiveness and accurate and quick market information are crucial in the export business. In addition, customer satisfaction could be improved by being able to communicate quickly. New information applications are essential, because relying on the telephone affects the sending of non-profitable messages back and forth, losing essential details and not being fully able to express the needed information precisely. However, modern equipment does not guarantee transparency of the supply chain if its members do not trust each other and understand the importance of information sharing. The sales manager's portable computer connected to a GSM phone, enabling faster, more secure and easier operation, belongs to today's business. In general, computerization has meant better planning and the ability to set sales targets further ahead. It offers the possibility of getting rid of the pitfall of selling mainly from stock.

Coordination is needed to cooperate with other companies. Sometimes it is beneficial to work with competitors to fulfil orders or make shipments to remote markets with greater volumes and the ability to build up loads to the specifications required.

Our informants request that the chain should be more transparent. The actions and performance of other members in the supply chain should be better known throughout the chain. E-tools could be used for sharing demand data, inventory sizes, capacity plans and production schedules as well as shipping schedules more efficiently. The systems can be developed so that this type of information could be available to appropriate members in supply chains on a real-time, online basis without significant effort.

There is a tendency for our company and the industry in general to focus on key customers. Personal contacts and the impact of people are underlined in making long-term relationships. Partners seem mainly to have remained the same but delivery systems have changed. Deliveries have become more frequent but shipments are much smaller than before. This means that information sharing, planning synchronization, such as collaborative planning and joint design, workflow coordination and evolution of new business models adopting e-business approaches are challenges for the current sawmill industry. New systems should be created for developing routes for out- and inbound transport from and to sawmills as well as services aiming at customizing sawn wood products more fully than before.

Communication and information sharing must be well organized between the members. It is necessary to make sure that all members of the supply chain see the benefits. The motivating incentives for building tight systems must be clear in order to develop partnerships, supply chains and networks. Tight cooperation cultivates strong mutual informational links that may lead to the adoption of modern IT applications.

Current aims at IT adoption

Not only big companies but also SMEs have noticed enterprise resources planning (ERP) systems' benefits. An ERP system is a system navigating business, and it may contain many different applications such as wages calculation, sales, inventory management and production management. The main benefit is the real-time control possibilities. The management know at every moment how the business is running, and can make corrections if necessary. However, these kinds of systems are really new ones in the wood processing business.

A wood processing company producing glue-lam beams announced a new element in their ERP system, namely, sales transactions connected to a production management system. This system covers the whole chain from sales to production and packaging. Every beam carries with it a great deal of information, which is recorded on the ID-code label stuck on the beam. From the moment a salesman has agreed to ship, it can be traced. The new thing is that the information concerns beams, not packages or items. Moreover, the salesman now has more opportunity to give instructions to production. Therefore, it is possible for the system to give options for scheduling transport.

ERP systems in one form or another are widely used in Finnish sawmills today. Usually, the system includes raw material procurement, production management, inventory management, shipments and sales phases, with document management and financial management. All packet labels include bar codes, so the log information can be tracked and inventories managed. And they can also be used for controlling payments, recording insolvency concerns and unpaid bills.

While ERP systems focus on the management of the company, the modern e-commerce tendency requires efficient data transfer among business associates. This data transfer consists of various business documents. The objectives are more effective and faster data transfer, less manual work, fewer mistakes and simpler processes. The implementation of IT frees up money and time, and provides more effective processes and better customer service.

EDI is common among larger companies and their suppliers, customers, and marketing channel members, but they are relatively cumbersome, expensive and time-consuming, so SMEs tend to avoid them. Instead, the sawmill industry has worked hard to develop standards for internet-based communication, with standardization giving flexibility. Different types of documents can be stored at dedicated websites, from where they are automatically downloaded to be used by business parties. While big enterprises have to deal with thousands of messages every day, more standardized messages can bring significant savings. The second natural step is to transfer that information with as little human intervention as possible directly into companies' ERP systems. According to our informants, leading sawmills are now at this stage.

Case study: steel industry

The mill is a relatively large European specialized steel producer and the workshop is one of the largest in Finland. The specific focus of the case is on steel processing, ie the hardening and marketing of steel plates and components.

The supply chain has evolved from a supply relationship between the mill and its parent company. A trustful relationship has existed between the mill, workshop and logistic provider for only about 10 years. After the individual steel plates and components have been hardened by the workshop, they are further processed by the mill and then sold on to customers.

Development of IT-based coordination mechanisms

In the beginning, no IT systems were used to coordinate activities in the supply chain. Telephone calls and occasional fax messages and meetings were the only ways to coordinate business besides daily mails. Then IT adoption started with internal applications. At first, various internal applications, from material resource planning (MRP) systems to office software, were acquired to manage materials flow in the mill. As stated, telephone and fax were the most important means to connect to other party when face-to-face interaction did not occur.

Already at that time, the early 1990s, the mill had a number of IT systems, which had been in use since the first punch card systems were acquired in the 1960s.

In the mid-1990s the company began to use IT more effectively, with e-mail being used in the supply chain to take care of routine communications. During the 1990s and 2000s the mill has invested heavily in various IT applications and solutions, including electronic marketplaces, point-to-point connections with customers and suppliers, and different software applications. The workshop, because of scarce resources, has invested only in some applications and those investments are carefully planned, but there is currently little integration.

The first issue that was solved with IT concerned order taking. Nowadays, the mill sends all orders over the internet. This makes business easier, eliminates errors and radically reduces costs. Use of the internet for order taking was made possible by the extension of MRP into small-scale ERP systems from the workshop side. This solution can be labelled as an extranet type of solution since it is secured and not available over the public internet. At the same time the mill has connected separate ERP systems to give more a coherent view of processes. The internet is still used for traditional e-mailing. However, currently billing is done physically owing to legal restrictions and the third-party logistic service provider is contacted by traditional means (ie fax, phone and e-mails).

A new step in coordination with the help of IT was gained when a mobile system using personal digital assistants (PDA) and mobile phones as terminals to log into the wireless internet (Wi-Fi) was introduced. Extensions of systems to the wireless world have helped the organizations in the chains to gain further efficiencies. First, steel hardness reports that were traditionally paper-based were digitized, eliminating the time it took to send reports from workshop to mill. Second, both the workshop and mill have an up-to-date view of the hardening capacity available when employees send reports using wireless devices. This means that the mill sales people can more easily fill the capacity available from the workshop. Overall adoption of this simple system provided considerable benefits to both parties of the chain with limited costs (Salo, 2009). Figure 14.2 depicts the different types of IT applications that adopted over time to manage coordination problems in the core supply chain between the mill and the workshop (Salo 2006). Missing from Figure 14.2 are third parties such as logistic providers and other suppliers to the mill and workshop.

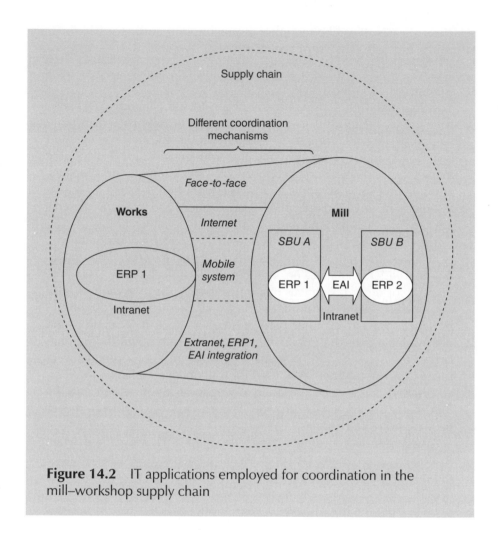

Figure 14.2 IT applications employed for coordination in the mill–workshop supply chain

CONCLUSIONS

Companies now work with many different types of supply chains and networks. Increasing pressure by competitors and globalization of business environment have caused managers to look for innovation and value from different places. Adoption and usage of IT within the supply chain in order to make supply chains more transparent is an obvious source of value and competitive advantage. Both sawmills and steel industries are adopting and using different types of IT, and the degree to which IT is used and for what purposes vary. At first sight it seems that the sawmill industry is lagging behind the steel industry, but this might be due to the selection of cases. It can be seen that in practice both industries are heavily adopting and using different types of mobile systems, RFID systems and laser-based systems to improve manufacturing and inter-organizational processes to coordinate interaction. Based on this, we can agree that IT, alongside specialization and outsourcing, is a key precondition for networking of organizations.

Our researches showed that the focus of the supply chain is turning towards more direct sawmill–industrial end-user relationships. The bigger sawmills are increasingly emphasizing short-term agreements, selection of market areas according to business cycles and price competition though customer orientation. In both industries it is clear that SMEs emphasize longer agreements as well as long-term and tighter supply chains including a win–win attitude, frequent interaction and open information sharing. This means that IT will play an increasingly important role in tightly structured supply chains and networks. Both industries' SMEs seem to be starting collaborative planning with their customers, aiming to avoid useless operations. For managers, we have provided new ways to think about the adoption and usage of IT to coordinate joint activities. These findings relate to particular industries, but there is clear overlap with other process industries such as chemical and paper.

References

Angeles, R (2000) Revisiting the role of internet-EDI in the current electronic commerce scene, *Logistics Information Management*, **13** (1), pp 45–57

Argyres, NS (1999) The impact of information technology on coordination: evidence from B-2 'stealth' bomber, *Organization Science*, **10** (2), pp 162–81

Arksey, H and Knight, P (1999) *Interviewing for Social Scientists*, Sage, London

Aungst, SG and Wilson, DT (2005) A primer for navigating the shoals of applying wireless technology to marketing problems, *Journal of Business & Industrial Marketing*, **20** (2), pp 59–69

Bensaou, M (1999) Portfolios of buyer–supplier relationships, *Sloan Management Review*, **40** (4), pp 35–44

Cecere, L (2006) A changing technology landscape, *Supply Chain Management Review*, **10** (1), pp 15–16

Chen, M, Chen, AN and Shao, BM (2003) The implications and impacts of web services to electronic commerce research practices, *Journal of Electronic Commerce*, **4** (4), pp 128–39

Christiaanse, E and Kumar, K (2000) ICT-enabled coordination of dynamic supply webs, *International Journal of Physical Distribution and Logistics Management*, **30** (3/4), pp 268–85

Christopher, M (1998) *Logistics and Supply Chain Management: Strategies for reducing costs and improving services*, 2nd edn, Pitman, London

Cripps, H, Salo, J and Standing, C (2009) Enablers and impediments to IT adoption in business relationships: evidence from Australia and Finland, *Journal of Systems and Information Technology*, **11** (2), pp 185–200

Croom, SR, Romano, P and Giannakis, M (2000) Supply chain management: an analytical framework for critical literature review, *European Journal of Purchasing and Supply Management*, **6** (1), pp 67–83

Curbera, F *et al* (2002) Unraveling the Web services web: an introduction to SOAP, WSDL, and UDDI, *IEEE Internet Computing*, **6** (2), pp 86–93

Davenport, TH and Brooks, JD (2004) Enterprise systems and the supply chain, *Journal of Enterprise Information Management*, **17** (1), pp 8–19

De Treville, S, Shapiro, RD and Hameri, A-P (2004) From supply chain to demand chain: the role of lead time reduction in improving demand chain performance, *Journal of Operations Management*, **21** (6), pp 613–27

den Hengst, M and Sol, HG (2002) The impact of electronic commerce on interorganizational coordination: a framework from theory applied to the container-transport industry, *International Journal of Electronic Commerce*, **5** (4), pp 73–91

Fawcett, SE and Magnan, GM (2002) The rhetoric and reality of supply chain integration, *International Journal of Physical Distribution and Logistics Management*, **32** (5), pp 339–61

Gadde, L-E and Håkansson, H (2001) *Supply Network Strategies*, John Wiley and Sons, Chichester

Garcia-Dastuge, S and Lambert, D (2003) Internet-enabled coordination in supply chain, *Industrial Marketing Management*, **32** (2), pp 251–63

Gardiner, S, Hanna, J and LaTour, M (2002) ERP and the reengineering of industrial marketing processes. A prescriptive overview for the new age marketing manager, *Industrial Marketing Management*, **31** (4), pp 357–65

Giannakis, M and Croom, S (2004) Toward the development of a supply chain management paradigm: a conceptual framework, *Journal of Supply Chain Management: A Global Review of Purchasing and Supply*, **4** (2), pp 27–38

Günther, H, Grote, G and Thees, O (2006) Information technology in supply networks. Does it lead to better collaborative planning?, *Journal of Enterprise Information Management*, **19** (5), pp 540–50

Houlihan, JB (1985) International supply chain management, *International Journal of Physical Distribution and Materials Management*, **15** (1), pp 22–38

Jones, TC and Riley, DW (1985) Using inventory for competitive advantage through supply chain management, *International Journal of Physical Distribution and Materials Management*, **15** (5), pp 16–26

Juslin, H and Hansen, E (2002) *Strategic Marketing in the Global Forest Industries*, Authors Academic Press, Corvallis, OR

Jüttner, U, Christopher, M and Baker, S (2007) Demand chain management – integrating marketing and supply chain management, *Industrial Marketing Management*, **36** (3), pp 377–92

Keith, OR and Webber, MD (1982) Supply chain management: logistics catches up with strategy, Outlook 1982, via Christopher, M (1992) *Logistics, the Strategic Issues*, Chapman and Hall, London

Kurnia, S and Johnston, RB (2003) Adoption of efficient consumer response: key issues and challenges in Australia, *Supply Chain Management: An International Journal*, **8** (3), pp 251–62

Lancioni, R, Smith, M and Oliva, T (2000) The role of the Internet in supply chain management, *Industrial Marketing Management*, **29** (1), pp 45–56

Langabeer, J and Rose, J (2002) *Creating Demand Driven Supply Chains: How to profit from demand chain management*, Spiro Press, London

Lapide, L (2006) Benchmarking best practices, *Journal of Business Forecasting*, Winter, 29–32

Lapide, L (2007) Optimally bridging supply and demand, *Supply Chain Management Review*, May/June

Lee, HL and Whang, S (2001) E-business and supply chain integration, *Standford Global Supply Chain Forum*, November, SGSCMF-W2-2001

Linthicum, DS (2000) *B2B Application Integration*, Addison-Wesley Professional, Reading, MA

Liu, S, Turban, E and Matthew, K (2000) Software agents for environmental scanning in electronic commerce, *Information Systems Frontiers*, **2** (1), pp 85–98

Mason-Jones, R and Towill, DR (1999) Total cycle time compression and the agile supply chain, *International Journal of Production Economics*, **62** (1–2), pp 61–73

McGrath, R Jr and Sparks, WL (2005) The importance of building social capital, *Quality Progress*, **38** (2), pp 45–49

Miles, MB and Huberman, AM (1984) *Qualitative data analysis: A sourcebook of new methods*, Sage, Beverly Hills, CA

Mills, J, Schmitz, J and Frizelle, G (2004) A strategic review of 'supply networks', *International Journal of Operations and Production Management*, **24** (10), pp 1012–37

Motwani, J et al (2002) Successful implementation of ERP projects: evidence from two case studies, *International Journal of Production Economics*, **75** (1–2), pp 83–96

Orlikowski, WJ (2000) Using technology and constituting organization science structures: A practice lens for studying technology in organizations, *Organization Science*, **11** (4), pp 404–28

Radosevich, L (1997) Early adopters hail extranet benefits, dodge pitfalls, *InfoWorld*, **19** (23), pp 65–66

Salo, J (2006) Business relationship digitization: what we need to know before embarking on such activities?, *Journal of Electronic Commerce in Organizations*, **4** (4), pp 75–93

Salo, J (2009) The role of mobile technology in a buyer–supplier relationship, *Journal of Business and Industrial Marketing* (in press)

Selen, W and Soliman, F (2002) Operations in today's demand chain management framework, *Journal of Operations Management*, **20**, pp 667–73

Spekman, RE, Kamauff, JW and Myhr, N (1998) An empirical investigation into supply chain management: a perspective of partnerships, *Supply Chain Management*, **3** (2), pp 53–67

Stern, L, El-Ansary, A and Brown, JR (1989) *Management in Marketing Channels*, Prentice Hall, Englewood Cliffs, NJ

Stern, L and Kaufmann, P (1985) Electronic data interchange in selected consumer goods industries: an interorganizational perspective, in *Marketing in an Electronic Age*, ed RD Buzzell, pp 52–73, Harvard Business School Press, Boston, MA

Stock, JR (1997) Applying theories from other disciplines to logistics, *International Journal of Physical Distribution and Logistics Management*, **27** (9), pp 515–39

Stoer, M *et al* (2003) IT infrastructure for supply chain management in company networks with small and medium-sized enterprises, in *Proceedings of the International Conference on Enterprise Information Systems*, France

Storey, J *et al* (2006) Supply chain management: theory, practice and future challenges, *International Journal of Operations and Production Management*, **26** (7), pp 754–74

Tarn, JM, Yen, DC and Beaumont, M (2002) Exploring the rationales for ERP and SCM integration, *Industrial Management and Data Systems*, **102** (1), pp 26–34

Vlosky, RP, Fontenot, R and Blalock, L (2000) Extranets: impacts on business practices and relationships, *Journal of Business and Industrial Marketing*, **15** (6), pp 438–57

Vollmann, TE, Cordon, C and Heikkilä, J (2000) Teaching supply chain management to business executives, *Production and Operations Management*, **9** (1), pp 81–91

Whiting, R (2003) Look within – business-intelligence tools have a new mission: evaluating all aspects of a company's business, *InformationWeek*, p 32

Wu, NC *et al* (2005) Challenges to global RFID adoption, *Technovation*, **26** (12), 1317–23

Yin, R (1989) *Case Study Research*, Sage, Thousand Oaks, CA

15

Delivering sustainability through supply chain management

Kirstie McIntyre, Hewlett-Packard

Supply chains span industry groups, cross industry boundaries, have a wide geographical spread and are an excellent vehicle for improving the environmental, social and economic performance of companies and industry sectors over the long term. Supply chain management functions are analysed for their potential impacts on the performance of a company. Practical examples from many industry sectors show the steps that can be taken to improve sustainability for the environment, for society and for the business. Specifically, the European Waste Electrical and Electronic Equipment (WEEE) Directive will have a significant and long-reaching effect on the supply chain. From purchasing decisions to reverse logistics, the whole supply chain will be reshaped by this new environmental law.

BACKGROUND

Sustainability has traditionally been a concept that is difficult to sell to senior management because it describes a state in the future that has never been experienced, rather than a specific process or methodology of how to get there. Theoretically, the concept makes sense, but translating it into actionable steps has proved a significant stumbling block for organizations (Preston, 2001). The concept of sustainability or sustainable development has been around for a while, but is a very recent customer requirement and one that many companies are trying to grapple with. Sustainability is a difficult concept to grasp in an industrial context, as shown by the definition (DETR, 2000):

Sustainable development is:

- social progress which recognizes the needs of everyone;
- effective protection of the environment;
- prudent use of natural resources; and
- maintenance of high and stable levels of economic growth and employment.

When a company considers what the above elements mean, it seems impossible to continue to do business and be sustainable. But sustainability is not just about being altruistic about the environment and workers' rights. It is also about ensuring the long-term viability of a business model and company. Shareholders, customers, suppliers and employees all want to see a future in their businesses. The functions that the supply chain organization manages are an ideal place for a company to begin putting together the actionable steps and investments that will demonstrate positive progress towards sustainable development.

Waste electrical and electronic equipment is one of the priority waste streams identified by the European Commission alongside batteries, tyres, vehicles and packaging. The directive has been written as part of the 'producer responsibility' set of laws, which demonstrates a shift in focus from process- to product-oriented environmental legislation. In the past, environmental legislation has focused on industrial emissions and air and water quality – but, owing to increasing waste generation and reducing disposal capacity, waste is now one of the top environmental issues in Europe. EU and UK waste policies increasingly involve the private sector. Producer responsibility legislation aims to increase product recycling by making producers financially responsible for their products at end of life.

WEEE has been specifically chosen as a priority waste stream for a number of reasons. There are perceived problems with the current state of waste management. Growing quantities of WEEE mean a higher contribution of WEEE to pollutants in municipal waste streams – and underdeveloped recycling technologies and infrastructure mean that there are limited ways of dealing with this. Diverging national legislation does not support a single European market or the ease of doing business in Europe. Therefore the general objectives of the WEEE legislation are to improve

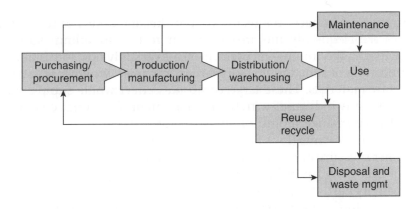

Figure 15.1   Common supply chain factors

waste management processes, eliminate hazardous substances, increase recycling capacity and introduce harmonizing legislation.

Supply chain management has risen high on the corporate agenda as companies recognize the potential that it offers for creating sustainable competitive advantage in an increasingly turbulent business environment. Customers' requirements are becoming more stringent and companies aim to be increasingly customer-focused – and it is often the supply chain that is able to provide the added value that customers are looking for. The 6th Business in the Environment Index of Corporate Environmental Engagement (BiE, 2002) identified the integration of environmental risk into supply chain management as a real challenge for many companies. Supply chain aspects of sustainable development resulted in the lowest management score, with 17 out of 38 industry sectors scoring below 50 per cent. There is a need to look strategically beyond the immediate environmentally driven aspects of supply chain management. With all stakeholders giving attention to the quality of management and corporate governance – demonstrated through supply chains and sustainability – this is an ideal time to look at combining the best of both disciplines. This chapter takes each of the major supply chain functions (shown in Figure 15.1) and discusses their ability to improve sustainability in terms of environmental, social and economic impacts.

PURCHASING OR PROCUREMENT

Purchasing is often the first place that companies start to integrate environmental issues into their management processes. This is especially true for service companies. Such companies often do not have large environmental impacts themselves – but the operations that use their services are frequently the area where there is a significant scope for improvement. Environmental performance is certainly now integrated into the procurement function of many large companies, whether for services or for raw materials. These large companies affect whole supply chains and cross many industries with their requirements for improved environmental performance. Some of this is being driven by environmental management systems (ISO 14000 or EMAS) and some is being driven by consumer pressure or even market differentiation. Toyota first laid out its goal of becoming an industry leader in environmental performance in 1992 with its Earth Charter. It is now imposing the same standards on its suppliers in its Green Supplier Guidelines – which are not so much guidelines as mandates. Toyota in North America demanded that all suppliers implement an environmental management system that conforms to ISO 14001 by the end of 2003. Suppliers must also obey a ban on 450 chemicals as well as comply with hazardous materials transport rules. Many of Toyota's suppliers welcome the tough standards as it brings them to the forefront of environmental performance in their own industries. Toyota has further environmental aspirations with long-term energy reduction and greenhouse gas and zero landfill targets (Zachary, 2001). Such strictures can apply a lot of pressure on suppliers, but Toyota's suppliers appear to have embraced the challenge and feel that they have gained from doing so. Toyota itself has improved its environmental performance by leveraging the effort of its suppliers. This seems an increasingly popular way of improving environmental and social performance, particularly by customer-facing organizations such as car manufacturers and retailers.

A growing number of European retail chains are developing their own safety initiatives by banning chemicals in their products. Many retailers are asking suppliers of own-label products to withdraw or phase out chemicals that have been put on priority lists for further research by the European Commission, national governments or environmental monitoring organizations. Fewer organizations have been successful at incorporating social issues into their procurement processes. However, with recent media attention on Nike and Gap over child-labour issues in their supply chains, the clothing retailers have taken a much more proactive approach to supplier assurance. Nike and Gap both have corporate compliance and monitoring teams who audit contract factories for fulfilment of stated aims and objectives. Many British retailers have joined the Ethical Trading Initiative (ETI), which identifies and promotes good practice in the implementation of codes of labour practice (see the ETI website, www.ethicaltrade.org). It is reasonable to expect more retailers to take these approaches to managing social impacts in their supply chain.

B&Q has been in the forefront of action in this area since the early 1990s when it realized that – as a DIY retailer – the majority of its environmental and social impacts came from its products and suppliers. The company uses both questionnaires and auditors to track environmental and social issues in its supplier base, and has decided that this approach is preferable to requiring an environment management system (B&Q, 1995). It submitted to suppliers, chemical companies and environmental groups a list of chemicals it wanted to ban in its products so that it could declare itself toxic-free by 2005. Some of the chemicals are among the 15 hazardous substances pinpointed for priority action by the Ospar convention, responsible for protecting the marine environment of the north-east Atlantic. Homebase, another DIY retailer, is going even further by planning to ban all the chemicals on the Ospar list – even though the governments that defined the list set a deadline of 2020 for ending these emissions.

The pressure to green the procurement function does not come only from companies; governments are also leveraging their purchasing power. The UK government has for some time produced a *Green Government Handbook*, which advises central and local departments on environmentally sound goods and services. The European Commission (2001) has issued guidelines that clarify the extent to which environmental criteria may be used in the public procurement process and still remain in line with procurement directives that regulate freedom of movement, competition and best value. A *Green Public Procurement Handbook* is being developed. The drivers for this are that the achievement of sustainable development requires that economic growth supports social progress and respects the environment, that social policy underpins economic performance, and that environmental policy is cost-effective. Public purchasing represents 14 per cent of EU GDP, and member states should consider how to make better use of public procurement to favour environmentally friendly products and services. The guidance goes beyond differentiating between products and services, and suggests that there are other possibilities for integrating environmental considerations into public purchases, notably when defining the technical specifications, the selection criteria and the award criteria of a contract. This means that public procurement departments may have the ability to change the way that goods are produced or manufactured or the supplies that service providers use.

Changing methods of public procurement are also being used to drive sustainability into goods and services purchased from the private sector. The construction sector in the UK has discovered that new procurement methods such as private finance initiatives (PFIs) and Prime Contracting (an MOD initiative) have long-term outlooks and responsibilities (25 years in the case of PFI), which means that designing, building and maintaining sustainable facilities become key to the successful tendering and managing of contracts.

PRODUCTION OR MANUFACTURING

The primary output of today's production processes is waste. Across all industries, less than 10 per cent of everything that is extracted from the earth (by weight) becomes usable products. The remaining 90 per cent becomes waste from production (Senge, Carstedt and Porter, 2001). Resource efficiency – or doing more with less – is the first place to start in improving sustainability performances. Through its 'waste-free factories' programme, Xerox has reduced landfill by over 75 per cent since 1993. Cornwell Parker Furniture's timber minimization programme has saved £250,000 per year and reduced waste by 20 per cent. Cornwell has also overhauled coating procedures, saving a further £180,000 per year, and cut solvent use by 21 tonnes per year. Instead of sending wood waste to landfill, a wood-fired incinerator with energy recovery has been installed. Although this cost £480,000, the reduction in landfill tax and heating fuel gives a payback period of four to five years (Envirowise, 2002). British Airways and its waste management contractor, Grundon, have created a strategic partnership to deal with waste arising from aircraft, engineering facilities and offices. The partnership means that, instead of being presented with an opaque final bill for services, BA receives a detailed breakdown of Grundon's waste handling costs. This has enabled both parties to identify opportunities for cost savings and then share in those savings (ENDS, 2002a).

Many argue that what we need is a different way of looking at products. Firms such as Dow Chemical, Carrier and IKEA believe that higher profits will come from providing better solutions, rather than selling more units. This creates a potential alignment between what is sound economically and what is sound environmentally. A company's business model no longer requires designed-in obsolescence to push customers into buying new products. Instead, producers have an incentive to design for longevity, efficient servicing, improved functioning and product take-back. Such design maintains relationships with customers by continually ensuring that products are providing the services that people desire, at the lowest cost to the producer.

The shift from valuing 'stuff' to valuing the service that the 'stuff' provides leads to a radical change in the concept of ownership. In the future, producers may own their products for ever and, therefore, will have strong incentives to design products to be disassembled and remanufactured or recycled, whichever is more economical. Owning products for ever would represent a powerful step towards changing companies' attitudes about product discard. When the production function is considered to be a part of the supply chain, there is obviously much that can be done to improve environmental and social performance at this stage. The environmental performance of manufacturing activities has been improving now for many years, much of it driven by easy cost savings.

Social impact assessments are common for large infrastructure projects (roads, pipelines etc) but are not yet a common part of manufacturing activities. However, many companies forget that social impacts include the health and safety of employees and neighbours, community relations or noise and congestion abatement processes. Many of these impacts are already part of environmental management systems. Human resource management processes also play a role in identifying and improving social performance – training, fair pay, equality and diversity activities all contribute to a company's sustainability performance.

The case of Scandic Hotels shows, first, that sustainable strategies and practices can be just as useful in service operations as in manufacturing and, second, that such strategies and practices can support a corporate turnaround. In the early 1990s, Scandic Hotels was turned from collapse by a new value system, embodied in the concept of sustainable development, which linked customers and employees. Through employee training programmes, environmental information systems and innovative collaborations with suppliers, Scandic was revived as a profitable corporation (Goodman, 2000).

DISTRIBUTION AND WAREHOUSING

Cooper, Browne and Peters (1991) maintain that the transport and storage of goods are at the centre of any logistics activity, and these are areas where a company should concentrate its efforts to reduce its environmental impacts. The authors claim that 24-hour transport is less environmentally damaging, as fuel consumption is more efficient with less congestion, and that just-in-time operations raise fuel consumption, as smaller lorries consume more fuel per tonne of goods moved than larger vehicles. This is an important point with the exponential growth of e-commerce and home deliveries. The use of combined transport options such as containers using road and rail links is advocated for environmental improvement. To begin the improvement process, the authors suggest a three-stage approach: an environmental audit of the logistics operation, a listing of actions to reduce impacts and a priority ranking of these actions. The problem with these recommendations is that they are not stakeholder-focused, but look only at fuel consumption and economic cost. Improving the efficiency of fuel consumption will indeed reduce environmental impact, but local community issues may become more important when using large lorries in a 24-hour operation.

Supermarkets are only just beginning to take into account the miles travelled by food from its country of origin to our plates. Consumer demand for fresh fruit and vegetables all year round and the falling costs of freight transport have not provided retailers with an economic incentive to reduce the transport associated with their products. However, climate change levies may change this as transport emissions are counted as part of a company's carbon dioxide burden. Drinks manufacturer HP Bulmer has identified that the second-biggest source of carbon dioxide and other air pollutants is transport – with outbound goods accounting for some 85 per cent of its total transport emissions. Currently 100 per cent of the company's transport is by road, but it has been testing ways of putting some back on the railway. A partial switch to rail appears to be cost-neutral and results in environmental benefits, with carbon dioxide emissions per tonne-kilometre reduced by 80 per cent. Such initiatives allowed Bulmer to set a target of reducing the environmental impacts of its transport operations by 75 per cent in 2004 (ENDS, 2002b).

Transport is often viewed as an activity with a negative environmental impact, yet the transport sector represents 7 per cent of the GDP of Western Europe and employs 7 per cent of the workforce. On the other hand, the cost to society in terms of congestion, pollution and accidents has been estimated to be 5 per cent of the GDP. The energy consumption of the transport sector is one-third of all the energy consumed by EU industry, and 85 per cent of this is used by road transport. Unfortunately, the recent troubles of Railtrack in the UK have done nothing to encourage goods to move from road to rail. And the sector is fragmented, very competitive and disinclined to act in concert to find solutions to its problems (Howie, 1994). Congestion is inflationary and decreases productivity through delays, stock-outs or over-stocking. So, there is a dilemma between reducing environmental impact and increasing financial cost. To some extent, this can be overcome by intermediaries such as consolidators (organizations that ship many companies' products together to maximize loading efficiencies).

Warehouse management is another key social and environmental factor in distribution. The siting of warehousing and distribution centres can be a major issue for local communities because of noise and congestion. The energy consumption or health and safety record in a poorly managed, temperature-controlled warehouse can eclipse all the other efforts that a company may make, yet it is often an overlooked function of the supply chain. Packaging and waste management are also important processes, often based at warehouse locations, which can have far-reaching impacts on the environment. The Packaging Waste Directive (94/62/EC) and national packaging laws now include all types of packaging in aggressive recovery and recycling targets for companies using over 50 tonnes of packaging a year. Anheuser-Busch, the US food processor, is looking at both in- and outbound materials to see how suppliers can improve the company's environmental performance as well as its bottom line. Suppliers have played a major role in its packaging programme, which has resulted in a reduction of aluminium use, saving $250 million per year. The company has also worked with materials-recovery suppliers to increase recycling rates as well as the quality of collected aluminium beverage containers. It is now the world's largest recycler of used aluminium drinks containers, currently recycling 130 per cent of the amounts it ships in the United States. Overall, the company has reduced the amount of solid waste to landfill by 68 per cent since 1991, saving $19 million. Such efforts take several years, require collaboration with suppliers and need to be integrated into existing quality programmes and new business initiatives (*Purchasing*, 2001).

USE AND MAINTENANCE

As many life cycle analyses have proved, it is the 'use' phase of a product or service that often creates the biggest environmental and social impact (McIntyre *et al*, 1998). It is also the use phase that many companies are recognizing as key to customer relationship management. As Volvo discovered years ago, when a company is selling cars its relationship with the customer ends at the purchase; when the company is providing customer satisfaction, the relationship just begins with the purchase. By interacting with the producer, the consumer can become a co-creator of value or, in some cases, a destroyer of value (Senge, Carstedt and Porter, 2001). Xerox found that it was not the electricity that its equipment consumed that caused the biggest environmental impact, but the consumption of paper and toner and the visits from the service engineer in a van (McIntyre, 1999). This indicated to Xerox that designing greater reliability into machines and then providing more training to customers would substantially mitigate the environmental impacts of its supply chain. Cooperating with paper and toner suppliers to reduce energy consumption at the production stage would result in greater cost savings and less environmental damage.

BASF's premise is that its products will have commercial advantage if they deliver environmental benefits as well as performing at the same level as the competition. The company examines all of its major products and processes every three years and assesses how they can be made more profitable or more environmentally friendly or, where necessary, replaced. The company has now undertaken more than 100 eco-efficiency analyses. One example introduced plastic fuel tanks for cars as being more eco-efficient than metal ones (because they are lighter and will reduce energy use and, therefore, cost to customers). Collaborations between BASF and its customers have become increasingly important in making choices about materials (Scott, 2001).

The examples above show that product stewardship is the key issue in the use phase of products and services. It is a key issue for a number of reasons, not only environmental and social impact, but also as added value to the customer. Corporate governance, ensuring that stated policies are adhered to and maintained, is also being extended by some companies into product stewardship. It is not enough for them to have products disappear on to the next stage in the chain: they are concerned about how their products are being used.

It may be difficult for service sectors to internalize product stewardship, but in practice 'service stewardship' can be applied equally. Understanding the environmental and social impacts that occur through the lifespan of a service is the first step to a reduction of those impacts. The hotel industry, for example, has understood that laundering towels is one of its biggest impacts. Many hotels now have a green hotel charter, which asks guests to consider whether they need clean towels on a daily basis. Although it is still the customer's choice, the hotel is using its relationship with its customers to mitigate environmental impacts from detergent, water and energy consumption.

DISPOSE OR REUSE AND RECYCLE?

Other organizations have focused their environmental efforts on the other end of the supply chain with recycling issues. Equipment is returned from the customers of companies such as IBM, Nokia, BMW and Xerox (Hopfenbeck, 1993: 139–73). These companies either recondition the old equipment or reclaim the materials they are made from, reprocessing them into raw materials. Logistics is well qualified to deal with cradle-to-grave issues because of its focus on the control of materials from suppliers, through value-added processes and on to the customer. The interface between logistics and the environment is embedded in the value-adding functions it performs (Wu and Dunn, 1995). To minimize total environmental impact, it must be evaluated from the total system perspective and reverse logistics may be the answer to improving the environmental impact of the supply chain by improving material use (Giuntini, 1996).

The requirements of the WEEE Directive emphasize that industry and governments should be driving towards individual producer responsibility, away from the collective responsibility of dealing with historical WEEE waste. This means that each producer would be responsible for only its own products, not a share of all WEEE within its market category. The aim of this is to achieve environmental benefits through encouraging innovative design and recycling technologies driven by producers. For example, Hewlett-Packard (2005) has been designing products for a number of years using the concept of extended producer responsibility. It is equally concerned about the design impacts on the cost of recycling the product at the end of its life as it is about the energy consumption and hazardous materials content. HP therefore assumes that its products will be easier and cheaper to recycle than its competitors' products and that it will be able to pass on this cost advantage to its customers.

The challenge for the supply chain is clear in this scenario. In order for HP to realize its cost advantage, it needs to recover and recycle only its own products. In these days of underdeveloped recycling infrastructure and technologies, it is difficult to see how this can happen without large amounts of manual handling to sort through piles of IT WEEE and select only HP branded products. Studies in the UK and other countries have shown that a significant proportion of WEEE returned by householders is unrecognizable or has no brand name left on it. This issue may be resolved with the advent of radio frequency identity (RFID) tagging, but this would require significant investment by producers to incorporate it into products, and by the recycling industry to invest in the sorting machinery needed to make the system efficient. However, it is only through producers being able to realize the benefits of eco-design at the end of life of products that the WEEE Directive will achieve one of its primary objectives – preventing so much electronic waste being generated in the first place.

The construction industry in the UK consumes around 6 tonnes of material per person per year and about 10 per cent of national energy consumption is used in the production and transport of construction products and materials. Some 250–300 million tonnes of material are quarried in the UK each year for use as aggregates, cement and bricks. Approximately 13 million tonnes of construction materials are delivered to site and thrown away unused every year (DETR, 2004). The construction industry produced an estimated 73 million tonnes of construction and demolition waste in 1999, representing 18 per cent of the total waste produced in the UK. Only 12–15 million tonnes of materials (less than 20 per cent) are recycled per year, as hardcore and landscaping fill. Using these materials more effectively, through reclamation and higher-grade recycling, would reduce the use of aggregates, save energy and reduce pressures on landfill sites (Vivian, 2001). For example, in 10 demonstration projects, MACE, Laing Homes, AMEC Capital, Wren & Bell, Schal, Scottish Executive, Try Construction, the Environment Agency and Carillion have all worked with CIRIA to minimize waste. Examples of waste minimization on these sites include (CIRIA, 2001):

- the recovery of 500,000 roof tiles for reuse in housing developments, saving £80,000;
- a house builder saving £600 waste disposal costs per housing unit built;
- a reduction in over-ordering by using just-in-time deliveries;
- the minimization of waste at the design stage of an office refurbishment;
- the segregation of waste on-site, saving 20 per cent on disposal costs; and
- better control of waste by the use of rigorous procurement and contractual measures.

MANAGERIAL AND FINANCIAL SUSTAINABILITY

What about all the support structures around supply chains, such as financial decisions, management systems and governance? Certain pre-conditions are necessary before an environmentally oriented value chain can be created. These include an environmentally oriented system of corporate management, a culture that allows learning, and a top-down principle with bottom-up support. Development and change aimed at the target audience are more likely to result in the environment (or sustainability) being considered from the beginning of the process (Steger, 1996).

Much of the influence on sustainability comes from outside the firm. Many in the fund management community probably think that sustainable development has little relevance to their decision making – but what about the energy company that is ignoring the rising tide of pollution legislation, or an automotive stockist that has not considered the implications of forthcoming vehicle recycling directives (Belsom, 2001)? When the cost of emitting climate-change gases is incorporated into the tax regime through the UK climate change levy, then the economics of doing business will change. The Society of Motor Manufacturers and Traders estimates that the extra cost for each new UK car after the implementation of the End of Life Vehicle Directive will be between £115 and £300. These uncertainties reduce the earnings from companies' stock and so their performance on the stock market.

Socially responsible investment aims to influence companies to adopt policies that benefit the environment and society at large. As investors, socially responsible investment funds have a great deal of influence over the way in which a company conducts business (CIS, 2002). An EIRiS/NOP (1999) survey found that over 75 per cent of UK adults think their pension scheme should operate an ethical policy, if it can do so without reducing the level of financial return. Of these, 39 per cent said their pension should operate an ethical policy even when it might reduce the size of their final pension. The growing prominence of ethical issues is also reflected in the spectacular growth in numbers and size of available funds that apply ethical criteria. Research by the Social Investment Forum indicates that, in 1999, more than $2 trillion was invested in ethical funds in the United States, up 82 per cent from 1997 levels.

Socially responsible investment is a growing trend and there are a large number of rating organizations that assess and screen companies to provide information on their operations. These rating organizations scrutinize factors such as environmental impacts and solutions, sustainability issues, management and external focus – and companies will need to consider the strategic responses in these areas (Walker and Farnworth, 2001).

Reputation and governance of a company and its supply chain are also key issues. Shell appeared very badly when it decided to sink an ageing oil platform, Brent Spar, even though it transpired that its solution for disposal was well researched and advised. Shell was unable to recover its corporate reputation and has since attracted more unwanted attention over its operations in Nigeria. Public and pressure group perception of a product is also important in laundry detergents. Suppliers of phosphates and linear alkyl benzene sulfonate (LAS) for laundry detergents in Europe are having mixed success in their fight to gain environmental support for their products. Denmark's environmental authorities are taking such a determined stance over LAS that Procter & Gamble has decided to stop marketing detergents with the surfactant in that country. It is not good for the image of its brands for the company to be seen to be opposing local authorities, even though research indicates that LAS is more biodegradable than the alternatives (*Chemical Market Reporter*, 2001).

BP looks at the challenge of sustainable development as a business opportunity. 'There are good commercial reasons for being ahead of the pack when it comes to environmental issues', says John Browne, BP's former Chief Executive. Business can play a leadership role in changes, with change driven through market innovation being easiest for our society to understand. The challenge is to develop sustainable business that is compatible with the current economic reality. Dell, Sun Microsystems and Cisco Systems have all identified supply chains as strategic differentiators, using them to forecast and plan future products and services by building trusting relationships through collaboration. As supply chains evolve from linear supplier–customer links to dynamic networking organizations, all members become involved in defining the processes and contributing to the value of the finished product or service. Innovative business models and products must work financially, or it will not matter how good they are ecologically or socially.

CONCLUSION

This chapter has shown that the pressures to be a more sustainable company in terms of the environment, economics and social responsibility are increasing. It has also shown that many companies have already started on the long road to sustainable development, some with huge success. Sustainable development is here to stay as a customer requirement, and the processes of supply chain management are ideally placed to respond to that requirement. However, meeting customer and market expectations, improving market access and increasing cost savings represent baseline expectations and are important simply to environmentally responsible companies remaining competitive. Control of the social and environmental aspects of supply chains will lead to better understanding of the supply chain as a whole. This in turn can lead to cost savings and better relationships between partners.

There are many challenges for the supply chain in the WEEE legislation in Europe. For some operators, little will change; for others, there will be a complete sea change. There are opportunities in data management, traceability and assurance, and in the potential development of interim sorting centres or platforms, for retailers and producers. The division of responsibility and accurate reporting is a challenge for members of specific product supply chains. Those parts of the supply chain that can respond to sustainability issues such as WEEE will generally be more proactive and able to meet changing customer requirements and market forces. By taking sustainability one step at a time – early in business planning – it is indeed possible to differentiate and innovate to create value. Supply chain management processes are an ideal place to start.

References

B&Q (1995) *How Green Is My Front Door?*, July, B&Q, Eastleigh

Belsom, T (2001) Unsustainable investors, *Global Investor*, **142**, May, p 142

Business in the Environment (BiE) (2002) *Sustaining Competitiveness*, 6th Annual Index of Corporate Environmental Engagement, 26 February, BiE, London

Chemical Market Reporter (2001) Phosphate and LAS eco profiles under siege in Scandinavia, **259**, 11 June, p 259

CIRIA (2001) www.ciria.org.uk

Cooper, J, Browne, M and Peters, M (1991) *European Logistics: Markets, management and strategy*, Blackwell, London

Co-operative Insurance Society (CIS) (2002), *Sustainability Pays*, Report by Co-operative Insurance and Forum for the Future, CIS, Manchester

Department of Environment, Transport and the Regions (DETR) (2000) *A Better Quality of Life: A strategy for sustainable development for the United Kingdom*, CM4345, DETR, London

DETR (2004) *UK Statistics*, DETR, London

EIRiS/NOP (1999) *Survey of Pension Scheme Members*, EIRiS/NOP Solutions, London

ENDS (2002a) BA's 'shared savings' scheme with waste firm, *ENDS Report*, **324**, January

ENDS (2002b) HP Bulmer: a ferment of sustainability ideas, *ENDS Report*, **324**, January

Envirowise (2002) *Furniture Workbook*, GG308, DETR, London

European Commission (2001), *Commission Interpretative Communication on the Community Law Applicable to Public Procurement and the Possibilities for Integrating Environmental Considerations into Public Procurement*, COM (2001) 274 final, 4 July, European Commission, Brussels

Giuntini, R (1996) An introduction to reverse logistics for environmental management: a new system to support sustainability and profitability, *Total Quality Environmental Management*, **Spring**, pp 81–87

Goodman, A (2000) Implementing sustainability in service operations at Scandic Hotels, *Interfaces*, **30** (3), May/June, pp 202–14

Hewlett-Packard (2005) *Design for Environment Programme Description*, www.hp.com

Hopfenbeck, W (1993) *The Green Management Revolution: Lessons in excellence*, Prentice Hall, London

Howie, B (1994) Environmental impacts on logistics, in *An International Review of Logistics Practice and Issues*, ed G Brace, pp 53–55, Logistics Technology International, London

McIntyre, K (1999) Integrated supply chains and the environment: establishing performance measurement for strategic decision making application – the case of Xerox Ltd, Engineering doctorate thesis, University of Surrey, January

McIntyre, K *et al* (1998) Environmental performance indicators for integrated supply chains: the case of Xerox Ltd, *Supply Chain Management*, **3** (3), pp 149–56

Preston, L (2001) Sustainability at Hewlett-Packard: from theory to practice, *California Management Review*, **43** (3), Spring, pp 26–37

Purchasing (2001) Anheuser-Busch 'greens' its supply chain for cost savings, 17 May

Scott, A (2001) BASF aligns R&D with sustainable development, *Chemical Week*, **163** (12), March, pp 39–40

Senge, P, Carstedt, G and Porter, P (2001) Innovating our way to the next industrial evolution, *MIT Sloan Management Review*, **42** (2), Winter, pp 24–38

Social Investment Forum (1999), *Report on Socially Responsible Investing Trends in the United States*, www.socialinvest.org

Steger, U (1996) Managerial issues in closing the loop, *Business Strategy and the Environment*, **5** (4), December, pp 252–68

Vivian, S (2001) Opportunities from environmental management, Paper given at the Institution of Highways and Transportation, June, Cambridge

Walker, J and Farnworth, E (2001) Rating organisations: what is their impact on corporate sustainable strategy?, Business Strategy and the Environment conference, Sept, ERP Environment

Wu, H-J and Dunn, S (1995) Environmentally responsible logistics systems, *International Journal of Physical Distribution and Logistics Management*, **25** (2), pp 20–38

Zachary, K (2001) Toyota prods suppliers to be green, *Ward's Auto World*, **37** (7), July

16

Performance measurement and management in the supply chain

Alan Braithwaite, LCP Consulting

INTRODUCTION

If you cannot measure it, you cannot improve it. (Lord Kelvin, 1824–1907)

The measurement of business performance is deeply grounded in the backward-looking accounting disciplines of recording profit. As a means to enhance future profits, management now measures and reports on a wide range of business performance from customer perception to strategy consistency and adherence. At the operational level of customer service, the supply chain is the kernel of the business. Indeed, the potential from supply chain thinking and practice is founded in realigning operations through the chain to reduce total cost and maximize service and return on assets. So measurement is a core discipline and capability to provide a framework for defining realignment and reporting progress as to its attainment.

The supply chain is a complex system with many interfaces and dynamic interactions. It is a significant challenge to define the measures at each point in the chain that are appropriate and consistent with the overall desired results. In addition, the desired outcomes in terms of profit, service, stock, assets and costs cannot be managed directly; while there is a general expectation that sales growth will drive profits, the connections to stock, service and cost are less direct.

Performance management in the supply chain is about setting goals within and between functions that will lead to the desired results with balance and without conflict. Ideally, these goals are then embedded in the fabric of the management measurement and reporting of the functions of the firm and its customers, suppliers and service providers. Each function is responsible for delivering its part of the chain to the performance objectives; and when things do not work as planned, the requirement is for failures to be identified and recovery actions mounted. Learning organizations will take the lessons of actual performance and the experience of failure and recovery to adjust the goals across the chain, acting as 'stewards' of the supply chain. This stewardship role is a key responsibility for supply chain managers, since they often do not have functional responsibility for all the chain, albeit they are judged and rewarded on its overall performance.

There are two requirements of performance measurement in the supply chain: 1) understanding and embedding the value and importance of measurement in a strategic framework for supply chain management; and 2) creating a predictive framework of supply chain risk.

KEEPING SCORE – A BASIC MANAGEMENT PRINCIPLE

Revenue is vanity, profit is sanity, and cash is reality. (Anon)

The essence of business is to generate profits and cash from satisfying customers through its investment in assets and capabilities. Compared with investing deposits in a bank, investors seek a premium return on investment that reflects the additional risk of trading with the assets as compared with the relative safety of the bank. Investors can mitigate risk by holding a number of investments in a portfolio – since some investments will go up while others may go down. Investors generally cannot run the businesses in which they participate so they appoint management to do this for them. They therefore want information on the financial health – or otherwise – of the business so that they can make judgements on the management and the prospects of the investment. Banks want the same information in order to assess the viability of making loans, and governments want information so that they can exact the tax due.

The requirement for compilation and disclosure of performance, in terms of financial health, is therefore vital for the stakeholders. For quoted companies there is an industry of financial analysis that picks over the reported results and attempts to forecast the prospects. Accounting standards bodies such as the Securities and Exchange Commission in the United States and the Accounting Standards Authority in the UK regulate the preparation of company information. The trend has been to require increasing disclosure – not just financially but also in respect of subjects such as equal opportunities and environmental compliance achievement.

The importance of trust and integrity in the preparation of financial statements has been brought into sharp focus with the exposures of corporate catastrophe and financial deceit at Enron, WorldCom and Parmalat. The scale of these cases was unprecedented, but there have always been such cases – with Maxwell Communications and Atlantic Computers being UK examples from the last 20 years. Setting aside these high-profile scandals, there are two major difficulties with financial reporting. The first is that even financial reports prepared with absolute integrity can stretch the notion of 'profit' to meet the aspirations of management and option holders, or to defer tax liabilities. The second is that reported performance is historical and has been likened to driving down a highway steering through the rear-view mirror.

Performance measurement, reporting and management, therefore, need to come closer to the reality of serving customers and the operational demands of day-to-day decision making. In the context of both business direction and the detail of the supply chain, the task of measuring performance unpacks into many layers of detail; it is a subject in its own right.

THE BALANCED SCORECARD – THE STANDARD FOR GOAL SETTING AND MEASUREMENT

Since neither historical performance nor company budgets can be assured to bear directly on a business's long-term strategic objectives, a considerable effort in the development of models and theories has been dedicated to this problem. Among these are the Deming Prize (Isixsigma, 2006a), the Malcolm Baldrige Award (Isixsigma, 2006b), the European Foundation of Quality Management's business excellence model (EFQM, 2006) and the balanced scorecard (Kaplan and Norton, 1996). In addition, theories such as the learning organization (Senge, 1990) and knowledge management (Snowden, 2000) devote much energy to similar issues. All these models have strengths, depending on the purpose for which they are being used.

However, the balanced scorecard offers a contained and comprehensive approach to strategic direction and control issues; it is the reference for many corporations and it fits especially well with supply chain thinking.

A balanced scorecard provides a picture of a business by combining financial measures with assessments for customer satisfaction, key internal processes and organizational learning and growth (see Figure 16.1). It requires specific goals for customers in terms of time, quality, performance, service and cost as well as relationship, brand and product leadership. The internal perspective provides focus on the core competencies, processes, decisions, and actions that have the greatest impact on attaining customer satisfaction. The learning and growth perspective measures continual improvements to people, systems and processes. Sitting above this framework are the financial measures, which are essential for showing whether executives have correctly identified and constructed their measures in the three preceding areas.

Fundamentally a balanced scorecard should have a balance between output measures (financial and customer) and input measures (performance drivers, such as value proposition, internal processes, learning and growth). Every measure selected for a scorecard should be part of a link of cause-and-effect relationships, ending in financial objectives that represent a strategic theme for the business. Kaplan and Norton (1992) outline four key processes that the balanced scorecard relies on to connect short-term activities to long-term objectives:

1. *Translating the vision.* Managers are required to translate their vision into actual measurements linked directly to the people who will realize the vision.
2. *Communicating and linking.* The scorecard indicates what the organization is trying to achieve for both shareholders and customers. The high-level strategy map is translated into business unit scorecards and eventually personal scorecards so that individuals understand how their personal goals and performance support the overall strategy.
3. *Business planning.* Once the performance measures for the four perspectives have been agreed, the company identifies the key drivers of the desired outcome and defines the milestones that mark progress towards achieving their strategic goal.
4. *Feedback and learning.* This allows for regular performance reviews to enable continuous improvement of the strategy and its execution.

In summary, the scorecard puts strategy and vision, not control, at the centre. The measures are designed to pull people towards the overall vision. This methodology is consistent with the approach of supply chain management by helping managers overcome traditional functional

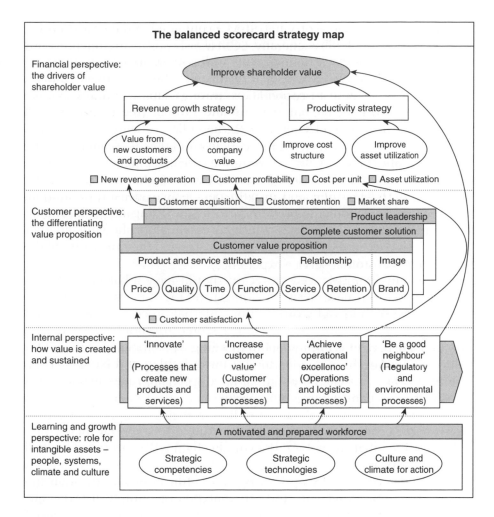

Figure 16.1 Kaplan and Norton's balanced scorecard framework

barriers and ultimately leads to improved decision making and problem solving.

FUNDAMENTAL CONCEPTS OF SUPPLY CHAIN MANAGEMENT AND MEASUREMENT

There are countless definitions of logistics and supply chain management in circulation, with the two terms broadly interchangeable – but there is not a consistent view of what SCM really is or should be (Cooper, Lambert and Pagh, 1997). Generally, SCM transcends firms, functions and business – with a working definition of 'A process orientation to managing business in an integrated way that transcends the boundaries of firms and functions, leading to cooperation, through-chain business process synchronization, effective ranging and new product introduction, as well as managing the entire physical logistics agenda'.

The mechanism by which the network of entities, which together make up the supply chain, works is through shared information and closely aligned processes. The vision for these networks is that they are characterized by high levels of communication and transparency supported by synchronous operations and performance measurement and management. This brings us to:

- improved customer service experience;
- reduced inventories;
- lower operating costs; and
- improved use of fixed assets.

The ultimate benefit is improvement in a mix of profitability, shareholder value and market share – depending on the strategic priorities of the firm. The implication is that the potential of supply chain management can transform a company in terms of its performance; the leverage through the combination of many small (albeit radical in their conception) improvements in the economic structure of a company can be remarkable.

The big idea that sits behind the supply chain concept is a move from function to process; the principle is that effectiveness of the chain is enhanced dramatically by optimizing across functions and through the whole chain compared with the accumulation of optimized functions. Striking a balance between functional and total business is a crucial dimension of SCM, although breaking down the barriers between functions to improve supply chain integration is not a substitute for functional excellence. Companies need to secure both dimensions – retaining and improving their competence in all the functions in the supply chain.

Optimizing individual functional performance can prevent the achievement of the most cost- and service-effective supply chain (Braithwaite and Wilding, 2004). Not only that, but it will also most likely insert further undesirable volatility and actually increase cost. Traditional functional methods of planning will never lead to breakthrough thinking in supply chain design and, indeed, are a cause of organizational problems. So the requirement is for the corporation to measure the end-to-end cost-to-serve – at least internally, but preferably looking inside both its customers' and its suppliers' operations – to enable a fundamental rebalancing on a holistic

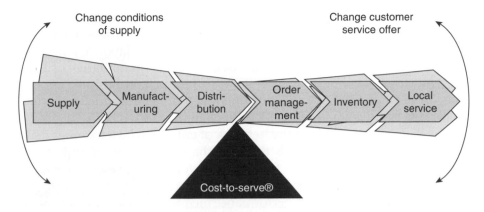

Figure 16.2   Balancing the supply chain
Source: LCP Consulting

basis that will deliver the required service at the lowest total cost (see Figure 16.2).

Performance measurement and management are a critical component of this rebalancing effort and a fundamental part of the supply chain concept. They require balance and overall goal setting. Supply chain performance measurement and management are the operational microclimate of the balanced scorecard of Kaplan and Norton.

MASTERING THE COMPLEXITY OF SUPPLY CHAIN AND LOGISTICS PERFORMANCE MANAGEMENT

Supply chain management at this microclimate level is complex in its detail. The biggest challenge in setting up measurement and management programmes is mastering that complexity, to create an internally consistent framework of goals that reflect the true relationships of cause and effect.

Figure 16.3 shows a framework of cost and performance based on structural determinants and management determinants. The idea of structural and management determinants – and the distinction between them – is important. Structural determinants relate to the 'business we are in' expressed as products and customers. Here the choices for management are limited; if you are in the fertilizer or seeds business you have farmers and merchants as customers and deliver to farms. The characteristics of the product are well defined and the nature of demand

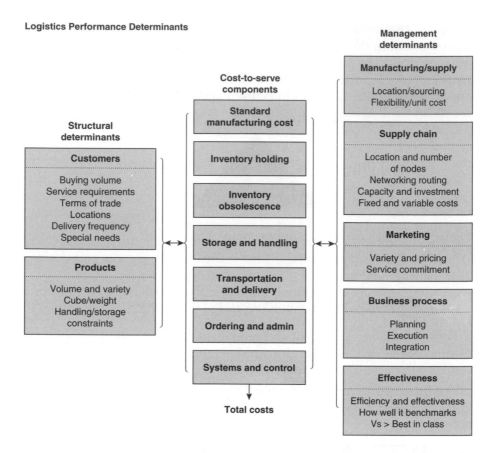

Figure 16.3 The complexity of supply chain and logistics, viewed through determinants

is broadly local and national. In contrast, microchip manufacturers operate on an international scale using airfreight and with billions of dollars invested in plant. The fundamental difference in the products is driven home by the cost per tonne of microchips being more than $500,000, whereas the cost per tonne for fertilizer is typically less than $300.

Management determinants reflect the areas where management has choices to make within the constraints of the nature of the business. There are big strategy decisions to be made here in relation to sourcing, capacity investment and characteristics, marketing positioning and service levels, business process design and operational effectiveness. These choices interact with each other and the structural determinants to drive the end-to-end cost and performance. The scale and degree of interaction across the various areas of cost and performance are multivariate and complex. The challenge that emerges for performance measurement and management in the supply chain is to define correctly the relationships and key drivers in the context of the choices that the company has made in its markets. From the definition of these relationships arises the precise specification of the measures to be used and the values to be set as goals for the individual functional managers.

THE PRINCIPLE OF INPUT AND OUTPUT MEASURES

The definition of cause and effect is important. The nature of the complexity illustrated in Figure 16.3 is such that the measures of effect are driven by the structure of the business and the key choices and designs that management make.

The implications of this observation are that the ultimate performance measures on which the stakeholders judge the business are not open to direct action. For example, we cannot act directly on:

- sales revenue and the economies that go with scale without dealing with the levels of customer satisfaction that are achieved in terms of inventory availability and service turnaround;
- inventory levels in the chain without dealing with processes such as forecasting accuracy and forecasting frequency and horizon, and inventory record accuracy;
- cost-to-serve by product and customer without having designed the network for sourcing and fulfilment.

These points make the distinction between input and output measures. Of course we need both to see if the actions taken have achieved the desired result. But there is limited value in just measuring the outputs without having first identified the cause-and-effect relationships, and the input measures that are likely to generate the desired change.

Figure 16.4 illustrates a simple example of input and output measures. The input measures reflect the major changes that were effected in a company, and the output measures were the consequences of these actions, and illustrate the shareholder value that was created. The strategic nature of the input measures is immediately clear, as is the improvement that was attained in this manufacturing business. All of these improvements were achieved through a long-term commitment to measurement, stock policy adherence and stewardship, leading to the rebalancing of the company's supply chain.

Measure	Start	Finish
Input measures		
Forecast accuracy	Poor	Improved but less important
Manufacturing change time	8 hours	15 minutes
New product introduction	Months	Weeks
Logistics structure	3 depots	Single national site
Output measures		
Sales		+10%
Customer service (OTIF)	96%	99%
Stock	12 weeks	2 weeks
Obsolescence	High	Minimal
Distribution costs	14% of turnover	9% of turnover
Manufacturing unit cost		Reduced by 20%

Figure 16.4 Input and output measures in a performance improvement case

SETTING GOALS ACROSS THE CHAIN THROUGH SERVICE LEVEL AGREEMENTS

The question most often asked in relation to performance measurement is 'How should functional goals be set in the chain to secure the potential?' And there is a further series of sub-questions arising from this major question:

- How does a function see its role and contribution to improving the whole supply chain?
- What levels of visibility should be given, between functions, of the goals and attainment by others?
- How does a function influence the performance of other members in the chain that can impact its own performance but are out of its direct control?
- Who sets the measures of performance across the chain?

The idea of inter-functional service level agreements (SLAs) is designed to resolve the first three of these questions. SLAs create a framework in which the various functions within a company and between organizations – both customers and suppliers – are measured against meaningful objectives that will generate overall performance improvement.

The first big idea embedded in such SLAs is that they are not just sequential between players in the physical chain, but also recognize the obligations of every member of the team to the others, whether or not they are next in line. The second big idea is that SLAs create a team environment; all players know their places in the side, the contribution that they make and the dependencies they have with other positions.

Figure 16.5 shows the standard conceptual framework of a sequential chain that, by this definition of SLAs, is incomplete; it also shows an example matrix of the SLAs that really need to exist. Each box in the SLA framework needs to be populated with input measures as they reflect the relationship that the functions have with each other. The entries are not symmetrical, as the obligations of the functions in the context of the overall goals are not mutual. So, for example, the relationship between sales and marketing and production planning is that sales and marketing must produce a forecast on time and to the agreed level of accuracy, while production planning's commitment to sales and marketing is to turn that forecast into available product through the creation of timely and economic schedules. Equally, manufacturing will have commitments to the business, including sales and marketing, that relate to adherence to schedule, yield and quality performance; but in return manufacturing is entitled to expect acceptable levels of demand volatility and schedule stability from sales and marketing and demand planning.

It is important to note that the SLAs are entirely about input measures such as adherence to schedule, quality and lead time. It is changes to these measures and improvements in performance that drive value through the company's supply chain and its output measures of profit and value.

The creation of this matrix, even in the most rudimentary form, and making it available to the entire business – together with published current performance and future targets – answer the first two of the sub-questions.

The process of setting up the SLA matrix and populating the targets and the performance actually achieved is the way that the functions can start to resolve the tensions relating to the impact they may have on each other. This is a crucial organizational process – correctly represented at board level – and it is this person (or small team) that sets the matrix in conjunction with the functional heads, and then monitors attainment and institutes corrective action where necessary. This is the idea of supply chain stewardship. The steward holds the total vision for supply chain improvement for the firm and the individual functional performances that will deliver the result.

Integrating the chain through SLAs

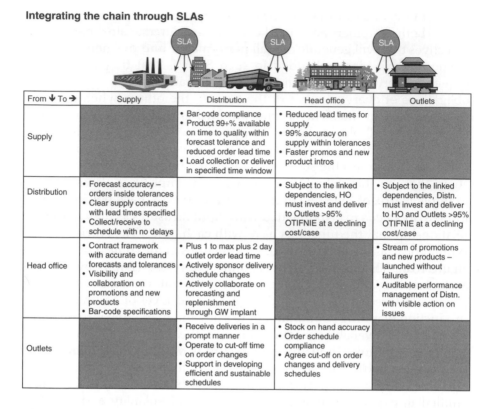

From ↓ To →	Supply	Distribution	Head office	Outlets
Supply		• Bar-code compliance • Product 99+% available on time to quality within forecast tolerance and reduced order lead time • Load collection or deliver in specified time window	• Reduced lead times for supply • 99% accuracy on supply within tolerances • Faster promos and new product intros	
Distribution	• Forecast accuracy – orders inside tolerances • Clear supply contracts with lead times specified • Collect/receive to schedule with no delays		• Subject to the linked dependencies, HO must invest and deliver to Outlets >95% OTIFNIE at a declining cost/case	• Subject to the linked dependencies, Distn. must invest and deliver to HO and Outlets >95% OTIFNIE at a declining cost/case
Head office	• Contract framework with accurate demand forecasts and tolerances • Visibility and collaboration on promotions and new products • Bar-code specifications	• Plus 1 to max plus 2 day outlet order lead time • Actively sponsor delivery schedule changes • Actively collaborate on forecasting and replenishment through GW implant		• Stream of promotions and new products – launched without failures • Auditable performance management of Distn. with visible action on issues
Outlets		• Receive deliveries in a prompt manner • Operate to cut-off time on order changes • Support in developing efficient and sustainable schedules	• Stock on hand accuracy • Order schedule compliance • Agree cut-off on order changes and delivery schedules	

Figure 16.5   The conventional sequential supply chain relationship and the SLA matrix
© *Source*: LCP Consulting 2005

The SLA matrix needs to be maintained as a living framework that responds to external forces, actual performance and continuous learning. This is a full-time organizational role. If supply chain management also has direct functional reports, then it will need to isolate the stewardship role within its own organization to ensure that balance and impartiality are achieved.

THE DELIVERY, RECOVERY AND STEWARDSHIP MODEL

Putting the SLA matrix into action is the process and activity of tracking performance against targets and identifying opportunities for improvement, not just looking back at past performance. The focus of performance

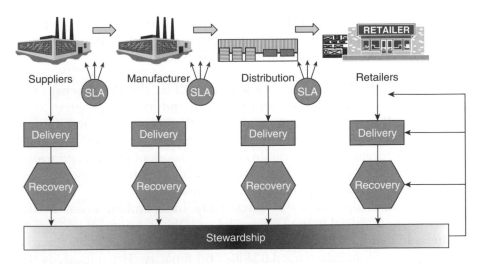

Figure 16.6   The delivery, recovery and stewardship (DRS) model
Source: Logistics Consulting Partners Ltd 2001 – all rights reserved

management should be the future: what do you need to be able to do and how can you do things better?

The delivery, recovery and stewardship (DRS) model is a way of institutionalizing measurement across the business. Figure 16.6 is a simple representation of the DRS model designed to illustrate the cycle of each function, measuring its delivery against its SLA in the matrix and including the cost performance goals. Reports including the identification of failures and the impact of recovery actions are produced at the functional level and then consolidated by the supply chain steward. Recovery is an important activity with the learning that comes with it. It is critically important for organizations to recognize and plan for things that go wrong. The stewardship role is to feed back to the functions the impact of overall performance and propose changes to the SLAs, delivery performance and the means of recovery.

The model is consistent with the so-called Shewhart or plan–do–check–act (PDCA) cycle, based on continuous improvement:

1. Business understanding and strategic directions: *plan* the process.
2. Running the operation to try to deliver in line with the plan: *do* the operation and record the results.
3. Performance reporting against plan and interpretation of results: *check* by analysis and reporting of performance according to key business drivers.

4. Tactical and strategic realignment: *act* to initiate improvement efforts based on the lessons learned from experience. These experiences feed into the new plan, since PDCA is a cyclical process.

In summary, the DRS model is a way to capture the supply chain improvement vision for the firm and to record and manage progress to its attainment. It may seem daunting and potentially complex – and if this is the case, the key is to start with the simplest possible framework and build from it as the organization learns. In other words, adopt the same principles of plan–do–check–act to the process of planning and measurement across the chain as are being applied to the chain itself.

The stewardship role as a functionally independent agent in the organization is crucial to the DRS model, and this is a difficult position to define and maintain in the organization. The person who holds the role will require vision, interpersonal skills and tenacity. The role needs the highest level of board sponsorship, and the results of DRS need to be a standard part of the board agenda. It is at this point that supply chain management and corporate strategy meet.

DEFINING SPECIFIC METRICS ACROSS THE CHAIN

The input and output measures described earlier are the high-level corporate cause-and-effect metrics for the supply chain. The measures in the SLAs are primarily about quality, compliance and time. The stewardship role requires these measures and adds cost measures to the portfolio. In this section, the specifics of the measures that can be applied across the supply chain are unpacked and described.

The supply chain and logistics professional and the corporate steward of the chain will want to develop an overview of the chain; a useful way to think about this is as a 'dashboard' or control panel for the business. This idea is illustrated in Figure 16.7, and many executives find the preparation of such diagrams valuable in identifying the performance issues in the chain and describing them to their colleagues. Measures may need to reflect both changes over time and performance across the product range of both customers and suppliers.

A further important point in relation to this overview is that, while supply chain rebalancing via SLAs will be one of the key drivers for competitive advantage, firms must also recognize that an equal and parallel emphasis should remain on attaining functional excellence. The goals of functional excellence, however, will be tempered at the margin through

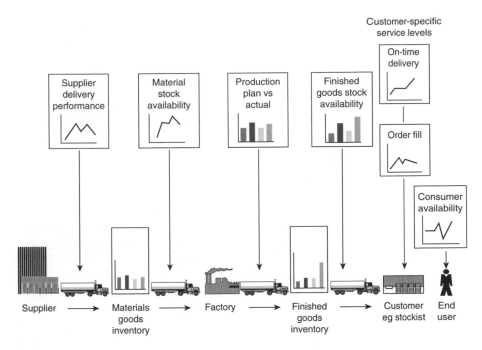

Figure 16.7 Viewing supply chain metrics across the chain

an understanding that such aims can lead to supply chain sub-optimization; the SLAs are developed over time to eliminate potential conflicts.

Although the measures themselves are generic for most businesses, the precise situation and issues for each firm will vary based on its competitive situation, technology and product-market characteristics. It is helpful to think of a hierarchy of measures across the chain in terms of both input and output measures:

- Level 1 measures should provide headline measures for the supply chain, such as orders on time in full with no invoice errors (OTIFNIE) and stock cover set in a balanced way that supports the vision for change.
- Level 2 measures should be used to provide further insight into the results of level 1, such as quantity fill percentage, line fill percentage and invoice accuracy.
- Finally, level 3 measures should provide diagnostics for use in problem resolution and improvement processes, such as requests for credit, clear-up rate and number of days out of stock by SKU.

Figure 16.8 provides examples of level 1 and 2 performance metrics across a typical retail supply chain.

Suppliers	Manufacturing	Forecasting	Inbound freight
▼ Unit cost ▼ OTIFNIE % ▼ Spread of failure ▼ Lead time of supply ▼ Fixed and firm schedule horizon ▼ Flexibility inside fixed horizon	▼ Plant utilization ▼ Output vs standard ▼ Cost/unit of manufacturing ▼ Overhead recovery to plan % time used in changeovers ▼ Conformance to plan ▼ Fixed and firm schedule horizons	▼ Forecast accuracy at +1 week, +2 weeks, +1 month, +2 months, +3 months ▼ By SKU and family ▼ Demand volatility coefficient of variation ▼ With and without promotions	▼ Truck utilization % tonnes or cube carried vs capacity % working time used ▼ Cost/delivery ▼ Cost/cu m or tonne ▼ Dispatch to delivery time

Suppliers Manufacturer ?

Distribution centre	Stock	Freight	Service
▼ Full cost per case ▼ Full cost per pallet ▼ Fixed cost/sq m ▼ Full cost/man hr ▼ Picks/man hr ▼ Labour utilization % ▼ Space utilization % ▼ Throughput utilization % ▼ Order-to-despatch time	▼ Weeks of cover ▼ Days of sale ▼ Stock turns ▼ OOS lines & % ▼ Stock > 26 wks ▼ Obsolescence/ write-offs % ▼ Stock accuracy (sku, qty and location)	▼ Truck util'n % tonnes or cube carried vs capacity ▼ Deliveries per day ▼ % working time used ▼ Cost/delivery ▼ Cost/cu m or tonne	▼ OTIFNIE % ▼ Order-to-delivery TAT days ▼ Line fill % ▼ Qty fill % ▼ Order fill accuracy % ▼ Invoice errors/ credit notes % ▼ % to schedule/ commitment

Manufacturer Distribution Retail distribution Retailers

Figure 16.8 Sample level 1 and 2 metrics containing both input and output measures

Figure 16.8 starts to provide insight into the levels of detail that are involved and can be used to challenge the connections between functions and the real drivers. So, for example, the figure shows both 'On time in full' (OTIF) and 'Order to delivery turnaround time' (TAT). It is immediately obvious that the longer the TAT, the higher should be the OTIF – since

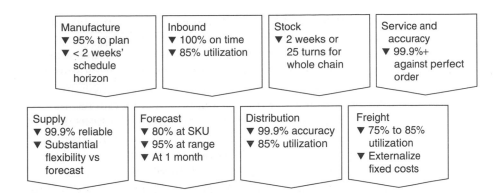

Figure 16.9 A sample logistical balanced scorecard

there is more time to get it right. But at the same time the longer the TAT, the lower should be the inventory, as the more time manufacturing has to respond to actual demand. TAT is therefore an input measure, and it is also one that management may want to change, as faster service is likely to be more competitive and create increased demand. In the same vein, measures of plant, distribution centre and transportation efficiency will be influenced by customer order turnaround time, forecast accuracy and plant changeover time – all of which are input measures.

Having decided on the appropriate metrics of performance, it is necessary to ensure that these individual measures are set in a balanced way to provide an overall picture of supply chain performance and support the business in moving to its goals. Figure 16.9 shows an example of a balanced set of objective measures for a fast-moving consumer goods company.

Very high service performance with low levels of stock is secured by quite high levels of forecast accuracy, very short manufacturing schedule horizons and exceptional supplier performance. High levels of accuracy are also essential, and the area sacrificed is that of distribution and freight utilization. Setting these measures consistently – having understood the relationships – is the key to avoiding functional conflicts that can cause sub-optimal performance. Examples of this are:

● Stockholding targets that are set too low will disable customer service attainment and reduce the number of orders fulfilled on time in full.
● Freight utilization and cost targets may delay shipments, leading to increased stock and a negative impact on customer service.
● Manufacturing unit cost goals may drive up stocks and downstream distribution costs because of long production runs and infrequent line changes.

With performance metrics established, greater focus can be put on supply chain issues. This also aids in benchmarking by identifying current and best practice in companies and their supply chains before using some of the level 3 diagnostic metrics to develop an improvement programme.

Two of the biggest barriers to a successful performance measurement and management programme are the compilation of data, and its analysis and interpretation. Typically this involves hundreds of thousands of transactions, many hundreds of general ledger codes, some thousands of stock-keeping units, and hundreds of customers and suppliers. All these can be linked through a number of plants and distribution centres.

Measurement and reporting used to be labour-intensive, but developments in mass data storage – often referred to as data warehousing – have provided a new platform. Changes in recent years have been revolutionary in terms of low-cost data storage, easy-to-program queries, and graphical programs to represent the outputs. Skills and experience in data warehousing are being accumulated, and new software environments are being launched to bring data together from different sources to give an end-to-end picture.

FUTURE DIRECTIONS IN PERFORMANCE MEASUREMENT

The major challenges for performance measurement in the supply chain for the future rest in: 1) integrating performance management into the fabric of the organization to drive supply chain strategy development and implementation; and 2) creating predictive measurement frameworks through which the corporation can identify the levels of risk that are inherent in its supply chains. Both of these areas are 'work in progress' in terms of the development of a complete understanding and operational frameworks through which they can be applied.

The word 'integration' is overused in supply chain management, without great clarity as to its meaning and implications. The LCP strategic crystal has been used successfully to address this question by describing the elements of an integrated supply chain strategy and showing how they interact to deliver business value in terms of customer satisfaction and economic value-add. Figure 16.10 shows the crystal, with the key elements:

- Business processes – the processes of generating planning and execution instructions through the chain that, if correctly designed, will increase customer service and reduce inventories and capital

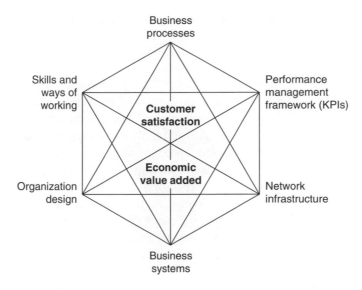

Figure 16.10   The strategic supply chain crystal
Source: LCP consulting 2002

applied. Business process redesign in supply chain management is focused on the principles of time compression and simplification. Business processes are crucially dependent on systems, organization and KPIs, three other points in the crystal. Business processes are key input measures and a major part of the SLAs.

- Business systems – the computer information systems that are applied must serve the business processes and the organization, support the network and inform the performance measurement environment.
- Network infrastructure – the supply chain network is the key to the cost performance in the chain and is enabled by the processes and systems. The organization design must align to the network to enable the lowest-cost operation.
- Performance management framework through consistent and appropriate KPIs is central to an effective supply chain strategy, as we have seen in this chapter. The process of performance management enables the organization and is dependent on the systems and the processes.
- Organization design is a most under-represented area of supply chain strategy. An organization that is aligned to the strategy and is served by the systems, processes and KPIs is central to realizing supply chain value. As businesses move from a functional to a process orientation, the boundaries of traditional functional power are challenged and tensions are exposed. The SLA approach can help resolve these tensions

Figure 16.11   The supply chain risk honeycomb

since functional control is not required under that model. However, the stewardship role is mandatory and, as discussed earlier, it must be positioned in the organization with both power and independence.

● Skills and ways of working are the final facet of the crystal and, like organization, are under-represented. The skills and behaviours to move to a supply chain ethic, from function to process, are profoundly different from those that have been trained into management over many years.

Another major challenge in performance management is for boards to recognize the risk that is endemic in their supply chains. Singhal and Hendricks (2000) have shown that supply chain catastrophes are common and that they destroy shareholder value by an average 20 per cent. With companies' supply chains being run ever more leanly, there is less room for unexpected errors. The requirement exists to evaluate the risk in a corporation's supply; Figure 16.11 shows a conceptual model (Braithwaite, 2003).

The underlying principle is that there are external determinants of risk that relate to the business environment, and there are internal determinants that relate to how the organization is aligned to its external environment. As an example of how this model works, it should be immediately clear that a company with a volatile market and supplies on long lead times with extended planning, scheduling and manufacturing processes and a poor record of performance management is riding for a fall. In contrast, a company operating in a market where demand is stable and competition well defined can accommodate longer lead times from suppliers and more rigid internal processes.

Risks external to the corporation can be summarized as follows:

- *Demand risk* relates to disturbances to the flow of product, information and cash emanating from within the network, between the focal firm and its market. In particular, it relates to the processes, controls, asset and infrastructure dependencies of the organizations downstream.
- *Supply risk* is the upstream equivalent of demand risk; it relates to disturbances to the flow of product or information emanating within the network upstream of the focal firm.
- *Environmental risk* is the risk associated with external and, from the firm's perspective, uncontrollable events.

Risks internal to the corporation relate both to how the firm addresses the external risks and to its competences to plan and execute its own business:

- *Processes* are the sequences of value-adding activities undertaken by the firm. The execution of these processes is dependent on internally owned or managed assets and on a functioning infrastructure. Process risk relates to disruptions to these processes.
- *Controls* are the assumptions, rules, systems and procedures that govern how an organization exerts control over the processes – and in the supply chain they may be order quantities, batch sizes, safety stock policies etc. Control risk is the risk arising from the application or misapplication of these rules.
- *Mitigation* is a hedge against risk built into the operations and, therefore, the lack of mitigating tactics is a risk in itself. *Contingency* is the existence of a prepared plan in the event of a risk being identified.

CONCLUSION

The potential for improvement through the development of performance management metrics across the supply chain is a key differentiator of change capability and organizational agility. Firms that develop supply chain measurement, as a core business competence associated with strategic objectives, will have a strong foundation for defining realignment internally and with both customers and suppliers.

The combined use of supply chain performance metrics, balanced scorecards, and the delivery, recovery and stewardship framework provides the capability to report on improvement, understand the factors that are driven by the change and identify supply chain management best practice.

There are six key points to hold in focus when developing a supply chain performance management framework:

- No single measure defines supply chain performance – there are many dimensions to measure.
- Measures can be in conflict – accentuating rather than breaking functional differences.
- The need is to obtain balance throughout the supply chain and be prepared to change.
- Measuring the overall performance at input and output levels is a key first step to making improvements.
- This requires considerable investment of time and commitment.
- Measurement and its interpretation are valuable and difficult skills that organizations should develop and nurture.

Organizations that have persevered with supply chain measurement and management have experienced sustained improvements in business performance.

References

Braithwaite, A (2003) Supply chain vulnerability self-assessment workbook, Cranfield School of Management on behalf of the Department for Transport, March, pp 249–59

Braithwaite, A and Wilding, R (2004) Laws of logistics and supply chain management, in *The Financial Times Handbook of Management*, 3rd edn, ed E Crainer and D Dearlove, Pearson, London

Cooper, MC, Lambert, DM and Pagh, JD (1997) Supply chain management: more than a new name for logistics, *International Journal of Logistics Management*, **8** (1), pp 1–4

European Foundation of Quality Management (EFQM) (2006) *European Quality Awards*, EFQM, wwwefqm.org

Isixsigma (2006a) *The Deming Prize Check List*, www.isixsigma.com

Isixsigma (2006b) *Malcolm Baldrige National Quality Award*, www.isixsigma.com

Kaplan, RS and Norton, DP (1992) The balanced scorecard: measures that drive performance, *Harvard Business Review*, January–February **70** (1), pp 71–79

Kaplan, RS and Norton, DP (1996) *Translating Strategy into Action: The balanced scorecard*, Harvard Business School Press, Cambridge, MA

Senge, PM (1990) *The Fifth Discipline*, Doubleday, New York

Singhal, VR and Hendricks, K (2000) *Report on Supply Chain Glitches and Shareholder Value Destruction*, December, Dupree College of Management, Georgia Institute of Technology

Snowden, D (2000) *Liberating Knowledge*, Institute of Knowledge Management, Toronto

17

Optimizing the road freight transport system

Alan McKinnon, Heriot-Watt University

INTRODUCTION

In an ideal world all trucks would run fully laden on every kilometre travelled. If this could be achieved the economic and environmental costs of road freight movement would be substantially reduced. Large potential benefits can therefore accrue to individual companies and the wider community from initiatives that improve the utilization of vehicle capacity.

In this chapter we will examine the various ways in which vehicle utilization can be assessed, consider the reasons why so many trucks run empty or only partially loaded, and outline a series of measures that companies can take to attain higher levels of vehicle fill.

ASSESSING THE UTILIZATION OF VEHICLE FLEETS

Different indices can be used to measure the utilization of vehicle fleets, each giving a different impression of transport efficiency.

Tonne-kilometres per vehicle per annum

This index generally presents the trucking industry in a positive light. It is essentially a productivity indicator, measuring the average amount of work done annually by trucks. In the UK, for instance, it increased fivefold between the early 1950s and late 1990s, mainly as a result of companies taking advantage of increases in maximum truck weight and running their vehicles for more hours of the day. Since 1999 this index has 'plateaued', suggesting that new initiatives may be required to intensify truck usage (DfT, 2009). This productivity measure, however, presents only a partial view of vehicle utilization. It takes no account of the proportion of the available carrying capacity actually used during the year. A vehicle with greater capacity could record higher productivity despite having inferior utilization, as illustrated in Table 17.1. This important difference between productivity and utilization is discussed in detail by Caplice and Sheffi (1994).

Weight-based loading factor

This is generally expressed as the ratio of the actual weight of goods carried to the maximum weight that could have been carried on a laden trip. When this ratio is plotted through time, a less rosy picture of transport efficiency emerges. In the UK, for example, average load factors (for trucks with gross weights over 3.5 tonnes) declined from 63 per cent in 1990 to 57 per cent in 2004. This load factor is only a partial measure of vehicle utilization, however. As it is an exclusively weight-based measure it takes no account of the use of vehicle space/deck-area or the proportion of vehicle-km run empty.

Space-utilization

Many low-density products fill the available vehicle space (or 'cube out') long before the maximum permitted weight is reached. In sectors

Table 17.1 Comparison vehicle productivity and utilization measures

Gross weight	Max payload (tonnes)	Annual distance travelled (km)	Average load tonnes	Productivity Tonne-km/ veh/year	% Capacity utilization Actual t-km/ Max t-km
32 tonnes	20	100,000	16	1,600,000	80%
40 tonnes	26	100,000	18	1,800,000	69%

characterized by low-density products, weight-based load factors tend to underestimate the true level of utilization. Where there are tight limits on the stacking height of the product, loading is usually constrained much more by the available deck area than by the cubic capacity. This deck area, for example, can be covered with pallets stacked to a height of 1.5 metres, leaving a metre or more of wasted space above them.

Very little research has been done on the space utilization of vehicles and few attempts made to collect volumetric data on road freight flows. In a study conducted in the Netherlands and Sweden, Samuelsson and Tilanus (1997) asked a panel of industry experts to estimate the average utilization of trucks, engaged in less-than-truckload deliveries, with reference to a series of space-related indices. This revealed that cube utilization was typically very low at around 28 per cent. On average, however, just over 80 per cent of deck area was occupied and 70 per cent of the available pallet positions filled. It was therefore mainly in the vertical dimension that space was being wasted, with average load heights reaching only 47 per cent of the maximum. A survey of 53 fleets, comprising roughly 3,500 vehicles, in the UK food supply chain in 2002 found that, on loaded trips, an average of 69 per cent of the deck area and 76 per cent of the available height was utilized, corresponding to a mean cube utilization of 52 per cent (McKinnon and Ge, 2004).

Empty running

The most obvious form of vehicle under-utilization is empty running. Typically around a third of vehicle-km are run empty, though this proportion varies with length of haul, type of vehicle, industrial sector and the nature of the delivery operation (McKinnon, 1996). Empty running generally occurs when operators are unable to find a return load. Unlike passengers, who usually return to their starting point, most freight travels only in one direction. In some countries, such as the UK, the proportion of truck-km travelled empty has been declining. In Britain, for example, it fell from 33 per cent in 1980 to 27 per cent in 2004, yielding significant economic and environmental benefits. Other things being equal, if the empty running percentage had remained at its 1980 level, road haulage costs in 2004 would have been £1.2 billion higher and an extra 1 million tonnes of CO_2 would have been emitted by trucks (McKinnon, 2006). In recent years, however, the downward trend in empty running has gone into reverse, raising the percentage of empty truck-km to almost 29 per cent in 2008 (DfT, 2009). This runs counter to an average forecast made by a panel of 100 logistics specialists surveyed in 2008 that the empty running percentage would drop from 27 to 22 per cent between 2007 and 2020 (Piecyk and McKinnon, 2009).

FACTORS CONSTRAINING VEHICLE UTILIZATION

The dominant constraints on vehicle utilization are as follows.

Demand fluctuations

Variability of demand over daily, weekly, monthly and seasonal cycles is one of the main causes of the under-utilization of vehicle capacity. Vehicles acquired with sufficient space or weight to accommodate peak loads inevitably spend much of their time running with excess capacity. Companies subject mainly to seasonal fluctuations can hire additional vehicles or outsource more of their transport at peak periods, allowing them to carry a regular base-load of traffic on their own vehicles during the year. For those exposed to demand volatility on a daily basis, the efficient management of transport capacity presents a much greater challenge. Figure 17.1, for example, shows fluctuations in the daily demand for trucks imposed on a major distributor of metal products over the period of a month. The average daily requirement was for 150 vehicles, but on particular days it varied between 96 and 190 vehicles. The company in question was often only informed at 4 pm on Day 1 how many vehicles would be required for deliveries by noon on Day 2. It is clearly very difficult to maintain high load factors across a vehicle fleet subject to this

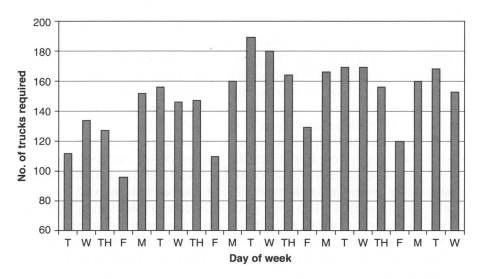

Figure 17.1 Variations in the daily demand for trucks experienced by a major distributor of metal products

degree of demand variability. Such variability is common in industries characterized by just-in-time (JIT) replenishment, as discussed under the next heading.

Just-in-time delivery

The replenishment of supplies in smaller quantities more frequently within shorter lead times has tended to depress vehicle load factors. Companies have often been prepared to accept lower vehicle utilization and higher transport costs in return for large reductions in inventory and other productivity benefits resulting from JIT. There is, nevertheless, disagreement in the literature over the extent to which JIT has impaired transport efficiency. Simulation modelling work by Swenseth and Buffa (1990), for example, suggested that transport costs were inflated by JIT, whereas Ansari and Heckel (1987) claim that, in practice, they were reduced. By reconfiguring their inbound logistics, companies can mitigate the adverse effects of JIT on transport efficiency, as illustrated by Nissan car company (Energy Efficiency Best Practice Programme, 1998a).

Unreliability of delivery schedules

Where schedules are unreliable, transport managers are naturally reluctant to arrange backhauls or more complex collection and delivery routes within which higher degrees of load consolidation can be achieved. Companies understandably prioritize outbound distribution to customers and fear that a vehicle engaged in backhauling may not be repositioned in time to handle the next delivery. Available survey evidence suggests that the probability of a delivery being delayed can be relatively high. In the course of seven transport 'key performance indicator' surveys conducted in the UK between 2002 and 2007, operational data were collected on 55,820 road journey legs in a range of freight sectors. Twenty-six per cent of these legs were subject to a delay and these delays averaged 41 minutes (McKinnon et al, 2009). Thirty-five per cent of these delays were caused mainly by traffic congestion on the road network. Most of the delays, however, occurred at the reception bays of factories, distribution centres and shops, where 'backdoor congestion' increases the average length and variability of loading and off-loading times. In other countries characterized by much longer journey length and transit times, delays of this magnitude would be unlikely to deter backloading and consolidation initiatives, particularly as the potential rewards would be much greater.

Vehicle size and weight restrictions

As noted above, some loads reach the maximum weight limit before all the space in the vehicle is occupied. Conversely, some low-density loads exhaust the available space before the legal weight limit is reached. This results in under-utilization of the vehicle in terms of either volume or weight.

Handling requirements

Many companies sacrifice vehicle utilization for handling efficiency. For example, by using roll-cages rather than wooden pallets supermarket chains can substantially reduce handling times and costs but at the expense of around 15–20 per cent lower space-utilization in shop delivery vehicles.

Incompatibility of vehicles and products

It is clearly not possible to transport a return load of bulk liquids in a box van or to consolidate part-loads of fertilizer and hanging garments. The need for specialist handling and/or refrigeration and rules governing cross-contamination restrict the proportion of the truck fleet that can be used for particular loads.

Health and safety regulations

The weight and dimensions of loads are partly constrained by health and safety regulations designed to ensure the welfare of employees.

Capacity constraints at company premises

Often the size of load is constrained by the available storage capacity at either the origin or the destination of the trip, more commonly the latter. Tanks and silos at farms or factories, for example, may not be able to hold a full truck load, while many retailers have compressed back-storeroom areas to maximize the front-of-shop sales floor. Warehouse racking systems, particularly in the fast-moving consumer goods sector, have a standard slot height for pallets of 1.7 metres. This limits pallets to a height significantly below the vertical clearance of at least 2.4 metres in most articulated trucks.

Lack of knowledge of backloading and load consolidation opportunities

Many of these opportunities are missed because carriers are simply unaware of them. It is hardly surprising, therefore, that roughly half the return loads carried by road in the UK are generated internally from within the same company (Lex Transfleet, 2002). Companies have traditionally relied on informal methods of finding external backloads, most commonly 'word-of-mouth'.

Poor coordination of the purchasing, sales and logistics functions

Opportunities for backloading are seldom discussed in the context of trade negotiations between companies. Purchasing departments typically regard inbound delivery as the responsibility of the supplier and fail to explore with logistics managers possible synergies with the transport operations of vendor companies. Sales staff, on the other hand, have a habit of making delivery commitments to customers that entail transporting part-loads often at short notice.

These constraints relate to five general factors: regulatory, market-related, inter-functional, infrastructural and equipment-related. Figure 17.2 maps the links between the constraints and the five factors, recognizing that the same factor can inhibit vehicle utilization in different ways. Physical infrastructure, for example, can affect reliability, the maximum size and weight of the vehicle and storage capacity at the delivery point. This network diagram illustrates the underlying complexity of the problem.

One of the most pervasive and influential factors is the inter-functional relationship between transport and other activities such as production, procurement, inventory management, warehousing and sales. Companies often quite rationally give these other activities priority over transport efficiency. For example, inventory savings from just-in-time (JIT) replenishment or reductions in handling costs accruing from the use of roll-cages may exceed the additional cost of running a truck only part-loaded. It can also be economically justifiable to deliver small orders to important customers in an effort to secure their longer-term loyalty.

Much under-utilization of vehicle capacity, however, is not based on careful analysis of logistical cost trade-offs and explicit calculations of any related sales benefits. It is often unplanned and reflects the relatively low status given to transport within corporate hierarchies dominated by production, marketing and sales. The most that a logistics manager can do is to optimize transport within the targets and constraints set by other

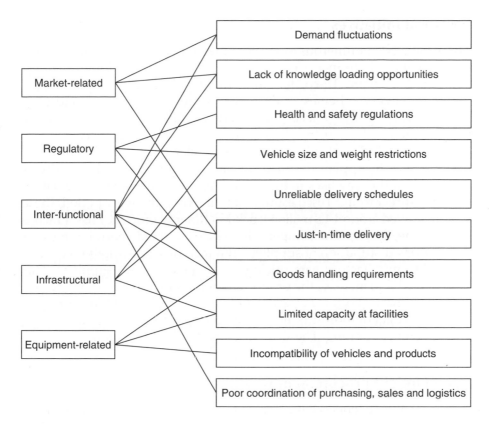

Figure 17.2 Five-fold classification of the constraints on vehicle utilization

departments (McKinnon, 2003). This may not be in the best interests of the company, however. It would be preferable if the cost of reduced vehicle utilization were objectively weighed against the benefits from the other activities which regularly impair transport efficiency.

MEASURES TO IMPROVE VEHICLE UTILIZATION

This section reviews a series of measures that companies can adopt, individually and in combination, to make better use of vehicle capacity.

Increase return loading

There are several ways in which companies can increase the level of backloading.

Logistical initiatives

There have been numerous examples in recent years of companies introducing initiatives to increase backloading. For example, Britain's largest supermarket chain, Tesco, has implemented 'supplier collection' and 'onward delivery' schemes. In the case of supplier collection, a returning shop delivery vehicle collects goods from a supplier's factory and carries them to the retailer's distribution centre. Onward delivery occurs where a supplier's vehicle offloads goods at the retailer's distribution centre and backloads with supplies destined for one of the retailer's shops. This is delivered on the way back to the factory, usually with minimal deviation from the direct route. Tesco estimated that over a five-year period, these schemes saved around 4.8 million truck-km (Energy Efficiency Best Practice Programme, 1998b). The company has since assumed control of most of the primary distribution of supplies from factories to distribution centres by establishing 'factory gate pricing' arrangements with suppliers. This has enabled it to increase the proportion of inbound supplies collected on a backload basis (Potter *et al*, 2004). Other, more balanced forms of intercompany collaboration can also increase opportunities for backloading and cut empty running. These are discussed in a later section.

Use of freight procurement services

Load-matching agencies have existed for several decades, providing road hauliers with a 'clearing house' service for potential backloads. They relied on market knowledge, personal networking and the telephone to broker deals between shippers and carriers. With the advent of the internet, a new generation of freight exchanges has emerged, providing web-enabled tendering, online auctions and bulletin boards for road haulage services (Lewis, 2002). This is making it easier to match loads with available vehicle capacity across much larger 'communities' of shippers and carriers on both a short- and medium-term basis. One online freight exchange estimated that companies using its procurement services were able to cut their transport costs by an average of 8 per cent by increasing 'carrier's asset utilization while protecting their margins' (Mansell, 2006, p 27). More sophisticated online procurement options are now available, involving the bundling of several companies' freight demands prior to the auction and the use of algorithms to improve the match between shippers' road freight demands and the available trucking capacity. Web-enabled tendering of large shippers' freight demands over periods of 3–12 months appears to have had a greater impact on the efficiency of road freight operations than short-term load-matching on a day-to-day basis. It has proved difficult for freight exchanges operating in this sector of the online market to generate the critical volume of vehicle movements needed to create a healthy supply of backloading opportunities (McKinnon and Ge, 2006).

Installation of vehicle tracking systems

Advances in information and communication technology (ICT) and telematics are facilitating the backloading of trucks (DfT, 2003). They can support collaborative initiatives where the participating companies and their logistics service providers operate from a common ICT plat-form. This makes it much easier to find backloading and load con-solidation opportunities and to coordinate the activities of the various fleets. Also, by making transport operations more 'visible', telematics can give both shippers and carriers greater confidence in delivery schedules, helping to overcome one of the traditional obstacles to backloading.

Reverse logistics

An increasing proportion of products is travelling back along the supply chain for repair, reuse, recycling or remanufacture. The growth in the recovery of waste packaging and life-expired product is partly the result of government regulations and directives. This is creating new opportunities for backloading in many industrial and retail sectors (McLeod *et al*, 2008).

Statistical evidence that around 30 per cent of truck-km are run empty can give the impression that there is huge inefficiency in road haulage and enormous potential for increasing backloading. A retrospective analysis of just under 9,000 road deliveries in the British food supply chain over a period of 48 hours, however, revealed relatively few opportunities for backloading after allowance was made for a series of operational con-straints (McKinnon and Ge, 2006). It may not be possible to extrapolate this result to other sectors and countries, though it does cast doubt on claims that empty running can be drastically reduced.

Maximize the available carrying capacity

Very few loads simultaneously reach vehicle weight and volume limits. Most fill out the vehicle space before the weight limit is reached or vice versa. Increasing the weight limit or the physical dimensions of the vehicle can, therefore, result in greater consolidation of loads.

Maximum vehicle weight

Within the EU, trucks engaged in cross-border transport have a weight limit of 40 tonnes. For domestic road haulage within member states, weight limits vary from 40 to 60 tonnes. In 2001 the UK government decided to increase the maximum weight of a six-axle truck from 41 to 44 tonnes, following a study that suggested that the resulting consolidation of loads in heavier vehicles could benefit both the economy and the environment. An impact study conducted three years after the implementation of this measure confirmed that significant savings in vehicle-km, cost and emissions have been achieved, with the greatest benefits enjoyed by industrial sectors producing and distributing dense products, such as coal, drinks, petroleum products and timber (McKinnon, 2005).

Vehicle size and design

It is generally acknowledged that the average density and 'stackability' of freight are declining. Table 17.2 lists the major reasons for these trends. This is partly reflected in the increasing use of taller 9'6" (2.9m) containers

Table 17.2 Reasons for the declining density and 'stackability' of road freight

---

1. *Change in the nature of the products*: Many consumer products have become lighter through time, as plastic and other synthetic materials have increasingly replaced metal, wood and leather.

2. *Increase in packaging*: As packaging is relatively light, increases in the ratio of packaging volume to product volume reduces the average density of freight consignments.

3. *Greater use of unitized handling equipment*: This handling equipment takes up space in the vehicle and reduces the average weight/volume ratio for the overall payload.

4. *Declining rigidity*: In some sectors the increasing fragility of the product and weakening of packaging material are limiting the height to which it can be stacked. In the food and drink industry, for instance, cans have become thinner, and rigid cardboard, plastic or even wooden boxes been replaced by cardboard trays, which offer little vertical support.

5. *Order-picking of palletized loads at an earlier stage in the supply chain*: The mixed pallet-loads that this produces tend to be lower, have an irregular profile and offer less opportunity for stacking.

6. *Tightening health and safety regulations*: These regulations have restricted the height to which pallets can be stacked to minimize the risk of injury to operatives during loading and unloading.

---

in deep-sea container operations and of drawbar-trailer combinations in European road haulage. Truck dimensions are constrained by the geometry of road layouts, bridge heights and loading bays and by the height of bridges and tunnels. Where the transport infrastructure permits an increase in vehicle height, the insertion of an extra deck can allow firms to make more effective use of vehicle space. In the UK, where most roads have height-clearances of 5 metres (mainly to accommodate double-deck buses), there are several thousand high-cube trailers, most of which have a second deck (McKinnon and Campbell, 1997). One major UK retailer demonstrated the benefits of double-decking by comparing operating parameters for deliveries using a double-deck vehicle and two single-deck vehicles with similar capacity. Unit delivery costs, vehicle-km and CO_2 emissions were all around 48 per cent lower (DfT, 2005).

Longer and heavier vehicles

In some countries, such as Sweden, Finland, the Netherlands and Australia, and in some US states, vehicle length and weight limits have been relaxed to allow companies to run so-called 'longer and heavier vehicles' (LHVs), typically 25 metres or more in length and with maximum gross weights in excess of 50 tonnes. In recent years, there has been much debate in Europe, both at an EU level and within individual countries, most notably the UK and Germany, on whether LHVs should be permitted. It is generally acknowledged that the resulting consolidation of loads can cut vehicle-km, fuel consumption and exhaust emissions, though concern has been expressed about possible displacement of freight to LHVs from other less environmentally damaging modes, particularly rail, and the possibility that the consequent cost savings might generate more freight movement. Studies of the environmental and economic impact of LHVs have been conducted in Germany (Umwelt Bundes Amt, 2007) and the UK (Knight *et al*, 2008). Partly on the basis of this research, the governments of these countries refused to legalize 25.25-metre vehicles, though Britain is currently considering relaxation of the maximum length of articulated vehicles with a single trailer from 16.5 to 18.75 metres. Another study undertaken for the European Commission concluded that LHVs could be widely introduced in Europe 'without harming European society as a whole', though it recommended that several 'countermeasures' be implemented to minimize the negative impact on alternative modes, allay safety concerns and prepare the road infrastructure (Transport and Mobility Leuven, 2008).

Vehicles can be redesigned in other ways to permit greater load consolidation. The compartmentalization of trucks has enabled grocery retailers and their contractors to combine the movement of products at different temperatures on a single journey. This form of 'composite distribution', for example, enabled the UK retailer Safeway to reduce the average number of vehicle trips required to deliver 1,000 cases from five in 1985 to one in 1995 (Freight Transport Association, 1995).

It is also possible to increase the maximum carrying capacity of a truck within legal restrictions on gross weight, by reducing the weight of the empty vehicle (or 'tare' weight). Use of lighter materials, such as aluminium or carbon fibre, and fittings can substantially cut the tare weight. The US Department of Energy and American Trucking Association aim to reduce the combined tare weight of the tractor and trailer in a Class 8 articulated truck by 5,000 lb (2.27 tonnes) (Eberle and Smith, 2004). Existing trucks already have widely varying tare weights. For example, a survey of trucking operations in Germany revealed that the average empty weight of trucks with a maximum 40 tonne gross weight was 14 tonnes, but the minimum only 11 tonnes (Leonardi and Baumgartner, 2004). The main performance indicator used in this study, the 'efficiency of vehicle usage' (E), made allowance for differences in the vehicle tare weights:

$$E = \text{tonne-km} / [(\text{vehicle tare weight} + \text{load weight})] \times \text{distance travelled}$$

If the lightest truck were used and fully laden, a theoretically optimal E value of 0.725 could be achieved. The best practice operator in the survey had an average E value of 0.56, while across the entire sample the mean value was only 0.36. There was therefore considerable scope for efficiency improvement, with much of the potential gain coming from the use of lighter vehicles.

Use more space-efficient handling systems and packaging

The efficiency with which the cubic capacity of a vehicle is used partly depends on the nature of the packaging and handling equipment. Companies must reconcile the desire to maximize vehicle fill with the need to protect products from damage in transit and to minimize handling costs. The following examples illustrate the effects that handling/packaging changes can have on the transport operation:

- Choice of loading method: A large mail order company managed to improve vehicle cube utilization and cut vehicle-km by 6 per cent by loading parcels loose rather than in bags.
- Pallet dimensions: It has been estimated that standardizing on a more efficient size and shape of pallet in the European grocery supply chain could cut transport costs by the equivalent of 0.25 per cent of sales revenue (A.T. Kearney, 1997).

- Stacking height: It was estimated in 1997 that if pallet-loads made full use of the 'vehicle inner heights' the European grocery distribution system would have required 15 per cent fewer trucks (Kearney, 1997). Often the maximum height of these loads, however, is constrained by the slot height in warehouse racking systems (typically 1.7 m) while articulated trailers commonly have internal heights of 2.4 m.
- Modular loads: A French food manufacturer was able to improve vehicle fill by 35–41 per cent by packing orders into modules of varying heights (University of St Gallen, 2000).
- Shape and dimensions of product packaging: If cans of food were square, rather than round, space utilization in vehicles, warehouses and shop shelves could be raised by 20 per cent (Buckley and Hoyle, 2005).

Employ computer-based planning tools

A wide range of software tools is available to help companies optimize the use of vehicle capacity. Over the past quarter century, computerized vehicle routing and scheduling (CVRS) software has vastly improved in terms of its functionality, flexibility, applicability, user-friendliness and the efficiency of the solutions it yields. While the quality of the product has dramatically improved, the real cost of the software and associated hardware has sharply declined. CVRS helps companies to optimize the use of vehicle assets with respect to various metrics, including distance travelled, driving time, vehicle loading and cost (DfT, 2007). It is difficult to estimate the average gain in transport efficiency from the use of CVRS as this depends on the complexity and variability of the delivery operation and the standard attained by the previous system of manual route and load planning.

Over the past 6–8 years, a new generation of higher-level modelling tools has been developed to optimize freight transport networks (rather than the multiple-drop delivery rounds to which CVRS packages are normally applied). Particular demand for such packages has come from large retailers, which have integrated their systems of primary (factory to DC) and secondary (DC to shop) distribution and are trying to maximize truck utilization across this entire network. This has presented a formidable analytical challenge. Currently available packages perform reasonably well, though the development of new software tools incorporating genetic algorithms should yield even more efficient solutions.

Adopt more transport-efficient order cycles

The nature of the order-fulfilment process can have a significant impact on the efficiency of the transport operation. There are ways in which this process can be modified to allow firms to increase the degree of load consolidation and hence improve transport efficiency.

Nominated day delivery system (NDDS)

Firms operating this system achieve much higher levels of transport efficiency by encouraging customers to adhere to an ordering and delivery timetable. Customers are informed that a vehicle will be visiting their area on a 'nominated' day and, that to receive a delivery on that day, they must submit their order a certain period in advance. The advertised order lead time is thus conditional on the customer complying with the order schedule. By concentrating deliveries in particular areas on particular days, suppliers can achieve higher levels of load consolidation, drop density and vehicle utilization. Some sales managers oppose this system, however, on the grounds that it will weaken their company's competitive position and probably result in sales losses in excess of the transport cost savings. The experience of many of businesses that have applied NDDS contradicts this view.

Abandoning the monthly payment cycle

Many companies invoice their customers at the end of each month, giving them an incentive to order at the start of the month and thereby obtain a longer period of interest-free credit. This can induce wide monthly fluctuations in freight traffic levels, making it difficult for firms to manage their vehicle capacity efficiently. Relaxing the monthly payment cycle and moving to a system of 'rolling credit', where customers were still granted the same payment terms but from the date of the order rather than the start of the month, suppliers could significantly improve the average utilization of logistics assets. This, however, 'would require a fundamental change in corporate culture and a relaxation of long-established traditions in sales and finance departments' (McKinnon, 2004).

Collaborate with other users and providers of transport services

There is a limit to how much any individual company can do to improve the utilization of vehicle capacity. To reach high levels of utilization it is often necessary to collaborate with other companies. This collaboration can be two-dimensional.

Horizontal collaboration

This occurs where companies at the same level in a supply chain combine their freight transport demands to increase average consignment size or create additional backloading opportunities. The need for such collaboration is well illustrated by an analysis undertaken by a large British fast-moving consumer goods (FMCG) manufacturer. It was concerned about the effects of JIT pressures in the retail supply chain on the efficiency of delivery operations. The company estimated that to be able to provide daily delivery of full trucks-loads to a retailer's distribution centre, it would need to supply the DC with approximately 750,000 cases annually. As Britain's main supermarket and grocery wholesale chains have a total of roughly 70 distribution centres, this would require an annual distribution throughput of approximately of 50 million cases. Only a small group of very large FMCG manufacturers have annual sales volumes as large as this. To maintain full load deliveries on a daily basis, other manufacturers would have to combine their loads.

More and more examples are emerging of companies sharing transport capacity. Kelloggs and Kimberly-Clark, for example, firms with similarly low-density products and complementary transport demands, have jointly saved around 430,000 vehicle-km per annum by coordinating their transport (Anon, 2008). A collaboration between United Biscuits and Nestlé has been more radical as these companies are direct competitors in the biscuit/confectionery market. They nevertheless took the view that they 'compete on the shop shelf and not in the back of a lorry' and have been able to achieve transport savings of around 280,000 vehicle-km per annum mainly through eliminating empty journey legs (Hasting and Wright, 2009) .

Firms can also merge their logistics operations at a shared distribution facility. For example, Unilever and Kimberley-Clark channel products for the Dutch retail market through a distribution centre in Raamsdonksveer operated for them by a logistics service provider (LSP) (ACR Logistics). As a result of this collaboration the companies have been able to cut their logistics costs by 12–15 per cent while responding to retailers' demands for faster and more frequent delivery. Many LSPs now operate 'primary consolidation centres' at which manufacturers can consolidate their orders for onward delivery to retailers' distribution centres in full loads. It has been estimated that the number of 'shared supplier consolidation centres' in the UK grocery supply chain increased from 11 in 1998 to over 100 in 2003 (Potter *et al*, 2003). Multi-company load consolidation also occurs at the secondary distribution level (between distribution centre and shop). Exel, for instance, operates a retail consolidation centre for shops located at Heathrow Airport. It was estimated that when fully implemented this retail consolidation scheme would cut the number of shop delivery vehicles visiting the terminal by 75 per cent and raise vehicle load factors 90 per cent (Energy Efficiency Best Practice Programme, 2002).

To take advantage of horizontal collaboration many companies must change the basis on which they outsource their transport. During the 1980s and 1990s, there was a sharp increase in the proportion of trucking services provided on a dedicated basis for individual clients. Dedication denies carriers the opportunity to perform their traditional 'groupage' role and, as a result, carries a vehicle utilization penalty. Many users of dedicated services have now granted LSPs the freedom to carry other firms' traffic in their vehicles. Several company-sponsored studies of the potential benefits of shared-user services in the automotive, consumer electrical and clothing sectors in the UK, in each case replacing four or five separate dedicated services, have indicated that this can reduce truck-km by around 20 per cent.

Vertical collaboration

This involves collective action by trading partners at different levels in a supply chain, often with the assistance of LSPs. It can help to ease the first two constraints on vehicle utilization listed earlier, namely demand fluctuations and JIT pressures. In the United States, the term collaborative transportation management (CTM) has been used to describe a formal initiative to encourage collaboration and the sharing of information between manufacturers, retailers and carriers to cut transport costs while improving service quality (Murphy, 2003). This is an extension of collaborative planning, forecasting and replenishment (CPFR), which has focused on the management of inventory across the supply chain. Key features of CTM are the sharing of demand information with carriers and the closer involvement of carriers in the replenishment process. As Browning and White (2000) explain, 'CTM... re-engineers the whole process so that the carrier is now part of the larger, more focused buyer/seller team' (p 3). By giving carriers an 'extended planning horizon' some have been able to increase the utilization of their regional truck fleets in the United States by between 10 and 42 per cent, mainly as a result of improved backloading (Esper and Williams, 2003).

Another initiative relating to the management of product flow through the vertical channel is vendor managed inventory (VMI). This gives suppliers control over the replenishment process, enabling them to phase the movement of products in a way that makes more efficient use of vehicle capacity. Simulation modelling has been used to demonstrate the potential transport benefits of VMI over a 'traditional supply chain' (Disney, Potter and Gardner, 2003). Sometimes it is also necessary to increase storage capacity at the customer's premises to accommodate the delivery of supplies in full truck-loads. This applies particularly to the movement of bulk commodities in process industries.

CONCLUSION

Transport optimization is the term now being widely used in business circles to describe efforts to maximize vehicle utilization (ECR UK, 2003). It is partly a reaction to the JIT trend, which has swept through manufacturing and retailing over the past quarter century. In the headlong rush to cut inventory, many companies were prepared to sacrifice transport efficiency. Now that low-inventory strategies are firmly in place, attention is shifting to freight transport operations to see what can be done to improve their efficiency. This is being reinforced by mounting concern about fuel costs, driver shortages, traffic congestion and the environmental impact of logistical activity, particularly on climate change.

Transport will inevitably be optimized within a range of constraints. This chapter has examined these constraints and the series of measures that companies can take to ease or overcome them. If properly implemented, these measures can yield a combination of economic and environmental benefits and help to make logistics more sustainable in the longer term.

References

Anon (2008) Collaboration brings savings for Kelloggs and Kimberly-Clark, *Logistics Manager*, 13 October

Ansari, A and Heckel, J (1987) JIT purchasing: impact on freight and inventory costs, *Journal of Purchasing and Materials Management*, **23** (2)

A.T. Kearney (1997) *The efficient unit loads report*, ECR Europe, Brussels

Browning, B and White, B (2000) *Collaborative Transportation Management – A Proposal*, White Paper, Logility Inc, Atlanta

Buckley, C and Hoyle, B (2005) Is this really the shape of tins to come? *The Times*, 30 March

Caplice, C and Sheffi, Y (1994) A review and evaluation of logistics metrics, *International Journal of Logistics Management*, **5** (2)

Department for Transport (DfT) (2003) *Telematics Guide*, Good Practice Guide 341, Harwell

DfT (2005) *Focus on Double Decks*, Transport Energy Best Practice report, London

DfT (2007) *Computerized Vehicle Routing and Scheduling for Efficient Logistics*, Freight Best Practice Programme, DfT, London

DfT (2009) *Road Freight Statistics 2008*, DfT, London

Disney, S, Potter, A and Gardner, B (2003) The impact of VMI on transport operations, *Transportation Research part E: Logistics and Transportation,* **39**, pp 363–80

Eberle, C and Smith, MT (2004) *Heavy Vehicle Mass Reduction Using Composite Polymers,* Oak Ridge National Laboratory, Oak Ridge, TN

ECR UK (2003) *Transport Optimization: Sharing best practice in distribution management,* Institute of Grocery Distribution, Letchmore Heath

Energy Efficiency Best Practice Programme (1998a) *Efficient JIT Supply Chain Management: Nissan Motor Manufacturing (UK) Ltd,* Good Practice Case Study 374, Harwell

Energy Efficiency Best Practice Programme (1998b) *Energy Savings from Integrated Logistics Management: Tesco plc,* Good Practice Case Study 364, Harwell

Energy Efficiency Best Practice Programme (2002) *Heathrow Airport Retail Consolidation Centre,* Harwell

Esper, TL and Williams, LR (2003) The value of collaborative transportation management (CTM): its relationship to CPFR and information technology, *Transportation Journal,* **42** (4), pp 55–65

Freight Transport Association (1995) *JIT: Time sensitive distribution,* Freight Matters 1/95, FTA, Tunbridge Wells

Hasting, R and Wright, R (2009) *Working with your Competitor to Remove Empty Trucks from the Roads,* Presentation to IGD Sustainable Distribution conference, London, 10 June

Knight, I et al (2008) *Longer and/or Longer and Heavier Goods Vehicles (LHVs) – a Study of the Likely Effects if Permitted in the UK: Final report,* TRL Published Project Report 285, TRL, Berkshire

Leonardi, J and Baumgartner, M (2004) CO_2 efficiency in road freight transportation: status quo, measures and potential, *Transportation Research Part D,* **9**, pp 451–64

Lewis, CN (2002) Freight exchanges: how are the survivors faring, *e.logistics magazine,* issue 16

Lex Transfleet (2002) *The Lex Transfleet Report on Freight Transport 2002,* Coventry

Mansell, G (2006) Transport tendering comes of age, *Transport and Logistics Focus,* **8** (4), pp 26–28

McKinnon, AC (1996) The empty running and return loading of road goods, *Vehicles Transport Logistics,* **1** (1), pp 1–19

McKinnon, AC (2003) *Influencing Company Logistics Management in European Conference of Ministers of Transport. Managing the Fundamental Drivers of Transport Demand,* OECD, Paris, pp 60–74

McKinnon, AC (2004) *Supply Chain Excellence in the European Chemical Industry,* European Petrochemical Association, Brussels

McKinnon, AC (2005) The economic and environmental benefits of increasing maximum truck weight: the British experience, *Transportation Research part D*, **10** (1), pp 77–95

McKinnon, AC (2006) Government plans for lorry road user charging in the UK: a critique and an alternative, *Transport Policy*, **13** (3), pp 204–16

McKinnon, AC and Campbell, J (1997) *Opportunities for Consolidating Volume-Constrained Loads in Double-deck and High-cube Vehicles*, Christian Salvesen Logistics Research Paper no 1, School of Management, Heriot-Watt University, 1997 [Online] http://www.sml.hw.ac.uk/logistics/s1.html

McKinnon, AC and Ge, Y (2004) Use of a synchronized vehicle audit to determine opportunities for improving transport efficiency in a supply chain, *International Journal of Logistics: Research and Applications*, **7** (3), pp 219–38

McKinnon, AC and Ge, Y (2006) The potential for reducing empty running by trucks: a retrospective analysis, *International Journal of Physical Distribution and Logistics Management*, **36** (5), pp 391–410

McKinnon, AC *et al* (2009) Traffic congestion, reliability and logistical performance: a multi-sectoral assessment, *International Journal of Logistics: Research and Applications*, **12** (5), pp 331–45

McLeod, F *et al* (2008) *Developing Innovative and More Sustainable Approaches to Reverse Logistics for the Collection, Recycling and Disposal of Waste Products from Urban Centres*, University of Southampton [Online] http://www.greenlogistics.org

Murphy, J (2003) CTM: Collaborating to weed out transportation inefficiency, *Global Logistics and Supply Chain Strategies*, November

Piecyk, M and McKinnon, AC (2009) Forecasting the carbon footprint of road freight transport in 2020, *International Journal of Production Economics* (forthcoming)

Potter, A *et al* (2004) Modelling the impact of factory gate pricing on transport and logistics, in *Transport in Supply Chains*, ed C Lalwani *et al*, Cardiff Business School, Cardiff

Potter, M *et al* (2003) *ECR UK Transport Optimization: Sharing best practices in distribution management*, Institute of Grocery Distribution, Letchmore Heath

Samuelsson, A and Tilanus, B (1997) A framework efficiency model for goods transportation, with an application to regional less-than-truckload distribution, *Transport Logistics*, **1** (2), pp 139–51

Swenseth, SR and Buffa, FP (1990) Just-in-time: some effects on the logistics function, *International Journal of Logistics Management*, **1** (2), pp 25–34

Transport and Mobility Leuven, TNO, LCPC and RWTH Aachen University (2008) *Effects of Adapting the Rules on Weights and Dimensions of Heavy Commercial Vehicles as Established within Directive 96/53/EC*, Report for the European Commission, Brussels

Umwelt Bundes Amt (2007) *Longer and Heavier on German Roads: Do megatrucks contribute towards sustainable transport*, UBA, Dessau-Roßlau

University of St Gallen (2000) *The Transport Optimization Report*, ECR Europe, Brussels

18

Retail logistics

John Fernie, Heriot-Watt University

The principles behind logistics and supply chain management are not new, but it is only in the last 10 to 15 years that logistics has achieved prominence in companies' boardrooms. This is primarily because of the impact that the application of supply chain techniques can have on a company's competitive position and profitability. Retailers have been in the forefront of applying best-practice principles to their businesses, with UK grocery retailers being acknowledged as innovators in logistics management. This chapter discusses:

- the evolution of the logistics concept;
- QR/ECR and managing supply chain relationships;
- the application of supply chain concepts in different international markets;
- future trends, including the impact of e-commerce upon logistics networks.

THE EVOLUTION OF THE LOGISTICS CONCEPT

The starting point for any discussion of logistics invariably centres around Drucker's (1962) description of 'the economy's dark continent', which suggested that distribution was one of the last frontiers of business to be 'discovered'. He noted that distribution was viewed as a low-status activity by managers, yet major cost savings could be achieved by managing this function more effectively. His ideas stimulated much debate, and most of the early research emanated from the United States as techniques developed in the context of military logistics began to gain acceptance in the commercial sector.

By the 1970s and 1980s, the supply chain was still viewed as a series of disparate functions – with materials management dealing with the 'back end' of the supply chain and physical distribution management focusing upon the flow of product from manufacturers to their customers (retailers and wholesalers). As a result, the literature on the subject has developed along two distinct routes: one pertaining to industrial and the other to consumer markets. The materials management literature has its roots in the management strategies of the Japanese and the application of total quality management, just-in-time (JIT) production and supplier associations. More recently, the 'Europeanization' of the concepts includes 'lean supply' and 'network sourcing'.

The 'front end' of the supply chain achieved greater prominence from the 1970s, initially as physical distribution management (PDM) but more recently as supply chain/logistics management. Initial work focused upon manufacturers' distribution systems, but as retailers centralized their distribution and began to exert control over the retail supply chain, most research focused upon retailers' logistics strategies. In both industrial and retail logistics research, the emphasis since the 1990s has been on viewing the supply chain as an integrated whole rather than a series of disparate parts. There is no point in taking cost out of one part of the supply chain, only to add costs somewhere else in the chain!

In the context of retail logistics, several authors have sought to explain the transformation of logistics practices since the 1970s. McKinnon (1996) identified six trends to account for this:

- retailers increasing their control over secondary distribution (warehouse to shop) – in the UK this process is complete in most sectors;
- restructuring of retailers' logistical systems through the development of 'composite distribution' and centralization of certain commodities into particular supply chain streams;
- adoption of quick response techniques to reduce lead times through the implementation of information technology, especially electronic data interchange (EDI), electronic point of sales (EPOS) and sales-based ordering (SBO);
- rationalization of primary distribution (factory to warehouse) and attempts to integrate this and secondary distribution into a single 'network system';

- introduction of supply chain management and efficient consumer response (ECR);
- increasing return flow of packaging material and handling equipment for recycle or reuse.

Fernie, Pfab and Marchant (2000) have built upon the work of Whiteoak (1993), who charted the evolution of UK grocery distribution from the 1970s to the early 1990s, and identify four stages:

1. supplier control (pre-1980);
2. centralization (1981–89);
3. just-in-time (1990–95);
4. relationship (1995 onwards).

The first stage, supplier control, is widespread in many countries today, and was the dominant method of distribution to UK stores in the 1960s and 1970s. Suppliers manufactured and stored products at the factory or numerous warehouses throughout the country. Direct store deliveries (DSDs) were made on an infrequent basis (7 to 10 days), often by third-party contractors that consolidated products from a range of factories. Store managers negotiated with suppliers and kept this stock in 'the back room'.

The second stage, centralization, is now becoming a feature of retail logistics in many countries and was prominent in the UK in the 1980s. The grocery retailers took the initiative at this time in constructing large, purpose-built regional distribution centres (RDCs) to consolidate products from suppliers for onward delivery to stores. This stage marked the beginning of a shift from supplier to retailer control of the supply chain, with clear advantages for retailers:

- reduced inventories;
- lead times at stores reduced from weeks to days;
- 'back-room' areas released for selling space;
- greater product availability;
- 'bulk discounts' from suppliers;
- fewer invoices and lower administrative costs;
- better utilization of staff in stores.

Centralization, however, required much capital investment in RDCs, vehicles, material handling equipment and human resources. Centralization of distribution also meant centralization of buying, with store managers losing autonomy as new headquarter functions were created to manage this change. This period also witnessed a boom in the third-party contract market, as retailers considered whether to invest in other parts of the retail business rather than logistics. All of the UK's 'big four' grocery retailers – Sainsbury, Tesco, Asda and Safeway – contracted out many RDCs to logistics service providers in the mid- to late 1980s.

In stage 3, the just-in-time phase, major efficiency improvements were achieved as refinements to the initial networks were implemented. The larger grocery chains focused upon product-specific RDCs, with most temperature-controlled products being channelled through a large number of small warehouses operated by third-party contractors. By the early 1990s, temperature-controlled products were subsumed within a network of composite distribution centres developed by superstore operators. Composites allowed products of all temperature ranges to be distributed through one system of multi-temperature warehouses and vehicles. This allowed retailers to reduce stock in store as delivery frequency increased. Furthermore, a more streamlined system not only improved efficiency but reduced waste in short-shelf-life products, giving a better-quality offer to the customer.

Initial projects were also established to integrate primary with secondary distribution. When Safeway opened its composite in 1989 at Bellshill in Strathclyde, it included a resource recovery centre that washed returnable trays and baled cardboard from its stores. It also established a supplier collection programme, which saved the company millions of pounds during the 1990s. Most secondary networks were established to provide stores with high customer service levels; however, vehicle utilization on return trips to the RDC were invariably poor, and it was efforts to reduce this empty running that led to initiatives such as return trips with suppliers' products to the RDC, or equipment or recycling waste from stores.

Although improvements to the initial networks were being implemented, RDCs continued to carry two weeks or more of stock of non-perishable products. To improve inventory levels and move to a just-in-time system, retailers began to request more frequent deliveries from their suppliers in smaller order quantities. Whiteoak, who represented Mars and therefore suppliers' interests, wrote in 1993 that these initiatives gave clear benefits to retailers at the expense of increased costs to suppliers. In response to these changes, consolidation centres have been created upstream from RDCs to enable suppliers to improve vehicle utilization from the factory.

The final stage, the relationship stage, is ongoing but is crucial if further costs are going to be taken out of the supply chain. In the earlier, third, stage, Whiteoak had noted that the transition from a supplier- to a retail-controlled network had given cost savings to both suppliers and retailers *until* the just-in-time phase in the early 1990s. By the mid-1990s, retailers had begun to appreciate that there were no more 'quick wins' to improve margins. If another step change in managing retail logistics was to occur, it had to be realized through supply chain cooperation.

ECR initiatives launched throughout the 1990s have done much to promote the spirit of collaboration. Organizations are having to change to
accommodate and embrace ECR and to dispel inherent rivalries that have
built up over decades of confrontation. The UK has been in the vanguard
of implementing ECR, with Tesco and Sainsbury claiming to have saved
hundreds of millions of pounds. The key to the relative success of UK
companies has been their willingness to share EPOS data with their suppliers through internet-based information exchanges.

LOGISTICS AND COMPETITIVE STRATEGY IN RETAILING

Many of the current ideas on supply chain management and competitive
advantage have their roots in the work of Porter (1985), who introduced
the concept of the value chain in relation to competitive advantage. These
ideas have been further developed by academics such as Christopher
(1997). Now we have a supply chain model (Figure 18.1) where each stage
of the chain adds value to the product through manufacturing, branding,
packaging, display at the store and so on. At the same time, at each stage
cost is added in terms of production, branding and overall logistics costs.
The trick for companies is to manage this chain to create value for the
customer at an acceptable cost.

According to Christopher there are three dimensions to time-based
competition that must be managed effectively if an organization is going
to be responsive to market changes:

- *time to market:* the speed of bringing a business opportunity to market;
- *time to serve:* the speed of meeting a customer's order;
- *time to react:* the speed of adjusting output to volatile responses in
  demand.

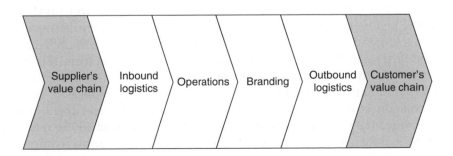

Figure 18.1   The extended value chain

He uses these principles to develop strategies for lead-time management. He argues that, if the lead times of the integrated web of suppliers necessary to manufacture a product are understood, a 'pipeline map' can be drawn to represent each stage in the supply chain process from raw materials to customer. In these maps it is useful to differentiate between value-adding time (manufacture, assembly, in-transit etc) and non-value-adding time (when nothing is happening, but products and materials are standing as inventory).

It was in fashion markets that time-based competition had most significance, because of the short time window for changing styles. In addition, the prominent trend in the last 20 years has been to source products offshore, usually in low-cost Pacific Rim nations, which lengthened the physical supply chains. These factors combined to illustrate the trade-offs that have to be made in supply chain management and the need to develop closer working relationships with supply chain partners. Christopher has used the example of The Limited in the United States to illustrate his accelerating 'time to market'. The company revolutionized the apparel supply chain philosophy in the United States by designing, ordering and receiving products from South-East Asia to stores in a matter of weeks rather than the months of its competitors. New lines were test-marketed in trial stores, and orders communicated by EDI to suppliers, which used CAD/CAM technology in modifying designs. The products, already labelled and priced, were consolidated in Hong Kong, where chartered 747s air-freighted the goods to Columbus, Ohio, for onward dispatch to stores. The higher freight costs were easily compensated for by lower markdowns and higher inventory turns per annum.

Quick response

The term 'Quick Response' (QR) was coined in the United States in 1985 (Fernie, 1994; Hines, 2001) when Kurt Salmon Associates (KSA) recognized deficiencies in the fashion supply chain. According to KSA, only 11 weeks out of the 66-week lead time were spent on value-adding processes, and the rest were wasted in the form of WIP and finished inventories at various stages of the complex system (Christopher, 1997, 1998; KSA, 1997; Christopher and Peck, 2003). The resultant losses arising from this were estimated at $25 billion – due to stocking too large an inventory of unwanted items and too small an inventory of the fast movers.

In response to this situation, the US textiles, apparel and retail industries formed the Voluntary Interindustry Commerce Standards Association (VICS) in 1986 as their joint effort to streamline the supply chain and make a significant contribution in getting the in-vogue style at the right time in the right place (Fernie, 1994, 1998) with increased variety (Lowson,

1998; Lowson, King and Hunter, 1999; Giunipero *et al*, 2001) and inexpensive prices. This is done by applying an industry standard for information technologies (eg bar code, EDI, shipping container marking, roll ID etc) and contractual procedures among the supply chain members (Ko, Kincade and Brown, 2000). QR adopts an IT-driven systematic approach (Hunter, 1990; Forza and Vinelli, 1996, 1997, 2000; Riddle *et al*, 1999) to achieve supply chain efficiency from raw materials to retail stores – and each member of the supply chain shares the risks and the benefits of the partnership on an equal basis to realize the philosophy of 'the whole is stronger than the parts'.

QR, in principle, requires the traditional buyer–supplier relationship, which is too often motivated by opportunism, to transform into a more collaborative partnership. In this QR partnership, the objectives of the vendor are to develop the customer's business. The benefit to the vendor is the likelihood that it will be treated as a preferred supplier. At the same time, the costs of serving that customer should be lower as a result of a greater sharing of information, integrated logistics systems and so on (Christopher and Jüttner, 2000).

The last, and perhaps one of the most important, of the tenets of the original proposition of the QR concept sees it as a survival strategy of the domestic manufacturing sector in the advanced economies against competition from low-cost imports (Finnie, 1992; MITI, 1993, 1995, 1999; METI, 2002).

With the basic fashion category, relatively steady demand is a feature of the market; therefore the US-born QR concept places much focus on the relationship between retailers and the apparel manufacturers. The eventual benefits to both parties are detailed in Table 18.1. Giunipero *et al* (2001) summarize the hierarchical process of QR adoption (Table 18.2). This model – most appropriate for the apparel–retail linkage in basic clothing – has become a role model for QR programmes in other advanced economies.

Table 18.1   Retailers' and suppliers' QR benefits

Retailers' QR benefits	Suppliers' QR benefits
Reduced costs	Reduced costs
Reduced inventories	Predictable production cycles
Faster merchandise flow	Frequency of orders
Customer satisfaction	Closer ties to retailers
Increased sales	Ability to monitor sales
Competitive advantage	Competitive advantage

Source: Quick Response Services, 1995

Table 18.2   Technological and organizational QR development stages

Stage 1	**Introduction of basic QR technologies** SKU-level scanning JAN (standard) bar code Use of EDI Use of standard EDI
Stage 2	**Internal process re-engineering via technological and organizational improvement** Electronic communication for replenishment Use of cross-docking Small amounts of inventory in the system Small lot size order processing ARP (automatic replenishment programme) JIT (just-in-time) delivery SCM (shipping container marking) ASN (advance shipping notice)
Stage 3	**Realization of a collaborative supply chain and win–win relationship** Real-time sales data sharing Stock-out data sharing QR team meets with partnerships MRP (material resource planning)

Source: Giunipero *et al*, 2001; KSA, 1997

Having achieved many of the QR goals, VICS implemented a collaborative planning, forecasting and replenishment (CPFR) programme, to synchronize market fluctuations and the supply chain in more real time. Through establishing firm contracts among supply chain members and allowing them to share key information, CPFR makes the forecasting, production and replenishment cycle ever closer to the actual demands in the marketplace (VICS, 1998). While US practices have played a leading role in QR initiatives in the apparel industry, much of their success is in the basic fashion segment – where the manufacturing phase is normally the first to be transferred offshore. In this sense, the philosophy of QR as the survival strategy of fashion manufacturing in the industrial economies has not been realized.

QR in Japan

The US fashion industry essentially produces for the international market that is mostly controlled by the largest retailers – which are the real

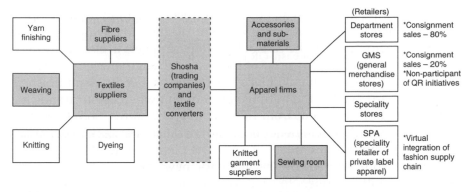

HIGHLIGHTED – (Partial) participation in the industry-wide QR initiatives

Figure 18.2 The structure of the Japanese fashion industry

promoters and the first to profit from QR (Taplin and Ordovensky, 1995; Scarso, 1997). Japanese apparel firms have forged their success on flexible specialization in a subcontracting network of process specialists (Piore and Sabel, 1984; Azuma, 2001). Harsh competition from offshore, and stagnant domestic consumption have come to highlight the costly structure and the lack of partnership in the Japanese fashion supply chain. This led to the formation of the Quick Response Promotion Association (QRPA) in 1994, as a joint endeavour to regain competitiveness of the domestic industry, and effectively and efficiently serve ever-changing customer needs.

Since the introduction of the first QR initiative in the Japanese fashion industry, a series of programmes have been implemented from 1) the retail–textiles, 2) the textiles–apparel, to 3) the apparel–sewing interfaces (see Figure 18.2). With an increasing adoption of industry-standard platforms for EDI, department stores and apparel firms have achieved some of the expected QR benefits. Elsewhere in the supply chain, however, there are fewer QR initiatives – and QR initiatives have not necessarily worked throughout the domestic apparel sector.

Benetton and Zara

The importance of supply chain integration cannot be overstated; however, much depends on the degree of control a company has over the design, manufacture, marketing and distribution of its supply chain. Two of the most successful fashion retailers in Europe – Benetton and Zara – illustrate how an integrated supply chain can enhance the retail offer.

Both companies draw heavily on lean production techniques developed in Japan. Their manufacturing operations are flexible, involving a network of subcontractors and, in the case of Benetton, suppliers in close proximity to the factory. Benetton was one of the first retail companies to apply the 'principle of postponement' to its operations, whereby semi-finished garments were dyed at the last possible moment when colour trends for a season became apparent from EPOS data at the stores. So rather than manufacture stock to sell, Benetton could manufacture stock to demand.

Zara's operation has similarities with The Limited in the United States in that the company scours the globe for new fashion trends prior to negotiating with suppliers to produce specific quantities of finished and semi-finished products. Only 40 per cent of garments – those with the broadest appeal – are imported as finished goods from the Far East; the rest are produced in Zara's automated factories in Spain. The result of its supply chain initiatives is that Zara has reduced its lead-time gap for more than half of the garments it sells to a level unmatched by any of its European or North American competitors.

Benetton, Zara and The Limited – as the latter's name suggests – have narrow product assortments for specific target markets. This streamlines and simplifies the logistics network. For general fashion merchandisers, the supply chain is more complex, with thousands of suppliers around the globe. Nevertheless, quick response concepts are being applied to these sectors in an effort to minimize markdowns due to out-of-season or unwanted stock in stores.

Although grocery retailers are more orientated to their national or super-regional markets – such as the EU – than their clothing counterparts are, the internationalization of grocery retailers and their customers has led to changing sourcing patterns. Furthermore, the increased competition in grocery markets, with the resultant pressure on profit margins, has acted as a spur to companies to improve supply chain performance.

Efficient consumer response

ECR emerged in the United States partly through the joint initiatives between Wal-Mart and Procter & Gamble, in response to recession and increased competition in the grocery industry in the early 1990s. Kurt Salmon Associates were again commissioned to analyse the supply chain of a US industrial sector, and they found similar features to those identified in their earlier work in the apparel sector – excessive inventories, long uncoordinated supply chains and an estimated potential savings of $30 billion, 10.8 per cent of sales turnover (see Table 18.3).

ECR programmes commenced in Europe in 1993, and a series of projects and pilot studies were commissioned – for example, a Coopers & Lybrand

Table 18.3 Comparison of scope and savings from supply chain studies

Supply chain study	Scope of study	Estimated savings
Kurt Salmon Associates (1993)	US dry grocery sector.	10.8% of sales turnover (2.3% financial, 8.5% cost). Total supply chain $30 billion; warehouse supplier dry sector $10 billion. Supply chain cut by 41% from 104 days to 61 days.
Coca-Cola supply chain collaboration (1994)	127 European companies. Focused on cost reduction from end of manufacturer's line. Small proportion of category management.	2.3%–3.4% of sales turnover (60% to retailers, 40% to manufacturer).
ECR Europe (1996, ongoing)	15 value chain analysis studies (10 European manufacturers, 5 retailers). 15 product categories. 7 distribution channels.	5.7% of sales turnover (4.8% operating costs, 0.9% inventory cost). Total supply chain saving of $21 billion. UK savings £2 billion.

Source: Fiddis, 1997

(1996) survey of the grocery value chain estimated potential savings of 5.7 per cent of turnover. Since then ECR has been adopted in countries around the world.

The European ECR initiative defines ECR as a 'global movement in the grocery industry focusing on the total supply chain – suppliers, manufacturers, wholesalers and retailers, working closer together to fulfil the changing demands of the grocery consumer better, faster and at least cost' (Fiddis, 1997). Despite the apparent emphasis on consumers, early studies focused on the supply side of ECR. Initially reports sought efficiencies in replenishment and the standardization of material-handling equipment to eliminate unnecessary handling through the supply chain. The Coopers & Lybrand report in 1996 and subsequent reprioritizing towards demand management – especially category management (McGrath, 1997) – have led to a more holistic view of the supply chain. Indeed, the greater cost savings attributed to the Coopers study compared with that of Coca-Cola can be attributed to their broader perspective of the value chain.

The main focus areas addressed under ECR are category management, product replenishment and enabling technologies. Figure 18.3 breaks

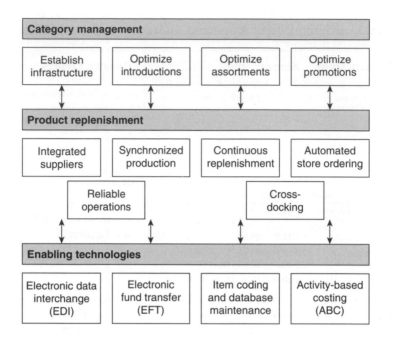

Figure 18.3 ECR improvement concepts
Source: Coopers & Lybrand, 1996

these down into 14 further areas where improvements can be made to enhance efficiency.

After the success of ECR Europe's annual conferences from 1996, a series of initiatives encouraged much greater international collaboration. ECR movements began to share best-practice principles, most notably the bringing together of different versions of the 'scorecard' that was used to assess the performance of trading relationships. These relationships were measured under four categories – demand management, supply management, enablers and integrators (see Figure 18.4). Comparing this with Figure 18.3 shows how ECR has developed in recent years to accommodate changes in the market environment. Retailers are becoming more sophisticated in their approach to demand and supply management, and there has been considerable progress in moving from traditional 'bow tie' relationships between retailers and their suppliers to a multi-functional team structure (see Figures 18.5 and 18.6).

Although logisticians would prefer a consistent flow of product through the supply chain, tactical promotions remain a feature in many retailers' marketing strategies. Research by Hoch and Pomerantz (2002) on 19 food product categories in 106 supermarket chains in the United States shows

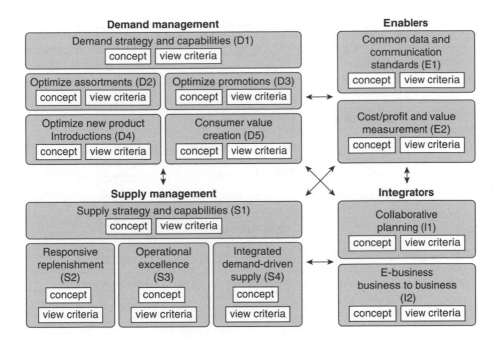

Figure 18.4 ECR concepts
Source: www.ecr-sa.co.za

Current relationship	Target relationship
• Adversarial relationship	• Collaborative relationships
• Price	• Total cost management
• Many suppliers	• Few 'alliance' suppliers
• Functional silos	• Cross-functional
• Short-term buying	• Long-term buying
• High levels of just-in-case inventory	• Compressed cycle times and improved demand visibility
• Expediting due to problems	• Anticipating due to continuous improvement
• Historical information	• 'Real-time' information (EDI)
• Short shipments	• Reliability focus
• Inefficient use of capacity	• Run strategy and synchronization

Figure 18.5 Changing relationships between manufacturers and suppliers
Source: Coopers & Lybrand, 1996

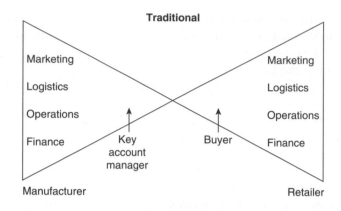

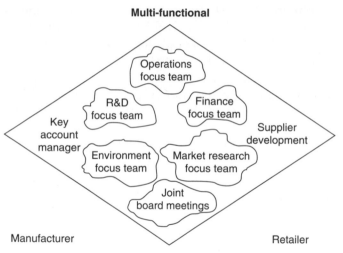

Figure 18.6 Transformation of the interface between manufacturer and retailer
Source: Fiddis, 1997

that price sensitivity and promotional responsiveness are much greater with high-frequency, staple purchases. These staple products benefited from range reduction, compared with more specialist niche products where greater variety and range built store traffic.

In order to integrate this demand-side planning with continuous replenishment, collaborative planning is necessary. The main catalyst for this was the VICS initiative on CPFR, which drew its primary support from US non-food retailers and their suppliers until the late 1990s when the grocery sector embraced the CPFR model. For example, Wal-Mart and Warner-Lambert are usually cited as key partners in sales forecast collaboration in the early to mid-1990s. The shift into grocery is hardly surprising in view of Wal-Mart's move into food through its supercentres in the United States and its overseas acquisitions of grocery businesses such as Asda in the UK.

By the late 1990s, VICS had produced a nine-step generic model bringing together elements of ECR initiatives – the development of collaborative arrangements, joint business plans, shared sales forecasts and continuous replenishment from orders generated. Although the tenets of CPFR have been established, the implementation of the model remains patchy and, like ECR initiatives, tends to focus on 'quick wins' where measurable profit enhancement or cost savings can be achieved. Most pilot schemes have involved a handful of partners dealing with specific categories. Companies come from a variety of technical platforms and cultures of collaboration. Indeed, the likes of Wal-Mart, Tesco and Sainsbury with their own intranet exchanges could actually impede more universal adoption of common standards!

To implement CPFR, it is a prerequisite that a close working relationship has been fostered between trading partners, in order to invest the necessary human resources to develop joint plans to generate real-time forecasts. There is clearly more volatility of demand with price promotions and seasonal and event planning. CPFR generates greater benefits in these heavily promoted channels where over-stocks or out-of-stocks are more evident than in high-volume, staple, frequently purchased items where demand is more predictable.

DIFFERENCES IN LOGISTICS 'CULTURE' IN INTERNATIONAL MARKETS

ECR principles have been adopted at different stages by different companies in international markets – and new entrants to a market can change the distribution culture of that market. Differences in such markets are more likely to exist in the context of fast-moving consumer goods, especially groceries, because of the greater variations in tastes that occur in both national and regional markets. The catalyst for much of the interest in these international comparisons was the revealing statistic from Kurt Salmon Associates (1997) that it took 104 days for dry grocery products to pass through the US supply chain from the suppliers' picking line to the checkout. With the advent of ECR, it was hoped to reduce this to 61 days – a figure that was still behind the lead times encountered in Europe, especially in the UK, where inventory in the supply chain averaged around 25 days (GEA, 1994).

Mitchell (1997) explains the differences between the United States and Europe in terms of trading conditions, stating that:

- The US grocery retail trade is fragmented and not as concentrated as in parts of Europe.
- US private-label development is primitive compared with that in many European countries.
- The balance of power in the manufacturer–retailer relationship is very different.
- The trade structure is different, with wholesalers playing a more important role in the United States.
- Trade practices such as forward buying are more deeply rooted in the United States than in Europe.
- Trade promotional deals and the use of coupons in consumer promotions are unique to the United States.
- Legislation, especially anti-trust legislation, can inhibit supply chain collaboration.

Fernie (1994, 1995) cites the following factors to explain these differences in trading conditions:

- the extent of retail power;
- the penetration of store brands in the market;
- the degree of supply chain control;
- types of trading format;
- geographical spread of stores;
- relative logistics costs;
- level of IT development;
- relative sophistication of the distribution industry.

Of these eight factors, the first three can be classified as relationship factors and the remainder as operational factors. Clearly there has been a significant shift in the balance of power between manufacturer and retailer during the last 20 to 30 years, as retailers increasingly take over responsibility for product development, branding, packaging and marketing. As mergers continue in Europe, retailers have grown in economic power to dominate their international branded manufacturer suppliers. While there are different levels of retail concentration at the country level, the trend is for increased concentration – especially as Southern and Eastern European markets are targeted by the major Western European retail chains.

By contrast, Ohbora, Parsons and Riesenbeck (1992) maintain that this power struggle is more evenly poised in the United States, where the grocery market is more regional in character, enabling manufacturers to wield their power. This, however, is changing as Wal-Mart develops its supercentres and acts as a catalyst for the 'consolidation wave' throughout the 1990s and early 21st century (Wrigley, 2001). Nevertheless, the immense size of the United States has meant that there has never been a true national grocery retailer.

Commensurate with the growth of these powerful retailers has been the development of distributor labels. This is particularly relevant in the UK where supermarket chains have followed the Marks & Spencer strategy of strong value-added brands that can compete with manufacturers' brands. British retailers dominate the list of top 25 own-label retailers in Europe.

The net result of this shift to retail power and own-label development has meant that manufacturers have been either abdicating or losing their responsibility for controlling the supply chain. In the UK the transition from a supplier-driven system to one of retail control is complete compared with some parts of Europe and the United States.

Of the operational factors identified by Fernie (1994), the nature of trading format has been a key driver in shaping the type of logistics support to stores. For example, in the UK the predominant trading format has been the superstore in both food and specialist household products and appliances. This has led to the development of large RDCs for the centralization of stock from suppliers. In the grocery sector, supermarket operations have introduced composite warehousing and trucking whereby products of various temperature ranges can be stored in one warehouse and transported in one vehicle. This has been possible because of the scale of the logistics operation – namely large RDCs supplying large superstores. Further upstream, primary consolidation centres have been created to minimize inventory held between factory and store. The size and spread of stores will, therefore, determine the form of logistical support to retail outlets. Geography also is an important consideration in terms of the physical distances products have to be moved in countries such as the UK, the Netherlands and Belgium compared with the United States and, to a lesser extent, France and Spain. Centralization of distribution into RDCs was more appropriate to urbanized environments, where stores could be replenished regularly. By contrast, in France and Spain some hypermarket operators have widely dispersed stores, often making it more cost-effective to hold stock in store rather than at an RDC.

The question of a trade-off of costs within the logistics mix is, therefore, appropriate at a country level. Labour costs permeate most aspects of logistics – and not surprisingly dependence on automation and mechanization increases as labour costs rise. Scandinavian countries have been in the vanguard of innovation here because of high labour costs – and similarly it can be argued that UK retailers have been innovators in ECR because of high inventory costs, caused by high interest rates, in the 1970s and 1980s. This also is true of land and property costs. In Japan, the United Kingdom and the Benelux countries, the high cost of retail property acts as an incentive to maximize sales space and minimize the carrying of stock in store. In France and the United States, the relatively lower land costs lead to the development of rudimentary warehousing to house forward-buy and promotional stock.

In order to implement ECR, there are 'enabling technologies' (Coopers & Lybrand, 1996) but their implementation is patchy both within and between organizations. For example, McLaughlin, Perosio and Park (1997) comment that 40 per cent of order fulfilment problems in US retailers are a result of miscommunications between retail buyers and their own distribution centre personnel. In Europe, Walker (1994) showed that EDI usage was much greater in the UK than in other European countries – notably Italy with its high cost of telecommunications, lack of management commitment and insufficient critical mass of participants. Since then, widespread ECR initiatives have led to greater use of 'enabling technologies', including web-based technologies, to enhance collaboration.

One area of collaboration that is often overlooked is that between retailer and logistics contractors. The provision of third-party services to retailers varies markedly by country according to the regulatory environment, the competitiveness of the sector and other logistics culture factors. For example, in the UK the deregulation of transport occurred in 1968, and many of the companies that provide dedicated distribution to RDCs today are the same companies that acted for suppliers when they controlled the supply chain 20 years ago. Retailers contracted out because of the opportunity cost of opening stores rather than RDCs, the cost was 'off-balance sheet', and there was a cluster of well-established professional companies available to offer the service. The situation is different in other markets. In the United States, third-party logistics is much less developed, warehousing is primarily run by the retailer, and transport is invariably contracted out to local hauliers. Deregulation of transport markets has been relatively late in the United States, leading to more competitive pricing. Similarly, the progressive deregulation of EU markets is breaking down some nationally protected markets.

THE INTERNATIONALIZATION OF LOGISTICS PRACTICES

The transfer of 'know-how' proposed by Kacker (1988) can be applied to logistics practices. Alternatively, companies can pursue an organic growth strategy by building up a retail presence in target markets before rolling out an RDC support function. For example, Marks & Spencer's European retail strategy initially was supported from distribution centres in southern Britain. As French and Spanish markets were developed, warehouses were built to support these stores in Paris and Madrid respectively. Another dimension to the internationalization of retail logistics is the internationalization of logistics service providers, many of whom were commissioned to operate sites on the basis of their relationship with retailers in the UK. With Marks & Spencer, Exel was the contractor operating the RDCs in France and Spain.

The expansion of the retail giants into new geographical markets is leading to internationalization of logistics. The approach to knowledge transfer is largely dependent upon the different models of globalized retail operations utilized by these mega-groups. Wrigley (2002) classified these retailers into two groups: one following the 'aggressively industrial' model, the other the 'intelligently federal' model (see Table 18.4). In the former model, to which Wal-Mart and to a lesser extent Tesco can be classified, the focus is upon economies of scale in purchasing and strong implementation of the corporate culture and management practices.

In the UK, Wal-Mart's impact on Asda's logistics has been mainly in enhancing IT infrastructure and reconfiguring its distribution network to supply the increase in non-food lines. By 2005, 20 supercentres had been opened, with 50 per cent of their space devoted to non-food items – and existing stores will release more space for these with the release of space from enhanced IT systems. Project Breakthrough introduced new EPOS and stock data systems from 2000, and their retail link system has allowed greater coordination of information from till to supplier, reducing costs and enhancing product availability.

Ahold, by contrast, adheres to the intelligently federal model. It has transformed logistics practices through retail alliances, and through synergies developed with its web of subsidiaries. In the United States, for example, it has retained the local store names post-acquisition and adopted best practice across subsidiaries.

Another method of transferring 'know-how' is through retail alliances, a large number of which exist throughout Europe, most of which are buying groups (Robinson and Clarke-Hill, 1995). However, some of these alliances have been promoting a cross-fertilization of logistics ideas and practices. In the case of the European Retail Alliance, Safeway in the UK has partnered with Ahold of the Netherlands and Casino in France. Not surprisingly, the exploitation of UK retail logistics expertise has enabled distribution contractors to penetrate foreign retail markets, not only in support of British retail companies' entry strategies but also for other international retailers. Harvey (1997), chairman of Tibbett and Britten,

Table 18.4 Alternative corporate models of a globalized retail operation

'Aggressively industrial'	'Intelligently federal'
Low format adaptation	Multiple/flexible formats
Lack of partnerships/alliances in emerging markets	Partnerships/alliances in emerging markets
Focus on economies of scale in purchasing, marketing and logistics	Focus on back-end integration, accessing economies of skills as much as scale, and best-practice knowledge transfer
Centralized bureaucracy, export of key management and corporate culture from core	Absorb, utilize/transfer, best local management acquired
The global 'category killer' model	The umbrella organization/corporate parent management acquired model

Source: Wrigley, 2002

argued that the success of his company – and other UK logistics specialists – is derived from the success of fast-moving consumer goods, but, as with UK retailers, success for the future lies with global opportunities.

THE FUTURE

Clearly there has been a transformation of logistics within retailing during the last 25 years. Centralization, new technologies, ECR, QR and CPFR, and the implementation of best-practice principles have resulted in logistics becoming a key management function within retailing. But what of the future? With the exception of e-tail logistics, there is a feeling of déjà vu about the concerns expressed by senior logistics managers on the key issues to be addressed. Product availability – or the 'last 50 yards' issue – is of prime concern. It is somewhat alarming that on-shelf availability for some of our major grocery retailers is no better than it was 30 to 40 years ago for many key value items (KVIs). In the 1960s and 1970s, customers could easily go to the nearest store to pick up a manufacturer's brand unavailable at their preferred store. In the days of car-orientated supermarkets it would seem that store switching is less likely than in the days when a greater number of outlets and companies prevailed. Continual non-availability of key items can be a major factor in diminishing store loyalty. It is not surprising, therefore, that much of the focus of CPFR initiatives is not only on promotional items but also on KVIs to enhance on-shelf availability. In order to sell in-store, replenishment times need to be reduced so that the overall supply chain is more flexible to meet changing consumer demands.

In many ways this is a rerun of issues originally raised in the 1970s and 1980s. The main difference now is that retailers have a range of tools that allow massive supply chain savings to be realized. The problem is that the infrastructure changes required and the systems enhancement needed involve massive capital investment at a time when competition is fierce and achieving sales growth is difficult. All of these initiatives are also resource-hungry in terms of management time, and have considerable implications for the relationships among people, processes and technology. In retailing, competitive advantage is invariably achieved on the successful implementation of initiatives that are available to all – but only realized by companies with the quality of management to achieve results.

Tesco has been particularly innovative in seeking new solutions to improve on-shelf availability and reduce stockholding levels. Shock stock-outs in the 1970s emphasized the importance of supply chain management to the company and drove recognition that the supply chain was an integral part of company strategy. In the 1980s Tesco was in the forefront in creating composite distribution centres, and in the 1990s it implemented ECR and CPFR. Since the late 1990s much of Tesco's management philosophy has been linked to 'lean thinking', and further improvements are ongoing. One initiative that has created a high degree of controversy has been the advent of factory gate pricing. Although backhauling and consolidation of loads was a feature of the previous decades, this was organized on a fairly ad hoc manner with a series of bilateral transport contracts between logistics service providers and retailers and manufacturers. Now the larger grocery retailers are sourcing products 'ex-works', thereby managing the entire transport operation from factory to consumer.

The concept of factory gate pricing is not just being applied to the grocery sector. Similar principles are being adopted in non-food, and especially the fashion sector. Instead of FOB, retailers are seeking to source ex-works, liaising with LSPs to consolidate loads and prepare floor-ready merchandise to minimize handling at the downstream part of the supply chain. The fashion sector has a longer and more complex supply chain than groceries, but lead times to the EU can be reduced (relative to Pacific Rim sources) by sourcing from the Middle East and Eastern Europe. As Marks & Spencer has acknowledged, however, the quest for low-cost sourcing is only one solution to competing in highly competitive pricing markets. Other developments in fashion have seen time-based competition become more critical, with retailers such as Zara emerging and competing successfully, in part on supply chain speed and excellence.

Advances in information systems over the last two decades have acted as enablers facilitating supply chain efficiency. Bar codes, EDI, enterprise resources planning (ERP) systems and internet-based exchanges have all reduced the administrative costs of communication among supply chain partners. The next potential major technological breakthrough that will have a significant impact upon supply chain costs is radio frequency identification (RFID) technology. Potential benefits to retailers are claimed to be immense. RFID could lead to the effective tracking of goods from factory to the home. Issues of cost and concerns over consumer privacy threaten the implementation of RFID, but it may also be that proponents have minimized some of the management and data use implications.

It is probable that the technology will be rolled out in stages, focusing on obvious issues and bottlenecks in supply chains. Initially the focus will be on tracking pallets, dollies and bins as they move from picking to the back room of the store. This will give cost savings in labour through greater automation of tracking and more visibility. Shrinkage (which costs retailers 1–2 per cent of sales a year) and stockholding levels should be reduced. As the costs of tags reduce – and if fears over consumer privacy are addressed – RFID tags will be used at the item level and implemented at store level. For retailers seeking to maximize on-shelf availability, this should give up-to-date information on sales and in-store inventory, with consequent supply chain benefits.

E-tail logistics is one area where activity is considerable – though perhaps not yet at the level anticipated by most commentators. Major changes may still occur, particularly when the e-tailing sector achieves greater stability. In the last few years a shake-out of the dot.com sector has occurred. In the non-food sector, a well-established delivery system is now in place and this system is being refined to accommodate the multi-channel strategy that is being adopted by most successful retailers. Traditional catalogue retailing incurred a high rate of 'returns' through the logistical network. This is being reinforced by online retailing, where around one-third of non-food products delivered to the home are returned. The reverse logistics task of retrieval, repackaging and returning or re-routeing merchandise is complex enough from home to warehouse, but web shoppers are also returning merchandise to their nearest store. 'Bricks and clicks' may increase customer spend and enhance loyalty but it also adds to costs. The need to invest in systems and infrastructure to accommodate such changes is leading to the formation of alliances among retailers to share these costs and build upon their relative expertise in supply chain functions.

E-grocery logistics has posed more formidable challenges. The initial 'hype' associated with the dot.com boom led to much investment into dedicated picking centres. In retrospect this was a flawed strategy based on unrealistic demand projections. Store-based fulfilment offered a more risk-averse approach to e-grocery, with demand met from existing assets and the e-grocer able to refine its systems and customer service as it gained experience. Nevertheless, there are questions about the long-term sustainability of such a model if online grocery sales continue to grow at current rates. The sharing of the same inventory between store and online shopper could aggravate the on-shelf availability problem and ultimately lead to poor customer service levels for both. As the market matures, investment in 'stand-alone' picking centres will be necessary in specific geographical markets, and the market leader, Tesco, intends to open such a centre in Croydon, near London, in 2006.

Regardless of the fulfilment model used, the 'last mile' problem is far from being resolved. Customers prefer narrow time slots for attended delivery; retailers prefer to utilize their transport assets around the clock. Ideally, the unattended delivery option is best for most parties, as customers are not constrained by delivery times, retailers can reduce their transport costs, and local authorities can reduce van congestion with 24-hour deliveries. But will customers invest in home reception facilities or be willing to pick up groceries in communal reception boxes? Initial reactions to such proposals have been lukewarm to say the least, leaving key problems to be overcome.

References

Azuma, N (2001) The reality of quick response (QR) in the Japanese fashion sector and the strategy ahead for the domestic SME apparel manufacturers, *Logistics Research Network 2001 Conference Proceedings*, pp 11–20, Heriot-Watt University, Edinburgh

Christopher, M (1997) *Marketing Logistics*, Butterworth-Heinemann, Oxford

Christopher, M (1998) *Logistics and Supply Chain Management*, 2nd edn, Financial Times, London

Christopher, M and Jüttner, U (2000) Achieving supply chain excellence: the role of relationship management, *International Journal of Logistics: Research and application*, 3 (1), pp 5–23

Christopher, M and Peck, H (2003) *Marketing Logistics*, Butterworth-Heinemann, London

Coopers & Lybrand (1996) *European Value Chain Analysis Study: Final report*, ECR Europe, Utrecht

Drucker, P (1962) The economy's dark continent, *Fortune*, April, pp 265–70

Fernie, J (1994) Quick response: an international perspective, *International Journal of Physical Distribution and Logistics Management*, 24 (6), pp 38–46

Fernie, J (1995) International comparisons of supply chain management in grocery retailing, *Service Industries Journal*, **15** (4), pp 134–47

Fernie, J (1998) Relationships in the supply chain, in *Logistics and Retail Management*, ed J Fernie and L Sparks, Kogan Page, London

Fernie, J, Pfab, F and Marchant, C (2000) Retail logistics in the UK: planning for the medium term, *International Journal of Logistics Management*, **11** (2), pp 83–90

Fiddis, C (1997) *Manufacturer–Retailer Relationships in the Food and Drink Industry: Strategies and tactics in the battle for power*, FT Retail and Consumer Publishing, Pearson Professional, London

Finnie, TA (1992) *Textiles and Apparel in the U.S.A.: Restructuring for the 1990s*, Special Report 2632, Economist Intelligence Unit, London

Forza, C and Vinelli, A (1996) An analytical scheme for the change of the apparel design process towards quick response, *International Journal of Clothing Science and Technology*, **8** (4), pp 28–43

Forza, C and Vinelli, A (1997) Quick response in the textile-apparel industry and the support of information technologies, *Integrated Manufacturing Systems*, **8** (3), pp 125–36

Forza, C and Vinelli, A (2000) Time compression in production and distribution within the textile-apparel chain, *Integrated Manufacturing Systems*, **11** (2), pp 138–46

GEA Consultia (1994) *Supplier–Retailer Collaboration in Supply Chain Management*, Coca-Cola Retailing Research Group Europe, London

Giunipero, LC *et al* (2001) The impact of vendor incentives on quick response, *International Review of Retail, Distribution and Consumer Research*, **11** (4), pp 359–76

Harvey, J (1997) International contract logistics, *Logistics Focus*, April, pp 2–6

Hines, T (2001) From analogue to digital supply chain: implications for fashion marketing, in *Fashion Marketing: Contemporary issues*, ed P Hines and M Bruce, Butterworth-Heinemann, Oxford

Hoch, SJ and Pomerantz, JJ (2002) How effective is category management?, *ECR Journal*, **2** (1), pp 26–32

Hunter, A (1990) *Quick Response in Apparel Manufacturing: A survey of the American scene*, Textile Institute, Manchester

Kacker, M (1988) International flows of retail know-how: bridging the technology gap in distributions, *Journal of Retailing*, **64** (1), pp 41–67

Ko, E, Kincade, D and Brown, JR (2000) Impact of business type upon the adoption of quick response technologies: the apparel industry experience, *International Journal of Operations and Production Management*, **20** (9), pp 1093–111

Kurt Salmon Associates (KSA) (1997) *Quick Response: Meeting customer needs*, KSA, Atlanta, GA

Lowson, B (1998) *Quick Response for Small and Medium-Sized Enterprises: A feasibility study*, Textile Institute, Manchester

Lowson, B, King, R and Hunter, A (1999) *Quick Response: Managing the supply chain to meet consumer demand*, John Wiley & Sons, New York

McGrath, M (1997) *A Guide to Category Management*, Institute of Grocery Distribution, Letchmore Heath

McKinnon, AC (1996) The development of retail logistics in the UK: a position paper, Technology Foresight's Retail and Distribution Panel, Heriot-Watt University, Edinburgh

McLaughlin, EW, Perosio, DJ and Park, JL (1997) *Retail Logistics and Merchandising: Requirements in the year 2000*, Cornell University Press, Ithaca, NY

Ministry of Economy, Trade and Industry (METI) (2002) *Seni Sangyo no Genjo to Seisaku Taiou* [The current status of the Japanese textile industry and the political responses], METI, Tokyo

Mitchell, A (1997) *Efficient Consumer Response: A new paradigm for the European FMCG sector*, FT Retail and Consumer Publishing, Pearson Professional, London

Ministry of International Trades and Industries (MITI) (1993) *Seni Vision* [Textile vision], MITI, Tokyo

MITI (1995) *Sekai Seni Sangyo Jijo* [MITI world textile report], MITI, Tokyo

MITI (1999) *Seni Vision* [Textile vision], MITI, Tokyo

Ohbora, T, Parsons, A and Riesenbeck, H (1992) Alternative routes to global marketing, *McKinsey Quarterly*, **3**, pp 52–74

Piore, MJ and Sabel, CF (1984) *The Second Industrial Divide: Possibilities for prosperity*, Basic Books, New York

Porter, ME (1985) *Competitive Advantage*, Free Press, New York

Quick Response Services (1995) *Quick Response Services for Retailers and Manufacturers*, Quick Response Services, Richmond, CA

Riddle, EJ *et al* (1999) The role of electronic data interchange in quick response, *Journal of Fashion Marketing and Management*, **3** (2), pp 133–46

Robinson, T and Clarke-Hill, CM (1995) International alliances in European retailing, in *International Retailing Trade and Strategies*, ed PJ McGoldrick and G Davies, Pitman, Harlow

Scarso, E (1997) Beyond fashion: emerging strategies in the Italian clothing industry, *Journal of Fashion Marketing and Management*, **1** (4), pp 359–71

Taplin, IM and Ordovensky, JF (1995) Changes in buyer–supplier relationships and labor market structure: evidence from the United States, *Journal of Clothing Technology and Management*, **12**, pp 1–18

Voluntary Interindustry Commerce Standards Association (VICS) (1998) *Collaborative Planning, Forecasting, and Replenishment Voluntary Guidelines*, VICS, Lawrenceville, NJ

Walker, M (1994) Supplier–retailer collaboration in European grocery distribution, Paper presented at the IGD Conference on Profitable Collaboration in Supply Chain Management, London

Whiteoak, P (1993) The realities of quick response in the grocery sector: a supply viewpoint, *International Journal of Retail and Distribution Management*, **21** (8), pp 3–10

Wrigley, N (2001) The consolidation wave in US food retailing: a European perspective, *Agribusiness*, **17**, pp 489–513

Wrigley, N (2002) The landscape of pan-European food retail consolidation, *International Journal of Retail and Distribution Management*, **30** (2), pp 81–91

19

Internet traders can increase profitability by reshaping their supply chains

Robert Duncan, B & C Business Services

INTERNET TRADING IS FORECAST TO ACCOUNT FOR A QUARTER OF ALL PURCHASES IN 2006

The volume of internet trading grew significantly in the final years of the last century. It continued to grow in the early years of this century and is forecast to grow even further in the next few years. Forrester (2001a) forecast that global online trade, a combination of both business-to-business (B2B) and business-to-consumer (B2C) sales, will account for 18 per cent of all sales by 2006. Furthermore (Forrester, 2001b), two-thirds of the $12.8 trillion expenditure will be accounted for by purchases in the United States, representing 27 per cent of all their goods and services purchased. It is estimated that this increase will add 1.7 per cent to US transport service revenues. The US Department of Commerce reported continuing growth in 2004 with e-commerce sales up 21 per cent for the year. The growth is forecast to continue. US internet retail sales are predicted to grow at a compound annual rate of 14 per cent a year until 2010 (Forrester, 2005b). It is recognized that the United States leads the way in most e-commerce-driven initiatives and, therefore, the scale of increases in the United States is likely to be seen in other developed countries shortly – followed by less developed countries. The UK reported a 30 per cent increase in year-on-year e-retail sales in the third quarter of 2004 (GVA, 2004). The level of sales during the first half of 2004 reflected a fivefold increase in the level experienced in 2001. The route to market, particularly with the introduction of broadband, is seen as so important that in the United States it is forecast that, by 2010, 8 per cent of all advertising spend will be directed at internet advertising in various forms (Forrester, 2005c). This sum will rival that being spent on cable and satellite TV and radio.

CUSTOMER SATISFACTION IS LESS THAN SATISFACTORY

Such growth predictions lie against a background of dissatisfied customers, press reports that many internet traders do not fully understand their order fulfilment costs, and transport service providers complaining that their customers tend to be cost- rather than service-driven. This leads them to suggest that their customers do not fully understand the complexity of home delivery – or B2C operations – and consequently the added value that they provide. This background has been created by internet traders trying to operate effectively utilizing traditional distribution methods and networks. There has been a tendency to concentrate too much effort on websites, and not pay enough attention to the business processes needed to integrate order capture with other business systems and order fulfilment.

Dissatisfaction in the mind of the customer can be created in a number of ways. Late delivery, damaged goods, poorly handled financial transactions and bad-tempered delivery people are just a few. It is generally accepted that because the placing of an order via the internet is extremely quick, simple and in many cases pleasurable, the expectation in the mind of the customer is that all aspects of the transaction will be of a similar nature. Customer expectation has been heightened. The ordering process was slick and customers, not unreasonably, expect the rest of the process to be undertaken with the same efficiency. Under these circumstances, it is more likely that the customer will not be fully satisfied unless particular steps are taken to ensure that the level of service provided meets the heightened level of expectations. It is all too easy to undo the excellent work done by the website in winning the customer – and the order – by inadequate business processes and order fulfilment procedures.

INTEGRATION OF BUSINESS PROCESSES HAS NOT ALWAYS RECEIVED ENOUGH ATTENTION

Many organizations are now realizing – often too late – that they should have paid as much attention to their internal business processes, their order fulfilment resources and systems, and the integration of these processes and systems with those of their suppliers and order fulfilment services as they did to their customer-facing website. The need is for a seamless, end-to-end 'order-to-cash' process incorporating the website, the business's accounting systems and the delivery mechanism. The accounting needs should embrace, as a minimum, accounts payable, accounts receivable, inventory, purchase orders, invoicing and credit control.

In many organizations, when internet trading is added to the traditional market offering the delivery mechanisms cannot cope with the requirement for a large number of small orders that require, to all intents and purposes, instant shipping. They may historically have been shipping relatively large orders to a few intermediate supply chain points with a two- to three-day lead time. The business processes – and perhaps more importantly the business systems that are required to manage a large number of small orders – are different from those required to manage the traditional business. The potential for making mistakes is high when an organization attempts to manage the internet business in the same way as the traditional business. And all the effort and resources that went into winning the business are wasted by losing that business due to the inadequate processes and systems to support order fulfilment.

MOVING AWAY FROM TRADITIONAL SUPPLY CHAINS ADDS COMPLEXITY BUT PROVIDES AN OPPORTUNITY FOR PROFIT

The situation is made even more complex by the fact that the rise in internet trading has provided the potential to restructure traditional distribution networks, supply chains and product flows. Much of the thinking to date relates to the traditional ways of moving products from manufacturers to customers. In the B2C area this has reflected traditional mail-ordering concepts as typified by those organizations selling products such as books and music CDs. In simple terms, rather than ordering from a catalogue received in the mail and posting their order back to their suppliers, customers are placing their order via the internet. Their products are delivered to them in much the same way as they were with traditional mail order. The key differences are that the ordering process has been shortened and the manufacturers' order capture and processing costs have been reduced. Food retailers offering home-delivery services typically rely on the order that has been received via the internet being printed in the branch nearest to the customer, picked from the shelves in that branch and delivered, by a branch-based vehicle, to the home of the customer.

Internet trading has enabled improved supply chains

Recent supply chain trends have reflected changes made possible by the internet as a means of communicating between buyers and sellers. When the simple scenario described above is related to books, it no longer requires a supply chain involving the printer and publisher, an intermediate stockholding location and an organization to promote the offer, capture the order and execute the delivery. Potential customers can place their orders using either their own PC at home or a terminal in the branch of a high-street book retailer specifically provided for browsing and order capture. The order is then transmitted to the relevant publisher – not an intermediate stockholding point – for picking, packing and shipping directly to the customer.

Books and CDs lend themselves ideally to this type of trade as, apart from some minor exceptions, they can easily be shipped across borders and they do not require particular shipping conditions in terms of temperature control. The situation for foodstuffs is very different. A single customer order may be relatively heavy, consist of a number of different-size cartons and bottles, require a range of temperature regimes and need to be delivered within a tightly defined time frame. As volumes increase, the industry is beginning to introduce home-delivery picking and delivery depots located away from the prime retail sites. Such facilities enable the use of sophisticated warehouse techniques, made possible by the automatic entry of customer orders into the warehouse system. The advantages created by customers ordering over the internet include more effective picking operations in a depot rather than a branch, improved product availability through monitoring the particular purchasing patterns of internet shoppers, lower delivery costs as the increased volumes allow sophisticated routing and scheduling techniques, and less congestion in the branches.

The monitoring of individuals' consumption patterns – and the retailers' websites both prompting and reminding their regular customers of those patterns as they go through the ordering process – could further extend the concept.

Such changes could be introduced into other market sectors

The two examples above – books and CDs – suggest modifications of current practices and adjustment to supply chains that result from the ability to place orders over the internet. The concepts could be used by other manufacturers not currently fully embracing the potential of electronically capturing orders and shipping customer orders directly to them. Figure 19.1 shows a general supply chain for the distribution of prescription drugs from a manufacturer to a patient.

The main characteristic is the use of wholesalers and retailers to make the delivery to the patient once a doctor has prescribed the particular drug. In the case of hospitalized patients, there is usually another stockholding point in the hospital's pharmacy, between the manufacturer and the patient. Large hospitals using large amounts of particular drugs receive deliveries directly from the manufacturers, but these are the exception rather than the rule.

The level of service provided is extremely high, with wholesalers making multiple deliveries a day to retailers to ensure that particular drugs – from the plethora potentially available – are delivered to the patients as soon as possible. However, patients often have to return to the pharmacy for either all or part of their requirements once they have

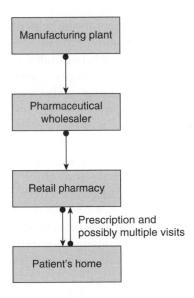

Figure 19.1   A typical pharmaceutical manufacturer's distribution network

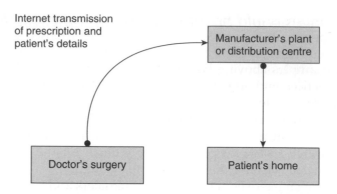

Figure 19.2 A possible pharmaceutical manufacturer's distribution network

presented their prescription. Owing to the nature of the products, the flows are highly regulated, and some form of control is obviously necessary. However, a more streamlined approach could be envisaged using the internet as the means of communication. Figure 19.2 illustrates a possible use of the internet to facilitate the order fulfilment of prescription drugs.

The scenario starts with the doctor prescribing the drugs in an electronic format and sending details via the internet to the manufacturer once the consultation with the patient has finished. The manufacturer simply picks, packs and ships the products to the patient's home. The shipping process would utilize the best means available to suit the characteristics of the product. Small and light packets of tablets, for example, could be shipped using conventional postal services; more sophisticated products requiring careful handling may use specialist express parcels services. A less radical version of the concept may result in the wholesalers providing the home-delivery service on a regional basis. In each case, the distribution supply chain is simplified and the patient does not have to go to the retail outlet, sometimes more than once, to obtain his or her medication. This is particularly advantageous for elderly and infirm patients.

Many retail pharmacists have introduced a prescription collection and delivery service, but their aim is not to simplify the supply chain, but to maintain the status quo. The supply chain change outlined not only provides an improved service to customers and a reduction in the complexity of the manufacturers' supply chains, but also helps overcome some of the issues associated with the parallel importing of pharmaceuticals. Pharmaceuticals are sold at varying prices around the world, so traders can buy cheaply in some areas, ship the products to areas of high selling prices and make a profit. Pharmaceutical companies experience lower sales in those areas with high selling prices, reduced profit levels – and, therefore, potentially lower research budgets. The proposed supply chain change gives pharmaceutical companies greater control through disintermediation, with less buying and selling of product by third parties, and less cross-border movements. The use of RFID technology, effectively electronically 'tagging' products, will also assist with the control of pharmaceuticals from the manufacturing plant to the point of use by the patient. This will increase service levels, reduce costs and sustain pharmaceutical research and development in the future.

The concept can also be applied in the B2B context

The B2B area also provides opportunities to restructure traditional supply chains. For many years, supply chain organizations have exchanged information electronically regarding production schedules, raw material and component stock levels and forecast levels of demand and production capacity. Suppliers and buyers, particularly in the automotive sector, have practised just-in-time techniques relying on electronic communication. They have developed and introduced order fulfilment techniques reshaping the structure of the distribution supply chains, enabling minimal inventories to be maintained through line-side delivery and rapid communication.

Other organizations have centralized their storage operations as a result of being able to communicate rapidly and fulfil orders using efficient transport services. The emergence of cost-effective and reliable, high-speed transport services has played an important role in achieving the ambitions of those players embarking upon an internet trading journey. The systems used by such organizations enable their customers to track their own shipments. This is essential in the early stages of using a changed network to give customers – both internal and external to the organization – the confidence that the remote operation will provide the required levels of service. More importantly, the systems enable carriers themselves to be proactive on the rare occasion that some corrective action is needed.

The impact will not be as large in all industry sectors

The reshaping of the supply chain as a result of internet trading and the emergence of reliable and cost-effective rapid-transport service providers will not affect all industry sectors to the same extent. While communications may improve – a worthwhile end in itself – it is difficult to envisage the network for bulk building supplies (such as sand, ballast and cement) changing significantly. The biggest impact is likely to be in the order

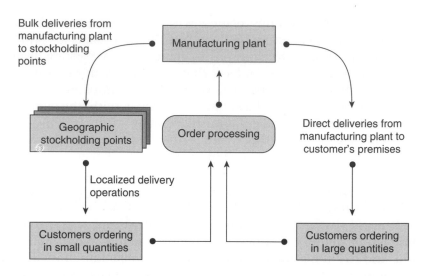

Figure 19.3 A traditional industrial supplier's distribution network

fulfilment of those products that are relatively high in value and easily transported. The B2B environment is more stable than B2C, with a more defined customer base and a better understanding of demand patterns. The traditional distribution supply chain of an industrial company is shown in Figure 19.3. It is characterized by the direct delivery of large orders from factory to customer and the use of distributors, agents or wholesalers for the delivery of small orders to customers on a geographic basis.

The internet can capture and process orders more cheaply and quickly, so manufacturers are beginning to consider reducing the number of middlemen that they use to fulfil customers' orders. Companies that supply consumables to other companies for use in their manufacturing can provide monitoring devices that send material usage statistics to them, via the internet, triggering automatic replenishment orders. Once a history of usage has been established, order fulfilment can be achieved more cost-effectively, with better planning to minimize the effects of peaks in demand. The customer does not need to maintain a purchasing function to place orders, and the supplier does not need to incur the costs of an order processing department – a 'win–win' scenario.

There is likely to be an increase in centralized operations

The biggest changes in order fulfilment infrastructure as a result of internet trading are likely to be in the area of centralized operations. Establishing a small number of order fulfilment centres – with associated software to integrate the website ordering process with the organization's business systems – is likely to be more cost-effective than the establishment of a larger number of local operations. Although transport costs are likely to increase as a result, they will be more than offset by lower order processing costs, inventory-related costs and warehouse facility costs. At constant volume, increased margins will be attainable or lower prices can be charged to increase market share and enhance profitability.

In Europe, organizations that typically operated on a national basis are establishing more regionalized operations. Products that are of relatively high value and easily transported tend to support larger regions than those that have low value and require specific transport resources. For example, companies with spare-part operations tend to centralize activities, as field engineers and customers can communicate with a central point via the internet, and inventory control is much simpler with a central stock than several stockholding locations. The enlarged membership of the EU has resulted in many organizations revisiting their infrastructure and designing regionalized structures.

As the infrastructures change and the traditional role of intermediaries declines, a new group of internet traders is emerging offering purchasing function services. In general terms, they negotiate prices with a range of suppliers and offer, over the internet, a one-stop service for the products of those suppliers to their customers. Once they have taken an order from a customer it is converted to an order with a supplier. That supplier then fulfils the order in the conventional manner. The benefits of this scenario are that the customers obtain better prices, the suppliers do not have the costs of the customer-facing activities and the internet trader makes money by providing an added-value service to both customer and supplier without stocking and handling the products.

The challenge is becoming greater

The growth in internet trading has not been accompanied by tales of delighted customers or order fulfilment processes to match the heightened customer expectation. Early experience suggested that organizations were not particularly good at integrating their website order capturing activities with their internal business systems and those of their order fulfilment service provider. And many organizations did not realize the potential of the internet for streamlining their supply chains. Changing business processes and introducing the necessary systems to trade over the internet provided a challenge within existing business relationships and infrastructures. The challenge is being made all the more difficult as business relationships and the physical infrastructure within which those relationships operate are changing.

HOW CAN INTERNET TRADERS TAKE ADVANTAGE OF OPPORTUNITIES?

In this ever-changing world not all of the potential internet-driven supply chain changes will be appropriate for all internet traders. Even within an industry sector, patterns will emerge, but the same solution may not be suitable for all of the players in that sector. There are, however, four activities that all internet traders can complete as a starting point for optimizing their benefits:

1. *The establishment of a vision of the future:* 'Where are we going and what is it going to be like when we get there?'
2. *The definition of the partnering arrangements needed for success:* 'Who is going to help us get to where we are going and how are we going to manage them?'
3. *The reviewing of their business processes and electronic systems:* 'Can our processes and systems enable us to achieve our long-term objectives?'
4. *The undertaking of trade-off calculations:* 'What options are open to us and how much will they cost?'

These four activities form the key steps of an overall route to success outlined in Figure 19.4.

The establishment of a vision of the future

It is perhaps a little obvious to say that an organization must be able to define the direction in which it intends to go. This vision of the future is not a loose collection of statements amounting to little more than a wish list. It is, however, several statements describing – in quantifiable terms – the nature of the business at some point in the future. That point will vary depending upon the nature of the marketplace in which the organization is operating. In the high-tech sector, the foreseeable future may be only a few months, or a year at the most. In traditional industry sectors that do not expect a significant percentage of their business ever to be undertaken over the internet, the vision may take several years to come to fruition.

The statements should cover the total volume of business both in terms of value and in physical terms, the share that is undertaken over the internet, the size of both the customer and the supplier bases, the profitability of the internet business, the costs associated with order fulfilment, and the delivery profile in terms of order numbers and the amount in each order size band appropriate to the business. Any individual organization

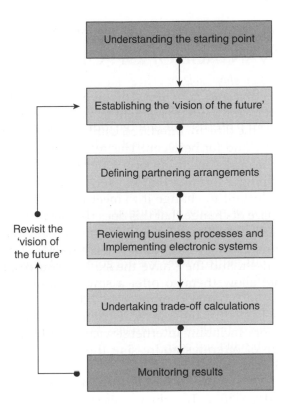

Figure 19.4 A route to success

will have many other metrics particular to its industry sector and product range. The key issue is that they should be measurable. They will be used to establish key performance indicators (KPIs) for the business. These KPIs will be monitored, and the organization can establish the extent to which it is achieving its vision and reaping the rewards from the changes it has made.

The definition of the partnering arrangements needed for success

Organizations wanting to trade over the internet, with a few exceptions, are unlikely to have all of the required skills in-house to establish the website effectively, integrate it with their business systems, and manage the order fulfilment activities. Partners are, therefore, essential for the vast majority of organizations. A number of options are available to potential electronic traders:

- *A single 'one-stop shop' able to deliver the website, integration with a commerce platform, and order fulfilment.* This gives the advantages of a single point of contact for the management team, and an organization that manages all of the difficult interfaces. Until recently, such organizations have been few and far between. This made selecting partners and a successful outcome something of a lottery – with service providers often developing a formula that worked for their original customer, and being reluctant to change it to meet the needs of new entrants. Such is the pace of change that this does not provide as large a barrier to progress as it did a few years ago. The investment in IT by a number of major value-adding order fulfilment contractors is now beginning to manifest itself, and they have the skills, resources, hardware and software that allow them to offer a single end-to-end service. The second wave of internet commerce in 2004 saw an increase in the demand for hosted or outsourced e-commerce solutions (Forrester, 2005a). Vendors, including internet service providers, have responded with a range of offerings addressing the supply chain in either its entirety or its component parts.
- *Partnerships with a number of specialist service providers to source all of the services that they require.* To achieve this successfully, project management and outsourcing management skills need to be in abundance in the organization. While the individual elements of website design, systems integration and order fulfilment may be readily available in the market, the required in-house skills of project and outsourcing management may not. With a trend to more outsourced resources, this issue will gain in significance for many organizations.
- *An organization that has already done all the hard work, but is not in competition with the market entrant.* It is likely that potential partners are traditional 'bricks and mortar' traders that have extended their offering to include an electronic commerce element. Perhaps niche players could partner with major players in their own industry to provide a wider offering to the major players' customers. In the past, small niche players would not have attempted to partner the major industry players, as they would have regarded them as competitors – and unequal partners. For example, the online market for books is dominated by mega-sites such as Amazon and Barnes & Noble. Alibris, a small organization specializing in used and hard-to-find books, now works with the major organizations as a supplier of titles that are not their mainstream business – to the mutual benefit of all of the supply chain partners (Internet.com, 2003).

Thus, there are many ways of developing a partnership. An organization that expects a rapid growth in volume over a short period may favour an added-value service provider, as it could overwhelm a traditional business that currently has only a small part of its business handled by the internet. Organizations that are hoping to move into new markets and/or geographies are likely to favour the added-value service provider. Organizations that see a relatively slow but steady growth may favour managing the situation themselves or partnering with an organization that has already made the leap to internet trading.

The reviewing of their business processes and electronic systems

When reviewing in-house systems, internet traders should include both electronic software systems and the business processes. In terms of the electronic software, the simplest questions include:

- Can our systems cope with a significant increase in transactional volume?
- Can our systems interface with modern websites?
- Can our systems interface with those of our suppliers of both goods and services?
- Can our systems enable us to deliver the required level of customer service?

A few years ago, some of these questions would have sent shivers down the spines of would-be internet traders. Thankfully, modern systems do not generally present significant difficulties with interfacing, and extra capacity is no longer the hugely expensive item that it was in the past. However, the critical area for most organizations is not the software systems and supporting hardware networks, but their business processes. Will any of the order processing, credit checking, inventory allocation, manufacturing, warehousing, shipping, invoicing and cash collection processes within the overall order-to-cash process negatively affect the requirements of the internet business?

If an organization is a true middleman and does not expect to hold stock, but converts a sales order from a customer into a purchase order for a supplier, its internal processes will need to be able to cope with this. It may be necessary to have a different process for internet trade from that used for conventional business in organizations handling both routes to market. The questions needing to be answered under these circumstances include:

- Who will design the required processes to ensure that all customers' requirements are met?
- What will be the impact of those new processes on existing processes and the consequent risk to our traditional business?
- Will we achieve the predicted levels of economies of scale employing two or more order-to-cash processes?

These questions will be easier to answer if a clear understanding of the business direction has been established. When the internet business is seen to grow steadily but will never be a significant part of the business, the duplicated process route may be the easiest way of dealing with matters. Alternatively, if the internet business is expected to grow rapidly and both the conventional and the internet trades become significant elements of the total business, a single process route would have merit.

Trade-off calculations

Analyses of the overall network and the options available to achieve the required levels of customer service are essential. To undertake the trade-off calculations associated with changing supply chains and distribution networks in order to select the best route to market for any individual internet entrepreneur, a full knowledge of the current and potential operating costs is needed. Again, the importance of a vision of the future can readily be appreciated. While having that vision is important, understanding the starting point is also extremely important. Key questions to be answered include:

- What volumes are being dispatched?
- What levels of service are being achieved?
- What costs are being incurred?
- Do we feel that we are obtaining value for money from the resources being employed?

The vision will be able to provide answers to the questions about future volumes and expected margins. The internet trader must then define a number of options for delivering the future volumes within the required customer service level constraints. They are likely to be network models with decentralized or centralized, direct delivery or delivery via distributors, and stockless or inventory-holding themes. A number of evaluation criteria – in addition to those that are strictly cost-related – will be required to establish the most appropriate solution for each particular trader. While industry sectors may find similar solutions, an individual organization in that sector will be driven by its vision of the future and its culture in achieving that goal.

OPPORTUNITY WAITING TO BE EXPLOITED

Internet trading is here to stay and, if recent experience is any guide, volumes are set to grow significantly in the very near future. Given the growth predictions, suppliers to both the consumer and the business markets have a tremendous opportunity. They are setting out on the journey against a background of heightened customer expectation and a history of failure to meet those expectations. The winners will be those organizations that take the opportunity afforded by the internet to change the manner in which they capture and fulfil their customers' orders.

To date, many traders have implemented an internet 'front end' to their existing business processes. Consequently, the initial limited volumes have been treated in the same way as their mainstream volumes. Those customers ordering via the internet have different customer service level needs and expectations from most traditional customers – hence the levels of disappointment expressed.

The internet allows for different trading relationships and physical networks to be established. Those traders that develop a vision of the future incorporating the available potential, enter into partnering arrangements to enhance their internal skill base, review their business processes to meet their customers' needs, implement electronic systems to support those new business processes, and undertake the trade-off calculations to identify the most appropriate ways of meeting all of their customers' needs will reap the benefits. Newcomers can learn from those organizations that are acknowledged industry leaders and advance quickly up the learning curve.

The opportunity is real. The winners will be those that grasp the opportunity by using the internet as a means of gaining competitive advantage, rather than continue to use it as a bolt-on extra to existing traditional operating methods.

References

Department of Commerce (2004) *Ecommerce-guide.com: E-commerce business is booming*, November, US Department of Commerce, Washington, DC

Forrester (2001a) *Techstrategy Brief*, December, Forrester Research, Cambridge, MA

Forrester (2001b) *Techstrategy Report: eBusiness propels productivity*, November, Forrester Research, Cambridge, MA

Forrester (2005a) *A Buyer's Guide to Hosted eCommerce Solutions*, January, Forrester Research Paper, Cambridge, MA

Forrester (2005b) *US eCommerce, 2005 to 2010*, September, Forrester Research Paper, Cambridge, MA

Forrester (2005c) *US Online Marketing Forecast, 2005 to 2010*, May, Forrester Research Paper, Cambridge, MA

GVA (2004) *Retail Trends*, Third Quarter, Grimley Research, London

Internet.com (2003) *Case Study: Alibris*, August

20

Time as a trade barrier

Hildegunn Nordås, OECD[1]

INTRODUCTION

It is no coincidence that cities and industrial clusters are located around good harbours or other nodes in transport networks. Easy access to food, industrial inputs and markets goes a long way in explaining the location of economic activities. One would, however, expect that with improved transport and communication technology, economic activity would become more evenly spread across the globe. This has not happened. Geographical clustering of economic activities has actually increased while the world's most peripheral countries have become increasingly economically remote.[2]

This paradox is first due to the fact that as transport, communication and other trade costs come down, more is traded and trade costs remain as important as ever for location of production.[3] A major reason why firms choose to increase their expenditure on transport is that this is more than compensated by savings on input prices and inventories. Thus, manufacturers increasingly outsource non-core activities to outside suppliers who often are expected to deliver their goods or services several times per day while only minutes of delay on each delivery are tolerated.

Second, remote areas become relatively more economically remote when infrastructure and logistics are improved in central areas. Better roads will encourage investment in bigger trucks that cannot economically service remote areas, better ports encourage investment in larger and faster vessels that bypass smaller ports and so on. For many developing countries this means that integration into world markets requires a long leap forward as far as availability and quality of transport and other logistics services are concerned.

Another factor disadvantaging peripheral countries is the diffusion of just-in-time (JIT) production systems beyond their application to advanced manufacturing. JIT is also increasingly important in the retail sector, where the practice has been coined 'lean retailing'. One example is fast fashion, where new models designed on the basis of observed consumer behaviour are introduced at frequent intervals. This usually requires that suppliers are located close to the market, where production costs can be relatively high.[4] However, fashionable products that are available only for a short season fetch a higher price in the market and this compensates for higher costs, it is claimed.

This chapter analyses lead time as a barrier to entry in foreign markets, using the gravity model. It is argued that the decision to enter a new export market is different from the decision to expand in an existing market. Or, seen from the importers' point of view, the decision to look for a new supplier in a different country is different from extending a contract with an existing supplier.[5] In either case, a new supplier/customer relationship requires fixed upfront costs on both sides. If, for instance, firms cannot meet foreign customers' lead time and reliability requirements, they will not be short-listed for bidding on contracts unless investments in better supply chain management systems and better quality control are made, sometimes involving hefty ICT expenditures. Furthermore, such investment will only pay off if infrastructure, transport and logistics services can support JIT delivery.

TIME, LOGISTICS AND TRADE – HOW ARE THEY RELATED?

Time for exports and imports

There are three concepts related to time that need to be considered when discussing time as a trade barrier: lead time, time variability and JIT. Lead time is the amount of time between the placement of an order and the receipt of the goods ordered, while time variability is measured by the (statistical) variation in lead time. JIT refers to a way of organizing production where inbound as well as outbound inventories are kept to a bare minimum and inputs arrive in the factory at the point where they enter the production process. Lead time and its variability are determined on the supply side, while JIT is a requirement on the demand side.

Both lead time and time variability constitute trade and entry barriers and these are more important the more widespread JIT technologies are. Lead time depends on the nature of the product, eg whether it is made to order or if it is a 'from the shelf' product. It also depends on planning and supply chain management, logistics services and, of course, distance between customers and suppliers. Long lead time does not need to be a problem if time variability is low and demand is stable.[6] However, if there is uncertainty about future demand, long lead time is costly even when the customer knows exactly when the merchandise will arrive. If future demand has been underestimated, running out of stock has costs in terms of forgone sales and the possibility of losing customers. If future demand has been overestimated, excess supply must be sold at a discount.

The impact of lead time and time variability also depends on the number of varieties of the product in question, since separate stocks will be required for each variety. Thus, for products for which product differentiation is important, lead time is likely to have a strong impact on the choice of suppliers. Finally it is important to notice that competitiveness, as far as timeliness is concerned, is not a static concept. When a critical mass of suppliers is able to deliver just in time and the customer finds it safe to reduce inbound inventories to a couple of days' – or in some cases even a couple of hours' – supply, those who are not able to deliver just in time will no longer be invited to bid on contracts. Therefore, it is time *relative to competitors* that matters for market entry.

Transit time in international trade has come down over the past decades due to faster ships, more effective multi-modal transport and a sharp fall in the cost of air transport. The relative cost of air transport in fact declined by 40 per cent between 1990 and 2004 (Harrigan, 2005). This induced a shift from sea to air transport and a reduction in the average shipping time to the United States from 40 days in 1950 to 10 days in 1998 (Hummels, 2001; Hummels and Schaur, 2009).[7]

The World Bank has since 2004 conducted an annual survey of freight forwarders in most of its member countries on freight time and costs from the factory gate until the cargo is loaded on a ship, including administrative procedures such as acquiring an export or import licence, customs clearance and inspection of goods. Table 20.1 presents regional averages and the top and bottom countries ranked by time for exports from the 2009 survey. Time for exports varies between 5 and 102 days, with Denmark, Estonia and Singapore sharing the top rank and Iraq having the longest time for exports.

Manufactured exports contain a considerable amount of imports, and time for imports is also highly relevant for the competitiveness of a

Table 20.1   Time for exports and imports, 2009

	Time for export (days)	Time for import (days)
East Asia & Pacific	22.1	24.3
Europe & Central Asia	26.8	28.4
Latin America & Caribbean	18.6	20.9
Middle East & North Africa	22.5	25.9
OECD: High income	10.5	11.0
South Asia	32.4	32.2
Sub-Saharan Africa	33.6	39.4
Denmark	5	5
Estonia	5	5
Singapore	5	3
Iraq	102	101
Uzbekistan	80	104

Note: Among OECD countries Mexico is included in Latin America & Caribbean, the Czech Republic, Hungary, Poland and the Slovak Republic are included in Europe and Central Asia.
Source: World Bank

country's exports. Many manufacturing industries, notably electronics, automotive and clothing, are characterized by elaborate international production networks where timely delivery is of utmost importance. In 2001, the import content was 32 per cent of export value in the electronics sector in China, 55 per cent in Ireland, 65 per cent in Thailand and 72 per cent in the Philippines. In the clothing sector, the import content of exports was 43 per cent in Sri Lanka, 40 per cent in Vietnam, 54 per cent in Ireland, 80 per cent in Botswana and 38 per cent in the Philippines, to mention but a few (Nordås, 2008).[8] Singapore ranks on top on time for imports with 3 days only, while Uzbekistan has the longest time for imports at as much as 104 days.

Depending on at what point in the production cycle the administrative procedures related to exports can start and whether or not the necessary permits and documents are specific to each shipment or are given to an exporting or importing company for a defined time period, the time for exports and time for imports could overlap to various degrees. In a worst-case scenario, the administrative procedures are repeated for each shipment and the procedures for imports start when an order is received, whereas procedures for exports start only when the goods are finished. If so, an Iraqi business that would need to import intermediate inputs would have a lead time of almost seven months due to time for imports and exports alone.

The role of logistics services

Just-in-time combined with small inventories requires sophisticated logistics. An example of this is Ford's factory in Toronto which receives 800 deliveries a day from 300 different parts makers who deliver to 12 different points along the assembly line, without any delivery being more than 10 minutes late. A specialist firm has been contracted to organize the inbound logistics system.[9] Supplies must be kept close to the assembly line in such cases. Another study reports that Ford in Valencia, Spain was linked to 50 suppliers with specifically designed aerial tunnels (Lukman Susanto, 2003).

Fast fashion is another sector where firms close to the market are at an advantage in spite of having high production costs compared to developing countries. Two examples are American Apparel and Zara. American Apparel is a vertically integrated clothing firm with production facilities in Los Angeles, employing 5,000 people in Los Angeles and 10,000 globally. It is the largest sewn products facility in the United States, and the average wage paid to sewers is $12 per hour. The company also has a distribution centre in Canada and offers two-day air-freight to Europe. It markets itself as a socially responsible company, which appears to be a successful competitive factor in addition to the speedy response to consumer tastes.[10]

In Europe, Zara, a Spanish vertically integrated fashion clothing firm, has rapidly gained market share based on the fast fashion concept. It takes two weeks for a skirt to get from Zara's design team in Spain to a Zara store almost anywhere in the world. Clothing is largely manufactured in Spain and Portugal at higher production costs than rivals that produce in China, India or other low-wage countries. Nevertheless, the company claims that higher labour costs are more than compensated by higher productivity, lower distribution costs and greater flexibility.[11]

A good example of the opportunities that efficient logistics services can open for developing countries is the recent entry of African countries, notably Kenya, in the European market for cut flowers. A chill chain from the farm gate to the final customer and efficient airline services are pre-conditions for this trade. At first, flowers were transported by passenger flights, creating linkages between the tourism and the floriculture sectors. As export volume grew, dedicated cargo flights became commercially viable. However, south-bound flights run almost empty owing to lack of demand for time-sensitive imports in Kenya. This could become a constraint on future expansion in floriculture as competition increases and margins decline. Recent developments towards direct imports by retailers are also a challenge to Kenyan exporters because this would shift more of the logistical activities, including packaging and testing, to exporters.[12]

Devlin and Yee (2005) provide some interesting case studies of the role of logistics services for lead time. For example, an Egyptian exporter of cotton clothing imports yarn from India and Pakistan and the time for terminal handling, customs clearance and transport from Alexandria to the company's storage facilities is 30 days. Customs clearance, including waiting time, takes at best two weeks. However, time variability when including the lead time of Indian and Pakistani suppliers is substantial and the company keeps storage of yarn corresponding to four months of supply in order to avoid stoppages. When the clothing is ready for export, export documents are prepared (the time unknown). Time for packaging into a container is four hours and it takes two days from the time that the container leaves the factory gate until it is loaded on a ship in Alexandria, 220 km away. The sailing time to the export destination (New York) is 21 days, which is about average for shipments to the United States. It could, however, be shorter if export volumes allowed direct shipping, as there are many stops along the route that also goes via Canada.

Testing can be a critical service for exporters from developing countries where accredited test laboratories can be scarce and waiting time for testing can consequently be quite long. Worse, in small and shallow markets testing facilities that satisfy the customer may simply not exist. An example of this was reported in a study of the car industry in India. A local manufacturer of switches for passenger cars could not sell to a foreign affiliate in India because thermal shock tests that satisfied the multinational company's requirements were not available locally and the equipment to perform the tests was too expensive for in-house testing (Humphrey and Memedovic, 2003).

Finally, the price a low-technology consumer good fetches in the market critically depends on to what extent it is differentiated from competitors' products. In mass consumer markets differentiation is often added late in the process, sometimes as late as at the packaging and marketing stage. Lack of expertise and speed in these areas adversely affects the price the exporter receives in the market.

The dynamics between market size, the cost of logistics services and depth of the services market constitute a virtuous cycle. As export volume increases, there is space for more logistics service suppliers operating at lower costs, allowing for more timely delivery and further export expansion. Finally, it should be stressed that improvements in one link in the supply chain will not shorten lead time or reduce time variability unless improvements are made in complementary links as well. More efficient customs clearance services will, for instance, not reduce lead time if local transport and logistics services remain inefficient and uncompetitive.

Relations to previous literature

The idea that time constitutes a trade barrier in its own right is relatively new in the academic literature. The seminal contribution was Hummels (2001). He argued that time to market has two distinct effects on trade. First, it is a determinant of whether or not a manufacturer will enter a particular foreign market. An increase in shipping time of one day was found to reduce the probability that a country will export manufactures to the United States by 1.5 per cent. Second, time affects the volume of trade once a market entry is made in a similar way as tariffs and transport costs. The tariff equivalent per day in transit was estimated at 0.8 per cent for imports to the United States. This amounts to a tariff rate of 16 per cent on a 20-day sea transport route, which is the average for imports to the United States. It is far and away above the actual average tariff rate. In this chapter a similar technique is used to estimate the importance of time for exports and imports for market entry as well as trade volumes for all countries in the world for which data are available.

The idea that JIT practices can create entry barriers has been discussed in the industrial relations literature for some time. A particularly interesting approach is the so-called O-ring theory proposed by Kremer (1993). He models production as a sequence of tasks and operations, all of which are essential. This means that if one task, operation or input is missing, the product cannot be finalized and it generates no revenue. The missing task or input will consequently nullify the value of all the tasks and inputs that have been performed in previous production stages. A less extreme version of the theory assigns a quality to the final product and assumes that in order for the final product to have the desired quality all inputs must have the minimum required quality. Examples of this abound. A producer of upmarket clothing with high-quality fabric and elaborate designs would not choose low-quality thread, zippers or buttons. Likewise, upmarket car producers would not dream of fitting a hundred thousand dollar car with a $50 radio or a plastic dashboard. By the same token, there is no point in using high-quality fabric in a bright orange T-shirt made to last for the few months that bright orange is in fashion. Consequently, an optimal strategy for an assembler will be to choose the same quality of all inputs.

Adapted to JIT production processes, the O-ring theory implies that if JIT is introduced at one stage of the production process, it is optimal to synchronize the entire supply chain in order for it to operate smoothly. The chain is only as strong as its weakest link and therefore all links should have the same strength. When JIT technology is introduced, delayed delivery of a component can hold up the entire production and cause costs that are much higher than the market price of the delayed component. Therefore, no discount can compensate the customer for unreliable delivery time, and firms with high variability of lead time will not be short-listed for contracts that require JIT delivery.

Two recent studies have introduced time for exports from the World Bank's Doing Business Survey into a gravity model of trade flows. Hausman, Lee and Subramanian (2005) and Djankov, Freund and Pham (2006) find that a 10 per cent increase in time reduces bilateral trade volumes by between 5 and 8 per cent. Compared to estimates of the impact of transport costs on trade flows, these are small effects.[13] A possible explanation is that these two studies suffer from a selection bias since they ignore zero trade flows, and that this bias is more serious for time costs than for transport costs since fixed costs are a more important element of the former.

ECONOMETRIC ANALYSIS

This section estimates the sensitivity of time for exports and imports to international trade flows, using the gravity model. The estimates are made for intermediate inputs to highlight the relevance of time in international supply chains. Presumably time for exports and imports, defined as the time it takes from the factory gate until the cargo is loaded on a ship and the time it takes from the cargo is offloaded from the ship until it reaches its final destination, is closely related to the effectiveness of the logistics system in the exporting and importing country.[14] The sectors chosen for the analysis are processed industrial suppliers (BEC category 22), parts and components of capital goods (BEC category 42) and parts and accessories of transport equipment (BEC category 53). The results are compared to the results for total merchandise imports. The gravity model is extended by incorporating time for exports and imports and the most recent estimation techniques are applied.

The data assembled for this analysis consists of a panel of 157 countries covering the period 2004 to 2007. Data on time for exports and imports are from the World Bank's Doing Business survey for the years 2004–7. Trade data are from the UN Comtrade database, the geographical indicators routinely included in gravity regressions are from CEPII,[15] and data for GDP are from the World Bank Development Indicators.

The gravity model simply states that trade between two countries is proportional to the product of their GDP, which captures the impact of market size, and inversely proportional to bilateral trade costs. Formally the model can be written as follows:

$$T_{ij} = \alpha_0 Y_i^{\alpha_1} Y_j^{\alpha_2} D_{ij}^{\alpha_3} \tag{1}$$

Subscripts *i* and *j* signify the country pair, *T* trade flows between them, *Y* their income (GDP) and *D* trade costs which in turn are assumed to be proportional to geographical, cultural and institutional distance. The parameters α_1 and α_2 are expected to be positive while α_3 is expected to be negative. Until quite recently this equation was habitually log-linearized and estimated using ordinary least squares (OLS). Recent literature has, however, revealed a number of problems with simple OLS estimation, and has suggested alternative estimation techniques. The regressions below apply the Poisson pseudo maximum likelihood (PPML) estimator, a methodology suggested by Santos Silva and Tenreyro (2006, 2008). It solves problems of heteroschedasticity in bilateral trade data and provides efficient estimates of the coefficients. The regression equation is as follows:

$$M_{ijt} = \exp(\lambda_j + \chi_i + \gamma_t - \beta d_{ij} - \beta_2 txm_{ijt} - \beta_3 txm_{jit} * dist_{ij} + \varepsilon_{ijt}) \qquad (2)$$

The first three terms are importer and exporter time-invariant fixed effects, and a dummy that captures time trends. The fourth term is a vector of geographical bilateral variables (distance, common border, common language and common colonial past). The fifth term is the one of particular interest: a constructed bilateral variable summing time for export in the exporting country and time for imports in the importing country.

The PPML estimator does not distinguish between market entry (the extensive margin) and expansion of existing trade flows (the intensive margin), however. It is argued here that decisions on the extensive and intensive margins can be distinct. Entry barriers are related to fixed or sunk costs that firms incur upfront before they enter a contract with a foreign customer, a contract that usually specifies the time of delivery and required time regularity. In order to meet these requirements, investments in better supply chain management tools are often necessary. In addition, fixed costs can be related to setting up a distribution network, establishing after-sales services, learning about and complying with product standards in the foreign market etc. The possibility that time for exports and imports may also reflect entry barriers is explored by estimating a probit function where the left-hand-side variable is whether or not a country pair trades.

Santos Silva and Tenreyro (2006) showed that the PPML yields unbiased and effective results and allows the inclusion of zero trade flows. The zero-inflated Poisson technique (zip) preserves the benefits of PPML, but allows for distinguishing between the intensive and the extensive margin. It does so by distinguishing 'true zeros' from zeros that are explained by the same mechanisms as the positive trade flows. The 'true zeros' in this setting would be those where trade flows are zero because time costs are

Table 20.2 Regression results using zero-inflated Poisson

Poisson	Total trade		BEC 22		BEC 42		BEC 53	
Ln importer GDP	0.787***	(0.017)	0.733***	(0.012)	0.693***	(0.027)	0.821***	(0.018)
Ln exporter GDP	0.761***	(0.011)	0.756***	(0.012)	0.838***	(0.022)	0.982***	(0.016)
Ln distance	0.147	(0.097)	0.015	(0.083)	1.077***	(0.180)	0.714***	(0.167)
Ln distance* ln time	−0.185***	(0.029)	−0.177***	(0.026)	−0.465***	(0.058)	−0.396***	(0.051)
Common border	0.829***	(0.076)	0.832***	(0.076)	0.520***	(0.158)	1.137***	(0.092)
Common language	0.236***	(0.055)	0.261***	(0.053)	0.470***	(0.100)	−0.028	(0.064)
Common colonial history	0.988***	(0.126)	0.785***	(0.104)	1.670***	(0.259)	0.374**	(0.167)
Ln time	1.348***	(0.244)	1.321***	(0.219)	3.304***	(0.526)	2.736***	(0.407)
Probit								
Ln importer GDP	−0.304***	(0.003)	−0.307***	(0.003)	−0.319***	(0.003)	−0.267***	(0.003)
Ln exporter GDP	−0.355***	(0.004)	−0.440***	(0.004)	−0.467***	(0.004)	−0.496***	(0.004)
Ln distance	−1.995***	(0.080)	−1.728***	(0.077)	−1.485***	(0.072)	−1.102***	(0.070)
Ln distance* ln time	0.520***	(0.020)	0.485***	(0.019)	0.431***	(0.018)	0.356***	(0.018)
Common border	−6.928***	(0.047)	−7.223***	(0.054)	−8.825***	(0.062)	−8.742***	(0.052)
Common language	−0.470***	(0.020)	−0.464***	(0.018)	−0.507***	(0.018)	−0.494***	(0.018)
Common colonial history	−0.180***	(0.021)	−0.323***	(0.021)	−0.170***	(0.022)	−0.183***	(0.023)
Ln time	−4.068***	(0.174)	−3.691***	(0.168)	−3.177***	(0.158)	−2.542***	(0.154)
Non/zero observations	6753		56042		47527		39297	
Zero observations	19757		31210		39658		47865	
Vuong test	85.97***		117.76***		118.13***		98.1***	

Note: Robust standard errors in parentheses. ***, ** and * signify statistical significance at a 1, 5 and 10% level respectively.

too high relative to the market in the importing country, whereas the 'false zeros' are country pairs that happen not to trade with each other at a particular point in time because among all possible trading partners there may be some randomness in which partners are actually chosen, given that firms do not have resources to establish trade links with all potentially profitable markets.

The distinction between the extensive and intensive margin using zip can be made without the need for an identifying variable, which has proved to be difficult when applying Heckman regressions, a commonly used methodology for distinguishing between the extensive and intensive margin. The zip technique starts with fitting a constant-only model, predicting whether a country pair is in the group of 'true zeros', using a probit model. It next fits the full model, starting with the fitted constant-only model and adding the Poisson count model. The Vuong test indicates whether zip estimates are preferred over PPML. The estimated probit function reads as follows:

$$\rho_{ijt} = \Phi(\kappa_j + \theta_i + \varphi_t - vd_{ij} - v_2 txm_{ijt} - v_3 txm_{it} \, {}^*dist_{ij} - v_4 txm_{jt} \, {}^*dist_{ij} + \eta_{ijt}) \quad (3)$$

The results for both the PPML and the probit regressions are reported for total trade in Table 20.2.

The standard gravity variables take the expected signs and similar values as in previous studies using the PPML estimator. Thus GDP increases bilateral trade and reduces the probability that a country pair will not trade with each other, and the same applies to common border, common language and common colonial history.[16] It is noted that almost 80 per cent of the country pairs included in the database trade with each other. But this share diminishes when we look at particular sectors, as should be expected. About a third of the country pairs do not trade processed industrial supplies and about 45 per cent do not trade parts and components of capital goods, while more than half do not trade parts and accessories of transport equipment, underscoring the importance of considering the determinants of entry into export markets as well as trade volumes.

The regression results show a complex relationship between trade, time for exports and imports and distance between trading partners. It is first worth noticing the strong tendency to trade with immediate neighbours. The probability of no trade is almost zero for country pairs that share a common border, and the effect is strongest for intermediate inputs in capital goods and transport equipment. Likewise, next-door neighbours tend to trade more than twice as much with each other than other country pairs everything else being equal, and for parts and components of transport equipment country pairs sharing a common border trade three times as much with each other.

The trade-reducing effect of distance depends on how long it takes to ship the goods, and vice versa. On average (ie for total trade), trade falls off with distance at an elasticity of −0.42 if time for trade is 10 days (close to the minimum observed eg for Denmark's imports from Estonia), increasing in absolute value to −0.99 if time for trade is 200 days (the maximum observed for eg Iraq's imports from Uzbekistan). In other words, countries that take a long time to ship goods will have difficulties exporting to distant markets. Notice that the measures of time do not include the time it takes to transport the goods between the two countries. This is probably proportional to the distance, and time for exports and imports as measured here constitutes a larger share of time from the factory gate of the exporter to the storage facilities of the importer the shorter is the distance. The result suggests, therefore, a rising marginal impact of time for trade. The impact of distance on the probability of zero trade also increases sharply with time for trade.

The same effect is found for trade in intermediate goods, parts and components. The impact of distance on the probability to trade depends on time for trade in a similar way for all sectors included. Furthermore, the rate at which trade falls off with distance depends on time in a similar manner as for trade on average for processed industrial suppliers (BEC category 22). The effect on trade flows is much stronger for sectors that are renowned for their JIT supply chain management, however. For parts and components of capital goods (BEC category 42), trade does not fall off with distance if time for trade is 10 days or less, while it falls off at a rate of 14 per cent for every 10 per cent increase in distance if time for trade is 200 days. For parts and accessories of transport equipment (BEC category 53) trade falls off at a rate of 2 per cent for every 10 per cent increase in distance if time for trade is 10 days, increasing to about 14 per cent if time for trade is 200 days.

The regression results show that countries can significantly broaden their export base through reducing the time it takes from imported parts and components leaving the port of entry until they reach the factory gate of the manufacturer and the time it takes from when the good leaves the factory until it is loaded on a ship, plane or truck headed for the export market. Better logistics, transport and customs procedures would contribute substantially to bringing down time for trade.

POLICY IMPLICATIONS AND CONCLUSIONS

This chapter has shown that lengthy times for exports and imports can be a substantial obstacle to entering export markets for entrepreneurs in developing countries. At the same time, products for which developing countries have a comparative advantage are becoming increasingly time-sensitive owing to consumer demand for new and differentiated products, lean retailing and JIT production technologies. Importantly, it is lead time and time variability relative to competitors rather than absolute time for exports that matter for market entry as well as export volumes. Therefore, developing countries with long and variable lead times need to shorten their lead times and reduce time variability faster than their competitors, if further marginalization in time-sensitive products is to be avoided.

What sort of policy measures could contribute to shortening relative lead time and improving the export performance of low-income countries? It is first noted that the measure of time for exports and imports used in the analysis covers the time from the factory gate until the merchandise is loaded on a ship destined for the foreign market. Therefore, the most relevant policy measures are behind the border and hence in the realm of domestic reforms. Furthermore, the dynamics between trade and lead time and time variability may constitute either a virtuous or vicious circle. In the latter case, poor trade performance yields low demand for effective transport and logistics services, resulting in shallow and underdeveloped logistics services and uncompetitive firms. Economies of scale in the transport and logistics sector will reinforce this low-export, poor-logistical services trap.

Lead time and time variability depend on the smooth operation of a number of services within a broadly defined logistic services sector. In addition, a well-functioning customs service and other public services related to trade are needed. These activities form a logistics chain where the speed of material flow is determined by the slowest activity. Identifying the bottleneck in the supply chain and focusing the reforms on opening these is likely to yield an early harvest and could generate support for further reforms.

Where customs and related procedures constitute the weakest link in the logistics chain, trade facilitation can have a large impact on trade flows. Earlier OECD work has documented benefits and costs of trade facilitation in developing countries. This work has emphasized that more efficient and modern customs services tend to stimulate trade as well as enhancing customs revenue. Therefore, the expenses related to trade facilitation, including investment in information technology, are quickly paid back when reforms are successfully implemented. The costs of not undertaking trade facilitation in a situation when trade becomes more complex and demands on customs for a timely and efficient response increase can be substantial.[17] The findings in this chapter strengthen this argument by showing that doing nothing, while others reform, would leave firms in the non-reforming country at an increasing competitive disadvantage. In countries where time-costs-related customs procedures constitute a bottleneck and where in addition the probability of exporting is close to 0.5, trade facilitation can remove barriers to entry and induce a leap forward in terms of exports of time-sensitive goods. Furthermore, trade facilitation can in that case trigger a demand-driven expansion of logistics services in the private sector, initiating a virtuous circle.

If logistics services represent the weakest link in the chain, trade facilitation will not break the vicious circle.[18] Instead, reforms in the transport and logistics sector are a necessary first step. In low-income countries, this often involves privatization of the transport sector combined with regulation in order to ensure that a public monopoly is not replaced by a private monopoly. Opening up to trade and foreign investment in transport and logistics services could also in many cases contribute to better services. In this study I have shown that such reforms can have large repercussions on other sectors in countries where logistics is a bottleneck and the probability of entering new markets is close to the critical value. Therefore, when considering reforms in the transport and logistics services sector, the benefits to other sectors should be factored in.

In cases where the entire logistics chain is weak, as is often the case in low-income countries, a reform package including trade facilitation and measures that stimulate the development of a diversified logistics services market is needed. These measures should aim at making the best use of existing infrastructure and institutional capacity, but this is not always enough. In many cases costly investments in infrastructure are also needed. Many of the initiatives that have been discussed under the aid for trade agenda relate to improving export capacity through better infrastructure and technology transfer and could support a reform and investment package. However, when resources are limited and the logistics chain very weak, scarce resources could be invested in special economic zones as a first step towards market entry.

The special economic zones in South East Asia and China have, for instance, contributed to creating a critical mass of skills and services inputs for the electronics sector (Kimura and Ando, 2005). Lessons can also be drawn from the role that trading houses in Hong Kong have played for the emergence of China as one of the world's largest traders. During the period 1988–98 as much as 53 per cent of China's exports were re-exported through Hong Kong where the Hong Kong trading houses added value through sorting, packaging, testing and marketing. The Hong Kong trading houses also played an important role in matching suppliers and customers. The mark-ups on Hong Kong re-exports averaged 24 per cent, indicating that the value of these services accounted for almost a quarter of the fob price (Feenstra, Hanson and Lin, 2002). However, examples of unsuccessful special economic zones abound. When zones are special mainly due to tax holidays and few regulatory restrictions they often end up becoming export processing enclaves at best. What is advocated here is well-located special economic zones, which are special in the sense that they have good infrastructure and related services.

To summarize the study, it has shown that time is an important competitive factor and hence also a trade barrier in its own right. It not only affects the volume of trade, but also the ability of enterprises to enter export markets. Furthermore, it has been shown that it is lead time and time variability relative to other exporters that matter for competitiveness. In order to avoid further marginalization, reforms are urgently needed since the status quo on lead time and time variability is likely to cause many low-income countries to fall further and further behind. Improving logistics could also help exporters to move up the quality ladder. Many developing countries have time for exports and imports that exceeds the level that enables local entrepreneurs to enter international production networks or to become regular suppliers to lean retailers, a situation that discourages investment in raising product quality.

Notes

1   This chapter builds on and updates an article in the OECD Economic Survey published in 2006. Views expressed herein are the author's and should not be attributed to the OECD or any of its member countries.
2   Duranton and Storper (2005) document that while transport costs have gone down over the past century, total trade costs have gone up due to more transport-intensive ways of organizing production.
3   World trade increased from 24 to 57 per cent of world GDP from 1960 to 2006, according to the World Bank's World Development Indicators.
4   See Evans and Harrigan (2005) for a study on US trade in textiles and clothing.
5   See Hummels and Klenow (2005) for a discussion and empirical evidence.
6   If demand was known months in advance, orders could be placed months in advance as well, and lead time would not matter much.
7   The shipping time is the weighted average of ocean shipping and air freight.
8   These ratios are calculated from the GTAP database for 2001, which is the only available database that distinguishes between imported and locally sourced intermediate inputs for developing as well as developed countries.
9   *The Economist*, 7 December 2002, Special Report Logistics.

10   See http://www.americanapparel.net/mission/workers.html, accessed 13 September 2009.
11   See http://www.inditex.com/en, accessed 12 September 2009.
12   See Nordås, Pinali and Geloso-Grosso (2006) and Nordås (2008) for a discussion.
13   Limao and Venables (2001), for instance, find that a 10 per cent increase in transport costs reduces trade volume by 20 per cent.
14   Time for exports and imports of course also depends on the effectiveness of the customs administration.
15   http://www.cepii.fr/francgraph/bdd/distances.htm
16   GDP is included in the reported regressions, which are run without country fixed effects. The reason is that it is difficult to get convergence of the zip regressions with such a vast number of dummies. Running Poisson regressions and probit regressions with country fixed effects yielded similar results.
17   See OECD (2003a, 2003b, 2004, 2005a, 2005b) and Engman (2005) for further discussion.
18   Recent modelling exercises analysing the gains from trade facilitation do not capture such complementarities and in some cases they underestimate the gains from trade facilitation and in others they overestimate the gains, depending on which are the weakest links in the supply chain. See Engman (2005) for a discussion of these studies.

References

American Apparel, http://www.americanapparel.net/mission/workers.html
CEPII (2006) *Distances*, http://www.cepii.fr/francgraph/bdd/distances.htm
Devlin, J and Yee, P (2005) Trade logistics in developing countries: The case of the Middle East and North Africa, *World Economy*, **28**, pp 435–56
Djankov, S, Freund, C and Pham, CS (2006) *Trading on Time*, World Bank Policy Research Paper No 3909
Duranton, G and Storper, M (2005) *Rising Trade Costs? Agglomeration and trade with endogenous transaction costs*, CEPR Discussion Paper No 4933, February, Center for Economic Policy Research
The Economist (2002), 7 December, Special Report Logistics
Engman, M (2005) *The Economic Impact of Trade Facilitation*, OECD Trade Policy Working Paper No 21, OECD, Paris
Evans, C and Harrigan, J (2005) Distance, time and specialization: lean retailing in general equilibrium, *The American Economic Review*, **95**, pp 292–313
Feenstra, RC, Hanson, GH and Lin, S (2002) *The Value of Information in International Trade: Gain to outsourcing through Hong Kong*, NBER Working

Paper No 9328, November, National Bureau of Economic Research, Cambridge, MA

Harrigan, J (2005) *Airplanes and Comparative Advantage*, NBER Working Paper No 11688, October, National Bureau of Economic Research, Cambridge, MA

Hausman, WH, Lee, LL and Subramanian, U (2005) *Global Logistics Services, Supply Chain Metrics and Bilateral Trade Patterns*, Mimeo, World Bank, Geneva, October

Hummels, D (2001) *Time as a Trade Barrier*, Mimeo, Purdue University, July

Hummels, D and Klenow, PJ (2005) The variety and quality of a nation's exports, *The American Economic Review*, **95**, pp 704–23

Hummels, DL and Schaur, G (2009) *Hedging Price Volatility Using Fast Transport*, NBER Working Paper No 15154, July, Cambridge, MA

Humphrey, J and Memedovic, O (2003) *The Global Automotive Industry Value Chain: What prospects for upgrading by developing countries?* UNIDO Sectoral Studies Series, UNIDO, Vienna

Inditex, http://www.inditex.com/en

Kimura, F and Ando, M (2005) Two-dimensional fragmentation in East Asia: conceptual framework and empirics, *International Review of Economics and Finance*, **14**, pp 317–48

Kremer, M (1993) The O-ring theory of economic development, *The Quarterly Journal of Economics*, **118**, pp 551–75

Limao, L and Venables, AJ (2001) Infrastructure, geographical disadvantage, transport costs and trade, *World Bank Economic Review*, **15**, pp 451–79

Lukman Susanto (2003) *Just in Time in Ford*, www.susanto.id.au/papers/JITFORD.asp

Nordås, HK (2008) Vertical specialization and its determinants, *Journal of Development Studies*, **44**, pp 1037–55

Nordås, HK, Pinali, E and Geloso-Grosso, M (2006) *Logistics and Time as a Trade Barrier*, OECD Trade Policy Working Paper No 35, OECD, Paris

OECD (2003a) *Trade Facilitation Reform in the Service of Development*, TD/TD/WP (2003)11FINAL, OECD, Paris

OECD (2003b) *Role of Automation in Trade Facilitation*, TD/TD/WP (2003)/21FINAL, OECD, Paris

OECD (2004) *Trade Facilitation Reforms in the Service of Development*, Country case studies, TD/TC/WP (2004)4FINAL, OECD, Paris

OECD (2005a) *The Cost of Introducing and Implementing Trade Facilitation Measures*, TD/TD/WP (2005)27FINAL, OECD, Paris

OECD (2005b) *Trade and Structural Adjustment: Embracing globalization*, OECD, Paris

Santos Silva, JMC and Tenreyro, S (2006) The log of gravity, forthcoming in *Review of Economics and Statistics*

Santos Silva, JMC and Tenreyro, S (2008) *Trading Partners and Trading Volumes: Implementing the Helpman–Melitz–Rubinstein model empirically*, Economics Discussion Paper 662, University of Essex, Department of Economics

World Bank, *Doing Business Database*, http://www.doingbusiness.org/

World Bank, *Governance Indicators*, http://www.worldbank.org/wbi/governance/govdata/

World Bank, *World Development Indicators*, CD ROM, Washington, DC

21

Learning from humanitarian supply chains

Rolando Tomasini and Luk Van Wassenhove, INSEAD

INTRODUCTION

In a globalized economy business networks have become more inter-connected, with companies operating in multiple time zones. The global expansion of these business networks has brought about many more options when selecting the actors that will be part of a supply chain. Suppliers come from different continents and manufacturing takes place in several locations, eg China, Mexico and Bulgaria. Transportation providers need to be well coordinated with the company's activities in the different locations to receive the raw materials and distribute the goods to a number of sites, where the product will be sold.

The multiplicity and diversity of actors in the global supply chain equal multiple risks for the network. For example, any disruptions in the material, information or financial flow in one area of the world can have immediate repercussion in the supply chain throughout different time zones. These events could be anything from a simple delay in a process, up to a major catastrophe like a hurricane that closes an airport or an earthquake or flood that destroys a warehouse. Regardless of their nature, dealing with the repercussions and learning to plan for them is a constant concern for supply chain managers. Lessons for these types of challenges to the supply chain can come from different sources. In this chapter we focus on examples from companies learning from the processes of humanitarian agencies.

DISASTERS ARE CHALLENGING LEARNING SETTINGS

Humanitarian organizations are driven by unpredictable events, constantly moving from one setting to another to attend the needs of affected populations all over the world. The speed at which they move is as irregular as the event occurrence. The magnitude of their involvement will also vary, depending on the impact the event had on the population, the number of actors engaged in the response, and the local coping mechanisms. Combined, this makes humanitarian operations fairly complex learning labs for companies to acquire or develop new knowledge. To illustrate this point, consider the example of the events from Lebanon 2006.

Lebanese/Israeli Crisis of 2006[1]

On 12 July 2006, the Lebanese guerilla group Hezbollah captured two Israeli soldiers patrolling the Lebanese–Israeli border. Later that day, Hezbollah's leader Hassan Nasrallah appeared in a broadcast TV announcement, confirmed the capture of the soldiers and stated his terms for their release. He threatened to escalate the violence if a prisoner exchange was not negotiated with the Israelis.

The Lebanese population expected a reaction from the Israelis,[2] as in the past, in the form of low-intensity bombings or riots. Instead, the Israeli Air Force (IAF) started a large-scale bombing campaign of major bridges in the southern suburb of Beirut, a Hezbollah stronghold,[3] on the same evening.

On 13 July, the IAF proceeded with the bombing of Beirut International Airport, the only operational airport in Lebanon, in addition to a couple of unused airfields in northern Lebanon and the Bekaa Valley in the east. The Beirut Port was also targeted along with several commercial and tourist ports. Severe damage put the airport out of operation, while the Beirut port was paralyzed and brought to a halt.[4]

Frightened by the massive bombings of populated areas, many people from southern Beirut or southern Lebanon fled their homes and took refuge in empty schools and public buildings. These families were in need of everything, from water and food to medicines and baby supplies. While people fled their homes in south Lebanon in the first days of the conflict, those who hesitated were unable to do so days later. With the fierce fighting between Hezbollah and the Israelis there was no way in or out of the battlefield.

Residents of southern border villages left to go to cities in the south like Tyre and Saida, others to Beirut and other parts of the country. Residents of Beirut's southern suburb also had to leave their homes, fearing strikes on the area. Those who could afford it left the country to go to Syria and Jordan mainly, until the access roads were targeted and blocked. Tourists from neighbouring countries left Lebanon by land as soon as the hostilities started. Other foreigners had to wait for their country's evacuation plans which started on 20 July, conscious that they could be targeted as well.

The attacks continued. On 30 July the main eastern crossing into Syria linking Beirut to Damascus was targeted again and the road was put out of action. The remaining northern crossings into Syria were also targeted, blocking all access into the country. International humanitarian aid was blocked at the borders until a safe passage through the humanitarian corridor was negotiated with the Israelis. The negotiations to access the country were primarily channelled through the United Nations Joint Logistics Center (UNJLC),[5] an interagency coordination platform working in close collaboration with all the aid agencies.

The war officially lasted until 14 August, two days after the United Nations Security Council issued resolution 1701 calling for a permanent cease fire. Although there was a clear call to lift the blockade, Israel kept its siege on Lebanon until 9 September. Trucks were able to enter from Syria and circulate within Lebanon, but ships were still forbidden to dock at ports, and civilian planes were only allowed to land in or depart from Lebanon after stopping in Jordan. Upon re-establishing peace, official figures issued by the Lebanese government[6] estimated the number of internally displaced people to be 947,184 at the peak of the war, and at least 30,000 destroyed houses. Ninety-five bridges all over Lebanon were destroyed, mainly in the south of the country. Civilian casualty figures vary between 850 to 1,190 dead[7] and 4,409 injured[8] at the end of the war.

The case of Lebanon illustrates the complexity that humanitarian agencies face when trying to set up a relief operation. For natural crises the security constraints may be lower and coordination among the actors easier. However, the relief operation remains a challenging setting where limited resources and priorities are constantly revisited to update planning and operations.

HUMANITARIANS AND THEIR SUPPLY CHAINS ARE DIFFERENT

The humanitarian sector, unlike the business sector, focuses on developing capabilities to respond to high-impact events with unpredictable resources. Organizations like the International Federation of the Red Cross (IFRC),[9] World Food Program (WFP),[10] United Nations Children's Fund (UNICEF),[11] CARE,[12] World Vision International (WVI),[13] among others in a long list, have a specific mandate to raise funds, recruit and train staff, set up agreements with business and governments, and develop relationships with communities to respond to natural and political disasters affecting communities. This mandate is an exceptional licence to focus on saving human lives by mitigating the impact of disasters and facilitating the return to normality.

The way these humanitarian organizations implement their mandate varies given their primary focus areas (eg food distribution, water sanitation, medical support, education, childcare) and their geographical priorities. However, the process of accessing the beneficiaries and delivering the aid remains the same. It comes down to developing a supply chain that is agile enough to adjust to changes in the types of goods and quantities required, and adaptable enough to react to changing conditions (eg security) and new actors (eg different NGOs, the military, or government).

Even though the focus areas and priorities may be different, humanitarian organizations and private companies at the core may share similar operational concerns. For humanitarian organizations, logistics (and the functions related to supply chain management) represents approximately 80 per cent of the activities. Humanitarian managers debate similar issues to private companies about how to negotiate the best supplier agreements, where to position warehouses, whom to choose as transport provider, how to improve delivery, and what investment is required to stay competitive. For example, over the past years the IFRC[14] has undergone a restructuring exercise to decentralize their supply chain, with regional logistics units (RLUs) in Panama, Dubai and Kuala Lumpur. The new structure was designed to improve their regional response capacity by reducing lead times and costs. The regional focus enables them to take advantage of local warehouse and transport providers, develop better relations with partners in the region, including donors, suppliers and governments, and forecast supply and demand more accurately.

In contrast to commercial supply chains, humanitarian supply chains are usually established without a precedent. They do not to respond to pre-existing or constant demand. Humanitarian organizations are responsible for reacting as quickly as possible, usually with little or no anticipation. As they establish their presence and become operational, they start to focus on the reduction of cost. For example, following a major disaster air transportation is used, incurring high costs, while humanitarian staff on the ground look for alternatives in the local markets and options for ground transport that could help lower the cost of the operation as it unfolds.

Finding ways to lower the cost can be a challenging task, as the humanitarian organizations experienced while preparing for the return of millions of refugees to south Sudan.[15] In 2005 a peace agreement was signed between the government of Sudan in the north and the Sudanese People Liberation Movement (SPLM) in the south, ending a 21-year civil war that had devastated most of the infrastructure in the south. Bridges, roads, rails and airports were destroyed, making land transport impossible. Under those conditions air transport was the only, and most expensive, option. However, it was unsustainable considering the size of the southern region, the distances to reach it and the number of people expected to return that would need humanitarian aid. The agencies engaged in a long exercise to design a distribution network from scratch, using funds from government donors and the expertise of private companies, eg to repair roads.

Another contrasting point is the motivation that brings the different actors together. Commercial supply chains are primarily held together by the profit incentives that the different organizations share. Humanitarian supply chains lack that incentive and yet they manage to bring together different actors and coordinate the interaction in a system where there is no formal command and control structure. Several coordination mechanisms have been institutionalized in the humanitarian sector for complex emergencies. One example is UNJLC, whose mandate is to consolidate the information from the different organizations involved, de-bottleneck and negotiate on behalf of the humanitarian community with the authorities, and assist in the allocation and consolidation of resources in light of changing priorities. Since 2005 it has been operating in Sudan, coordinating the pipeline for non-food items (eg blankets, mattresses, cooking kits, soap) to beneficiaries. The pipeline is an interagency project that balances the core competencies and local capacity of different agencies operating in Sudan. During its initial setup UNICEF was responsible for the procurement of goods, WFP served as the consignee for in-kind donations, and CARE assumed responsibility for warehousing and transportation to the refugee camps where an implementing NGO would be assigned to do the last-mile distribution.

Companies interested in getting involved with humanitarian organizations are immediately faced with the complexity of the sector and are forced to define how they will add value with their participation, and what motivates them. Over the past decade we have seen a number of examples of companies establishing close collaborations with the humanitarian sector to provide support for relief operations. In this chapter we review examples of companies that invested in developing relationships with the humanitarian sector as part of their corporate social responsibility programmes, getting exposed to the numerous lessons from disaster management.

CORPORATIONS MOVING IN TO HELP FIND THEY CAN ALSO LEARN

Initially motivated by the will to contribute with their core competencies and capacity to a greater good, several companies from the transport and logistics sector have developed over the past decade a series of corporate social responsibility (CSR) initiatives and partnerships with the humanitarians. These partnerships were designed to support the humanitarian agencies to fulfil their mandate, giving them access to the companies' know-how, resources, global presence, and network. Over time these companies have also realized that the humanitarians have complementary skills that would be valuable to their own organizations.

Two major examples in the sector are the partnership between TNT and WFP, also known as Moving the World, and the Humanitarian and Emergency Logistics Program (HELP) set up by Agility.

Moving the World[16]

As a leader in the industry, TNT was conscious of the consequences of globalization and the responsibility it inherited as a major player in the global economy. Since 1946 TNT has expanded through takeovers and acquisitions from its Dutch roots in the public mail service to a global company present in 63 countries with over 160,000 employees operating its own airplanes. In 2002 CEO Peter Bakker expressed his concern to a team of senior executives when he decided to develop a global CSR programme. He had recently learned that every five seconds a child dies from hunger and that logistics could help to alleviate that figure, especially in emergency situations. His call went out to the team of executives explaining that:

> It's not enough to be socially responsible within our company. We should strive for social leadership outside our business. If through our business we can help improve people's living conditions, it is our responsibility to do so.

Following a six-month selection process, Bakker and the team of executives decided to partner with WFP for an initial period of five years to form Moving the World. The choice of partner was made on several bases that confirmed the complementary fit between the two leading organizations. As a global provider of mail, express and logistics services, TNT wanted to make sure its partner would have similar appreciation and interest in its capabilities and global presence. WFP fitted the bill as the largest humanitarian organization that provides 'food aid to an average of 90 million people, including 56 million hungry children, in more than 80 countries every year'.[17]

To define projects and goals for Moving the World, TNT and WFP teams made a visit to WFP's Tanzania operations. They visited emergency operations and noted the logistics challenges. The observations led to a series of discussions in which both partners agreed to collaborate in the areas of emergency relief, joint supply chain, transparency and accountability, employee volunteering, and the school feeding programme.

Between 2002 and 2007 Moving the World mobilized staff globally from both organizations to participate in fundraising campaigns, secondments and volunteer opportunities, and support for disaster relief operations. Among these activities is support for the relief operations of the Indian Ocean tsunami, where TNT contributed with its local staff, offices and equipment, helping WFP to become operational quickly. Similarly, in 2008 during the Myanmar floods, TNT facilitated access to the country through its local network while WFP struggled to overcome the bureaucratic challenges imposed by the government. During these operations, and a long list of many more, field staff from both organizations worked very closely towards to same goal, borrowing equipment, tapping into each other's expertise and developing new contacts.

Throughout the five years the partnership evolved, with €38 million invested by TNT in the different projects and an additional €9 million raised by employees. Lessons from each project were reshaping the collaboration guidelines. Following an independent evaluation of the first five years, both organizations decided to renew their engagement indeterminately.[18] To facilitate the collaboration they reorganized the partnership into four pillars: awareness and fundraising, transport for goods, hands-on support for disasters, and knowledge transfer for best practices. These four categories were more representative of the value exchanged between both organizations and the activities involved. Inherent in this new structure is the idea that TNT could also learn and benefit from WFP's knowledge. Throughout the partnership history, 70 TNT specialists have been seconded to WFP to contribute and acquire new experiences and best practices.

Agility: Humanitarian and Emergency Logistics Program[19]

The notion of risk and vulnerability is one that Agility knows well and seeks to master. This is reflected in its history, strategy and CSR programme. Agility was founded in 1979 in Kuwait as the Public Warehousing Company (PWC Logistics). In 1997 it was privatized and became publicly traded, marking the beginning of eight years of expansion. Through a series of acquisitions the company became the largest logistics provider in the Middle East and a global industry player. In 2006 the company rebranded itself as Agility to represent 550 offices in 100 countries and 32,000 employees.

Agility's presence in the industry is unique in different aspects. Agility is the world's eighth-largest logistics company and the only global top ten industry player with roots outside of Western Europe or the United States. Among the top players it is also the main one focusing on emerging markets, a strategy that has exposed it to a series of risks and social issues it aims to address through its CSR programme. Chairman and CEO Tarek Sultan explained his vision of the company by saying:

> We work in difficult countries in challenging situations; therefore we need to be ready to add value in tough places, whether it be on commercial terms or not. We understand risk, and we have an appetite and knowledge to thrive on it and do business. When you are sitting in Kuwait, you have Iraq to one side and Saudi Arabia to the other. The minute something happens, you see, you listen ... you are used to working with difficult, uncertain and constantly changing conditions. When you are sitting in Kuwait, you understand that everything can change overnight and affect not only your business but people around you.[20]

Aware of the opportunity to help and the responsibility his company has in the areas where it is present, Sultan hired in 2005 Mariam Al-Foudery, to design and implement a global CSR programme. From her discussions with managers and knowledge of the company and humanitarian sector she pointed out the potential that Agility had to contribute with its logistics competencies and capacity. These could be used towards disaster relief or employee volunteer programmes. The focus on disaster relief was seen as fitting with the company presence and experience in emerging markets, and a natural fit for local staff willing to volunteer their knowledge and time.

The test for Agility's CSR plans came in 2006 when the Lebanese crisis erupted, affecting 120 of its employees, destroying the warehouses of several clients and disrupting all commercial activity in the country. Sultan immediately agreed with Al-Foudery to create a team to address the crisis. Accompanied by experienced logisticians, she joined the humanitarian agencies at the Syrian–Lebanese border to define how Agility could help.

Security constraints in Lebanon discussed earlier had blocked all access to the country and forced humanitarian agencies to hold all aid at the border until access was safe. The challenge for the humanitarian agencies became how to stock all this aid safely and efficiently, so that it could be moved into Lebanon with the shortest possible delay when the situation improved. Through their network of contacts with commercial suppliers in the region, Al-Foudery and her team identified warehouses and transport operators in the region. They listed them in a database, visited them and evaluated them using Agility's standards for capacity and quality. They also engaged in the negotiations to review the contracts and ensure the necessary flexibility needed by the agencies in terms of payment schedules, responsibilities and insurance. Over two weeks the Agility team helped the humanitarians to develop a warehouse–transport network, enabling the agencies to focus on other pressing tasks.

The Lebanese experience validated that Agility had a role to play in disaster relief, and that lessons could be learned from it. The next steps were to design a programme that would enable Agility to systematically engage in these types of activities while producing value for the humanitarian organizations. Upon return to the headquarters, Al-Foudery and the rest of the team discussed lessons learned from the experience to structure the Humanitarian and Emergency Logistics Program.

HELP became the platform for Agility to provide support to humanitarian agencies responding to natural disasters in countries where the company is present. The programme has been successful, 'approximately 15% of the company's global workforce volunteered for a total of 168 community projects in 62 branch offices in 45 countries around the world, reaching about 396,000 people on the ground with some type of service activity involving disaster relief, education, food, and/or health'.[21]

THE VALUE OF CROSS-SECTOR LEARNING

The commitment from companies like TNT and Agility to support activities of the humanitarian world requires significant investment in terms of money, skills and time. The value of this investment is hard to quantify, especially with indicators that are shared by both parties. For example, the companies can quantify the value of the media exposure they received from their support to the humanitarian agencies, but that figure is added value to the company and not to humanitarian organizations. On the opposite side of the argument, the humanitarian agencies could quantify the value of the transport services they received pro bono, but these savings would only reflect the benefits to the humanitarian organization, leaving out of the equation the private company.

One area in which they both agree to have reciprocity in the creation of value is learning. Through their interaction both sectors confirm that they have gained a new perspective on their capabilities. Staff from TNT and Agility have been seconded on missions to humanitarian operations where they put their skills to use in a completely different context. The employees, confident of their knowledge, are faced with experiences that test the limits of their skills by demanding them to adapt to different settings and conditions. Through these experiences the employees are able to see new applications of their knowledge and skill set.

The interaction has a similar impact on the humanitarian staff working with the private partner. A great percentage of the learning for humanitarian workers is experiential, from one relief operation to another, and informal. Through the interaction with the private sector, the humanitarian workers benchmark their knowledge and identify gaps in their skill set that they can set as targets for their professional development. In some cases, the companies have made their training sessions and agreements available to staff from their humanitarian partners, helping them to address those gaps and acquire new tools.

However, learning is not without challenges. For the most part, learning happens at the interpersonal level first. Even though this is still beneficial for the organizations that employ the individuals, the fullest value of the learning experience cannot be attributed to the interaction until it is captured at the organizational level. The challenge is how to capture the knowledge that resides in the individuals and use it in the process to create added value for the organization. Private companies could benefit from that knowledge to develop new products and services, or simply to better manage their relations in some regions or with certain stakeholders.

LESSONS FOR COMPANIES

Humanitarian organizations are established to meet needs in settings and conditions very different from the private sector. They are also driven by a different set of values, objectives and funding mechanisms. However, these differences are a source of numerous lessons that can be adapted and transferred to the private sector.

In this chapter, we have focused on the lessons that can be learned from the humanitarian supply chain through long-term CSR programmes. As the examples cited show, the humanitarian supply chain can offer lessons to companies operating in global markets to help them prepare for high-impact low-probability events affecting their operations.

Acquiring these lessons can be difficult, as they will be found in areas where it is challenging to operate and where risks like security can be very high. They also require a serious investment from the companies. This starts with the senior leaders clearly communicating their motivation for the CSR programme, making it a company-wide priority, and financing their commitment. Finally, the lessons from the humanitarian sector extend beyond the personal level, and should be lifted to the organizational level. Capturing the richness of these experiences for the organizations from the individuals is an additional investment that the company needs to make to be receptive to the new ideas, provide the means for staff to transfer them into the company, and build upon those lessons internally.

Notes

1 Excerpt from INSEAD Case No. 09/2008-5495: *Humanitarian Response to the 2006 Lebanese/Israeli Conflict*
2 A similar event took place 10 days earlier in Gaza and led to a full military operation by the Israelis who were refusing to negotiate based on the no-negotiation with terrorist organizations policy.
3 Beirut's southern suburb is home of the Hezbollah headquarters and television station.
4 Except for the evacuation of foreigners, no ships were allowed to dock at the ports in the early days of the war.
5 www.unjlc.org
6 Numbers published on the Higher Relief Council website, www.lebanonundersiege.com
7 Respective sources: Israeli and Lebanese governments
8 Source: Lebanese government
9 www.ifrc.org
10 www.wfp.org
11 www.unicef.org
12 www.care.org
13 www.wvi.org
14 INSEAD Case Study No. 2009-5590: *Yogyakarta Earthquake: The IFRC's first experience with the decentralized supply chain*
15 INSEAD Case Study No. 06/2008-5363: *Moving the World-UNJLC: Transport optimization for South Sudan*

16 Section inspired by INSEAD Case Study No. 03/2004-5194: *TNT-WFP Moving the World: Learning to dance*

17 Source: www.wfp.org

18 INSEAD Case Study No. 03/2009-5596: *TNT/WFP Partnership: Moving the World five years on. When the music changes, so does the dance*

19 Section inspired by INSEAD Case Study No. 03/2009-5559: *Agility: A global logistics company and local humanitarian partner*

20 INSEAD Case Study No. 03/2009-5559: *Agility: A global logistics company and local humanitarian partner*

21 www.agilitylogistics.com

22

Global sourcing and supply

Alan Braithwaite, LCP Consulting

BACKGROUND

Global sourcing and supply is now a central part of many companies' business strategies. It has proved essential to sustaining competitiveness and maintaining net margins. Indeed, global sourcing and supply is probably both the biggest economic trend of the past 20 years and a key ingredient for corporate survival.

The adoption of low-cost sourcing and supply areas has displayed an exponential trend which, despite recent economic turmoil, is forecast to continue over the longer term. However, the dynamics of this new type of operation are only just being understood and have not been documented extensively. Global sourcing implies long-distance supply chains, multiple interactions and extended lead times. As companies move to increase their share of global sourcing beyond the current entry levels, there will be major implications for how these extended chains are managed; security of supply, demand responsiveness and product life-cycle management all take on greater significance.

Global sourcing is an established fact of business life and is a dominant market-driven trend. But the challenge for every individual corporation is to implement it in a way that secures a sustainable advantage. This means organizing to manage risk alongside commercial and competitive advantage. All of the principles of supply chain management still apply;

the specifics of global sustainability have many additional dimensions that are not experienced in more conventional local chains.

GROWTH IN GLOBAL TRADE

The expansion of global trade in manufactured goods has been one of the most pronounced and remarkable economic trends of the past 40 years. It has both fuelled and enabled the growth in gross domestic product (GDP) of most developed countries: exporting jobs to countries with large pools of increasingly skilled and low-cost labour. The capacity of the labour pool in developed countries is being released to higher value or essentially local activities and the service sector. The scale of this shift is shown in Figure 22.1.

Despite recent economic problems, the long-term trend of growth in global trade shows no sign of abating. It has been reinforced by the reduction in tariff barriers and the expansion of low-cost international logistics in the form of container freight. Moreover, there is no correlation between growth and the absolute scale of imports and exports, meaning that there is opportunity for global trade and economic benefit to both mature and emerging economies. If we set aside the natural tensions of self-interest that have been evident in recent world trade negotiations, it is clear that there are enormous benefits for buyers and sellers alike.

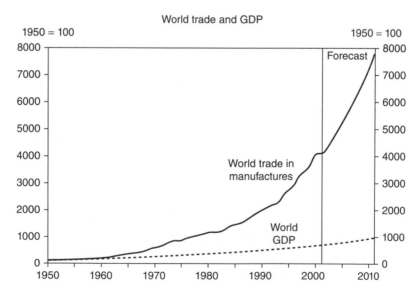

Figure 22.1 Growth in global trade in manufactures
Source: WTO/OEF

China has been describing its GDP growth as 8–9 per cent a year, but on the whole this is felt to be an underestimate. It refers to itself with pride as the 'factory to the world'. No one can ignore this trade potential and global sourcing is now a matter of board strategy for all businesses in developed economies.

Statements in relation to planned increases in this trend are a regular feature of annual reports and analyst briefings. Wal-Mart, the world's largest retailer, made the trend to direct international sourcing a key feature of its 2002 annual report, saying: 'We also are making exciting strides in … global procurement. Last year we assumed responsibility of global procurement from a third party. This allowed us to better coordinate the entire global supply chain from product development to delivery. In addition, our global procurement program allows us to share our buying power and merchandise network with all our operations throughout the world.'

Dyson closed its entire manufacturing in the UK and moved to Asia as a key element of its entry strategy for the US market. New origins for the garment trade are Turkey and Morocco where companies can still leverage low-cost labour, but without full Far East sacrifices on lead time and flexibility.

Figure 22.2 shows the critical contribution of the automotive industry, engineering and electronics to globalization. In reality, companies like

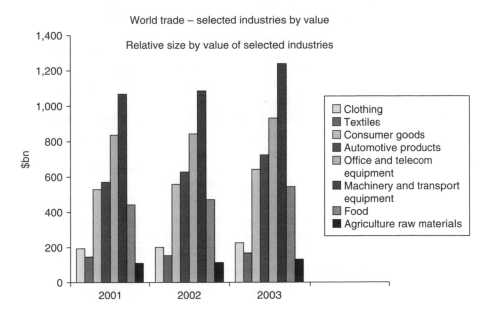

Figure 22.2   Global trade growth by product category
Source: WTO, 2004

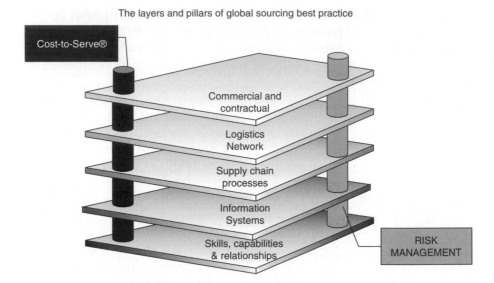

Figure 22.3 The layers and pillars of global sourcing
© *Source*: LCP Consulting, 2005

Wal-Mart are only catching up and this will likely be at the expense of both importers and local manufacturers.

The WTO predicts that global supply is the future. Indeed, it is an irreversible trend since capacity is leaving developed markets because it cannot compete with low-cost imports. This global sourcing dimension of strategy is now a cornerstone of companies' plans to generate value for customers and shareholders alike. Few can envisage a sustainable future without an increasing level of global supply.

Given this landscape of major change, this chapter brings together some key dimensions of the practice of global sourcing. It reviews the 'layer and pillar' model (Figure 22.3), which proved useful as a means to describe the multifaceted nature of global supply chain management. Supply chain management in global sourcing must address all of the layers. Best practice is bound together by a requirement to understand and manage through a structured approach to risk and through the total 'Cost-to-Serve' (a registered mark of LCP Consulting), which is a supply chain costing methodology that can quickly capture the true logistics cost drivers and identify activities that are intrinsically uneconomic.

GLOBAL SOURCING AS A WAY TO CHANGE BUSINESS STRATEGY

The central role of global sourcing in transforming business strategies can be understood by comparing the relative wage rates in regions of the world. Because of difficulties with exact comparisons, these figures as indicative rather than definitive. For skilled labour per hour in Germany the cost is $18 to $25; in the Czech Republic it is $3–5; in the United States it is $9–15; in Asia and India it is often less than $1. The cost of support services, construction, capital investment and management are in proportion, which means that the cost of an equivalent article made in an emerging economy can be as little as half of that sourced locally.

Traders have been taking advantage of this arbitrage potential for many years and have used their local relationships, buying skills and logistics know-how to make a margin. That margin was their return for taking risk, including quality, financing and marketing. The ultimate price differentials were reduced to 10 to 20 per cent to the end customer.

The surge in growth of global trade is the result of more companies going into markets to deal direct – cutting out the middleman. The effect of this has been to increase margins and also to increase the buyer's risk. The business strategy has been to plough back the margin benefit into lower prices, which in turn has increased volumes and market share. The trick has been – and will be – to exploit the elasticity of demand by just enough to get more volume than the margin that has been conceded. Getting this right makes both sales and profits grow.

Across industry as a whole, the trend has been for lower real prices as value is passed on to customers. The open question is the extent to which this trend is now played out. The next step in global sourcing will involve another doubling of activity levels and this will require improved levels of control and integration. The skills of supply chain management will become increasingly central.

IDENTIFYING AND SELECTING SOURCES

The practice of sourcing depends on the commodity and product. For example, chemicals display different supply characteristics from clothing, which in turn is different from micro-electronics. Entering a new sourcing arrangement is a moment of risk and there are many factors to be considered. These include the following:

- *Quality is a key issue.* Vendors are increasingly able to deliver to quality – but this ability cannot be taken for granted. The implications of a long-distance quality failure are much greater than a local one, as the problem may not be discovered soon enough to avoid serious disruption. Increasingly, companies are insisting on more comprehensive quality control at vendors, alongside detailed specification and engineering integration.

- *Ethical supply*. The marketing and PR impacts of the use of child labour and the environmental conditions surrounding production are now important for consumers. Media disclosures can damage the brand with consumers, and shake investor confidence. Increasingly, companies are conducting regular audits and inspections of their sources to make sure that they do not get surprises and damage to their reputations.
- *Patent protection*. The leaking of design and technology advantage has become a common experience. Companies have outsourced to places where respect for patents and know-how is rather less than the standard they would expect. Often designs, ideas and products reappear through different channels and can erode markets and price levels. This risk requires a very careful approach to ensure that key differentiators are protected and that contractual guarantees that can be enforced are obtained.
- *Operational excellence*. Vendors' capabilities can vary widely and it is crucial to understand the extent they will be able to perform to expectation. For example, late new product introductions can significantly impact the buying and marketing organization, and there is evidence of share price erosion when international chains fail.

These points require a higher level of due diligence and ongoing management than many might expect. Dealing across cultural boundaries is a major part of this challenge – and the word 'yes' in many languages cannot be taken as an unequivocal agreement.

COMMERCIAL MODELS

Global trade is by definition more remote than buying locally. A problem with local supply can prompt a whole range of quite simple actions, including refusing to pay and taking legal action. With global sourcing and supply these actions are more difficult, since the goods may already have been paid for, and legal action is less likely to be successful. Commercial models are, therefore, a key part of supply chain design. These are about the point of payment for the various activities along the chain, where the risk is taken, and the margin that is taken or conceded for that risk and credit period. These terms can vary enormously by both sector and companies' preferences. Traditionally traders took title to the goods at the side of the ship and paid with a currency instrument (letter of credit) that was guaranteed by a bank and cross-guaranteed by the buyer. Then they organized their own freight and paid any duties and tariffs at the destination. This model is often called FOB (Free on Board) and has been adopted by retailers who are progressively replacing their traders and agents.

Another common option is CIF (Cost of goods plus Insurance and Freight) where the vendor charges for the cost of goods plus the insurance and freight to get them to the final destination. Any duties and taxes in this model are for the buyer to arrange to pay when the goods arrive in the origin country. DDP is the most equivalent option to local supply. It stands for Delivered Duty Paid and it is where the vendor takes total responsibility for all costs until the product is delivered. Financing is invariably part of this package.

These are the most common of many models that are referred to as IncoTerms. The precise selection of the right IncoTerm is a critical decision for the specific trade on extended supply chains, with many hidden risks and the requirement for extended financing. It will be influenced by a whole range of factors, including the buyers' balance sheet, the vendors' financial capacity, the risk in the trade, and the relative cost of financing and operating the chain under the different models.

INTERNATIONAL LOGISTICS

The importance of international logistics cannot be overemphasized. The flexibility of container freight to make efficient, shared capacity available to many users has been a huge driver of global trade. But with scale in global trade have come new issues that require new approaches.

Even with container freight, traditional methods of managing international logistics can involve as many as 10 to 12 hand-offs in movement and documents. If just one or two of these fail, with no effective way of putting it right, the unreliability of global logistics becomes the reality that is often a subject of comment and complaint.

With scale and growth, inbound management at the destination now requires central coordination. Correspondingly, management at the origin also needs to be controlled to ensure the right flow at the destination, and to enable the buyer to take advantage of the scale of its activities. The management of documentation, customs clearance and compliance can also benefit from a single centralized administrative and forwarding set-up.

Finally, the question of security against terrorism is now a major concern in international trade. There are onerous requirements for certification of cargoes, especially into the United States, under the CT-PAT scheme (Customs and Trade – Partnership against Terrorism). Failure to comply can lead to cargoes being refused carriage or blocked for lengthy inspection and clearance.

The result of these factors is that major buyers are tending to appoint a global 'lead logistics service provider' (LLP). These are often offshoots of the container shipping lines or international freight forwarders who have extended their services, and are especially appropriate where a buyer is maintaining many trading relationships. In companies where there are a smaller number of very large trading relationships, the tendency is to adopt an in-house forwarder.

In all circumstances, the operational need is for integrated management of many remote origins, providing information visibility, certification, and the capability to respond to factors in the supply chain.

FLOW MANAGEMENT

Flow management and control is often executed, but seldom planned, by the LLP. Someone, generally the buyer, has to make the planning, forecasting and ordering decisions. The key feature of global sourcing is that chains become extended, with longer lead times and less agility to respond to changes in the actual marketplace. This needs improved forecast accuracy and more integrated supply chain planning. The consequences of poor planning are a combination of service failures and increased cost from emergency deliveries and associated expediting.

Global best practice is to introduce a sales and operations planning process, part of which is to identify the products whose demand characteristics makes them particularly vulnerable during extended lead times. With these products there is generally the potential to implement supply chain strategy options such as postponement, capacity booking or switch sourcing:

- Postponement is where the product is made and shipped in a generic form so that it can go into a number of different final products. The generic parts are then localized in the final market to meet real customer orders (HP and Dell are renowned for using this approach).
- Capacity booking is where a vendor is 'booked' to provide capacity on a fixed cycle; the exact mix of product to be made is decided at the last minute. This reduces lead times and ensures that the product made is the one that is most needed.

- Switch sourcing is where the initial quantity is made in the lowest-cost source and if demand forecasts are exceeded any patterns or moulds are flown to higher-cost sources where the product can be made and shipped with much shorter lead time.

ORGANIZATION DESIGN

The organization of global sourcing is a major issue, with companies that have global sourcing creating organizations in their main origins which they now feel are 'disconnected' from the core organization at the destination. The dilemma seems to be whether the offices in the origins are buying functions, logistics functions, technical functions – or some combination of these. Each of these relates to different functions in the parent organization – and ownership and control appears to become an issue. Furthermore, the relationship of the origin offices and capabilities with the main organization is inevitably challenged by distance, communications, systems issues and – most of all – goals and key performance indicators (KPIs).

It is clear that the next stage of maturity in global sourcing and supply will require a greater definition of the organizational lines and responsibilities than exists in many businesses today. This will most likely be based on team-based structures working on categories, technologies and product life-cycle projects as appropriate; it will be fully integrated with the core business at the right points and work actively to overcome the barriers of geography and culture.

INFORMATION TECHNOLOGY

Extended chains require information technology that can manage the long-distance 'purchase to pay' cycle, and all the steps along the way. The key is to make available a single version of the order and its status to every point along the chain. It must allow the appropriate people and organizations to make amendments, update status and provide a history of events. This is beyond enterprise resource planning (ERP) as the various players along the chain (such as vendors, service providers, and Customs & Excise) all have many relationships with other parties. They also have particular information needs that will not fit with the customers' ERP systems – and the attributes of the data are rather different from that in conventional ERP systems. The data architecture needs to be able to handle consignments, waybills, containers, tariffs, providers, VAT and duty as well as orders, stock-keeping units (SKUs), vendors, and locations.

Data interchange between systems is essential to provide the visibility needed for flow control. Internet technology has provided the ideal platform on which many-to-many relationships can be maintained. It is low cost and provides widely based connectivity. However, every major shipper then needs a single reference point for its international trade, and this is unlikely to be the main ERP system. Some of the major shippers and forwarders have invested heavily in such event management systems and the associated connectivity. The early versions of these systems have added considerable value and the new generation is expected to provide another step change.

However, the systems world is full of tensions as providers compete to promote their systems and lock in their clients. It is unwise to expect that the international technology (IT) world of global trade is an open and transparent one. There are many barriers, including the operational excellence (or lack of it) with which the technology is fed.

OPERATIONAL EXCELLENCE

With as many as 12 operational hand-offs in the extended international supply chain, there is much that can go wrong – so operational excellence is critical to a smooth supply chain. Typical issues that must be done with excellence are:

- product labelling and bar coding – right code, right box, right quantity;
- invoicing – right product, right cost, right consignee;
- customs – right classifications;
- advanced shipping notices for right product;
- schedule and date required compliance;
- container packing accuracy;
- handling quality.

Surveys have shown very high levels of non-compliance and operational variability in global supply. Quite simply, the origin participants do not understand the requirements for supply chain management by their customers and, therefore, often do not comply. The use of an LLP can be combined with more proactive vendor management to make sure that due dates and data quality are achieved – and to impose charges when standards are missed. Case material has demonstrated the downstream value of upstream excellence. The cost is tiny in relation to the value, and the barriers to excellence are more about culture and understanding than deliberate obstruction.

RISK MANAGEMENT

Risk management should be continuous for buyers. There is much to be concerned about, for example:

- the basics of vendor viability;
- sudden and unadvised changes in priorities by vendors and service providers;
- quality and timeliness issues;
- introduction of unauthorized materials or child labour;
- loss/leakage of technical know-how and patents;
- sudden and unexpected duty and quota constraints as a result of political and economic pressures;
- currency variations;
- sudden and un-forecast changes in customer demand.

A lot of these would apply to local supply as well, but their scale and impacts would generally be less. The combination of culture, language, distance and complexity conspires to make a formal risk management process with regular checks essential. This requirement will expand further as global sourcing moves into its next phase of growth.

CRITICAL SUCCESS FACTORS

The measures to manage global chains and mitigate risk require six capabilities. These capabilities form the critical success factors:

1. Total acquisition cost management – the ability to analyse and predict the total cost-to-serve from the source of supply to its final point of sale. The capability in this analysis is not simply to build up the logistics costs from freight, inventory holding, duty, applicable customs regimes and so on. It is more important to analyse and build into the costing the risk of markdown and lost sales through a market-risk-cost profile. This analysis identifies products that should never be traded on a long lead time, or that should be the subject of a postponement strategy. It is also likely to show that there are some products where actions to reduce lead time and increase flexibility will justify a higher initial purchasing cost.
2. One-touch information flow – to avoid double entry, duplication, mistakes and inconsistency as the same transaction moves through the many points of contact in the chain. Accuracy of information is a precondition of proactive management. This capability is systems

enabled – and it is critical to have the widest view of the total chain on one information platform with the ability to recognize inconsistencies.

3. Total product identification and compliance – to ensure fast accurate product and handling unit identification that feeds the 'one-touch information' requirement. The use of bar codes and radio frequency identification (RFID) to the correct standards is the enabling technology.

4. Real-time routing through dynamic visibility – the capability to see through the chain, know what is coming, and test for events that have not happened as planned; to interpret the implications of failures in a proactive way and make decisions to minimize their impact. This is the 'traffic control' of global supply chain, and it must be managed transparently and with the cooperation of all the parties in the chain.

5. Vendor development – the capability to understand and improve the long-term performance of vendors in terms of cycle times, timeliness, quality and accuracy. Based on historical performance of the chain, it is possible to identify improvement programmes to develop supplier reliability. The ultimate goal is to issue orders and schedules on shorter lead times, reflecting real demand or more accurate forecasts. Understanding the underlying performance of vendors and their category of products in the marketplace is the starting point for this.

6. Information platform to provide consistent and timely information – the capability to put in place, operate and maintain a full supply chain visibility solution. All of the above capabilities are anchored by the operational skill to secure and maintain the information backbone, with the diverse data structures that are needed by each supply chain function.

GLOBAL SOURCING – SUSTAINING THE TREND

It is clear that first movers to global sourcing have gained a competitive advantage. Often these were traders who had an intimate knowledge of a supply market in terms of the vendors and their capabilities – as well as the logistics to get the product to the market. They committed to stock risk and knew where to dispose of product if the original channel did not work. For this they earned a respectable margin for the risks they took.

In the context of the explosion of global sourcing and the further potential, the conclusion is that the 'land grab' is over (Figure 22.4). The figure suggests that we are moving from initial exploitation to putting in place stable structures that can handle the next phase of growth. This will be essential as companies become more dependent on long-distance supply chains with all the risks and issues that we have identified.

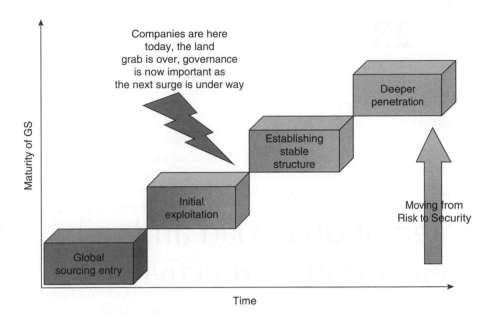

Figure 22.4 Maturity development of global sourcing

The increased penetration of global sourcing will make its management a core skill and capability. This chapter has attempted to provide an initial view of the emerging landscape and issues.

Reference

WTO (2005) International trade statistics, *World Trade Organization* [Online] www.wto.org

23

International road and rail freight transport activity

Jacques Leonardi, Allan Woodburn, Julian Allen and Michael Browne, University of Westminster

INTRODUCTION

International road and rail freight transport activity is a complex field where existing structures and rules concerning goods transport are mainly driven by developments at the national or European level, such as the introduction of new social or environmental legislation, or by global trends, for example adopting new technologies or developing new vehicles. Little attention has been paid so far to the specific problems and trends governing cross-border, international traffic by land.

This chapter first establishes the recent trends in international trade volumes. It then aims to identify the main ways in which this trade growth has impacted on road and rail freight transport activity at the international level, and considers the factors influencing the future direction of international land-based transport. The 'international' focus is on cross-border road and rail transport, rather than on comparisons of trends and prospects across a range of different countries. In talking about international freight transport it is important to be aware of the diversity of trip types included, and the impact that the attributes of the trip can have on its organization and cost.

As far as possible, experience from around the world is identified and discussed, although the main focus is on cross-border flows between countries in Europe, Asia and North America since these three regions are where the majority of land-based international transport takes place. While the assessment is evidence-led where possible, there are limitations relating to differing definitions and measurement units, both spatially and temporally, and inadequate data relating to cross-border freight transport activity.

The structure of the chapter is as follows. The next section deals with recent trends in international trade activity since this is a driving force in the development of international transport. This is followed by three sections presenting a more detailed discussion of road and rail, within which aspects such as infrastructure issues, policy and regulation, and operations are assessed. Future perspectives are discussed in the concluding section.

RECENT INTERNATIONAL TRADE ACTIVITY AND TRANSPORT: ECONOMIC FACTORS AND TRENDS

The World Trade Organization (WTO) provides the most comprehensive data on trade volumes and trends. This section highlights some of the main aspects of world trade that affect freight transport activity and mode choice. Figure 23.1 reveals the long-term growth in international trade volumes in all product categories, but most notably in manufactures.

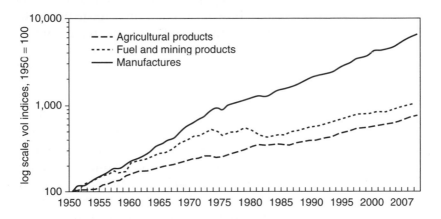

Figure 23.1 World merchandise trade volume by major product group, 1950–2007
Source: WTO, 2008

Table 23.1 Annual percentage change of value of goods in world merchandise trade by region, 2000–06

Exports	Region	Imports
20	CIS	23
16	Middle East	15
16	Africa	14
14	South & Central America	10
12	Asia	12
11	Europe	11
11	World	17
5	North America	7

Source: adapted from WTO, 2007

In general, trade growth has exceeded the increase in gross domestic product (GDP) over this time period; between 2000 and 2006, trade growth was approximately twice the GDP increase (WTO, 2008). In terms of the value of products, the top six flows between world regions involve just three regions, Europe, Asia and North America, with trade within and between these regions accounting for three-quarters of world trade value. Internal European flows alone make up almost one-third of all international trade. Six of the top 10 countries involved in international trade are European, with two each from North America and Asia.

Table 23.1 shows the average annual growth in trade to and from each of the world regions for 2000–06. Globally, the value of goods traded increased by an average of 11 per cent per annum. North America recorded lower than average growth, and those regions less involved in international trade experienced higher than average growth rates, but remain relatively insignificant in comparison to Europe, Asia and North America.

International road and rail transport movements were greatly influenced by the introduction of regional trading blocs. The two most significant trading blocs are the European Union (EU) and the signatories to the North American Free Trade Agreement (NAFTA). The EU has expanded and has removed internal trade barriers while developing unified trade agreements for extra-EU trade. EU countries were involved in 38 per cent of global merchandise trade by value in 2006. Of this, two-thirds was traded internally between EU countries (WTO, 2007). By contrast, trade between NAFTA countries (Canada, Mexico and the United States) comprised just over 40 per cent of the total merchandise trade of those countries.

In their own right, road and rail modes are mainly dealing with intra-regional flows, given that two of the three main inter-regional flows (Asia–North America and Europe–North America) are not possible by land-based routes, so maritime transport dominates. For the third (Asia–Europe), land transport is possible though currently very limited, with the majority of goods again being moved by sea. Considerable use is made of road and rail as feeder modes for these inter-regional maritime services, connecting with inland flow origins and destinations and, in some cases, acting as land bridges. As noted by Kopp (2006), 'there is widespread agreement that the reduction in long-distance transport and communications costs has been an important determinant of today's globalization'.

Trade costs can be influenced by different factors, described by Deardorff (2005). Trade costs (especially transport costs) can be important and can reduce the amount of international trade by making it unprofitable. This is a problem that is often faced by landlocked, developing countries, which as a result of their geographical disadvantage face 'specific challenges in their attempts to integrate into the global trading system, mainly because goods coming from or going to a landlocked country are subject to additional trade barriers such as lengthy border-crossing procedures' (UNCTAD, 2007).

The costs of transporting goods from one international location to another (the resource cost of transportation) is probably the most important cost of trade for most products. This cost varies with distance, weight and bulk density of the product, and its handling requirements in transit. Other costs of international trade include insurance (which is related to size and value), financing (which varies depending on the elapsed time between production and receipt of payment), and financial fees (resulting from trading across national borders and often using more than one currency) (Deardorff, 2005).

Time is another important factor in the cost of international trade (Deardorff, 2005). Time is required to transport the good from its origin to its destination, as well as to load and unload it, and to process the good and the vehicle through customs clearance and border crossings. Given that it takes time to carry out international transport of goods, it is necessary for companies to hold stock. This stockholding incurs several costs in terms of warehousing costs, interest payments, and depreciation costs associated with physical deterioration or change in consumer tastes. In trying to minimize these time-related costs, it is important to choose the fastest possible means of transport.

Hummels (2001) has noted that time delays and the variability of transit times are of greater concern to shippers than direct transport costs, as they affect companies' ability to meet agreed delivery schedules and therefore necessitate large stockholding. The author has used the costs of different modes of transport to infer the costs of time from the amount that firms are prepared to pay to reduce it. His results suggest that a one-day delay in shipping leads to an average cost equivalent to a 0.8 per cent tariff.

Trade costs are high. Broadly defined, trade costs include all costs incurred in getting a good to a final user other than the cost of producing the good itself. An estimate of the 'representative' tax equivalent of trade costs for industrialized countries is 170 per cent of the 'original' value. This estimate includes 74 per cent international trade costs (such as transport costs and border-related trade barriers) and 55 per cent local distribution costs. The international transport costs comprise direct freight transport costs as well as a 9 per cent tax equivalent of the time value of goods (Anderson and Wincoop, 2004).

Traditionally for international goods movement, air transport has been used for products that are time-sensitive and valuable, and sea has been used for lower-value products that are less time-sensitive. However, ever-longer international road and rail transport options are becoming viable as a result of infrastructure improvements and international agreements. These land-based modes are likely to increase their modal share of international goods movements as they offer services that are cheaper (but slower) than airfreight and faster (but more expensive) than sea.

However, the quantity of goods transported internationally by land modes is still very small in comparison with domestic road and rail freight movements.

RECENT TRENDS IN INTERNATIONAL FREIGHT TRANSPORT VOLUMES BY ROAD AND RAIL

European Union (EU)

For the 11 EU Member States with consistent data, the proportion of tonne kilometres for international road haulage increased slightly from 22 per cent in 1995 to 26 per cent in 2005 (European Communities, 2004, 2007). This represented an increase of 52 per cent in absolute terms, given the overall growth in road activity during this period. Of the cross-border volume for this sub-set of member countries, 90 per cent in 2005 was between adjacent countries. For the EU-25 countries (excluding Greece and Malta), 30 per cent of road freight volumes in 2005 were cross-border in nature, with 15 per cent of the cross-border volume being cross-trade, representing the greater incidence of transit traffic in certain Eastern European countries (European Communities, 2007).

By contrast, international flows are more significant in the rail market. Fifty-one per cent of rail freight volumes in the 25 EU countries in 2005 were cross-border in nature (European Communities, 2007). As with road, the vast majority of this volume was between adjacent countries, with just 20 per cent of the total international volume transiting intermediate countries. While no consistent statistics over time exist at the European

Table 23.2 US trade with Canada and Mexico by road and rail, 2006, in million (m) tonnes per year

Exports from United States			Imports to United States	
Mode share (%)	Tonnes (m)		Tonnes (m)	Mode share (%)
		Canada		
42	59	Road	62	21
21	30	Rail	76	26
		Mexico		
38	31	Road	28	20
26	21	Rail	11	8

Source: adapted from NATSD, 2009

level, analysis of trends in individual countries reveals the growing share of international flows for national rail systems. For example, international rail freight increased from 37 per cent of all rail freight in Germany in 1995 to 47 per cent in 2005, and in the Netherlands the increase was from 76 to 79 per cent (European Communities, 2003, 2007).

North America

The North American Transport Statistics Database (NATSD) does not contain detailed and consistent time series data relating to intra-North American trade by transport mode; these data have been published only since 2004 (NATSD, 2009). Table 23.2 summarizes the road and rail freight flows between the United States and Canada and Mexico in 2006. These two modes are dominant for exports from the United States, where 60–65 per cent of tonnage is by road or rail, whereas water transport and, in the case of Canada, pipeline, are important modes for imports to the United States.

In 2002, international road freight accounted for just 2 per cent of total road freight lifted to, from and within the United States. The corresponding figure for international rail was 6 per cent (measured in tonnes lifted – freight delivered to a port will be counted as national rather than international for road and rail movements). In combination, road and rail represented 32 per cent of international tonnes lifted to and from the United States (imports and exports combined) (Office of Freight Management and Operations, 2007).

Europe to/from Asia

Travel distances between Europe and Asia are generally far shorter by land than they are by sea. This is especially true if the origin and/or destination

Table 23.3 Estimated transport of full-load containers between Europe and China in 2005 (million full-load TEUs)

	Westbound	Eastbound	Total
Sea transport	4.5	2.5	7.0
Rail	< 0.2	< 0.1	< 0.3
Road (truck)	< 0.03	< 0.03	< 0.06

Source: US Chamber of Commerce, 2006

are inland. Rail services from China to Europe via Central Asia that take approximately 20 days could be provided, whereas this takes approximately two weeks by sea. It has been estimated that travelling from Europe to Asia by road would take approximately two weeks (ECMT, 2006).

At present, the major trans-Asia land routes are rail routes, including the Trans-Siberian, the TRACECA corridor, and the southern route via Turkey and Iran. Road routes can be preferable to rail routes in Asia in terms of the denser coverage they provide to larger towns. In addition, the physical terrain in the south of the continent is often better suited to road than rail.

China is currently developing a country-wide network of road and rail infrastructure that will link up with connections to Kazakhstan, Mongolia and Russia. The reopening of the border between China and Kazakhstan for commercial trade has resulted in the recommencing of long-distance freight flows by (road and rail) land between the two continents. However, volumes of intercontinental freight flows remain small at present. These land routes are mostly used for the transport of commodities such as coal, agricultural products, iron and oil, and bulk goods. Only very limited quantities of containerized cargo are transported over these land routes. Table 23.3 shows the estimated modal split for containers between Europe and China. This reflects the fact that maritime transport still dominates these container flows by far (US Chamber of Commerce, 2006).

INTERNATIONAL ROAD FREIGHT TRANSPORT: RECENT DEVELOPMENTS AND CHALLENGES

Infrastructure developments

The basic infrastructure for international road transport is available, but 'missing links' constrain route choice. In addition, insufficient capacity on some corridors and the poor quality of infrastructure add to the cost and time of road transport. There is also a general lack of infrastructure facilities, such as inland container depots, particularly at border crossings, to support the consolidation and distribution of goods and transhipment between road and rail services (UNESCAP, 2003).

The International E-road Network in Europe (E-road = a European road numbering system) lists the road routes followed by the traffic arteries defined in the European Agreement on Main International Traffic Arteries (AGR) signed at Geneva in November 1975 (UNECE, 2007). The AGR was extended in 2000 to include the E-road network for the then new UNECE member countries in the Caucasus and Central Asia. This resulted in the international road network in these countries, which extend right up to the borders with China, also being ascribed 'E' numbers As well as establishing a coherent road network, the AGR set in place minimum technical requirements to which E-roads should be constructed.

Asia also has a dense road network which links major cities, especially in the southern part of the continent (including India, Pakistan and the South-East Asian peninsula). The planned Asian Highway Network (UNESCAP, 2009) aims to provide road transport infrastructure linkages to and through the region. It is already a network of 141,000 km of standardized roadways joining 32 Asian countries with linkages to Europe.

One of the leading European infrastructure policy is the Trans-European Transport Network 'TEN-T', established in 1993, which involves transport infrastructure projects to help put in place high-quality trans-European transport networks. It is intended to overcome problems associated with missing transport links and existing bottlenecks. Fourteen priority projects were established in the EU-15 in 1996; this was extended to 30 priority transnational axes in 2004 following the accession of new Member States (EU-27). In 2007, discussions commenced on modifications to the major TEN-T axes to neighbouring countries. This involves TEN-T being re-defined to include the EU's neighbours, towards the CIS and Central Asian countries along key transport corridors (ECMT 2006, European Commission 2005).

While the construction and improvement of road infrastructure is important in the development of international road freight, there are additional factors necessary in order to create a successful and efficient road network. This includes standardization and harmonization of many other factors besides the quality of road construction, such as traffic regulations, vehicle regulations and traffic technologies. Specific factors that need to be taken into account in standardizing and harmonizing the road network include:

- the systems adopted for traffic management (including the policies and technology used);

- border-crossing arrangements and dwell-time caused by customs policies;
- road signage and information, including traffic conditions and roadworks;
- truck stop facilities (including eating and resting locations and services for drivers);
- emergency operations – calling a single number, minimum guarantee response time etc;
- repair, maintenance and emergency vehicle services (in case of vehicle breakdowns);
- disaster management systems (fire brigades etc).

Several conventions concerning international road transport can help in the standardization and harmonization of international road networks. These include the Convention on Road Traffic, which helps to harmonize road traffic rules, the Convention on Road Signs and Signals, which has produced a large set of common signs and signals to use, and the TIR Convention, which allows trucks loaded with goods to cross several borders without customs controls and without payment of duties or taxes.

Policy/regulation

Agreements between countries in international road freight transport

International road freight operations by definition involve goods vehicles moving between two or more countries as part of a delivery or collection. Some international trips can involve the vehicle or goods passing through (ie transiting) many different countries in order to get from the point of collection to the point of delivery. Different countries tend to have developed varying national rules governing goods vehicles, goods movement and driver regulations. In order to overcome the main differences, it was necessary to develop conventions that govern international road freight operations. The international community has, over the years, adopted several international legal instruments that contain provisions intended to assist international road freight operations, including gaining access to seaports via transit traffic through neighbouring countries.

The four main legal instruments addressing transit traffic and customs transit are (UNCTAD, 2007):

- Convention and Statute on Freedom of Transit, 1921 (entry into force 31 October 1922; 50 parties);

- General Agreement on Tariffs and Trade (GATT), 1947, now part of GATT 1994 (provisional entry into force 1 January 1948; 150 members of the World Trade Organization (WTO));
- Convention on Transit Trade of Land-Locked States, 1965 (entry into force 9 June 1967; 38 States parties);
- United Nations Convention on the Law of the Sea, 1982 (entry into force 16 November 1994; 155 States parties).

In addition, the General Agreement on Trade in Services (GATS) extends the GATT's principles of freer and fairer trade in goods to services as well, which includes freight companies looking to do business abroad (Latrille, 2007).

International legal instruments are complementary to regional, corridor and bilateral transport and transit agreements and are often referred to in such agreements on transport as well as in those on infrastructure, storage and general trade terms (UNCTAD, 2007). Several regional cooperation organizations have established transit and/or transport agreements. Many countries have traditionally entered into bilateral agreements on particular aspects of cooperation. In road transport, such agreements have often been needed to allow a transport operator in one country to carry out bilateral transport operations, third-country transport operations or transit transport operations through another country.

A transit corridor agreement is an agreement concerning a designated route between two or more countries along which the corridor countries have agreed to apply specified procedures. These agreements tend to be very focused on corridor and transit issues, such as infrastructure, customs, border crossings and vehicles. An example of this type of arrangement is the Walvis Bay Corridor Group, which was established in 2000. This comprises public and private stakeholders along four transport corridors in southern Africa, all connecting with the port of Walvis Bay in Namibia.

Liberalization of international road freight transport

The European Union provides an example for liberalization of international road freight transport movements between Member States. The Treaty of Rome provided for the establishment of a common transport policy, based on principles of free market economics, which was intended to remove obstacles to free competition between transport operators from different countries. Multilateral Community authorizations were introduced in 1969, which gradually replaced bilateral agreements between countries. The establishment of the Single European Market was the catalyst for full liberalization in international road freight, with the removal of these multilateral authorizations and the introduction of European Community licences.

Full liberalization of international road freight was completed by 1998. Operators based in a Member State need only comply with two requirements to be able to carry goods between any EU countries: i) to be recognized as a professional road transport operator and ii) holding a European Community licence. To be recognized as a professional operator it is necessary to meet three qualitative criteria: good repute, financial standing and professional competence. Any operator who meets these requirements, and who meets any other national market access regulations, obtains a Community licence. This then allows it to carry out international transport operations in the entire geographical area of the EU (ECMT, 2005).

The European Commission has put in place harmonized social regulations to ensure that full liberalization does not lead to competition distortions brought about by national differences in factors such as labour rates. These regulations cover issues such as working hours, driving time and rest periods for drivers, and periodic technical inspection of motor vehicles and their trailers.

A recent study tended to show that deregulation had a large positive effect on the growth of international trucking and that EU liberalization was not leading to a shift in the demand for international road freight towards low-wage countries (Lafontaine and Malaguzzi, 2009). However, there is an ongoing controversial debate about policy design, modalities and rules of road freight liberalization, since cross-border traffic between many countries is still facing elementary operative problems due to diverse dysfunctions at the infrastructure, technology, security and policy compliance levels (Snitbhan et al, 2004).

Operations

Coping with growth in international road freight transport

Growth in world trade together with road and rail infrastructure improvements has made the possibility of land-based international freight solutions easier over time. One way in which logistics service providers can enter into foreign markets is through the establishment of operating centres in other countries and gradually increasing their networks. Other firms prefer mergers, takeovers or strategic trading alliances with operators based in other European countries as a means of becoming more international.

The growing internationalization of business has forced companies providing logistics services to consider their own strategies to meet these new needs. Service providers need to determine the extent to which they can meet all the service requirements of a European business or whether they can realistically meet only part of those needs. There is a potential mismatch between the logistics demands of European companies and the ability of any service provider to meet these demands. This often results in disappointment when a manufacturer decides to rationalize its logistics network and seeks to reduce the number of service providers. In many cases the manufacturer finds that there are few logistics service providers that wish to take on the commitment of handling all its European activities.

Providers of logistics services need to be concerned with two dimensions to their activities in the first instance: geographical scope and range of services. A consideration of these two dimensions highlights how challenging it really is for the logistics service company to be able to provide 'one-stop shopping' for a customer. Some companies already provide what can be described as European services, in the sense that they are the long-distance links in a network used by manufacturing companies. This provision of services is evident in the case of airlines, shipping lines, freight forwarders and integrators. It is clearly at the level of local and national distribution that internationalization of service provision has been slowest to develop.

A broad range of logistics activities can be found. Freight transport and warehousing services have been widely available for many decades, together with documentation services to support the flow of products. In recent years, logistics services providers have begun to offer a wider range of services, such as final assembly of products, inventory management, product and package labelling, product tracking and tracing along the supply chain, order planning and processing, and reverse logistics systems (which tackle the collection and recovery of end-of-life products and used packaging in the supply chain).

The very different nature of global markets means that logistics providers wishing to provide for a growing demand for international services adapt their approaches for different markets. International transport companies engaged in cross-border work already understand that strategies may need to be tailored to the particular country of operation. Clearly the most ambitious strategy is to provide a truly global service. Several major logistics services providers are working towards achieving this, but it is a challenging goal. The foundations for the multi-domestic strategy appear to lie in the successful duplication of domestic services in other countries. The original services are, of course, adapted as required.

Tackling crime against road freight

International road freight drivers are prone to criminal attacks on their vehicles and the goods they carry as well as attacks on themselves. The fact that such operations are taking place in foreign countries, and sometimes in isolated locations, makes drivers more prone to such attacks than in domestic operations. A recent study investigated assaults on international road freight drivers in 2005/6 (IRU, 2008). The main findings included (IRU, 2008; Crass, 2007):

- 17 per cent of all drivers interviewed have suffered an attack during the five-year period;
- 30 per cent of attacked drivers have been attacked more than once;
- 21 per cent of drivers were physically assaulted;
- 60 per cent of the attacks targeted the vehicle and its load, while the remaining 40 per cent were related to theft of the driver's personal belongings.

Preventative measures to reduce crime and theft problems are challenging since only a few success stories have been reported within the road transport network.

FACTORS INFLUENCING RECENT TRENDS IN INTERNATIONAL RAIL FREIGHT TRANSPORT

Infrastructure

The most critical physical requirement to allow cross-border rail freight traffic is an active network connection. In some countries, rail networks are domestic in nature, and cross-border links have either never been constructed or have ceased operation. For example, in Latin America, links that previously existed between Colombia and Venezuela, and between Guatemala and El Salvador, are no longer present (ECLAC, 2003). In Europe, the various national railway networks are relatively well interconnected, although the quality of the international links can often be sub-standard compared to domestic corridors. Where a physical cross-border connection does exist, one of the biggest infrastructure constraints for international rail flows is the historical decision made by different countries to adopt a different track gauge (ie the distance between the two rails) when constructing their rail system. Two main gauges exist, metric (1,000 mm) and standard (1,435 mm), but there are others in certain parts of the world. Where different gauges are found, time and cost are added to the rail cross-border transfer because the goods themselves need to be transferred between rail wagons, or the wagons need to have their axles changed for onward transport on the other gauge.

Examples where gauge differences exist at international borders include:

- Southern Brazil is metric gauge whereas Uruguay and Argentina have standard gauge networks; only the link to Bolivia is compatible with Brazil (ECLAC, 2003).

- France has standard gauge track, but traditional routes in Spain and Portugal have different gauges, 1,672 mm in Spain and 1,664 mm in Portugal; new high-speed lines on the Iberian peninsula are being constructed to the standard gauge (European Commission, 2005), but freight will have to continue using the traditional routes where the difference in gauge will persist for the foreseeable future.
- In Asia, at least five different track gauges exist, ranging from metric in much of South East Asia up to 1,676 mm in the Indian subcontinent; China has generally adopted standard gauge track, while Russia has a broader 1,520 mm gauge.

Another infrastructure-related issue is that of differing voltages on electrified lines, which have traditionally required a change of locomotive at border crossings. This tends not to be as significant an obstacle as track gauge differences, though, since a locomotive change can be completed in a shorter period of time than re-gauging the wagons on an entire train. In many cases, diesel locomotives are used for cross-border services (even where systems are electrified) and multi-voltage electric locomotives have been introduced to operate internationally.

A number of initiatives have been developed to try to better integrate domestic rail networks to provide higher-quality long-distance corridors, notably in Europe (RailNetEurope, 2009). Elsewhere, political alliances and/or disputes have had an influence on the continued use of existing cross-border infrastructure or the provision of new routes. For example, the break-up of the Soviet Union and subsequent unrest in much of the Caucasus region led to many of the rail routes linking Russia, Armenia, Georgia and Azerbaijan being abandoned and international rail freight volumes declining (Jackson, 2008). New links within this region are now proposed, together with external routes to Turkey and Iran which may eventually form part of strategic long-distance international corridors planned for the Asian continent. New routes are also planned within South East Asia, linking China to Thailand, Singapore and the Indian subcontinent (Briginshaw, 2007). Should the range of schemes currently proposed or under construction come to fruition, rail network connectivity across Asia will be significantly enhanced, opening up an array of new international journey opportunities (UNESCAP, 2009).

Policy/regulation

In many parts of the world, railways are viewed as the responsibility of the public sector. Over time, though, many countries have initiated a process of liberalization. Most noticeably, this occurred first in North America, but has also now taken place elsewhere, including Australasia,

Table 23.4   Institutional rail policy differences between North America and Europe

	North America	Europe
Rail policy orientation	Competition	Regulation
Rail competition	Parallel rail	On-rail
Infrastructure control	Operator	Regulator
Infrastructure funding	Private	Public

Source: Posner, 2008

South America and Europe. There has been no standard method of liberalization, but competition between rail freight companies is now prevalent in many countries. As Table 23.4 reveals, there are considerable differences in the processes implemented in North America and Europe. As a consequence, there remains a much greater role for the public sector in European rail provision. This may also result from the fragmented nature of the European market, rather than the more integrated North American situation where there are only three countries in a large land mass. Public policy remains an important issue regardless of the nature of the market.

The European Union sees the growth of international rail freight activity as a political objective, for economic, environmental and social reasons. Over the past decade, it has agreed a series of railway packages aimed at liberalizing the rail freight market, particularly concerning cross-border traffic.

Operations

There are various ways in which rail freight operations are being influenced by the internationalization of transport activity. Three of these show the range of effects:

- geographical expansion of operators;
- new international services provided by cooperation between operators;
- land bridge corridors.

With the liberalization of access to provide services over rail networks in different parts of the world, formerly domestic rail freight operators have started to become more international in nature. An early example in the 1990s was the expansion of Wisconsin Central, a US railroad company that is now part of Canadian National, into New Zealand, Canada, the UK and Australia, often through the purchase of rail freight operations being privatized by governments (Canadian National, 2008). America Latina Logistica (ALL), a private Brazilian operator, has expanded its operations across the border into northern Argentina (Kolodziejski, 2005). Recently, the German operator Deutsche Bahn realized a significant growth in other EU countries.

In addition to rail operators expanding their own territorial coverage, there have been developments in international services provided through cooperation between infrastructure and/or service operators, where two or more rail freight companies are responsible for transit from origin to destination. For example, RZD, the Russian public rail company, has been developing partnerships with a number of neighbouring countries, not least with the setting up of the Eurasia Rail Logistics joint venture, which also includes Germany, Poland and Belarus (Lukov, 2008). Partnerships and service quality initiatives have been developed in Europe, building on an international Freight Quality Charter which was implemented in 2003 (CER, 2005). The Charter focuses mainly on train punctuality and the implementation of quality contracts between railways and customers. CER (Community of European Railway and Infrastructure Companies) claims considerable success in improving service punctuality on international corridors, with steady improvement from 50 per cent of trains arriving within one hour of schedule in 2001 to 72 per cent in 2004.

The third example can develop either as a result of one operator's expansion or cooperation between a number of operators, demonstrating rail's abilities in providing a land-based link in international supply chains dominated by shipping, primarily for containers. The US land bridge, where containers shipped across the Pacific from Asia are moved across to the East Coast, is well established, with international containers accounting for the majority of the 15 million (approx) intermodal units moved by rail from the west to east of the United States (Briginshaw, 2007). The growth in traffic between Asia and North America has led to rapid land-bridge growth for North American operators, such as Union Pacific, BNSF Railway, Canadian Pacific and Canadian National (Lustig, 2006). In South East Asia, there has been growth on the land-bridge route between Malaysia and Thailand, in competition with feeder ships. A similar land-bridge proposal is now being developed in Saudi Arabia, linking the Red Sea and the Gulf, which will allow traffic from the key Jeddah Islamic Port on the Red Sea to move more directly to the Gulf region (Jackson, 2005).

More innovatively, plans are emerging for new long-distance services taking advantage of the network improvements and regulatory freedoms outlined earlier. For example, a case study reveals details of a trial through-container train service from China to Europe in early 2008, possibly marking the start of a concerted effort by rail companies to gain a share of the market for freight transport between the Far East and the European Union (Trans Eurasia Logistics, 2009).

CONCLUDING REMARKS

With developments to remove bottlenecks, combined with operational improvements, there is scope for considerable increases in the efficiency of international road and rail freight in many regions. Many past forecasts of improvements in transport technology and operations have been overtaken by events and, in some cases, rather than transport becoming easier and faster, it has become more complex and occasionally slower. Within the next 15 years, there seems to be limited opportunity to increase the speed of either shipping or air freight. There is a potential in rail freight in particular for shorter transit times and possibly reduced costs. Road freight times may not have the scope to be reduced to the same extent as rail freight, but there are still many opportunities to improve road operations and thereby improve both the economic and environmental performance of road freight transport over long distances.

As noted in the introduction, international road and rail freight transport is extremely diverse. Thus the developments that have implications for short-distance road freight are very different from those that affect long-distance rail. It is evident from this review that there remain many opportunities to improve the efficiency and to reduce the environmental impact of both international road and rail freight transport. Many of these developments require government intervention in the form of changes in policy and regulation or improvements to infrastructure. This is a complex area when considered within one country – when it concerns international developments it is, of course, even more complicated.

However, it is important when considering the developments that will happen in the next 15 years to note the growing role played in international transport by the major logistics companies. The consolidation that is evident means that single companies are now able to provide truly integrated services in a way that was not possible a few years ago. At the same time, it is important for policy makers and regulators to take note of these developments, in order to maximize the opportunities for more efficient international road and rail freight transport, and in order to ensure that developments meet the growing environmental constraints.

References

Anderson, J and Wincoop, E van (2004) Trade costs, *Journal of Economic Literature*, **42**, pp 691–751

Briginshaw, D (2007) Asian railways rise to meet the growth challenge, *International Railway Journal*, 1 January

Canadian National (accessed 20 February 2008) *The Wisconsin Central Story* [Online] www.cn.ca/about/company_information/history/en_AboutWisconsinCentral.shtml

CER (2005) *Rail Freight Quality: Progress in a competitive market – Update Report on the CER-UIC-CIT Charter, Community of European Railway and Infrastructure Companies (CER)*, Brussels

Crass, M (2007) Speech by Principal Administrator of the ECMT/International Transport Forum at the 4th IRU Euro-Asia Road Transport Conference, 14–15 June, Warsaw

Deardorff, A (2005) The importance of the cost and time of transport for international trade, paper in *ECMT Time and Transport*, Round Table 127, ECMT, Paris

ECLAC (Economic Commission for Latin America and the Caribbean) (2003) *Current Conditions and Outlook*, United Nations, New York

ECMT (2005) *International Road Freight Transport in Europe – Market Access and the Future of The Licence System*, Report of The Special Advisory Group, ECMT, Paris

ECMT (2006) *Transport Links Between Europe and Asia*, ECMT, Paris

European Commission (2005) *Trans-European Transport Network: TEN-T Priority Axes and Projects 2005*, European Commission, Brussels

European Communities (2003) *Europe in Figures*, Eurostat, Office for Official Publications of the European Communities, Luxembourg

European Communities (2004) *Europe in Figures*, Eurostat, Office for Official Publications of the European Communities, Luxembourg

European Communities (2007) *Europe in Figures*, Eurostat, Office for Official Publications of the European Communities, Luxembourg

Hummels, D (2001) *Time as a Trade Barrier*, GTAP Working Paper No 18, Global Trade Analysis Project, Purdue University, West Lafayette, IN

IRU (2008) 1 in 6 drivers attacked, press release, 18 February, IRU

Jackson, C (2005) Saudi landbridge ready to launch, *Railway Gazette*, 1 March

Jackson, C (2008) Railways realign in troubled region, *Railway Gazette*, 16 January

Kolodziejski, J (2005) Grain giant targets cross-border logistics, *Railway Gazette*, 1 June

Kopp, A (2006) Summary of discussions, in *ECMT Transport and International Trade*, Round Table 130, ECMT, Paris

Lafontaine, F and Malaguzzi Valeri, L (2009) The deregulation of international trucking in the European Union: form and effect, *Journal of Regulatory Economics*, **35** (1), pp 19–44

Latrille, P (2007) The role of market structure in the transport sector on the effects of liberalization: the case of the world trade organization, in *Market Access, Trade in Transport Services and Trade Facilitation*, ed ECMT, Paris

Lukov, B (2008) RZD adopts long-range development strategy, *Railway Gazette*, 22 January

Lustig, D (2006) Railroads invest in extra capacity to move Asian import windfall, *Railway Gazette*, 1 August

North American Transport Statistics Database (NATSD) (2009) North American Merchandise Trade [Online] http://nats.sct.gob.mx/

Office of Freight Management and Operations (2007) *Freight Facts and Figures 2006*, Federal Highway Administration, US Department of Transportation, Washington, DC

Posner, H (2008) *Rail Freight in the USA: Lessons for Continental Europe*, CER Essay Series, Community of European Railway and Infrastructure Companies (CER), Brussels

RailNetEurope (2009) *Annual Report*, Vienna

Snitbhan, N et al (2004) Study on cross-border transport of goods by road from Malaysia to Thailand, *TDRI Quarterly Review*, **17**, March [Online] http://www.tdri.or.th/library/quarterly/text/m04_3.pdf

Trans Eurasia Logistics (2009) Trans Eurasia Express – a new transport solution between Asia and Europe [Online] http://www.trans-eurasia-logistics.com/

UNCTAD (2007) Note by the UNCTAD secretariat, for the *Expert Meeting on Regional Cooperation in Transit Transport: Solutions for landlocked and transit developing countries*, 27–28 September 2007, UNCTAD, Geneva

UNECE (2007) *International E Road Network, European Agreement on Main International Traffic Arteries (AGR)* [Online] http://www.unece.org/trans/conventn/MapAGR2007.pdf

UNESCAP (2003) *Transit Transport Issues in Landlocked and Transit Developing Countries*, Note by the secretariat, E/ESCAP/1282, UNESCAP, Bangkok

UNESCAP (2009) *Asian Highway Route Map, and Trans-Asian Railways Network* [Online] www.unescap.org/TTDW/

US Chamber of Commerce (2006) *Land Transport Options between Europe and Asia: Commercial feasibility study*, US Chamber of Commerce, Washington, DC

World Trade Organization (WTO) (2007) *International Trade Statistics 2006*, WTO, Geneva

World Trade Organization (WTO) (2008) *International Trade Statistics 2007*, WTO, Geneva

24

The changing supply of logistics services – a UK perspective

Colin Bamford, University of Huddersfield

In the four years since the publication of the 4th edition of this book, there has been substantial change to the supply of logistics services in the UK. This change has in part been internal to the business through a significant consolidation of provision among the largest companies. This has included Exel's acquisition of the Tibbett and Britten Group (2004), closely followed by Deutsche Post's takeover of the greatly expanded Exel (2005) and further consolidation with Wincanton's takeover of P and O Trans European (2003). At the same time all companies have experienced difficult trading conditions as a result of:

- uncertainties over the price of fuel and the climbdown on lorry road user charging;
- lower operating profits in many cases despite an increase in turnover;
- driver shortages and concerns over the short- and longer-term effects of the EU's Working Time Directive on logistics providers.

External change and challenges have come about through the further globalization of supply chains and the demands for a high level of customer performance from the retail and manufacturing customers of logistics providers, as well as through the long-awaited geographical expansion of the EU in May 2004 to include eight new members in Central and Eastern Europe plus Cyprus and Malta.

In short, much has happened to change the way in which logistics services are supplied to customers in the UK.

UK MARKET TRENDS

Table 24.1 shows general trends in the overall market since 1994 (ONS, 2005). As this indicates, in terms of goods moved, the market has been relatively static since 1998. This is slightly surprising given the unprecedented and consistent growth in real GDP over the period. It is also in contrast to the period before 1998 when the total goods moved was broadly in line with the state of the economy.

The causes of this changing pattern are not easy to explain. An obvious one is the continued de-industrialization of the British economy. The manufacturing sector has experienced continued decline over the period shown in Table 24.1. Given the derived demand for freight transport, it is clear that there is now less demand from customers in those sectors of manufacturing that have experienced structural changes due to increased

Table 24.1 Freight transport by road – goods moved by goods vehicles over 3.5 tonnes, 1994–2004 (billion tonne-kilometres)

Year	Mainly public haulage[1]	Mainly own account[2]	Total	Percentage mainly public haulage
1994	100.8	37.0	137.8	73.0
1995	106.5	37.2	143.7	74.1
1996	109.1	37.7	146.8	74.3
1997	112.2	37.4	149.6	75.0
1998	114.3	37.6	151.9	75.2
1999	110.9	38.3	149.2	74.3
2000	113.0	37.5	150.5	75.1
2001	114.7	34.7	149.4	76.8
2002	110.6	39.2	149.8	73.8
2003	114.3	37.4	151.7	75.3
2004[3]	110.8	41.4	152.2	72.8

Notes: [1] Relates to carriage of goods owned by people other than the operator.

[2] Relates to goods carried by operators in the course of their own business.

[3] A minor reclassification means that data for 2004 are not strictly comparable with earlier years.

competition from the rest of the world. By 2004, the manufacturing sector was responsible for less than one-fifth of GDP.

A second reason for change though is the improvement in logistical efficiency as a result of better road vehicle utilization. This has been evidenced in a recent study by the Department for Transport that indicated that, since 1998, the intensity of road freight activity had increased by just 2 per cent while the economy had grown by almost 17 per cent (DfT, 2005). The increase since 2002 reflects the increased use of 44-tonne vehicles; the average length of haul in contrast has fallen slightly. Transport efficiency has also improved through a steady fall in empty running. This decreased from around 29 per cent in 1998 to 26.5 per cent in 2004. In part this can be explained through more supplier collections and factory gate pricing contracts from major retailers especially. In contrast, lading factors (the ratio of goods carried in relation to the maximum carrying capacity of the vehicle) have fallen. This is best explained by the increased use of less dense unitized loads through the greater use of roll-cages, tote boxes and so on, again mainly by the major retailers.

Table 24.1 also shows that, although there are minor annual variations, the 'mainly public haulage' sector, which includes third-party logistics providers (3PLs), has remained more or less static at around three-quarters of the total market. A tentative conclusion could be that this sector has more or less reached saturation level relative to the 'mainly own account' sector. If this is the case, it supports the view that the supply of logistics services through 3PLs has become even more competitive.

The arguments in favour of businesses using a 3PL are well documented (see Chapter 17, for example). This sector in the past has seen most of the growth of activity in goods moved. Although the data are not strictly comparable, in total terms, the own account sector would appear to be holding its own. This should not in any way undermine the importance of 3PLs (and in some cases advice from a fourth-party logistics provider, or 4PL) in offering a full range of supply chain management services to clients. As well as offering the usual transport and warehouse management services, 3PLs can provide for the assembly and management of inventory and the integration of business IT systems.

With a relatively static market, there are clear signs of increasing segmentation, particularly on the part of middle-sized operators, which are increasingly vulnerable to competition from the top tier of providers in the market. Typical segments are automatic parts, food services and home deliveries, to add to the more traditional ones of fuel oils and chemicals. The top-tier operators tend to have interests in most segments: primary and secondary distribution, temperature-controlled as well as ambient.

The annual round of contracts awarded attracts considerable attention in the trade press (see, for example, *Motor Transport* magazine). As market growth has slowed, the market has become even more competitive. The uncertainty over fuel prices, given their importance in contract terms, and the need to be price-competitive have meant that most providers have had a difficult time in maintaining margins. In 2005, for example, Analytica reported that around half of the main European providers in 2004 had experienced a small decline in operating margins (Analytica, 2005). This list included Exel, Wincanton, Christian Salvesen, TDG and GIST.

A crucial issue in any contract renegotiations is whether service levels are being met. It has been clear for some time that businesses invariably compete on the efficiency of their supply chains – getting it right is vital for business success, in the retail sector more than ever.

In a difficult marketplace, the challenge for the top logistics providers has been to meet the needs of supply chain globalization, while integrating the services that they are able to provide. As the Analytica study stated, 'This enables logistics providers to benefit from scale, creating competitive advantage and a greater breadth of expertise, both of which results in benefits to their customers ... customer service must come first. This is the only true base upon which a fully integrated service can be built.'

A further insight into outsourcing and globalization has questioned whether the former really is a magical solution in cases where businesses have sought to benefit from lower unit labour costs in Eastern Europe and Asia (Sweeney, 2005). It is argued that this has resulted in a shift away from controlling the supply chain through ownership to one based on management and control through effective supply chain relationship management. In some cases, the outcome has been a disaster. In other cases, particularly in clothing, textiles and hi-tech manufacturing, many companies have gained significant benefits from outsourcing various supply chain services. The key to success is to see outsourcing as part of an integrated approach to managing the supply chain, a task that increasingly is best carried out by one of the top tier of global logistics providers.

The need for customers to have strategies to exploit the global market is one that is increasingly being carried out by 3PLs. In some cases, this might be a 4PL, an outside organization that has the task of assembling and integrating supply chain capabilities for clients. Our largest 3PLs now see themselves as 4PLs, usually ensuring that much of the supply chain management function for clients produces an appropriate amount of business for themselves.

MARKET STRUCTURE – CONTINUING CONSOLIDATION AND GLOBALIZATION

The term 'market structure' is one that is used by economists to describe the way in which a market is organized. In distinguishing market structures, there are two key variables, namely the number of firms and the extent of barriers to entry for new firms seeking to join the market. The significance of these is that they determine the degree of competition in a market. The smaller the number of firms and the higher the barriers to entry, then in theory the less competitive the market will be.

In some markets such as grocery retailing, vehicle production and certain branches of food processing, the level of industrial concentration has been high. In others, such as road freight and distribution, the existence of thousands of small firms has meant that historically this has been a very competitive, low-concentration market. The continuing consolidation among the big players, particularly since 2000, has resulted in this market showing increasing signs of being an oligopoly (see Sloman, 2003).

What has happened over the past six years or so is that the 3PL market especially has become increasingly concentrated in the hands of a small number of very powerful providers. The experience of Exel and to a lesser extent Wincanton is typical of the behaviour of firms in an oligopolistic market. Exel, for example, merged with MSAS Global Logistics in 2000, took over the Tibbett and Britten Group in 2004 and was itself acquired by Deutsche Post World Net (DPWN) in 2005. In theory, an oligopolistic market has some or all of the following characteristics:

- a market leader that often takes the lead in pricing decisions;
- interdependence in so far as the actions of one firm can often determine the reactions of others;
- a strong brand image;
- although illegal, the possibility of collusion, for example to squeeze out would-be competition.

So, to what extent is the 3PL an oligopolistic market? Table 24.2 shows the top 10 providers in the UK market in 2003–04 (*Motor Transport*, 2004). As indicated, Table 24.2 incorporates Exel's acquisition of Tibbett and Britten; it also includes Wincanton's purchase of P and O Trans European. Exel had an estimated turnover of over four times that of its leading rival and was substantially greater than any of the remaining 3PLs shown in the table. This former state-owned business has more than maintained its pole position following its privatization in 1981.

Table 24.2   The UK's leading 3PLs, 2003–04

Company	Financial year end	Turnover[1] (£m)	Percentage change on previous year	Employees
Exel[2]	Dec 03	6,749	+44.2	104,200
Wincanton	Mar 04	1,681	+68.4	25,000
Hays Logistics[3]	Dec 03	854	−3.0	n/a[4]
Christian Salvesen	Apr 03	846	−3.6	n/a[4]
Autologic Holdings	Dec 03	701	+4.8	4,380
TDG	Dec 03	541	−4.5	7,990
TNT Logistics UK[5]	Dec 03	500	+32.5	8,000
GIST	Sept 03	292	+10.2	5,750
Kuehne & Nagel	Dec 03	276	+32.8	832
Securicor Omega Logistics	Sept 03	215	n/a	1,700

Notes: [1] Total turnover from UK market and elsewhere for UK companies only.

[2] Includes recently acquired Tibbett and Britten Group.

[3] Now ARC Logistics.

[4] Data not available for the logistics side of these companies.

[5] Estimates.

Tibbett and Britten was perceived as the rising star of the 1990s. Prior to the Exel takeover, its turnover had increased tenfold since 1990. It had also led the way among 3PLs in establishing a strong foothold in inter-modal distribution, both for international and for domestic movements, and in the way it had tackled the challenge of providing 3PL services to clients in the emerging Central and Eastern European markets.

Wincanton, unlike Exel and Tibbett and Britten, has traditionally concentrated its growth in the domestic market. Its acquisition of P and O Trans European was its first successful venture into the wider European market. Equally, there have been casualties. TDG, for example, has lost market share as the market has grown and, in late 2005, TNT announced that its logistics business was to be sold in order to allow it to concentrate its business activities on its mail and courier/express services. Although the reasons behind these changes must be complex, a simple conclusion is that both companies have been victims of the increasingly competitive market.

At a European level, as Table 24.3 indicates, in 2004 Exel became the largest single provider of logistics services (Analytica, 2005). As with all of the major players, its business is truly global. The acquisition of Tibbett and Britten gave Exel additional business in 13 countries, including Austria, Poland, Romania and Slovakia, where it had previously no

Table 24.3 Europe's leading logistics providers, 2004

Company	Turnover in 2004 (£m)	Change in turnover in 2003 %
Exel	8,961	25.2
Schenker	8,042	17.3
NYK	7,976	7.1
Kuehne & Nagel	7,432	21.2
Deutsche Post World Net	6,786	15.4
Logista	4,406	8.0
TNT Logistics	4,082	9.3
Panalpina	3,965	14.1
Ryder	3,776	7.2
Geodis	3,371	4.8
Wincanton	2,438	2.7

involvement. The growth in its contracts logistics business has been particularly strong in Europe, the Middle East, Africa and the Americas. In the Asia Pacific region, the provision of air and sea freight services accounted for 75 per cent of its turnover. Growth prospects for contract logistics in this region remain healthy. As in Europe, though, operating margins remain subject to external pressures such as the rising price of fuel (Exel, 2005).

The consolidation and integration of the logistics sector has brought substantial business benefits to global European players. These benefits include:

- Economies of scale. As a business increases in scale, it can put pressure on its supply partners to reduce longer-term average costs when purchasing fuel, vehicles, shipping capacity and so on. There are also financial and risk-bearing economies.
- Gaining competitive advantage through not only offering a wider range of services but also concentrating activities in key market segments such as clothing and textiles, automotive, retail, electronics and so on.
- Providing a fully integrated supply chain management service for global clients.

Analytica's recent research, though, adds a clear warning with respect to the last point in stating that 'Integration is not a licence to win new customers ... a "one size fits all" solution may not be acceptable to all global manufacturers. This sends out a clear message that customer service must come first.'

Finally, in September 2005, it was announced that Exel's shareholders had agreed a massive £3.6 billion takeover bid from DPWN. The logistics arm of Exel would be DHL, with Exel as a sub-brand (*Daily Telegraph*, 2005). At the time it was estimated that the combined Deutsche Post and Exel group would have between 6 and 7 per cent of the European logistics market.

The only concern about the takeover was whether it would be blocked by the European Commission on the grounds that it would impede effective competition in the European logistics market. Although total market share is small compared to other sectors of business, a dominant firm like DPWN/Exel could be against the interests of customers of logistics services. After only a brief period of investigation, the Commission approved the merger.

On the face of it, this deal is about logistics. Underneath, though, there would seem to be a very serious threat to the UK's Royal Mail, which in January 2006 saw its traditional postal business opened up to full competition. Deutsche Post is already a competitor to the Royal Mail in the bulk mail market. Its marriage with Exel's logistics expertise must surely enhance its opportunities to make further inroads into the UK postal market.

THE EU25 – NEW MARKET OPPORTUNITIES AND THREATS

Given the nature of the degree of change analysed in the last section, one might conclude that UK 3PLs have a strong hold over the domestic market and that they have little to fear from operators based elsewhere in the EU. This conclusion might also naively be made from the conclusions of research by the Institute of Grocery Distribution (IGD), which once again recognized that UK 3PL operators are the most efficient within the whole of the EU (IGD, 2005). This may well be the case, in particular for the retail grocery market, but in other sectors 3PLs from the rest of the EU and elsewhere are having an increasing share of the UK market.

Table 24.4 shows some such operators (*Motor Transport*, 2004). Most have particular strengths in the automotive and clothing sectors. In addition, the strength of companies such as DHL and UPS, both of which are major players in the express parcels and document sectors, should be recognized.

The geographical enlargement of the EU in May 2004 has presented increased market opportunities for 3PL operators, including those based in the UK. Prior to the formal accession of the eight countries in Central and Eastern Europe (CEE) plus Cyprus and Malta, various UK operators such as Exel (including in particular Tibbett and Britten) and P and O

Table 24.4   Non-UK-owned hauliers in the UK market

Company	Turnover 2003–04 (£m)	Change from previous year %
Autologic Holdings[1]	701.7	+4.8
Kuehne & Nagel	275.7	+32.8
DFDS Transport	157.0	+12.1
UK subsidiaries:		
TNT Logistics (UK)	500	+32.5
NYK Logistics (UK) MIR	135	+23.5
Gefco UK	110	+0.5

Note: [1] Includes Walon, Ansa and Acumen.

Trans European (now part of Wincanton) had penetrated the market in Central and Eastern Europe. All have recognized the considerable market opportunities in Poland, the Czech Republic and Hungary.

In these countries there are two main types of opportunity for UK 3PLs. These are:

1. *Non-food.* Unit labour costs in the joining countries are substantially lower than elsewhere in the EU. Consequently, automotive manufacturers such as VW Audi and Suzuki have established assembly plants in these countries and ship finished vehicles into the rest of the EU. Other typical manufacturers are those involved in chemicals, electronics and textiles. As well as producing for export, the domestic market in these countries is growing as local consumers become more affluent.

2. *Retail distribution.* This has been an obvious area of development. EU retailers such as Tesco, Metro, Carrefour and so on now have a strong presence in Poland, Hungary and the Czech Republic. It seems logical for them to follow the same logistics practices as in their domestic markets. In some cases, their 3PLs have moved into the market with them.

Getting a foothold in the CEE market is a risky and uncertain business. Some 3PLs have bought transport and warehousing companies in these countries, Tibbett and Britten being a particularly good example. An alternative means of entry is to go it alone and set up a brand new operation. This outcome, of course, is much less certain to succeed.

Realistically, UK companies may have the logistical expertise to make substantial inroads into the expanding CEE market. Geographically, though, German operators are far better placed to know the market and the opportunities that may be available. This is a major threat to UK operators.

TRANSPORT POLICY ISSUES

Businesses supplying logistics services are required to operate within a policy and regulatory framework that is increasingly laid down by the EU. It is beyond the scope of this chapter to look at recent issues in depth. It is, though, useful to indicate those that have been and remain of particular concern to UK 3PLs, for example:

- The Working Time Directive. From April 2005, all operators governed by drivers' hours regulations (excluding self-employed) must comply with these new rules (European Commission, 2002). Driver working time is now limited to an average 48-hour week over a reference period. No more than 60 hours can be spent working in any single week. Complying has raised fundamental problems of driver shortages, although last-minute concessions on 'periods of availability' have helped some operators.
- Drivers from new EU countries. The accession of eight new CEE member states to the EU has opened up the opportunity for drivers and warehouse operatives from these countries to work in the UK. This may help companies in places where there is a labour shortage, although there are concerns over the rates of pay that are being offered. Whether the current wave of activity by recruitment consultants becomes a flood remains to be seen.
- The comparative price of diesel fuel between the UK and the rest of the EU remains a major concern to all UK operators, not only those involved in international work. Given the importance of fuel costs in relation to total operating costs, any marked variation in fuel prices between the UK and the rest of the EU must damage the competitiveness of UK operators.

CONCLUSIONS

It should be clear from this chapter that the market for 3PL logistics services is subject to ongoing change. Demand-side influences – a highly competitive domestic market and opportunities in the CEE – require UK companies to become increasingly efficient to maintain pole position in the European market.

Simultaneously, supply-side factors have seen major changes in ownership, with increasing concentration in the top tier of operators. This has coincided with concerns over the impact of EU regulations on UK operators, although in context these are unlikely to halt the process of market consolidation and globalization.

References

Analytica (2005) *Profitability in European Logistics*, Analytica, London

Daily Telegraph (2005) Exel snapped up in £3.6bn takeover, 19 September

Department for Transport (DfT) (2005) *Continuing Survey of Road Goods Transport*, DfT, London

European Commission (2002) *Working Time Directive*, 2002/15/EC

Exel (2005) Delivering value across the supply chain, *Annual Report*, Exel

Institute of Grocery Distribution (2005) *Retail Logistics*, IGD, Watford

Motor Transport (2004), 30 September

Office for National Statistics (ONS) (2005) *Transport Statistics, Great Britain*, ONS, London

Sloman, J (2003), *Economics*, Prentice Hall, New York

Sweeney, E (2005) Outsourcing – a managerial solution?, *Logistics Solutions*, 8 (1)

25

Developments in Western European logistics strategies

Michael Browne, Julian Allen and Allan Woodburn,
University of Westminster

INTRODUCTION

Several political initiatives that have had major implications for logistics services throughout Western Europe have taken place since 1990:

- Border controls and customs arrangements within the EU were lifted following the creation of the Single European Market (SEM) under the Treaty of Maastricht in January 1993.
- On 1 January 1999, the euro was launched as an electronic currency and became legal tender on 1 January 2002. It has been implemented in 12 of the 15 EU Member States and these states represent the 'eurozone' (Austria, Belgium, Finland, France, Germany Greece, Italy, Ireland, Luxembourg, the Netherlands, Portugal and Spain). The European Central Bank is responsible for the monetary policy within the eurozone.
- New Member States have joined the European Union (EU). Austria, Finland and Sweden joined on 1 January 1995, increasing the number of Member States to 15. Ten more countries joined on 1 May 2004,

taking the total to 25. These countries were: Cyprus, the Czech Republic, Estonia, Hungary, Latvia, Lithuania, Malta, Poland, Slovakia and Slovenia. These 10 members increased the surface area of the EU by a quarter and its population by one-fifth, to 450 million. Bulgaria and Romania joined in 2007, taking the current membership to 27 countries.

Central to the logic of making the European Union free from unnecessary trading restrictions has been the desire to encourage the development of European companies able to compete on a global basis. It is often claimed that fragmented national economies within Europe have resulted in too many small companies in certain key industrial sectors. Dismantling barriers to trade and opening up new market opportunities allow companies to grow and become more competitive. Inevitably, this is also likely to result in the relocation of certain economic activities as some companies become larger and others fail. The collapse of communism in the former Soviet Union and the countries of Central and Eastern Europe, and the subsequent reorientation of these countries towards the free market, has also opened up new avenues of trade that extend beyond the borders of the EU.

This chapter addresses the ways in which company business strategies and manufacturing and retailing operations have been developing within Europe during this time of political, economic and geographical change, and the effect that this is having on the demand for logistics services. The extent to which logistics providers have been meeting these needs is also discussed. These developments as well as the similarities and differences in suitable logistics strategies for different European countries are illustrated by reference to the European grocery industry. The impacts of these emerging logistics services on freight transport patterns and activity levels within Europe are discussed, together with the policy initiatives and responses being generated at the national and European levels. Finally, future European logistics strategies are considered and the question of whether logistics service providers are able to match their customers' requirements is examined.

CHANGES IN THE DEMAND FOR LOGISTICS SERVICES

An enlarged and more integrated Europe has influenced the demand for logistics services. Indeed, markets for goods and services in Europe have become much less fragmented over the past 10 years and, at the same time, for many companies there has been a discernible shift away from a mainly national approach to a more unified European strategy. In general, companies increasingly regard the EU as their home market rather than having their trading horizons restricted to a single country. This in turn has important implications for logistics services. For example, increased trade between Member States creates new demands for logistics services such as transport and warehousing. However, the transition to a European pattern of operation has not been as smooth as many commentators expected and in some cases the benefits have been slow to emerge.

Market developments and retailer/manufacturer strategies

Increasing market integration enables large companies to pursue a number of strategies designed to take advantage of their size. The scope to concentrate production at a small number of carefully selected locations is one that has a special importance within Europe. Until recently, the strategy followed by many companies has been based on production for separate national markets. The requirement to produce product variants for different markets, the complexity of border-crossing formalities and the added costs of international trade transactions led, typically, to a rather fragmented approach to production. Although for many companies the changes in strategy have been part of a broader response to growing global opportunities and increased international competition, the abolition of border controls and the simplification of trading procedures has undoubtedly encouraged plant and warehouse rationalization.

Since the business ambitions of many companies are not confined to the existing EU, scope for inventory rationalization has grown as Europe becomes more commercially integrated. Dismantling trade barriers has allowed firms to reduce the number of warehouses within their logistics systems which, in turn, has important longer-term implications for transport patterns. Instead of looking at Europe on a country-by-county basis, firms have been able to consider more natural market demand patterns and adapt their warehousing accordingly. Significantly, these developments are not confined to the EU – many firms have already adopted a very wide definition of Europe in developing their logistics strategies. For example, Bosch-Siemens (manufacturers of domestic appliances with a head office in Munich) took its first steps in cross-market distribution by rationalizing its Scandinavian warehousing operations and consolidating stocks for Finland, Norway and Sweden in one regional centre located between Stockholm and Malmö, distributing to other Scandinavian countries from that single location (O'Laughlin, Cooper and Cabocel, 1993). There are many examples of this type of initiative as companies have changed their traditional views about the best way to serve markets. The sports equipment firm Nike has adopted a completely centralized strategy for storage within its European supply chain, despite increasing diversity of sourcing and continued demands for fast response to customer requirements (Kemp, 1997). Geest, the prepared food company, announced plans to consolidate production in 2001, with dressed salads being produced at one rather than two sites (European Logistics Management, 2001a). The French food group Danone also announced a restructuring plan for its biscuit production business in 2001, in which 6 of its 36 factories in Europe would be closed, with production levels increasing at the remaining factories (European Logistics Management, 2001b). The trend to centralization has taken a firm hold on management thinking and there are still many companies seeking further opportunities to reduce the number of stockholding points. Whether these initiatives can be justified against a background of pressure to develop more sustainable logistics strategies remains to be seen.

Many large companies now take a supply chain view when considering new ways to: i) integrate their own operations, and then ii) seek to extend this integration to their supply chain partners. Growing integration has profound implications for the role of external service providers since in many cases the physical flow of materials is one of the first areas of change when a supply chain view becomes more clearly developed. When companies start the process of considering the supply chain as a whole, it often becomes evident that there is scope to rationalize the number of service providers in much the same way as it may become possible to reduce the number of stockholding points.

In their drive to maintain and increase profit levels, retailers and manufacturers are trying to achieve more with less – this is epitomized for many companies by the application of the just-in-time (JIT) philosophy. A JIT approach emphasizes reliance on logistics partners. But service providers need to be able to match the increasingly demanding expectations of their customers not just in terms of speed but in terms of reliability, service monitoring and consignment tracking. Only by doing this will the benefits of a JIT approach really become apparent.

The survey of logistics costs that has been carried out by the European Logistics Association (ELA) and A.T. Kearney every five years indicates that costs as a proportion of sales fell by approximately 50 per cent for Western European companies between 1987 and 2003 (see Figure 25.1). This has been achieved at the same time that customer service has been rising. However, the survey results indicate that cost reductions were extremely limited between 1998 and 2003, and respondents' forecasts about likely logistics costs in 2008 suggest that they will remain at

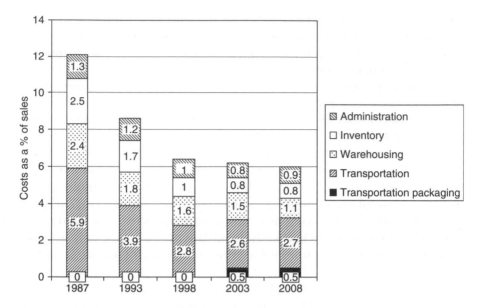

Figure 25.1 Logistics costs as a proportion of sales
Note: 2008 is a forecast.
Source: ELA and A.T. Kearney, 2004

approximately 6 per cent of sales revenue. More than 100 companies in 14 European countries responded to the survey. The results of this survey indicate that transportation is the single largest component of logistics cost; it represented 43 per cent of total logistics costs in 2003.

Market concentration has been occurring in the vast majority of European retail and manufacturing markets in recent years. In grocery retailing, for example, the market share of the top five national retailers in many European countries, including Austria, Belgium, Denmark, Finland, France, Germany, Hungary, Ireland, Norway, Sweden, Switzerland and the UK, is in excess of 60 per cent (Mintel, 2008). However, it is important to recognize that the degree of market concentration varies significantly between industries in any one country, and that the general degree of market concentration varies from one country to another.

Limitations on European integration

Despite growing similarities, there are still many differences between European countries; retailing is a case in point. The retail format used in different European markets varies significantly between countries, with very large stores playing the biggest role in some countries (eg hypermarkets selling food and non-food in France and out-of-town supermarkets in the UK) and small food stores and traditional grocers far more common in others (such as Spain and Italy). As a result of these different retail formats, the total number of stores operated by retailers varies between European countries; for example, in 2000 there were approximately 120,000 grocery stores in Italy compared with only 33,000 in the UK (WARC, 2002). In addition, patterns of consumption also vary widely between European countries for a range of cultural, demographic and economic reasons. If one argues that we are now operating within an integrated European marketplace, this ignores the special distinguishing features of Europe and, in particular, market complexity, market size, maturity of the market, density of population spread, number of separate nation states, and many languages. It must be acknowledged that in many cases these factors have acted as a brake on the introduction of European-wide supply chains and logistics systems to serve them.

However, many companies will continue to strengthen their European initiatives, resulting in further examples of corporations making dramatic changes to their European logistics networks – this in turn places new demands on logistics managers and logistics services. We need to be aware that there are often conflicting tensions within large organizations and, in some instances, initiatives to implement changes at a European scale will be overtaken by the desire to have in place a framework allowing global coordination of supply chains. Changing priorities can make it difficult to determine the most appropriate way to develop logistics management structures and this in turn has implications for the relationship with service providers (Hindson, 1998).

Eastern Europe and distribution centre locations

Alongside the move towards centralization noted earlier has been a move eastwards within European manufacturing and distribution. As Lenders (2005) notes, an increasing number of manufacturers have relocated from Western Europe towards Eastern Europe. Since most raw material shipments are arriving at ports in Western Europe, the logistics flows that follow from this change in strategy are potentially important. In turn there is a strong expectation that European distribution functions will also move eastwards from their present concentration in the Netherlands. This has led some to predict a new location for distribution 'hot spots' within Central and Eastern Europe (Lloyd, 2004). While it would be wrong to exaggerate the speed of this trend, it is nevertheless clear that this type of development reinforces the need for a more Europe-wide approach to the selection of European logistics services. In addition, from a policy perspective it poses some major challenges for existing European transport infrastructure (see below).

MARKET STRUCTURE OF LOGISTICS SERVICE PROVIDERS

Recent changes in the demand for logistics services in Europe pose a problem for logistics service providers as they are working with a range of companies all moving at different speeds towards what may well be rather varied objectives. Out of this challenge comes the advantage for the bigger organization that can match these requirements across and within different markets.

Company size and response to international opportunities

As we have noted, European deregulation, the abolition of internal frontiers, harmonization of fiscal and technical standards and the introduction of the euro have all helped to boost trade within an enlarged EU and made it simpler for all logistics service providers to participate in that activity. Many factors influence the response of logistics companies to these opportunities. Among the most important are:

- company culture and background (for example, the size of the company and their ability to absorb the financial and management consequences of rapid change);
- customer profile (industry, speed of reaction to European opportunities);
- customer culture (for example, the customers of the logistics service provider could purchase services either at the European level or purely on a national basis).

Company size is likely to have a special significance in determining the response to the opportunities created by an enlarged EU. For example, in the case of larger logistics providers there is the opportunity to continue to internationalize their activities in order to provide full national distribution services in more than one country. For smaller companies the impacts of an enlarged EU are far more limited and it is clear that, for example, the road freight industry has a preponderance of small companies. Many small companies operate at a local level serving local industry and expect to go on working in this way. Although these smaller companies predominate in terms of numbers, within the third-party sector it is the larger companies that dominate the market in terms of the total vehicle fleet and, therefore, capacity. In the UK, for example, 6 per cent of goods vehicle operators control approximately 53 per cent of the vehicles, and this is a trend which can be identified, albeit in some cases to a lesser degree, right across the EU (DfT, 2008).

Internationalization among larger carriers

One way in which logistics service providers can enter into foreign markets is through the establishment of operating centres in other countries and gradually increasing their networks. However, rather than follow this evolutionary and somewhat slow route to growth in foreign markets, some firms prefer the prospect of mergers, takeovers or strategic trading alliances with operators based in other European countries as a means of becoming more international.

The growing internationalization of business has forced companies providing logistics services to consider their own strategies to meet these new needs. Service providers need to determine the extent to which they can meet all the service requirements of a European business or whether they can realistically meet only part of those needs. In many cases there remains at present a potential mismatch between the logistics demands of European companies and the ability of any single service provider to meet these demands. This often results in disappointment when a manufacturer decides to rationalize their logistics network and seeks to reduce the number of service providers they deal with at a European level. In many cases the manufacturer finds that there are few logistics service providers that wish to take on the commitment of handling all their European activities (*Distribution*, 2002).

Providers of logistics services need to be concerned with two dimensions to their activities in the first instance: geographical scope and range of services. A consideration of these two dimensions highlights how challenging it really is for the logistics service company to be able to provide 'one-stop shopping' for a European company. Some companies already provide what can be described as European services in the sense that they are the long-distance links in a network used by manufacturing companies. This provision of services is evident in the case of airlines, shipping lines, freight forwarders and integrators. It is clearly at the level of local and national distribution that Europeanization of service provision has been slowest to develop.

A broad range of logistics activities can be provided by logistics service providers. Freight transport and warehousing services have been widely available for many decades, together with documentation services to support the flow of these products (eg delivery and customs documentation). However, in recent years, logistics service providers have begun to offer an ever-expanding range of services such as final assembly of products, inventory management, product and package labelling, product tracking and tracing along the supply chain, order planning and processing, and reverse logistics systems (which tackle the collection and recovery of end-of-life products and used packaging in the supply chain).

Despite a period of uncertainty about the benefits of scale for logistics service providers, there have been some important developments in the past few years. Larger logistics service providers have grown mainly through merger and acquisition and appear to be committed to developing more European and global capabilities. Box 25.1 provides details of the ways in which three major logistics service providers have expanded their services and geographical coverage in the past 10 years through organic growth, mergers and acquisitions, and alliances.

Box 25.1 Deutsche Post DHL

Deutsche Post DHL is the former state department responsible for German postal services. In 1995 it became a private company owned by the government, and was partly privatized in 2000 with 31 per cent of stock made available. Since becoming a private company, Deutsche Post has pursued a strategy of extending its geographical coverage in the mail and express sectors as well as expanding the range of logistics services offered.

The aim of the company has been to become an international player capable of offering an extensive range of mail, express and logistics services, and thereby providing one-stop shopping for national and international customers. It has integrated these newly acquired businesses. This has been a significant task and involved the integration of the companies' internal structures, products, brands, sales and IT systems.

Most of this growth has been achieved through acquisitions. Over a five-year period it spent billions of dollars purchasing other businesses (Harnischfeger, 2002). Companies that have been either wholly or partly acquired include many express companies with national and global networks (such as DHL (global), Securicor Distribution (UK) and Ducros (global)), and forwarders and distribution companies (such as Danzas (Europe's largest ground forwarder), ASG (Nordic countries), AEI (global forwarding) and Nedlloyd ETD (European coverage)). The most recent major acquisition was that of Exel plc, which Deutsche Post acquired in 2005 for €5.5 billion, making it the largest logistics provider of air freight, ocean freight and contract logistics in the world.

The combination of the two companies has created a group with over 500,000 employees, operating in 220 countries, with approximately €54 billion in annual sales in 2008 (Deutsche Post DHL, 2009). The operational merger of DHL Logistics and Exel took some time to complete. The enlarged logistics unit operates under the DHL brand and uses DHL's red and yellow colours. Since the merger DHL has been operating with two logistics sub-brands: DHL Exel Supply Chain and DHL Global Forwarding (Deutsche Post, 2005).

Exel had itself been involved in a major merger with Ocean Group in May 2000, creating the largest logistics service provider in the UK, and one of the largest in the world. The merger was viewed as highly appropriate, bringing together the contract logistics capabilities of Exel Logistics with the freight forwarding strengths of Ocean Group. Both of these companies had been active in the acquisition market over recent years, which had led to Exel Logistics' presence in several European countries, and to Ocean's services in both Europe and America. Bringing together these two companies into one expanded the range of services offered as well as the geographical coverage (Datamonitor, 2002).

Kuehne and Nagel

Kuehne and Nagel is a major logistics service provider. It has more than 55,000 employees based at approximately 900 locations in more than 100 countries (Kuehne and Nagel, 2009a). Traditionally the company was a significant presence in the sea and air freight markets. Recently it has been expanding its contract logistics expertise through acquisition.

An alliance was reached with SembCorp Logistics of Singapore. This helped to increase Kuehne and Nagel's presence in Asia. The acquisition in 2001 of USCO, a large logistics service provider in the United States, helped to increase the company's strengths, with these warehousing and distribution providers becoming part of Kuehne and Nagel's service offering (King, 2002).

The company examined how best to improve its trucking capability in Europe. This could be achieved either by acquisition or by alliance with existing carriers. It opted for the acquisition route. The acquisition of the overseas logistics division of French group CAT in January 2004 facilitated the expansion of forwarding activities in France as well as in Mexico and Belgium (Kuehne and Nagel, 2004).

In October 2005, Kuehne and Nagel acquired the contract logistics group ACR Logistics (formerly HaysLogistics), headquartered in Paris (France), for €440 million. ACR Logistics is a major contract logistics provider in Europe. The acquisition – which was the largest in Kuehne and Nagel's history – promoted it to among the top few global providers in this business sector. The takeover increased the number of employees in the logistics group by 15,000. Logistics services offered by ACR include supply chain management, distribution and transport management, factory support (eg pre-assembly) and value-added services (eg call centre management, repair management), as well as managing approximately 7 million m² of warehouse space (Kuehne and Nagel, 2009b).

TNT

TNT N.V. is a global provider of mail, express and logistics services. The group employs about 151,000 people and serves over 200 countries. For 2008 the company reported sales of €11.2 billion (TNT, 2009a). The company announced in December 2005 that it would increase its strategic focus on its core competency of providing mail and express network services. The company believed that it had competitive advantage and growth opportunities in these markets.

As a result of industry consolidation, TNT decided to sell its logistics business to Apollo Management and its freight management business to Geodis in 2006. TNT believed that the focus on its delivery networks and leaving the logistics market would allow simplification of the organization. TNT retained a limited amount of the logistics activities that fitted its core network strategy.

Also in 2006, TNT announced the acquisition of ARC India Limited (which operated under the trade name Speedage Express Cargo Services until it was re-branded as TNT in 2008), one of the leading road express companies in India. In the same year it also acquired the national road transport and freight business of the Hoau Group in China. These acquisitions were part of TNT's Focus on Networks strategy, to become a leading provider of express deliveries in the emerging markets in Asia (TNT, 2009b).

In 2007 TNT acquired Expresso Mercúrio, the market leader in the Brazilian domestic express market. In 2009 TNT signed an agreement to acquire Expresso Araçatuba Transportes e Logística (to build on its pan-Brazilian network) and also acquired LIT Cargo (a leading express delivery company in Chile). These acquisitions have helped TNT to develop its South American Road Network (SARN), linking services in Chile to Brazil and Argentina, which links 30 cities over 3,000 km (TNT, 2009c).

TRANSPORTATION IN EUROPE

European freight activity

The changing demand for logistics services in Europe outlined in the previous sections has had a significant impact on transportation patterns and activity within Europe. Europe's economic growth has gone hand

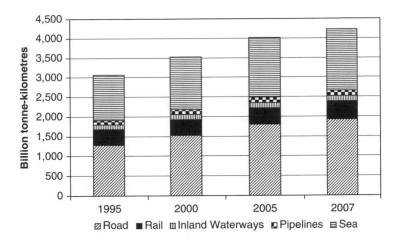

Figure 25.2 Growth in freight transport in Western Europe (EU-27; bn tonne-kilometres)

in hand with a growing flow of goods. The growth in freight transport in Western European countries between 1995 and 2007 is shown in Figure 25.2. During this same period there has been an ongoing shift towards road transport and, to a slightly lesser extent, short-sea shipping within and between Western European countries (see Table 25.1). These data relate to the 27 current Member States of the European Union. Although there are some important differences between individual countries, it is evident that road freight dominates the inland movement of goods within Europe and that road freight activity has increased in recent years. Short-sea shipping services have also grown in importance and account for almost as much freight activity as road. Rail, inland waterways and pipeline have all lost market share, though the decline has slowed in more recent years.

There is also an integration effect – for example, the EU countries trade four times more foodstuffs than other countries with identical production and consumption levels – and this has important implications for logistics demands. As already discussed, the prospect of a Europe free from internal borders spurred many companies to review and then reconfigure their logistics systems (Cooper, Browne and Peters, 1994). This has resulted in a rationalization of both production and stockholding sites among some large companies operating across Europe, thereby increasing the demand for national and, especially, international transport services. At the same time there has been a trend to reduce stock levels by managing production much more carefully and implementing just-in-time (JIT) production techniques. Both these developments lead to an increase in the

Table 25.1   Trends in market share of freight transport modes (EU-27; proportion of tonne-kilometres)

	1995	2000	2005	2007
Road	42%	43%	45%	46%
Rail	13%	11%	10%	11%
Inland Waterways	4%	4%	3%	3%
Pipelines	4%	4%	3%	3%
Sea	38%	38%	38%	37%
Total	100%	100%	100%	100%

Source: European Commission, 2009

consumption of transport services within the supply chain. This can occur as a result of either increasing trip length (as is the case with the concentration of production and storage) or greater frequency of deliveries (as occurs in a JIT system). In addition, there is greater pressure on transport services to achieve high levels of reliability.

Many developments in modern logistics tend to increase road transport (see Table 25.2). The growth in international trade and sourcing as well as the relevance of new business strategies will make policies aimed at reducing road transport difficult to implement. It is still not clear whether the concentration of production and warehousing will in fact open up new opportunities for rail and inland shipping – although in theory this should happen.

At the same time as this growth in road freight activity across Europe, most countries have also experienced significant growth in car traffic, resulting in increasingly congested urban and inter-urban road networks. Freight transport costs and operational efficiency are ever more affected by this road congestion, which is occurring on many key European transport routes and especially in urban areas.

Policy measures affecting logistics and transport in Europe

European Commission White Paper on Transport

The European Commission White Paper on Transport published in 2001 identified many potential policy measures that, if introduced, would have significant effects on freight transport and logistics services in the EU. The White Paper identified that lack of fiscal and social harmonization in the transport market has led to several key problems in transport within the EU:

Table 25.2   Developments in logistics and the impact on transport and traffic

Main development	Impact on transport and traffic
Modal shift towards road	More road vehicle trips
Spatial concentration of production and warehousing	Longer distances, increase in transport volumes on key routes
Adoption of JIT in manufacturing	Smaller shipments, faster transport (road), decrease in load factors
Adoption of Quick Response and ECR in retail distribution	Smaller shipments, faster transport (road), decrease in load factors
Wider geographical sourcing of supplies	Raw materials and components transported over greater distances
Wider geographical distribution of finished product	Finished products transported over greater distances
Supply chain integration	Decrease in number of suppliers and transport providers, increased road transport in the case of more outsourcing
Decrease in order cycle time	Demand-driven flows lead to increased number of trips, decrease in transport efficiency
Increase in assortments	Smaller shipments, increased number of trips
Reverse logistics	Additional transport of waste materials and end-of-life products
Retail market concentration	Fewer, larger out-of-town stores; encouraging the use of car journeys for shopping

Source: adapted from NEA quoted in Dutch National Spatial Planning Agency, 1997; and Technical University of Berlin *et al*, 2001

- Unequal growth in different modes of transport. This reflects that not all external costs have been included in the cost of transport as well as the fact that some modes have adapted better to the needs of a modern economy than others.
- Congestion on the main road and rail routes, in urban areas and at airports. Growth in the demand for goods transport is due to the shift from a 'stock' economy to a 'flow' economy.
- Harmful effects on the environment and public health.

In the view of the European Commission, 'sustainable development offers an opportunity, not to say lever, for adapting common transport policy. This objective, as introduced by the Treaty of Amsterdam, has to be achieved by integrating environmental considerations into Community policies' (European Commission, 2001, p 14). The White Paper proposed

60 specific measures to be taken at Community level as part of the transport policy, grouped under four main objectives. The measures likely to have the greatest impact on freight movement were incorporated into the following key themes:

- shifting the balance between modes of transport, addressing a wide range of issues such as: infrastructure charging; capacity utilization; regulations and enforcement; inter- and intra-modal competition; taxation; and integration of the different modes to achieve the best outcome in economic, social and environmental terms;
- eliminating bottlenecks, particularly through the development of the trans-European network and its corridors, with priority for freight together with traffic management plans for major roads;
- managing the effects of transport globalization, particularly the improvement of access to remote areas and the incorporation of the new European Union Member States into the existing transport networks and operations.

The White Paper included an action programme extending to 2010. The mid-term review of the 2001 White Paper emphasized the key role of logistics in 'ensuring sustainable and competitive mobility in Europe and contributing to meeting other objectives, such as a cleaner environment, security of energy supply, transport safety and security' (European Commission, 2006a). Several policy initiatives were jointly launched by the European Commission with this mid-term review to help improve the efficiency and sustainability of freight transport in Europe. One of these is the Freight Logistics Action Plan, which presents a number of short- to medium-term actions intended to help Europe address its 'current and future challenges and ensure a competitive and sustainable freight transport system in Europe' (European Commission, 2007). In the Action Plan these actions have been grouped under the topics of e-freight and intelligent transport systems; sustainable quality and efficiency; simplification of transport chains; vehicle dimensions and loading standards; and 'green' transport corridors for freight. Details of policies outlined in the 2001 White Paper relating to non-road modes, and road freight transport, are outlined below.

Policies encouraging the use of rail, inland waterway and short-sea shipping

The European Union anticipates considerable further growth in freight transport, but is developing policies to ensure that as much of this growth as possible is by non-road modes. It hopes to achieve higher shares for these modes through a combination of the measures outlined above so as to achieve two key objectives: regulated competition between modes and the integration of modes for successful intermodality. The policies essentially seek to ensure that the different modes of transport account for their true costs and compete on an equal basis, while investment is made in the infrastructure to support rail and waterborne traffic to ensure that the capacity exists to increase their share of the freight transport market.

At the international level, the European Union is implementing its Trans-European Network (TEN-T) programme (European Commission, 2005). This originated in the 1990s but the number of key projects has been added to in more recent years so that in total 30 key projects were included. In 2007, discussions commenced on modifications to the major TENs axes to neighbouring countries. This involved TEN-T being redefined to include the EU's neighbours, towards the CIS and Central Asian countries along key transport corridors (as has previously been carried out for Central Europe and Mediterranean countries) (ECMT, 2006). By 2020, the Network should include 89,500 km of roads and 94,000 km of railways, 11,250 km of inland waterways (including 210 inland ports), 294 seaports and 366 airports. The majority of new or enhanced infrastructure will be for modes other than road. Concern has been expressed at the slow progress with the development of the TEN-T programme and measures have been taken in the hope that the programme will be completed by the target date of 2020. A number of the TEN-T key projects are wholly or significantly focused upon rail and inland waterway freight transport, including:

- international intermodal (rail) corridors (eg Iberian peninsula to France);
- Betuwe railway line from Rotterdam to the German border;
- Rhine/Meuse–Main–Danube inland waterway axis;
- Seine–Scheldt inland waterway.

Significant capacity exists in the seas around Europe and this can be exploited subject to sufficient port capacity being available. The European Union has therefore promoted the concept of 'motorways of the sea', which is one of the TEN-T projects (European Commission, 2006b) and focuses primarily on the movement of freight. Four corridors have been identified for the development of projects, which aim to:

- develop more efficient, more cost-effective and less polluting freight transport;
- reduce road congestion at major bottlenecks across Europe;
- provide better-quality, more reliable connections for Europe's peripheral regions;
- assist in making Europe's economy stronger and more sustainable.

The four corridors are the Baltic Sea, Western Europe (Atlantic Ocean–North Sea/Irish Sea), south-western Europe (western Mediterranean Sea), and south-eastern Europe (Adriatic, Ionian and eastern Mediterranean Seas). It is intended that these sea corridors link with other modes of transport, particularly non-road ones, to encourage intermodal flows that make use of the appropriate transport mode for the appropriate stage of a journey.

The European Union is also concerned with charging for access to the transport infrastructure for different modes, since freight users do not always pay for the costs that they impose on others. Policies are being developed to integrate external costs into the charging regimes and to harmonize fuel taxation. It is widely expected that these policies will favour rail and waterborne modes, with their rates becoming more competitive relative to road haulage charges. Proposals for road-user charging are detailed below.

Particular issues exist for rail freight operations, which have been slow to adapt to the Single European Market. As a result, policies have been developed to encourage rail freight to become more competitive. These include open and non-discriminatory access to infrastructure for rail freight service providers so as to stimulate competition, transparent pricing regimes, interoperability between national transport networks, the development of priority rail freight corridors and quality assurance standards for freight services. Since railway privatization in Great Britain in the mid-1990s rail freight's mode share of the total road and rail market has increased from 9 to 12 per cent, representing an absolute increase in rail volumes of 45 per cent. Many factors have led to this increase, though the development of competition between an increasing number of operators is one important contributory factor. This British experience contrasts sharply with that in many other Western European countries, where liberalization of the rail network has tended to be much slower.

Other policy measures affecting road freight transport

There are two other policy measures that are having a significant impact on road-based freight and logistics services in EU Member States, and may also affect the location of logistics and other industrial activities: namely the EU Working Time Directive and road-user charging for goods vehicles. Policy developments in both of these areas are summarized below.

- The EU Working Time Directive (WTD) was applied to the freight transport sector in all EU Member States in 2005. These regulations introduce limits on weekly working time and a limit on the amount of work that can be done at night. They also specify how much continuous work can be done before taking a break and introduce daily and weekly rest limits. Under the new regulations, working time for goods vehicle drivers must not exceed: i) an average 48-hour week, ii) 60 hours in any single week, and iii) 10 hours in any 24-hour period, if working at night (DfT, 2005). This represents a reduction in the total number of hours that goods vehicle drivers can work in a week. In the UK it has reduced the average weekly working hours of a goods vehicle driver from 55 hours to 48 hours (a 13% reduction) (Pott, 2001). The WTD is resulting in the need for companies to employ more drivers in order to maintain the same quantity of distribution activity each week.

- Time or distance-based road-user charging for goods vehicles. Several EU countries have already implemented these charging schemes in place of annual licence fees for lorries. These schemes aim to relate the charge to the usage of the vehicle, and therefore better reflect the costs that they impose when using roads. Time-based road-user charges already exist in Belgium, Luxembourg, the Netherlands, Denmark and Sweden. Switzerland currently uses a distance-based road-user charge. In January 2005 a new toll system was introduced on the 12,000 km of German autobahn for all trucks with a maximum weight of 12 tonnes and above. The new toll system, called LKW-MAUT, is a governmental tax for trucks based on the distance driven in kilometres, number of axles and the emission category of the truck (the average charge will be €0.12 per kilometre). The tax is levied for all trucks using German autobahns, whether they are full or empty. Toll booths on the highways are not used in the scheme; instead, the scheme uses several methods: on-board units, manual payment terminals and via the internet (roadtraffic-technology.com, 2005). After a consultation in 2002 the British government planned to introduce a distance-based lorry road-user charge by 2008 that would ensure that lorry operators from overseas pay their fair share towards the cost of using UK roads (HM Treasury, 2002). The new charge was to be accompanied by a reduction of existing taxes, ensuring that the UK haulage industry does not pay any more than today. According to the UK government's provisional view, the charge would apply to all lorry operators regardless of their nationality, apply on all UK roads, vary according to the characteristics of the lorry (eg weight, axle structure, emission standard), vary according to the type of road (eg charging less for motorways) and have the potential to vary according to the time of the day (eg different tariffs at night and during daytime). However, the UK government announced in July 2005 that it would not proceed with the introduction of this lorry road-user charging scheme. National road pricing for cars and goods vehicles is now unlikely to be introduced before 2015.

OPPORTUNITIES AND PRESSURES FOR LOGISTICS PROVIDERS IN A NEW EUROPE

It is evident that many multinationals are rationalizing the number of logistics service providers they deal with across Europe – in much the same way as they have rationalized their production and warehousing operations (there is, of course, a link between these developments). This, together with the growth in intra-European trade, is leading to greater demand for transport and logistics services. Political changes have opened up new geographical markets, both for production and consumption. Devising and implementing the right logistics strategies lies at the heart of successfully capitalizing on these commercial opportunities available in Europe. Many of these changes are of significance to logistics service providers, especially those concerned with international markets.

The very different nature of European markets means that logistics providers wishing to provide for this growing demand for European services adopt suitable and appropriate approaches for different markets. International transport companies engaged in cross-border European work already understand that strategies may need to be tailored to the particular country of operation.

Naturally, what is right for one company will not be right for all. In particular, there are important differences between the sort of strategies and initiatives that need to be devised by larger companies and those of smaller ones.

Strategies for larger logistics service providers

In deciding how to take advantage of the new European opportunities, logistics service providers need to be clear about which of the following strategies they wish to adopt:

- Strategy A (Pan-Europeans) – providing a Europe-wide service offering distribution both within and between a number of European countries.
- Strategy B (Multi-domestics) – providing national services which are in several European countries.
- Strategy C (Eurolinkers) – providing a network (or part of a network) of mainly international services between major European markets.

The network implications of each strategy are illustrated in Figure 25.3.

Clearly the most ambitious strategy is the first – to provide a truly pan-European service. Several major logistics service providers are working towards achieving this, but it is a challenging goal. The foundations for

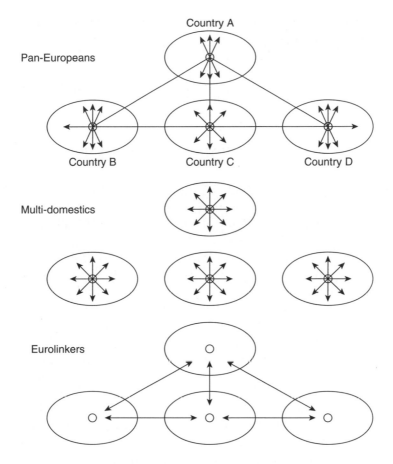

Figure 25.3 Network implications of each strategy
Source: Browne and Allen, 1994

the multi-domestic strategy appear to lie in the successful duplication of domestic services in other countries. The original services are, of course, adapted as required.

Strategies for small and medium-sized service providers

The smallest logistics service providers tend either to operate at a local level or to work for a few companies. The scope for these companies to develop strategies to take advantage of European opportunities will be rather limited. For medium-sized companies, and especially those already operating in the international marketplace, there are undoubtedly ways in which they can develop initiatives to take advantage of the growing opportunities in the EU. However, it is evident that many multinationals are seeking to rationalize the number of logistics providers that they deal with across Europe and, therefore, in response to this medium-sized providers should find ways to tie their operations into those of their customers so that they become a vital part of their customers' distribution operation.

CONCLUDING REMARKS

Cost-effective systems of goods distribution are often argued to be an essential prerequisite for competing in international markets and for delivering a good standard of living at a national level. Efficient distribution of goods and services influences market diversity, consumer choice, jobs and prosperity. Logistics can be viewed as critical to economic success in manufacturing, retailing and service industries in Europe. In addition, the scope for improved logistics strategies to promote higher service levels and reduced costs is also being pursued in public sectors such as health and defence. Logistics contributes to economic growth by: extending market reach thereby giving firms access to a wider range of raw materials and supplies and providing access to a wider market; and reducing waste – concepts such as just-in-time have a significant impact on reducing stock held within supply chains.

Logistics management and supply chain strategies play a critical role in the competitiveness of firms. Indeed, it has been argued that increasingly competition is between supply chains rather than between individual enterprises. Within logistics management the role of transport is an important one and is frequently the aspect of logistics affected by policy interventions (for example, deregulation of transport markets or decisions about infrastructure expenditure).

A number of logistics developments have tended to increase the consumption of transport services within the supply chain. This can occur as a result of either increasing trip length (as is the case with the concentration of production and storage locations) or greater frequency of deliveries (as can occur in a JIT system). However, there are also many positive logistics initiatives have taken place that combine both environmental and commercial benefits. Clearly companies at the leading edge already enjoy the benefits of these and contribute to sustainability. There would be much to be gained by improving the efficiency of companies that are not at the forefront of these initiatives. Therefore ways need to be found to encourage more companies operating in Europe to use logistics approaches and to ensure that those approaches, which contribute to sustainability, become more widely disseminated.

References

Browne, M, and Allen, J (1994) Logistics strategies for Europe, in *Logistics and Distribution Planning: Strategies for management*, ed J Cooper, Kogan Page, London

Cooper, J, Browne, M and Peters, M (1994) *European Logistics: Markets, management and strategy*, 2nd edn, Blackwell, Oxford

Datamonitor (2002) *Consolidation in the European Logistics Industry*, June

Department for Transport (DfT) (2008) *Road Freight Statistics 2007*, Transport Statistics Bulletin SB (08) 21, DfT, London

DfT (2005) *Road Transport (Working Time) Guidance*, March, DfT, London

Deutsche Post (2005) *Deutsche Post World Net Completes Acquisition of Exel*, press release, Bonn/London, 14 December

Deutsche Post DHL (2009) The world's leading mail and logistics services group, Deutsche Post DHL [Online] http://www.dp-dhl.de/dp-dhl?tab=1&skin=hi&check=yes&lang=de_EN&xmlFile=300000263

Distribution (2002) Europe yet to become a single entity, interview with Steve Allen – managing director of Securicor Omega Logistics, **15** (3), p 17

Dutch National Spatial Planning Agency (1997) *Spatial Patterns of Transportation: Atlas of freight transport in Europe*, Dutch National Spatial Planning Agency, The Hague

ECMT (2006) *Transport Links Between Europe and Asia*, ECMT, Paris

European Commission (2001) *European Transport Policy for 2010: Time to decide*, White Paper, Office for Official Publications of the European Communities, Luxembourg

European Commission (2005) *Trans-European Transport Network: TEN-T priority axes and projects 2005*, Directorate-General for Energy and Transport, Brussels

European Commission (2006a) *Keep Europe Moving – Sustainable mobility for our continent*, Mid-term review of the European Commission's 2001 Transport White Paper, COM (2006) 314 final, European Commission, Brussels

European Commission (2006b) *Motorways of the Sea: Shifting freight off Europe's roads*, Directorate-General for Energy and Transport, Brussels

European Commission (2007) *Freight Transport Logistics Action Plan*, Communication from the Commission, Brussels

European Commission (2009) *EU: Energy and transport in figures 2009*, Directorate-General for Energy and Transport, Brussels

European Logistics Association (ELA) and A.T. Kearney (2004) *Excellence in Logistics*, ELA, Brussels

European Logistics Management (2001a) Geest accelerates French acquisition, *European Logistics Management*, 19 February, pp 9–10

European Logistics Management (2001b) Danone's plan to revamp biscuit business includes closure of six manufacturing sites, 17 April, p 9

Harnischfeger, U (2002) Deutsche Post out to prove its gusto, *Financial Times*, 20 September, p 30

Hindson, D (1998) *The Pressure for Pan-European Logistics*, Pan-European Logistics Conference, London, 20–21 January

HM Treasury (2002) *Modernising the Taxation of the Haulage Industry*, Progress Report One, April, HM Treasury, London

Kemp, D (1997) *Competitive Supply Chain Structure: Nike – a case study*, World Logistics Conference, London, December

King, M (2002) We can be king of the jungle, *International Freighting Weekly*, 1 April, p 7

Kuehne and Nagel (2004) Expanding integrated logistics in France, *World magazine*, No 1, p 21

Kuehne and Nagel (2009a) Company Profile [Online] http://www.kn-portal.com/about/overview/

Kuehne and Nagel (2009b) Integrated Logistics Solutions [Online] http://www.kn-portal.com/

Lenders, R (2005) European DCs on the move, in *Capgemini Supply Chain and Procurement Newsletter* (November)

Lloyd, S (2004) Europe's DC hot spots, *Logistics Europe*, April, pp 38–42

Mintel (2008) *Food Retailing – Europe*, November, Mintel, London

O'Laughlin, K, Cooper, J and Cabocel, E (1993) *Reconfiguring European Logistics Systems*, Council of Logistics Management, Oak Brook, IL

Pott, R (2001) Working time: part one, *Croner's Road Transport Operation Bulletin*, No 53, May

roadtraffic-technology.com (2005) *LKW-MAUT Electronic Toll Collection System for Heavy Goods Vehicles, Germany* [Online] http://www.roadtraffic-technology.com/projects/lkw-maut/

Technical University of Berlin *et al* (2001) *SULOGTRA: Analysis of trends in supply chain management and logistics*, SULOGTRA Deliverable Report D1, Workpackage 1

TNT (2009a) TNT at a glance, *TNT* [Online] http://group.tnt.com/aboutus/tntataglance/index.aspx

TNT (2009b) Histor, *TNT* [Online] http://group.tnt.com/aboutus/history/index.aspx

TNT (2009c) *TNT launches first-to-market South American integrated road network*, TNT press release, 2 June

World Advertising Research Centre (WARC) (2002) *The Retail Pocket Book 2002*, WARC, Henley

26

Logistics in China

James Wang, University of Hong Kong

INTRODUCTION

In 1978 China started its transition from a centrally planned economy to a market economy. Since then, the country has witnessed a fast and relatively consistent growth: an average of 10 per cent growth in GDP, and 18 per cent in trade from 1980 to 2005. The growth has in fact accelerated since 2001 when China became a member of the World Trade Organization (WTO). By the end of 2008, China was ranked the third-largest economy in terms of the total gross domestic product (GDP), following the United States and Japan. With such a background, China's logistics sector has been experiencing a significant expansion never seen before.

Wuliu, the word for logistics in Chinese, has become popular, although it was very confusing when it began to appear in the 1990s. Literally, *wuliu* means 'material (*wu*) flow (*liu*)'. Many, including some officials in charge of the sector, took the term to be similar to 'transportation'. Suddenly, millions of companies such as removal firms renamed themselves as a *wuliu* firm, in order to take advantage of any government policies or incentives aimed at promoting the sector.

Indeed, government policies have been critical in nurturing the development of the logistics sector in China, as the state machine, including all levels of government, is still the most influential power driving and shaping changes in the economy, and the logistics sector is no exception. Two

Table 26.1   Proportion of logistics spending to GDP, 2000

Country/Region	Logistics spending/GDP %
China	20
Japan	14
EU	10–13
US	10.3

Source: China State Development and Planning Commission, 2006

recent developments show evidence of such power. First, the central government decided to promote the producer service industries and logistics activities in China's 10th Five-year Plan commencing in 2001. Therefore, each level of government – from county to city to province – needed to work out schemes and plans to boost the logistics sector. Second, at the time of joining the WTO in November 2001, China committed to opening its logistics market fully to the world within three years (which we discuss later in the chapter), indicating the strong willingness of the state to accelerate the reform of its logistics sector by introducing pressure from outside.

China has been left behind the most developed countries in logistics, as can be seen by examining the efficiency of logistics activities revealed by the ratio of logistics spending to GDP. A report by the State Development and Planning Commission (SDPC) (2006) shows that in 2000, logistics sector spending, including transportation, inventory storage, and loss and breakage, amounted about 20 per cent of China's total GDP. Such a proportion was much higher than those of the United States (10 per cent) and Japan (14 per cent) (Table 26.1). The three major cost components, namely, transportation, inventory storage and management cost, contribute roughly 57, 29 and 14 per cent, respectively, of the total.

Despite the central government's target to increase the efficiency of its logistics sector and reduce the proportion of that sector in the national GDP, the reality has been the opposite. China's logistics industry grew at an annual rate of 15–30 per cent during 2000–04, much faster than the national economic growth of 8–9 per cent annually for the same period. The total logistics cost accounted for 21.4 per cent of GDP in 2003, and 21.3 per cent in 2004, both higher than the 2000 figure of 20 per cent. Enterprises in the sector handled only 18 per cent of raw material supply, 16 per cent of semi-final product distribution and 17.6 per cent of final product distribution in 2000. In other words, more than 80 per cent of logistics activities were conducted by producers themselves. This indicates that China is in the taking-off stage of industrialization. At this stage, there is a huge potential market for logistics. Therefore, market expansion rather than increasing efficiency is and will continue to be the focus of most logistics firms.

The logistics operators in China come from five different backgrounds. The first group comprises former subsidiaries of relevant ministries, for example Sinotrans from the Ministry of Foreign Trade. These firms are generally large in size and have some 'natural' connections or *guanxi* advantages stemming from their previous freight forwarding or distribution networks. The second group comprises foreign logistics firms or freight forwarders such as DHL and APL Logistics. With the power and reputation of their brand names, they entered the Chinese market earlier than many others. They enjoy an advantageous position owing to regulations that favour foreign investors with large registered capital. The third group consists of the logistics departments of certain large conglomerates that expanded their logistics operations to serve both their parent companies and some others in the same or similar industrial sectors. Annto Logistics from Media Group is an example. It was once the logistics department of Media Group for national distribution of Media air conditioners, and has now extended its services to many other producers of home appliances. The fourth group basically consists of transportation firms that develop vertically in order to have their own agents doing freight forwarding and warehousing, such as China Railway Express Co. The last group consists of many private firms. Unlike in the other four groups, firms in this group tend to be small in size, and usually have their special area of coverage or focus of business. Some of these small private firms make a very important contribution in fitting into market niches and helping avoid monopoly. For example, Hercules Logistics in Shenzhen provides special logistics services between this fast-growing Special Economic Zone next to Hong Kong and Siberian cities at the Far East border of Russia.

THE MAJOR AREAS OF IMPROVEMENT

Infrastructure development

The market for logistics in China has three prominent features – infrastructure development, the prevalence of outsourcing activities with international players, and e-commerce-based distribution activities dominated by domestic firms.

Regarding infrastructural development, a total of 728.3 billion Yuan (about US$88 billion) was invested into fixed assets in the logistics industry in 2004, a growth of 24 per cent from the previous year (CFLP, 2004). Of this, transportation amounted to 604 billion Yuan (US$73 billion), or 82 per cent of the total (see Figure 26.1). This shows that the Chinese government

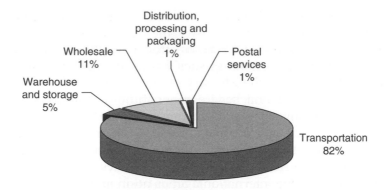

Figure 26.1 China's logistics industry: composition of total fixed assets investment in 2004
Source: Li & Fung Research Centre

has been placing huge emphasis on developing the transport sector. Most of these investments have gone to projects for new railways, highways, deep-water berths and civilian airports. However, the country still lacks a fully integrated transport network for intermodal transportation. For example, major ports such as Shanghai and Shenzhen, ranking third and fourth respectively in the world in container throughput, have less than 1 per cent of their containers going from or to the railways. This compares with 7–15 per cent in major European and American ports – keeping in mind that China is a huge country and its railway network plays a much bigger role than other modes of transport in its economy.

Another major area of investment has been the construction of logistics parks. As the sector has been largely pushed by government policies, building logistics parks is regarded as an important measure to promote and upgrade the sector. Starting with Shenzhen, the Special Economic Zone next to Hong Kong, every major city in China has several logistics parks, which have been planned and constructed quickly in the past few years through special incentives such as land rent exemption or deduction. These newly built logistics parks can be categorized into three types according to their expected roles: 1) serving gateway facilities such as airports and ports for international and national trade; 2) regional distribution centres, which are normally located near railway stations or highway conjunctions; and 3) local services centres for city logistics. From an operational perspective, not many of these parks are running as well as expected, for the following reasons:

● Positioning their role incorrectly. Some cities set up their logistics parks aiming at high-value-added logistics activities for regional or international distribution, but the reality is that, being cities with export-oriented processing industry, there is little need for regional or domestic distribution. The real logistics activities surrounding their ports, for example, are things such as empty container depots and truck parks.

- Lack of proper regulatory environment for borderless logistics. As the country is in a transitional period from a centrally controlled economy, customs is central government's key body to monitor imports and exports at all the local gateways where international logistics occur. When local governments try to reform their systems, with deregulation to create a true international articulation environment such as a real free trade zone, they need not only the permission of the State Council, but also local cooperation from customs. This often requires a much longer time to achieve than constructing a logistics park.
- Abuse of the concept of logistics parks. As China is the country with the world's largest population, urban land in cities with potentially large logistics activity is definitely a scarce resource. Some companies have taken advantage of government incentives for logistics parks by packaging commercial or residential property development into a 'logistics development project' to occupy the logistics parks. Such abuse is often allowed by the park authorities, when recognizing the risks of relying too much on logistics.
- Misinterpretation and misplacement of logistics parks. In some cities, it was expected that when a logistics park was set up somewhere in the city, logistics firms would come to work there together in order to achieve economies of scale. The reality, however, is that, owing to the different needs of their own supply chains, firms behave differently and do not move to the same location, even when incentives are provided.

Prevalence of outsourcing activities and foreign logistics operators entering China

Economic reforms and the open-door policy since the 1980s have made China a world factory for both domestic and foreign enterprises. Growing marketization and internationalization have led to huge demands for outsourcing activities and third-party logistics (3PL), particularly after China's entry to the WTO. Many foreign logistics service providers have established joint ventures (JVs) with domestic enterprises or wholly foreign-owned enterprises – such as APL Logistics, Exel, Kerry Logistics and SembCorp Logistics, which formed JVs with Legend Group Holdings, Sinotrans, Beijing Holdings and St-Anda respectively. These ventures offer 3PL services to most major Chinese cities.

Table 26.2 Post-WTO accession regulations in China

	By 2002	By 2003	By 2004	By 2005	By 2006	By 2007
Shipping and freight forwarding	–	Majority ownership by foreign firms	–	–	Wholly owned subsidiaries. No limit on foreign firms to international freight business	–
Maritime cargo handling, customs clearance	–	Majority ownership	–	–	–	–
Rail transport	Foreign PRC JV permitted	–	Majority ownership	–	–	Wholly owned subsidiaries
Road transport	Minority ownerships/JVs	Majority ownership	–	Wholly owned subsidiaries	–	–
Warehousing and storage	Minority ownerships/JVs	Majority ownership	–	Wholly owned subsidiaries	–	–
Courier services	Minority ownerships/JVs	Majority ownership	–	–	Wholly owned subsidiaries	–

Source: Accenture, 2002

China's accession to the WTO in 2001 set many 'deadlines' for opening up its logistics markets (see Table 26.2). This further opening of logistics markets is very tempting to foreign logistics enterprises, since the country is now in a stage of fast economic development and urbanization. On the one hand, the GDP growth rate was 10.3 per cent on average from 1979 to 2004 and is expected to continue at a speed of no less than 6 per cent for another decade or two, and its foreign trade volume is growing even faster (35.7 per cent in 2004, for example), as the economy depends more on the global market. It means that more global supply chains now have their first outsource linkages or production bases inside China. On the other hand, as there will be about half a billion of the population moving from the countryside to urban regions to work in the next 10 years, and 10 million people are entering the 'middle-income class' by world standards every year from 2005 to 2010, a huge market for domestic consumption is in the making. This is leading to a rapid expansion of China's retail sector and ample room for further development of its logistics industry – and 3PL in particular. Major transnational retail chains such as Wal-Mart, Carrefour, KFC, MacDonald's and Starbucks Coffee are already there, ready to set up more retailing stores; and major 3PLs or integrators such as FedEx, UPS, DHL and AT&T are opening offices and cargo collecting points in as many cities as possible. Mergers with successful domestic firms and the establishment of Asian distribution centres in China are becoming popular.

Express services boosted by online shopping

The most dramatic improvement found in Chinese consumer services since 2000 must be the boom in e-commerce. By September 2009, the number of internet users in China had reached 328 million, of whom a quarter, or 70 million, used e-shopping functions. Shanghai is said to have 60 per cent of the web surfers who go e-shopping (CNNIC, 2009). Total online sales reached 100 million Yuan (about 13 million US dollars) for the first six months of 2009, and most of the products sold online were delivered by Chinese private 3PL firms such as JZP Express and FS Express. How could a country with limited credit card ownership develop such high online purchasing demands and how could such demands be satisfied? The secret lies in the success of the 'Pay on Arrival' (POA) method. Since 1998, POA has gained popularity as it reduces the risk to both buyers and retailers.

The POA system, as shown in Figure 26.2, works in the following manner:

1. An e-commerce firm sets up a partnership with a 3PL firm that has a nationwide network established on a franchise basis.

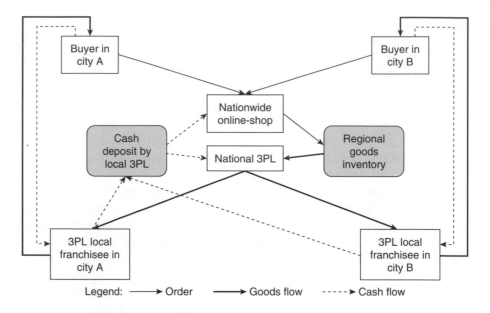

Figure 26.2 The pay on arrival (POA) system commonly used in China's online retailing
Source: compiled from personal interviews with the CEO of a leading Chinese e-commerce company on 27 September 2009

2. The local franchisees of the 3PL pay a cash deposit as a guarantee for the goods to be distributed by them.
3. When orders are placed by buyers in any city on the service network, the head or regional office of the 3PL is responsible for send the goods ordered to the city.
4. On arrival, the buyer pays for them, after verifying the quality and quantity of the goods.
5. Once it has received the cash, the local 3PL firm sends confirmation to its head office as well as to the e-commerce firm so that the cash and profit can be deducted from the deposit paid earlier by the local franchisee.
6. The local 3PL franchisee decides to deposit more cash for future business, depending on local demand for this service channel.

This method has the following characteristics:

1. The buyers do not need to worry about the credit and security issues of online purchase.
2. The online retailer gets paid quickly, as it gets the money immediately the sale is confirmed.

3. The willingness of local franchisees to participate is closely associated with local demand for online purchase, which means that the better the online shop, the more likely it is that the local 3PL will deposit enough cash to get more business.
4. The national 3PL and the online retail enterprise do not need to invest heavily nationwide, while small local distributors can participate in this retail market of great potential.

After a decade of use, the POA method has been proven as an effective tool to nurture a huge e-commerce-based logistics service market in China. Currently, this market is dominated by a few Chinese firms rather than transnational corporations (TNC). Different calculations of the risks inherent in the POA method seem to be the major reason for the TNCs being defeated by the younger and smaller domestic competitors in this area.

CHALLENGES IN DEVELOPING MODERN LOGISTICS

Huge geographical variations

The first and probably most challenging reality is the enormous variations within China. When talking about China as a world factory, often people are thinking of the whole of China – a country of 96 million km^2 of land and 1.3 billion people. In fact, this is not really true. Geographically speaking, the real world factory is just the coastal part of China, consisting of 332 cities and counties. Statistics in Table 26.3 show that the coastal provinces, and mainly their port cities, have become more and more important in the global market as their contribution to China's external trade keeps increasing. Up to 2007, 96 per cent of the total value of Chinese foreign trade was made in the coastal region of three autonomous cities (Beijing, Shanghai and Tianjin) and nine provinces. More than 83 per cent of foreign direct investment to China has been concentrated in the coastal cities. The country is thus clearly divided by the level of international trade and transport connectivity with the outside world. Production in the coastal areas is highly associated with the global economy, while that of the inland provinces is still largely for the domestic market. As this trend has been reinforced rather than weakened in the past two decades (as shown in Table 26.3), one can see that logistics development in China is currently a dual-track system. On the one hand, there is a fast track in its coastal region, where ports are equipped with the most up-to-date equipment and operated with the highest efficiency of any world top-class

Table 26.3 China: International trade by origin/destination region in China, 1998–2007 (million US$)

	1998	1999	2000	2001	2002	2003	2004	2005	2006	2007
National Total	324,046	360,630	474,296	509,768	620,768	851,207	1,154,792	1,422,118	1,760,690	2,173,800
Coastal Region*	268,477	332,654	438,866	471,923	576,304	789,848	1,073,807	1,324,560	1,515,409	2,079,539
	82.9%	92.2%	92.5%	92.6%	92.8%	92.8%	93.0%	93.1%	86.1%	95.7%
Inland Region	55,569	27,976	35,431	37,846	44,464	61,360	80,985	97,557	245,281	94,261
	17.1%	7.8%	7.5%	7.4%	7.2%	7.2%	7.0%	6.9%	13.9%	4.3%

* The coastal region consists of the three coastal autonomous cities of Beijing, Shanghai, Tianjin, and nine coastal provinces.

Source: China Customs, 1998–2007

container terminal operator. On the other hand, one rarely sees a container truck in an inland province, and competition in the transport and logistics sector there is still often achieved by overloading trucks or vessels in order to save on unit costs. The domestic markets of most products are still largely production-driven rather than buyer-driven.

As a result of such huge unbalanced development, either domestic or international logistics enterprises may need to have local strategies to deal with the situation. For example, Wal-Mart has decided not to have regional distribution centres in China, considering that inland transportation, including railways and highways, is not reliable enough for time-definite delivery. Haier, the top brand name and largest producer of electric home appliances in China, has been doing its own logistics rather than contracting out, as it sees that none of the 3PLs can do a better job than itself.

Absence of a fully integrated national transport network

Despite the fact that some effort has been made by the Chinese government in developing the logistics infrastructure for the entire nation, bottlenecks in transport hamper logistics efficiency. Among major transport modes, railways are the key links between the inland cities and the gateway port cities. They started to operate unit trains for containers in the late 1990s, but up to 2008, less than 3 per cent of container throughputs at major Chinese ports are associated with railway services. Upgrading railway systems for containerized transport is not easy, since the double-deck trains that are commonly used in the United States are not feasible on most routes in China, which is a mountainous country. Water-borne transport is not as feasible as in some European countries, as there are only a few provinces where river barging is economically viable. As a result, highways have become the backbone of land surface containerization. The economic distance of trucking is thus forming an invisible division between container-accessible coastal regions and the rest of China – the former being served by modern transport and logistics that match international standards, while the latter is served by conventional means. How to improve inland transport and logistics therefore becomes a critical issue not only for logistics firms, but also for the governments at various levels.

Multiple jurisdictions and local protectionism

The third challenge to developing modern logistics systems in China comes from local governments. The essence of logistics services is efficiency in getting things and information along the supply/demand chains and over land. Strong intervention by governments looking out for local interests has become probably the most difficult obstacle to overcome. Often improvement of logistics is regarded as an instrument to help generate more GDP within their own jurisdictions rather than a way to improve the efficiency of flows of cargo across them. Individual municipal governments are motivated to compete for logistics hubs regardless of their geographical locations – and none of them is willing to see the firms based in their cities set up distribution centres in other jurisdictions. Consequently, duplicated construction of regional logistics parks or distribution centres – even airports – in nearby cities is common. One scheme pursued by logistics firms serving nationwide markets is to register the firm at a city that charges the lowest tax – but locate their business wherever best fits their network needs. This may mislead local governments in both jurisdictions statistically and cause more duplicate investment in infrastructure.

Old-fashioned wholesale marketplaces remaining competitive

Conventional wholesale marketplaces do well in many cities and city-regions where low-end products are traded, and transport and logistics are often taken care of by the buyer. For example, in Foshan, a city near Guangzhou (Canton), there is a huge wholesale market for furniture, 9.5 km long and 150 m wide each side along Highway 325. Each day, thousands of individual consumers – such as new-home owners in the nearby cities – or groups come to this Le Cong Furniture Market to do a day's shopping. Most of them buy their furniture and truck it back home using their own means of transport. Le Cong has contributed to the local economy for more than 10 years and employed significant numbers of people, and many local governments wondered whether the same success could be achieved in their own town. As a result, many wholesale marketplaces (or 'professional markets' as they are called in China) have been set up to boost the competitiveness of the local economy by reinforcing the logistics and distribution systems. However, since the logistics services in China have been developed to different stages of maturity for different types of products, some of those marketplaces have had very a short life before fading away.

New government policies and future prospects

The Ministry of Commerce – together with other related ministries and commissions – released a communiqué on 5 August 2004, 'Notice on promoting the development of China's modern logistics'. This covers various areas such as administration, management, taxation, financing, market opening etc. Major policy initiatives suggested in the document include:

- standardizing registration and approval procedures for logistics enterprises;
- promoting the opening up of the logistics market, and adjusting administrative procedures – reducing to a minimum the entry requirements in the domestic railway freight forwarding agencies, marine freight forwarding agencies and other intermodal transport agencies;
- simplifying taxation on all logistics enterprises;
- improving current practices in regulation to establish a competitive, fair and regulated market environment.

All these initiatives aim at encouraging more foreign participation and more consolidation of the logistics industry in China. Although the economic growth of this country is expected to slow down from an average of 8.1 per cent for the past 25 years, the momentum of the growth is still high and would continue probably for another decade or two even with the impacts of the global financial crisis in 2007–08. It is expected that the following trends in development will appear:

- More penetration of foreign logistics enterprises. DHL, Federal Express, Maersk and Exel Logistics are investing more in this country. The penetration of these transnationals takes different forms. FedEx, for example, has committed itself to move its Asian hub from Subic Bay, Philippines to Guangzhou by 2008; Exel Logistics has invested in Sinotrans, in order to take advantage of being a partner of this leading Chinese logistics firm. Foreign firms may also follow APL Logistics and set up wholly foreign-owned enterprises. For example, FedEx announced in January 2006 that it would acquire all the shares of its partner DTW Logistics in Tianjin in order to turn their joint venture into a wholly foreign-owned enterprise. These TNCs have more advantages over their Chinese competitors in the area of supply chain management rather than in retail distribution logistics. They will appear strongly in supply chain management for medium to large Chinese firms or JVs.
- Consolidation and upgrading of domestic logistics firms. Except for Sinotrans, most leading domestic logistics firms are currently still more or less dependent on their parent firms. For example, Annto Logistics, a leading logistics firm established in 2000, originally a subsidiary of Midea Group, one of China's largest conglomerates with a focus on household appliances, still considers Midea its most important client,

and is based in Shunde where the headquarters of Midea is located. This will change in the near future when Annto's network stretches nationwide and its credit is recognized by more clients. This will eventually lead the firm – and others of this kind – towards real 3PL operations.

● Highly efficient intermodal logistics/transport corridors. To narrow the development gap in logistics services between the coastal and inland regions, intermodal corridors linking the major inland cities should be the first requirement. According to initiatives from the State Council, one can expect more inland cities to open up their airports to international connections, with the Ministry of Railways forced to operate fixed-schedule unit-trains for container shipments along major national corridors in order to meet national goals, even if such operations are not profitable in the short term. The building of a high-speed passenger railway network nationwide will release more capacity from the existing rail network for containers.

● More free trade zones opened at major ports and airports. An important new policy initiative from the State Council is called 'zone–port interaction'. Since the beginning of 2005, eight major port cities in China have been trying this out. The policy aims at establishing an integrated space within which there is a free trade zone together with some terminals for international transactions. Within such places, cargo can be handled as if it is outside the customs area, although it is physically present within the territory of China. This policy intends to set up several 'mini Hong Kongs' so as to facilitate international logistics – including transhipment, consolidation and even exhibitions.

● More advanced e-platforms and technologies. The late 1990s was an embarrassing period for China when it started to introduce new technologies such as electronic data interchange (EDI) to potential users. After spending a lot of time and resources on staff training and installation of equipment, most of the EDI systems did not work, since by the time everything was ready the systems were out of date – not compatible with the newer systems employed by major international organizations or government departments. Recognizing this problem of compatibility, China is now putting more effort into standardizing and upgrading e-platforms in government departments – such as the General Customs and their local offices – in order to improve the efficiency of logistics services, including documentation handled at all international gateways. Web-based platforms for freight forwarding and cargo monitoring are becoming popular as well. The country is also trying to catch up with the developed world by developing and employing the most advanced technologies in logistics, such as radio frequency identification (RFID).

CONCLUDING REMARKS

As a fast-growing economic giant, China is in a stage where advanced technologies and management in logistics coexist with backward or conventional ones – the former being employed in its global trading sector while the latter are largely for its domestic market. A bifurcation is also found between the transnational logistics companies and local firms: the former are penetrating from individual coastal major cities to more regional or inland markets, while the latter are upgrading themselves from transport providers to true 3PLs or even 4PLs.

Governments at all levels are keen on developing modern logistics, since it is widely believed in China that the logistics sector is one of the key sectors for the country and for the competitiveness of their own province or city in today's globalizing economy. Interestingly enough, however, the major obstacles to better provision of logistics services in China also come largely from the governments at various levels. They are putting too much effort into manipulating the sector, such as over-investment in logistics parks or protection of local interests through discriminatory regulations against non-local firms.

The injection of high-quality logistics services by international providers after China's accession to the WTO seems to be regarded as an effective means to uplift the quality of logistics services there. But such a strategy becomes problematic when tension accumulates between Chinese firms and transnational companies. After all, perhaps a more fundamental and long-term solution is to nurture a better market environment for fair play between domestic and foreign firms, and between the inland and coastal regions. For such a solution, improvements in infrastructure and governance are equally important.

References

Accenture (2002) *On the Edge: The changing pace of supply chain management in China*, Accenture, New York

China Customs (1998–2007) *China Trade Statistics*, China Customs, Beijing

China Federation of Logistics and Purchasing (CFLP) (2004) Circular released by CFLP

China Internet Network Information Center (CNNIC) (accessed 29 September 2009) *The 24th Statistical Report on Internet Development in China* (Report) [Online] http://www.cnnic.cn/html/Dir/2009/07/28/56 44.htm

State Development and Planning Commission (SDPC) (2006) National Statistics, China SDPC, Beijing

27

Logistics strategies for Central and Eastern Europe

Grzegorz Augustyniak, Warsaw School of Economics

INTRODUCTION

The fall of communism in Central and Eastern Europe (CEE) at the turn of the 1990s began a fascinating period of systemic transition. This period of transformation has coincided with unprecedented economic integration in Europe that, on the one hand, creates enormous opportunities and advantages, but, on the other, needs great – often painful – changes. Since 2004, eight former Soviet-bloc countries have joined the European Union (the Czech Republic, Estonia, Hungary, Latvia, Lithuania, Poland, Slovakia and Slovenia), another two (Bulgaria and Romania) joined in 2007 and most of the remaining ones strive to do so in the future. Both the new members of the Community and the candidates must follow or adapt quickly to EU standards at a time of slow economic growth in Western Europe, and intense competition resulting from globalization and the lifting of trade barriers within WTO member countries. The scale of changes in CEE countries, inherited gaps in infrastructure and limited access to financial resources make the implementation of logistics strategy – or any strategy – in this region very difficult.

When analysing the situation in CEE countries we should not forget that despite their numerous similarities – resulting from their common

Table 27.1   Comparison of salaries, labour standards and price indexes in selected cities (Zurich, Berlin and capitals of new EU members representing CEE)

City (country)	Salary index	Working hours per year	Vacations (days per year)	Price index
Zurich (Switzerland)	100	1,872	23	100.0
Berlin (Germany)	64	1,666	28	75.0
Lubljana (Slovenia)	21.2	1,830	22	55.0
Budapest (Hungary)	16.6	2,012	23	56.0
Warsaw (Poland)	13.0	1,901	26	50.7
Riga (Latvia)	12.6	1,862	20	43.0
Tallin (Estonia)	12.4	1,826	21	50.0
Prague (Czech Republic)	11.8	1,943	22	40.3
Vilnius (Lithuania)	11.2	1,833	26	49.0
Bratislava (Slovakia)	9.7	1,881	19	38.3

Source: Eurostat, 2005; Dudzik, 2004

fate as Soviet satellites – each is significantly distinct. The most often quoted differences between them include:

- the size of the respective markets (measured by population and per capita income);
- the size of territories and their geographical configuration (determining their logistics systems);
- different starting positions for reforms (determined, for example, by ownership and industry structures, foreign indebtedness etc);
- cultural and historical differences;
- different ways, degrees and effectiveness of reforms implemented (from a shock-therapy approach, through evolutionary progress, to almost giving up);
- different levels of salaries, productivity and price indexes (which in turn differentiate them from their richer partners in the West, as indicated in Table 27.1);
- degree of integration with NATO and the EU, with new EU members from CEE in a favourable position because of EU financial support for less developed regions and structural funds.

For these reasons, this description of logistics strategies for CEE is focused on those countries that are the most advanced in the transition process, and whose logistics strategies are the most similar. This primarily refers to the Czech Republic, Hungary and Poland. Just recently, Slovakia joined the team, with a high increase in investments due to favourable conditions for foreign investors and a flat, transparent tax system. These four countries share similar political strategies that are based on integration with NATO (as new members accepted in 1999), development within the European Union (since 2004), and joining the eurozone no later than 2011.

While focusing on those three, we should not forget that EU membership also affects other CEE and Baltic states that have recently joined the Community. All of these are similar in size but differ in per capita GDP, with Slovenia being the richest of all CEE countries. When talking of NATO enlargement we should mention states that are less advanced in reforms, but becoming strongly Western-oriented, such as Bulgaria and Romania, which aspire to join the EU in 2007. Such aspirations are also expressed by other Balkan states and Ukraine.

In other words, the CEE region constitutes a mosaic that is struggling with internal logistics problems, while aiming at integration of its logistics systems with both the EU and within CEE.

It would be hard to overestimate the impact of this integration on the countries' logistics strategies. However, the current conditions determining the development of logistics in CEE are to a large extent the result of the communist legacy, so it is necessary to take a brief overview of the 'old' system of working practices.

CONDITIONS OF ECONOMIC DEVELOPMENT OF CEE COUNTRIES BEFORE 1990

After the Second World War, the economic development of CEE countries focused on their reconstruction. This was accompanied by rapid industrialization based on heavy industry and mining. However, this industrial structure did not reflect the real needs of the economies but was rather dictated by the prevailing 'Cold War' doctrine. As a result, in the 1960s, while the West was experiencing its first consumer revolution, Comecon countries were still developing enormous industrial potential, with almost complete disregard for actual consumer needs. The problems were exacerbated by the measures of organizational effectiveness. The most common was based on the maximization of assets employed. In other words, the more you use resources (ideally, the entire amount assigned by the relevant central plan) the better. When economies were faced by shortages of supplies, the focus was shifted towards maximization of output – but abandoning any measures of quality. Other measures of performance were meaningless, since permanent shortages of consumer products – sold at fixed prices – gave producers absolute powers in the market. The ways of doing business in CEE countries stimulated waste and corrupted workers, whose intuitive efforts at rationalization were not only ignored but were, in many ways, punished (Kisperska-Moron, Kapcia and Piniecki, 1996).

Paradoxically, the wave of Western credit in the 1970s, when East–West relations were relaxed, deepened the economic crisis in CEE countries. Money was wrongly spent or consumed, and this resulted in huge indebtedness. Moreover, industrial plants built on Western technology made countries dependent on imports of spare parts, and when these became too expensive they could only be replaced by low-quality substitutes produced locally. Consequently, the efficiency and life span of production lines were significantly reduced. Further attempts at reform in the 1980s brought nothing but economic slump. Soon, the political system collapsed, and since 1989 CEE countries, one after another, have moved towards market economies.

The logistics system of CEE before 1989

In centrally planned economies, knowledge of logistics and other modern management concepts and techniques was practically useless. The only exceptions were found in those companies whose export orientation exposed them to operations in the West. In other companies, monopolistic producers, whose distribution was also in the hands of monopolies, dominated the quasi-market. The government set prices for products and services (with few exceptions where higher prices were allowed) and fixed the currency exchange rates. In these circumstances, the only business goal was to exist – at the expense of the state, which covered any loss.

The only concern of logistics was to obtain scarce resources from suppliers to secure the execution of centrally set plans (which meant that the logistics in CEE had a very strong supply orientation) and to deliver goods produced to customers. This sounds similar to the tasks of logistics in the West, but with the significant difference that the logistics system was not focused on quality. None of the logistics systems objectives (well known from the '7 Rs' definition) had to be fulfilled, and both effectiveness and customer satisfaction could be ignored without penalty. Ineffectiveness was officially explained by 'objective reasons' – or sometimes by firing or imprisoning selected managers, employees or 'speculators'. This approach led to enormous waste and technological obsolescence of companies, which treated investments and customer service as costs to be avoided rather than sources of potential improvement and revenue.

These facts indicate that the logistics system of CEE countries was extremely expensive, especially because of high transportation and inventory carrying costs. The transportation system consisted of a relatively dense, but low-quality, infrastructure serviced by obsolete and inefficient fleets. Another major factor contributing to the high cost of transportation was the commercially ridiculous (but politically motivated) location of production plants and other logistics facilities. The criteria for location were based on a theory of balanced development for all regions in a country. This meant that a factory could be erected anywhere, regardless of its proximity to suppliers or consumers, existing transportation, telecommunication infrastructure and the profile of the labour force available. In practice, every investment of this kind required huge investments in new roads and social infrastructure, eg workers' hotels, heating plants, sewage systems etc. This was rarely shared with any other local facilities. To make matters worse, the lack of money often meant that new infrastructure was incapable of serving the needs of the facility. The result of these poor locations – and supporting infrastructure – decisions was that distances travelled by transport were far greater than necessary, for both supply and distribution. This often had an impact on the quality of goods carried – while the fixed cost of investment was very high, the system generated a lot of pollution, and other environmental threats were totally ignored. Another major drawback for CEE countries lay in the poor telecommunication infrastructure, which came with a lack of incentive to improve information flows.

Shortages of supplies, combined with inefficient transportation, forced all companies in CEE to carry huge amounts of inventory to secure smooth production. This meant that inventory was treated more like an investment than a necessary evil. The quality aspect again had no impact on the system, since eventual waste was added into the cost of production. Final product defects did not harm the producers, since chronic shortages meant that customers were forced to accept any products they could find.

Overall, the 1990s found CEE countries with inefficient, fragmented and out-of-date logistics systems that did not meet their requirements as they moved towards market economies. The system was generally characterized by:

- a lack of customer focus;
- the underdevelopment of a transportation and telecommunication infrastructure;
- poorly located, ineffective and obsolete industrial plants and related logistics infrastructure (especially low-standard warehouses);
- a lack of specialized, integrated logistics services;
- inadequate and poor management education, especially in logistics and quality management across all levels;

- a lack of reverse logistics systems – as there were no environmental policies for, say, the reuse and recycling of packaging and hazardous waste;
- low employee morale and job satisfaction.

The clear conclusion is that the logistics system inherited from communism was a fundamental barrier to the transformation of these economies and their subsequent competitiveness. This is supported by an analysis of the cost of logistics of these countries – which is estimated at up to 30 per cent of GDP, perhaps twice as high as typical values in the West. Thus, poor logistics is a major counterbalance for the few advantages of the region, such as:

- a low-cost and technically well-educated workforce;
- incentives for investment in selected regions;
- the relatively low cost of land acquisition;
- favourable geographical conditions (part of the EU market and its transit location);
- the size of the market and its potential, accompanied by rapid economic growth.

Logistics has a huge potential for significant improvements and savings, and successful transformation in this area might be a key to success for CEE countries (especially those that have recently joined the EU) and investors.

DEVELOPMENT OF LOGISTICS IN THE PERIOD OF TRANSITION AND AFTER JOINING THE EU

At the beginning of reforms, all CEE countries suffered from similar problems – though on different scales. Their major effort in the early 1990s concentrated on stabilizing the macroeconomic condition, focusing on curbing inflation (or hyperinflation, as it was in Poland), high unemployment (a term that never existed in centrally planned economies) and social security. Simultaneously removing most barriers and curbs on entrepreneurship – accompanied by privatization of government-run industries – led to the rapid, but also chaotic, development of market economies. Government efforts to gain some sort of control over these changes were made on a trial-and-error basis. In general – regardless of the many limitations, mistakes and high social costs – those CEE countries that followed more radical approaches to reforms have become leaders in the transition to market economies.

Soon, the development of market economies and the need to compete globally raised new challenges for politicians and entrepreneurs, who realized that:

- the transition into market economies means that CEE markets will gradually adopt Western patterns;
- the relaxation or abandonment of trade barriers forces these countries radically to improve their productivity;
- the major impediments to the transition will be the underdeveloped banking, telecommunication and transportation systems that are heavily dependent on the state or are hard to privatize.

Unfortunately, the shaky political situation in CEE countries (both during the creation of democratic institutions and habits, and caused by changing governments) coupled with the need to pursue tough financial policies (based on IMF guidelines) was a major obstacle in implementing reforms. These problems were magnified by the sudden fall of production and replacement of local products by imports. This created an unfavourable trade balance with the West that could not be compensated for by trade with the East, since the Comecon system no longer existed and internal ties had been broken. Lower incomes for governments and inherited indebtedness (despite substantial reductions) limited their scope for investment in logistics infrastructure. While it was not a major problem at the beginning of transition, after a few years of rapid development the state of the deteriorating – or at best very slowly improving – transport and logistics infrastructure became the major obstacle for future development. To understand better the reasons for this, it is worth considering the major factors that stimulated the rapid growth in logistics and related areas, which include:

- the rapid growth of trade;
- productivity improvements, especially in inventory management;
- deregulation and liberalization in some modes of transportation;
- development of telecommunication and information infrastructure;
- development of management education;
- accession to the EU.

Developing trade

The general area of 'trade' was the first to adapt itself fully to the market economy, the main reason being that the consumer market was the weakest element of the previous system and attempts to deregulate it were implemented before the systemic changes of the 1990s. Trade was also the first area in which private capital was invested and entrepreneurship appeared. Growth of the sector was especially high in the retail industry. In Poland, the number of retail outlets (mostly small shops) tripled between 1989 and 1995, excluding the number of pedlars and market stalls that covered the streets of cities and villages. Of course, this growth reflected the great underdevelopment of these services during communist times.

Along with retail trade, wholesaling companies were reorganized and many new ones entered the market. At the beginning these were local firms or family business units. But they were soon confronted with aggressive competition from large wholesaling and retailing companies from the West (including large supermarket chains like Casino, Carrefour, Tesco and Metro), which also brought new technology. For these companies CEE is now one of the major markets (with hundreds of hyper- and supermarkets), with further expansion planned into Ukraine and Russia.

These new entrants had an inherent advantage, since the collapse of the old system caused paralysis in the former centralized and state-owned companies, but there is still some space for expansion.

Another sign of the gradual unification of CEE markets with the West is a behavioural change among consumers, who now prefer shopping at large supermarkets and department stores at the weekend (Rutkowski, 1996). This, in turn, has forced small shops to search for consolidation opportunities to enable them to compete with the large hyper- and supermarket chains. Another strategy, implemented by local grocery shops, is to make a transition into convenience stores that operate longer hours, offer wider ranges of products and improve customer service and shop layout.

Significant improvements in customer service, along with better consumer legal protection (increasingly matching EU standards), encourage more sophisticated systems of delivery, often aimed at achieving just-in-time, quick response (QR) and efficient consumer response (ECR). Joining the EU removed another significant obstacle that ruined many logistics strategies and lowered the attractiveness of the region: this was congestion at borders, which reduced vehicle performance by 15 per cent or more.

Among other positive changes in CEE logistics systems is the rationalization of costs, with significant improvements to stock levels and turnover, which have reduced the average costs of inventory by more than 20 per cent. The biggest improvement is in food products and other perishable items. This was achieved despite – as is typical in an emerging market – shifts of inventory from distributors and retailers to producers. Now, the producers are adopting innovative approaches to production and distribution, including flexible manufacturing and advanced management concepts.

Warehousing is also a dynamically developing area. There was an initial fall in numbers resulting from the bankruptcy of old, multi-storey and small warehouses. But then many companies, both local and foreign, started to develop modern and well-equipped warehouses, and provide services that go beyond the standard stockholding. The first state-of-the-art logistics platforms were created at the end of the 1990s, with many new logistics production centres already completed. In 2005, total modern warehousing and logistics space reached 1.2 million square metres, and the capacity of the recently planned logistics centre in Piotrków Trybunalski in central Poland is 500,000 square metres. In the Czech Republic, 110,000 square metres of new space is added annually (mostly around Prague and seven other major cities). In Hungary there are already around 200 industrial parks providing logistics services to manufacturing and service companies. Most of these centres are run by large, well-known companies, which start to consider them not only as centres for further expansion to the East (into Ukraine, Belarus and Russia) but also as logistics centres for Central Europe including some 'old 15' EU Member States. Such platforms not only improve services, but also create new employment opportunities. Logistics becomes a vital element of the whole economy, and the demand for logistics specialists – as a new profession in CEE – is very high.

As in the West, logistics centres have added activities, including final production activities outsourced by large manufacturers. These developments – along with a growing inflow of foreign investments, growth of local markets and exports – have created a basis for rapid growth in advanced logistics services. Third-party logistics services became a reality in CEE, and the introduction of fourth-party logistics is only a question of time. Another positive sign of change into more sophisticated contracts is the rising number of companies integrating their whole supply chains.

It is also worth mentioning that there has also been a rapid development of management and logistics education, both at university level and as a part of in-company training. This is also reflected in the growing number of professional logistics associations and clubs, and the many professional magazines popularizing logistics theory and practice.

Road transport

All these developments in logistics require parallel development of the transport network and services. After decades of state monopoly, transportation became a hot topic during liberalization, with road transport being the first mode to be substantially deregulated.

Domestic services were offered by almost anybody who held a driver's licence and registered the activity. In terms of international transport, some restrictions applied, but after joining the EU the market reopened, giving transport companies new opportunities of offering services between EU states. The liberalization of road transport led to the establishment of thousands of small, private carriers – and the prices for these services decreased significantly, taking most business away from the railways. However, this created some negative impact on safety, environmental protection and the profitability of the sector. The rush to attract more and more orders for transport services and the maximization of loads resulted in widespread violation of transport procedures – especially for the rest time of drivers and overloading trucks. The dynamically developing and deregulated road transport industry left government agencies unable to control safety standards. This gap, especially in Poland, forced the authorities to take radical measures to reorganize the system by investing in more truck weigh stations (including mobile ones) and the creation of a specialized agency – Road Transport Inspection – empowered to penalize any deviation from technical, legal and humanitarian (such as the movement of livestock) standards.

After joining the EU the regulations got stricter and forced many transport companies to reorganize and modernize their fleet and management systems. Of course, opening new markets created new opportunities for transport companies in CEE, but they also faced new and fierce competition from companies in other EU countries. This again resulted in a drastic reduction in profitability, and eventually the lowering of service standards. But now companies had begun to quit the 'cheapest-and-nearest' approach to carrier selection and looked for more integrated, dedicated services offered by respected and well-established logistics companies. Some of these are still independent and local – but the leading ones are country-wide, with long experience of international transport, or have emerged from forwarding agencies that are part of global companies like Schenker, P&O etc.

Despite concentration, small, private transport companies can still modernize themselves and succeed in market niches. They are obviously more vulnerable to competition, but prospects are good, since road transport remains the dominant mode (except in Estonia and Latvia, where sea transport is dominant) and there is no strong competition from other modes.

These changes are associated with a programme of construction of new roads and motorways supported by the EU. Unfortunately, progress still lags behind the growing transport needs, and the density of motorways is far behind that in former EU15 states (3 metres per square kilometre in CEE against 17 metres in EU15). Motorway construction in Poland attempts to use private–public partnership, but this appears to be ineffective, slow and very costly – both in construction and in use by motorists (because of high tolls). This in turn means that new motorways do not attract enough traffic to give a return on investment. More progress in this area has been made in the Czech Republic, Slovakia and Hungary, but it does not change the overall picture of a growing infrastructure gap between EU15 and new members. For example, the planned density of motorways in the Czech Republic in 2008 (12.8 kilometres per 1,000 square kilometres) is still below the EU15 average in 1999 (15.8 kilometres per 1,000 square kilometres). The situation requires more action both at the EU and at the local levels, since further deepening of this gap may adversely affect the investment attractiveness of CEE countries – and ultimately the development of Eastern markets.

Rail transport

Railways in CEE countries are still run by the state, and the restructuring process is not as advanced as other modes. Each country is searching for the best route to eventual privatization, but owing to large numbers of employees and the high cost of modernization the transformation changes are only gradually being implemented. In Poland, for example, the first step was to separate all services (such as maintenance facilities, construction companies etc) from the railways. This has already allowed a few non-state-run railway companies to act as carriers, paying for the use of the track – and hopefully fostering competition and allowing better allocation of resources for modernization and upgrades. But substantial modernization to allow heavier loads and higher speeds of transport will require enormous additional financial resources.

More progress has been made in separating cargo and passenger operations. At the moment, some local connecting passenger services are being closed, while vital commuter lines in cities are managed by local authorities alone, or in cooperation with the former monopoly. Fully owned state railways usually focus on intercity connections.

The major obstacle to restructuring comes from the trade unions, which realize that applying market principles will mean track closures and further reductions in employment (at a time when unemployment is high, reaching 18 per cent in Poland). The need for such a reduction paradoxically reflects the relatively high density of rail track (with the majority of the network electrified – 60 per cent in Poland, 45 per cent in Hungary, but only 30 per cent in the Czech Republic, compared to a 52 per cent average for EU15). But much of this is used exclusively for commuter passenger services, or has minimal use because of competition from road transport. It is also important to note that, to comply with AGC and AGTC European agreements, most of the existing tracks need to be upgraded for high-speed transport, higher axle load, and clearance profile of cargo movement.

Most CEE railways offer limited intermodal services – so there is a major opportunity for them to compete with road transportation (or to support its transit traffic) provided there are financial resources to finance such programmes. A good example is in Hungary, where intermodal carriages account for 7 per cent of all operations done by MAV (Hungarian state railways). Another initiative is to put more commuter carriages on to tracks by limiting or eliminating competition on such routes. And the European Commission's investigation of the true cost of transport and its strategy of supporting 'greener' modes of transport may encourage more cargo and passengers on to rail.

We should also note that the climate around railway privatization – influenced by the poor results from the UK – is not encouraging. We should expect more efforts towards the commercialization of state-owned railways, rather than their privatization, especially in larger CEE countries.

Air transport

Ownership changes in the turbulent air transport industry are also slow, but the modernization process is well advanced. Former flag carriers are still major players in this slowly deregulating market, but their share is substantially lower than a few years ago – largely because of the arrival of low-cost airlines. The response of full-service airlines is further restructuring of fleet and services, deeper cooperation with alliances (LOT Polish Airlines with Star Alliance, and CSA Czech Airlines with SkyTeam) and the creation of low-cost carriers (like Centralwings, which is a joint venture between LOT and Germanwings). All major CEE carriers started to replace Soviet-built aircraft with Western products in the 1980s, and when this process was completed it brought dramatic increases in passenger service quality and cargo capacity. CEE airlines continue to keep among the most modern and newest of aircraft fleets.

After 9/11 all CEE airlines have been exposed to enormous turbulence but, fortunately, few disappeared. Financial reports from 2005 show profits, but the situation – as in the whole airline industry – is still shaky. Uncertain economic conditions in the region and the threat of terrorism have slowed the rate of privatization – but not the investments and improvements in CEE airline operations. These actions are essential, so – despite higher productivity and an increased number of passengers – extra revenues are largely spent on tighter security in the airports and on planes.

Along with airline modernization, the air traffic control infrastructure is undergoing radical changes. New passenger and cargo terminals have been built, and air traffic control systems have been upgraded to improve safety and services in the increasingly crowded skies of the region. Some of these projects are supported by EU structural financial aid and the European Bank for Reconstruction and Development.

Other modes

The pipeline system is also expanding to deal with new sources of natural gas and crude oil. Conversely, there is a general decline in sea and inland water transportation because it is not being used to its full potential. This is largely due to the lack of proper terminals and underdevelopment of waterways, especially in Poland. However, in the Baltic States modern container terminals are being built, and the increase in operations exceeds 20 per cent a year. The rising costs of fuel revitalize many projects to integrate European waterways, especially on the River Danube.

Some progress has taken place in the development of telecommunication and information networks. In Hungary, the Czech Republic and Poland, the monopolistic service providers have already been privatized, but in other countries the networks are still under the control of the state. Economic recession and over-optimism about the uptake of the latest technology have slowed the rate of privatization, but recent changes in ownership (for example, Hungarian Matav sold to Deutsche Telecom) may indicate a return to previous policy.

Large investments in the latest communications technology – along with customer relationship management (CRM) strategies – have dramatically increased service levels. Increasing competition and anti-monopoly measures have resulted in lower tariffs, so prices may soon be at the same level as those in EU15. Unfortunately, consumer perception of telecoms is still of low quality at a high price (compared with salary levels), so access to the internet is still much lower than in EU15. There is a different situation in the mobile phone market, where there is more competition. The underdevelopment of landlines, along with the greater availability and lower prices of mobile services, make CEE one of the most dynamically developing regions. But even here, there are signs of saturation that are forcing mobile network companies to focus on effectiveness and more diversified services. To some extent (but not as obviously as in some Western companies), the financial position of mobile service providers has worsened due to investment in UMTS technology concessions. These were, however, relatively cheap, and government regulatory agencies were flexible about its introduction. Another clear trend in the mobile industry is the replacement of local brands by global logos – leading to the unification of marketing and service strategies across Europe.

The use of information networks – particularly fibre optics – is also increasing, and the first applications of electronic data interchange (EDI) in accordance with UN/EDIFACT standards are being introduced. In addition, more companies are using integrated management information systems – but with mixed results. This is not unique to CEE – but value for money seems to be lower here, and it requires more advanced management systems to use the technology as a support tool and not a solution in itself.

Summarizing

Regardless of the economic transformation and improvements in logistics infrastructure, statistical data – supported by everyday experience – show that logistics in CEE still requires rapid modernization. The gap with the West in the case of road infrastructure is still 10–20 years, but the accession to the EU should help gradually to close this. There are both advantages and disadvantages of the current situation. The advantages include:

- increasing recognition and application of modern logistics solutions in both manufacturing and services;
- increasing efficiency and effectiveness of logistics systems in companies;
- more investment in modern logistics infrastructure;
- the advent of logistics services providers (mainly from the West) promoting state-of-the-art logistics solutions; and
- significant progress in customer service and rapid development of the service sector.

A separate group of advantages results from the recent accession of some CEE countries to the EU:

- lifted border and customs barriers (accompanied by dynamic development of border infrastructure with non-EU neighbours);
- adoption of EU regulations and even greater access to the common European market;
- higher logistics productivity due to increasing competition and modernization;
- greater access to capital and financial support for logistics investment.

The disadvantages include:

- too slow development of a new transport infrastructure (especially roads) to upgrade the existing, and often very poor, system;
- financial instability and organizational weakness of companies (especially SMEs);

- the too-high cost of logistics activities (a result of the conditions described earlier), which lowers the attractiveness of CEE for potential foreign investors in industries requiring effective logistics;
- low demand for integrated logistics services (despite quite impressive supply of such operations); and
- fragmentation of logistics activities (resulting in constant sub-optimization of decisions) and not fostering a holistic approach to supply chains as the result of a complex and slow process of implementation of modern management concepts.

A full understanding of the problems and their causes is a key requirement for the design and successful implementation of logistics strategies in these countries. Despite the continuing process of assimilation of EU standards, this awareness is especially important to potential investors in the region, for whom the experience and challenges of CEE countries may still be new.

LOGISTICS STRATEGIES IN CEE COUNTRIES

The description of the existing logistics system in selected CEE countries indicates that it is affected by:

- the dynamics of their economic growth and the inflow of foreign investments (slowed down because of the recent global economic downturn and the threat of terrorism);
- development of the economic and political situation, mostly within the EU – the major trade partner of all CEE countries;
- the progress of CEE countries in utilizing their membership of the EU, and the process of opening up other EU markets to the new members;
- global trends;
- a focus on environment protection.

Obviously, all these factors are dependent on one another but the aim is clear: the logistics system of CEE has to adapt and be close to EU15 standards. It will be a long process – but inevitable for the creation of an integrated and pan-European logistics system that is ready to compete globally.

CEE countries enjoy higher economic growth than EU15 – partially boosted by accession – and the defective infrastructure and social conditions inherited from the communist system will be removed. Further inflows of modern technology and management methods give improving productivity and competitiveness – supported by the advantages of low-cost labour, which should continue for the next decade. But the high cost of logistics is a major constraint on the development of CEE economies. So investment in logistics – improving infrastructure and developing the logistics services market and logistics education – should be one of the major priorities of economic policies. The key objectives for developing logistics strategies are determined by the major challenges that exist in the region at the beginning of the 21st century, namely:

- further development of integrated supply chains;
- implementation of modern tools for forecasting and designing logistics systems in companies;
- a focus on achieving further synergy between cost reduction and customer service levels, especially in delivery times, reliability and flexibility;
- development of agile logistics systems based on transformation of companies' management systems to give process orientation and adoption of relevant information technology;
- acceleration of the development of transport, information, banking and customs infrastructure;
- integration of CEE logistics systems with those of other EU countries;
- recognition and development of logistics in service industries, especially in healthcare, banking, telecommunications and tourism – which all have potential for growth and expansion.

Successfully meeting these challenges will be a major test for CEE members' ability to capitalize on EU membership. The reality is that the willingness of EU15 to support the integration of the new members is lower than it was at the time of the accession of Spain, Greece or Ireland. Another fact is that logistics investments have to compete with other important reforms of administration, education, healthcare and pension schemes – as well as restructuring heavy industry, agriculture and so on. The economic growth that CEE enjoys at the moment is also too slow for a satisfactory rate of progress. In such complex situations, the logistics strategy implemented by the state should:

- focus on key investments that the private sector is unable to make;
- create a favourable climate for other investments to improve the logistics system;
- work out a joint strategy with NATO and the EU aimed at directing more structural aid for the development and integration of CEE logistics systems with the rest of Europe;
- limit or eliminate monopolistic practices, unfair treatment, corruption and bad practices in the logistics sector – which is the major threat expressed by SMEs in CEE.

This is why the logistics strategy at the macroeconomic level should focus on:

- expanding the liberalization and deregulation processes in logistics in accordance with EU regulations;
- finishing the privatization processes in the banking and telecommunication sectors, complementary to the proper organization of material and services flows;
- more active involvement of CEE governments in the construction of motorways and bypasses, along with modernization of border infrastructure;
- actively supporting environmental solutions in logistics by enacting the relevant legislation and incentives for companies dealing with reverse logistics and intermodal transport systems.

At the micro level, logistics strategies should reflect global trends and focus on:

- orientation towards, development of and participation in supply chains – aimed at continuously improving performance and similar to those that meet customer needs in the West;
- investment in modern management education that emphasizes the development of human resources and knowledge-based management;
- implementation of outsourcing strategies for logistics, as the development of owned operations is too expensive and risky;
- development of agile logistics in manufacturing and services;
- further investments in information technology linked with radical changes in managing the company towards process-oriented structures.

All these strategies have to be implemented simultaneously to bring maximum effect and significantly improve the ability of these countries to become strong and attractive partners in a united Europe. Any further delay in this sphere may destroy the whole effort and waste the sacrifices made during the transition process, especially in those countries that will still remain for some time outside the EU.

CONCLUSIONS

CEE countries are at different stages in their move towards market economies, but they are all still a long way from their desired targets. Logistics and the related infrastructure were the most neglected elements of the previous system. To upgrade and develop modern logistics systems,

CEE countries must use a significant part of their financial and human resources. They must realize that, after fixing the financial system, the second step is significantly to improve logistics. This would give enormous savings to help the economies of CEE gain further momentum in their development. Such reforms seem to be gaining support from countries already experiencing the negative aspects of underdeveloped logistics infrastructures.

Another important element of successful reforms concerns the development of human resources – and the change of 'inherited' thinking. The emerging market economies inspired individualism and entrepreneurship, but the simplest ways of improving productivity in the region have been almost exhausted. Further development requires more teamwork, a holistic view of enterprise and better education. Changes must be implemented in a smart way, so that capital will be acquired and used in the most efficient and effective way. Modern logistics, along with developed management concepts, offers a variety of solutions.

These challenges have now been recognized in CEE countries. Logistics associations have reached maturity – and more universities and companies offer logistics training and consultation. In technology, state-of-the-art solutions are becoming available, and companies are making better use of them. These initiatives are a prerequisite for the rapid development of both the internal markets and the external environment. Only effective implementation of the presented strategies will ensure that this region becomes an attractive platform linking the West with the East.

Finally, it is worth emphasizing that – regardless of some criticisms and real problems faced by the region on its path to joining the EU – enormous progress has already been made. Even when politicians prefer short cuts and focus on the elimination of symptoms rather than causes, effort and resources have shifted towards the future – towards better infrastructure and management of resources.

Not all the countries have used their time of transition equally well, and new EU members fall below some standards (as was the case with Spain, Greece, Portugal and Ireland), but they are attractive places for investment, with most of the market rules and institutions already functioning. It is a stable region that more companies should discover. And, in turn, major companies from CEE can expand into the established markets of the West.

We hope that progress in CEE logistics systems and their unification into a pan-European logistics network will allow us to stop discussing the legacy of communism and focus on the discovery of Central and Eastern Europe as a good place to develop business.

References

Dudzik, M (2004) Magiczna data 1 maja 2004? [1 May 2004 – a magic date?], *Gospodarka Materialowa i Logistyka*, 5

Eurostat (2005) *Euro-Indicators*, Statistical Office of the European Communities, Brussels

Kisperska-Moron, D, Kapcia, B and Piniecki, R (1996) Badanie kwalifikacji kadry logistycznej w polskich firmach [Evaluation of logistics staff qualifications in Polish enterprises], *Zeszyty Naukowe*, 5, TNOiK Poznan, pp 117–24

Rutkowski, K (1996) Tendencje rozwojowe logistyki w Polsce – od dezintegracji do integracji [Logistics development trends in Poland – from fragmentation to integration], 3rd International Conference, Logistics 96, on Logistics Systems as Key to Economic Development, Polish Logistics Association, Poznan

28

North American logistics

Jean-Paul Rodrigue, Hofstra University
Markus Hesse, University of Luxembourg

NORTH AMERICAN LOGISTICS: A REGIONAL REALM

Attributes of North American logistics

Globalization induces the transport sector and supply chains to adapt to new functional and operational considerations. This is particularly the case for North America because of the geographical scale and scope of its production, distribution and consumption activities (Brooks, 2008; Rodrigue and Hesse, 2007). In a context where transport technology such as containerization has been a powerful force of homogenization in supply chain management, geography remains an important factor shaping freight distribution. The operational characteristics of freight distribution have to be reconciled with the regions in which they are taking place. Regional characteristics, ranging from basic physiography to the regulatory framework, thus have a notable influence on how supply chain management is taking place. Modal preferences and locational behaviour of terminals and distribution activities are among issues being influenced by regions in which logistics are taking place. Four fundamental attributes characterize North American logistics:

1. *Two major commercial orientations.* The first is longitudinal and concerns national (commodities and manufactured goods) and global distribution (mostly manufactured goods for imports and commodities for exports). The second is latitudinal and related to the North American Free Trade Agreement (NAFTA) and a specialization of the factors of production within the North American economy, particularly along border regions.
2. *Three maritime fronts serviced by a system of multimodal gateways.* They include the Atlantic seaboard, the Pacific Coast and the Gulf of Mexico to a lesser extent. These gateways, such as Los Angeles and New York, provide an interface between global and regional systems of maritime and air circulation.
3. *Long-distance inland freight distribution serviced by rail corridors controlled by large private rail operators.* These corridors service and connect inland freight distribution centres such as Chicago, Kansas City or Winnipeg.
4. *A system prone to economies of scale in distribution (corridors and distribution centres) because of the geographical extent and the relative homogeneity of the market.* This has favoured the setting of high-capacity highway and rail corridors as well as vast logistic parks.

An important commercial trend that impacted North American logistics in recent years has been the rapid industrialization of Pacific Asia, particularly China, and the enduring growth in the consumption of foreign goods in North America and Europe. Up to 2008, global trade has steadily been growing despite the increase in the average distance of trade relations. Parallel to this growth, the need to reconcile spatially diverse demands for raw materials, parts and finished goods has placed additional pressures on freight distribution and logistics. The North American system of freight transport and logistics is developing as an outcome of changes in trade and industries, regional distribution of growth and the ratio of import and export in the economy. The development of a globally oriented production and distribution system has involved a greater share of long-distance international traffic handled at major gateways. The performance of the freight system bears major challenges to infrastructure, gateways and other issues internal and external to the transportation system.

A realm facing regional and global changes

Historically, the setting of national rail and highway systems has supported the emergence of a North American freight distribution market. Yet, this scale is being expanded further by NAFTA as well as by the globalization of production. Jointly, they have created an environment where the transport sector is coping to adapt to higher volumes, particu larly at major gateways, as well as more stringent requirements in terms of frequency and reliability of these expanded supply chains. Among the most common factors of change in supply chain management are those related to the exploitation of comparative advantages, mainly in terms of labor, information and telecommunication technologies, foreign direct investments and technology transfers (Hesse and Rodrigue, 2006). All these have helped create a clustered and spatially diffused global economy, particularly in terms of production and consumption.

Yet, the conditions behind globalization that were supported by the setting of long-distance intermodal transportation chains have signifi- cantly changed in recent years. The current macroeconomic context is uncertain, volatile and prone to risks. It must be acknowledged that the surge of American imports was based on a debt-driven process supported by a massive wave of asset inflation, namely in real estate, enabling many consumers to borrow against the paper value of their equity. As long as this process was taking place international trade and trans-Pacific container flows were growing, placing pressures on the North American intermodal transport system to provide capital for additional and im- proved transport and logistical infrastructures. From 2006, as the real estate bubble started to deflate, intermodal traffic started to level off at major import gateways. By late 2007, the global financial system began a phase of deflation with massive defaults and downward revisions of asset prices, which cumulated in late 2008 and early 2009. The process of debt-based consumption was substantially curtailed, which led to a notable drop in port and rail traffic. Oil prices also surged to about $140 per barrel in mid-2008 to retract to the range of $60–80 in 2009, which is well above the $20–30 range that prevailed until 2003. This has made long-distance trade more costly and is forcing many suppliers to reconsider their strategy, which over the last two decades has depended in low input costs, particularly from China.

While supply chain management remains relatively illusive and supply chains tend to be more effective when loosely integrated in a competitive environment (Bretzke, 2009), logistics deals with tangible flows that need to be functionally and operationally organized. The chapter thus addresses how freight distribution is organized in North America to fulfil capacity, time, flexibility and reliability requirements of global, continental and regional supply chains.

NORTH AMERICAN GATEWAYS

Trade synchronisms and imbalances

The emergence of China in the global manufacturing market had profound impacts in terms of the volume and pricing of a wide variety of goods. There was a strong impetus, either implicit or explicit, to undertake strategies, many potentially macroeconomically unsound, aimed at accelerating economic growth and the modernization of China. This strategy turned out to be highly successful in turning China into a major manufacturing centre and exporter. China also applied an export-oriented currency debasement strategy, particularly because the Yuan was kept devalued compared with other currencies, particularly the US dollar (USD). For instance, the Yuan was purposely debased by almost 50 per cent in comparison with the USD between 1993 and 2003. During that period, China mostly focused on the lower range of the added-value manufacturing process in addition to having low labour costs. The unfolding recession created pressures to maintain the value of the Yuan in order to maintain a competitive advantage for exports even if normally the devaluation of the USD should continue in light of the staggering trade imbalances and accumulated debt.

The usage of China as a privileged location in the global manufacturing system has thus been linked with low input costs (mainly labour) as well as low long-distance transport costs brought by containerization. The longer distances of shipping freight from China were positively compensated by lower input costs as well as the setting of massive economies of scale in maritime shipping through larger containerships. This explains why integration processes in North America, namely the use of Mexico as a low-cost manufacturing base, were mainly bypassed in the past decade. Also bypassed was the setting of regional North American supply chains in light of the dominance and efficiency of global supply chains. However, from 2005 the price of oil surged, which started to erode the comparative advantages of China in freight-intensive goods (such as steel and other ponderous goods). North American supply chains may be positively impacted by such a trend, which will put a greater emphasis on NAFTA as a comparative advantage structure. Changes in the structure and direction of freight flows in North America are to be expected with a higher level of regional orientation.

Trade gateways

Gateways remain a relatively constant component in the global space of flows. They can be seen as semi-obligatory points of passage linking global,

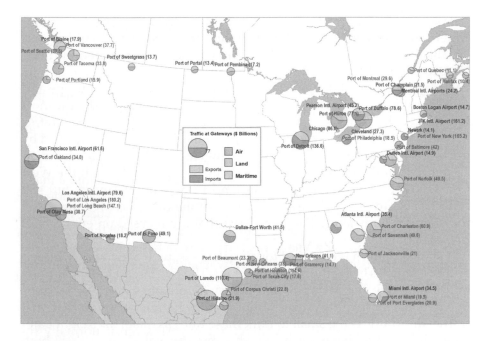

Figure 28.1 Major North American gateways, 2007

regional and local freight distribution. Gateways come in three major categories linked with the mode of entry, whether land, maritime or air. Like other gateway systems around the world, North American gateways (see Figure 28.1), particularly maritime and air gateways, have been quite stable in time, implying that the dominance of gateways such as Los Angeles or New York has not been much challenged. Still, this does not prevent new gateways emerging, capturing opportunities and consolidating their position, such as Savannah and Prince Rupert (maritime) or Laredo (land).

Land gateways have experienced the most changes, as NAFTA helped restructure commercial flows in North America. They commonly have a simple transit function with some nearby logistics and manufacturing activities, particularly when there are significant wage and regulatory differences, such as is the case between the United States and Mexico. The Maquiladoras, a border region system of manufacturing activities mostly servicing North American supply chains, are interfacing with the North American transport system through a series of land gateways, mainly centred around Southern California, El Paso and Laredo. They are dominantly servicing an import function, expanded under NAFTA trade, and connected to corridors of continental freight circulation. Manufacturing tends to take place on the Mexican side and logistical activities managing this freight take place on the US side.

Trade and physical flow imbalances are clearly reflected at major American modal gateways. Almost all the gateways – land, maritime and air alike – are characterized by traffic imbalances where inbound traffic far exceeds outbound traffic. This is particularly the case for maritime gateways linked with long-distance international trade with Europe and more specifically Asia. The West Coast is notably revealing and is the most imbalanced both in the concentration and the direction of the traffic. Inbound traffic accounts for about 80 per cent of all the traffic handled by ports (a 3 for 1 ratio). The ports of Los Angeles and Long Beach handled 75 per cent of the total freight dollar value brought in through the West Coast. NAFTA land trade gateways tend to be more balanced, but still reflect a negative flow. A surge in oil and commodity prices has increased the share of ports along the Gulf Coast that are focused on energy and raw material trade.

A similar pattern is observed for air gateways, with New York, Chicago and Los Angeles being the most important. The two largest freight airports in the United States, Memphis and Louisville, are not gateways, but hubs in a national air freight system. Although they handle some international traffic, this traffic is too small to rank these hubs as major air freight gateways. What also characterizes North American gateways is their high level of concentration in a limited number of gateway systems; a set of modal gateways within a relatively defined region that acts as a functional system linking that region to international trade. Logistical activities obviously congregate around these gateways.

The North American port system illustrates a concentration of container traffic in a limited number of ports and clusters. The share of containers handled by the five largest ports has remained unchanged for the past 20 years at around 55 per cent, underlining the cumulative advantages of capital investment in container-handling facilities and access to the hinterland. The system is articulated along port clusters, representing a set of ports oriented along a coastal corridor such as Vancouver–Portland and San Francisco–Los Angeles along the West Coast and New York/New Jersey–Hampton Roads, Charleston–Jacksonville and Palm Beach–Port Everglades along the East Coast (de Langen, 2004). All those clusters are connected to a North American land bridge and also include small but growing Canadian and Mexican components. However, inland freight distribution is challenging the relationships between many ports and their hinterlands and represents one of the most acute freight transportation problems (Notteboom and Rodrigue, 2005). Ports along the southern East Coast façade (Charleston–Jacksonville range) also anticipate higher volumes because they have additional transhipment capacity and uncongested hinterlands. Further, the potential enlargement of the Panama Canal could expand the Gulf of Mexico ports because maritime shippers

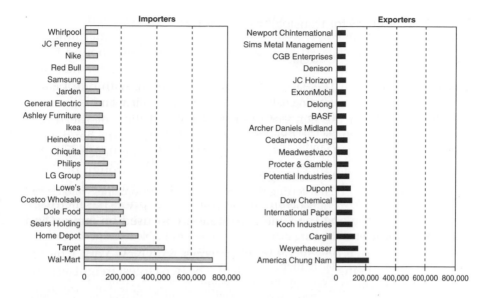

Figure 28.2 American foreign trade by maritime containers, 2008 (in TEUs)

would benefit from economies of scale in addition to the untapped port capacity.

Inbound logistics

An important characteristic of North American logistics is the imbalanced traffic, a reflection of the negative trade balance that has endured in the United States since the 1990s. For instance, of the total value of trade handled in 2007 by American maritime gateways, imports accounted for a staggering 73 per cent. The structure of global trade thus impacts heavily on the operations of North American gateways that are essentially a system dealing with the intricacies of inbound logistics.

North American retailers account for a substantial share of containerized imports, mostly involving finished consumption goods bound to major inland freight distribution centres. The largest importers, such as Wal-Mart, Home Depot, Target, Sears, Costco, Ikea and Lowe's, are all mass (Big Box) retailers relying on high-volume and low-margin goods, which are dominantly produced abroad. It is worth mentioning that about 60 per cent of all Chinese trade surplus with the United States is the outcome of American-owned firms operating in China and importing their output in the United States. Exporters show a completely different profile and thus completely different supply chains. A major category of containerized

Table 28.1 Causes for transloading containers

Cause	Outcome
Weight compliance	Transferring the contents of heavy containers into loads meeting national or regional road weight limits.
Palletizing	Placing loose (floor loaded) containerized cargo unto pallets. Adapting to local load units.
Demurrage	Handing back containers to owner (maritime shipping or leasing company) by transferring its contents into another load unit (eg domestic container).
Consolidation	Transferring the contents of smaller containers into larger containers (eg three maritime 40-foot containers into two 53-foot domestic containers). Cost savings (number of lifts).
Equipment availability	Making maritime containers available for exports and domestic containers available for imports. Trade facilitation.
Supply chain management	Terminal and transloading facility as a buffer. Delay decision to route freight to better fulfil regional demands.

exports concerns recycled products with exporters such as America Chung Name, Potential Industries or Cedarwood-Young. Other major exporters include forest and paper products (eg Weyerhaeuser, International Paper), agribusiness (eg Cargill, Archer Daniels Midland) and chemicals (eg Dow, Dupont).

Two important logistical functions are linked with inbound logistics: transloading and empty container repositioning. Transloading involves the transfer from one load unit to another, which can be a complex task if the load units are significantly different. Repositioning involves making a container available for export activities once its import function has been fulfilled. If export cargo is unavailable, for example due to trade imbalances, then the container needs to be repositioned globally, which comes at a cost. There are several causes that may favour container transloading, which tends to take place in the vicinity of port terminals or inland (satellite) terminals (see Table 28.1).

- *Weight compliance.* Simply involves shifting the contents of heavy containers into lighter loads such as domestic containers or 20-footers. This is particularly the case for the containerized movement of commodities.
- *Palletizing.* Very common for the shipment of consumption goods. To gain shipment space in imbalanced container flows many containers are 'floor loaded' and once arriving near consumption markets, the shipments are broken down and assembled into manageable pallets. This also gives the opportunity to adapt to local load units that involve

different sizes, such as the difference between North American and European pallets. Doing such a task at the point of origin would be logistically complex.

- *Demurrage.* Containers are commonly rented for a specific time period and/or the leasing contract specifies that the maritime container cannot leave the vicinity of the port (or cannot spend more than a specific amount of time inland). Transloading is thus performed to ensure that the leased container is handed back to the maritime shipping company or the leasing company without additional charge.
- *Consolidation.* In many cases where this is a significant market for domestic containers and the domestic load unit is larger than the maritime load unit, a consolidation of the shipments is often performed. For instance, in North America the largest domestic load unit is 53 foot, which represents the maximal legal size of a truck load on the highway. Thus, in distribution centres in the vicinity of several major ports the contents of three maritime containers are transferred into three domestic containers. This enables cost savings as shipment costs, including terminal costs, are established in terms of loads. A domestic rail terminals charges by the number of lifts, which means the costs are the same to handle a 40-foot or a 53-foot container.
- *Equipment availability.* This often takes place in conjunction with demurrage. Transloading enables a more efficient use of both container assets (international and domestic) and can facilitate international trade by freeing transport capacity. For instance, moving maritime containers over long distances in the North American transport system can be considered a suboptimal usage of transport equipment. Conversely, the global maritime shipping industry is mainly designed to handle 40-foot containers.
- *Supply chain management.* A transloading facility can act as a buffer within a supply chain, enabling shippers some room to synchronize the delivery of goods with the real-time needs of their customers. This is particularly the case for long-distance trade where a shipment can be in transit for several weeks while the demand conditions at the destination may have changed.

Transloading thus offers an opportunity to delay the decision about routing freight to the final destination by using the facility as an opportunity to do last-minute adjustments in terms of which shipments should go to which markets. Transloading accounts for a substantial activity at major port terminals. For instance, more than 25 per cent of all the containerized traffic handled by the ports of Los Angeles and Long Beach is transloaded into domestic containers. In many cases transloading requires specialized equipment and a facility where it can be performed.

NORTH AMERICAN CORRIDORS AND INLAND FRIGHT DISTRIBUTION

The North American lattice

Although North America has a lattice of highways connecting all the major metropolitan areas, the long-distance rail corridors supported by an intermodal rail system play the most significant role in commercial flows. They account for close to 40 per cent of all the ton-miles transported in the United States, while in Europe this share is only 8 per cent. Rail freight in the United States has experienced a remarkable growth since deregulation in the 1980s (Staggers Act) with a 102 per cent increase in volume between 1985 and 2008. The main growth factors for rail activity in recent years have been linked with a surge in international containerized trade, particularly across the Pacific, a growth in the quantity of utility coal moving out of the Powder River basin and a growth of the Canadian and Mexican transborder trade. Intermodal and coal represent the two most important sources of income for most rail operators. The two largest North American railroads, UP and BNSF, derive a sizable share of their operating revenue from long-distance intermodal movements (land bridge) originating from the Pacific Coast. The construction and upgrade of intermodal rail terminals have been a prevalent trend to support this system of freight distribution.

A North American lattice of trade corridors where freight distribution is coordinated by major gateways (container ports) and inland freight distribution clusters (IFDCs) has emerged in the recent decades (Figure 28.3). While gateways and IFDCs are significant markets, they also command distribution within the market areas they service as well as along the corridors to which they are connected. They thus have a significant concentration of logistics and intermodal activities. The extent of the market area of an IFDC is mainly a function of the average length of domestic truck freight haul, which is around 550 miles (880 km). About a third of the American trade took place within NAFTA, mainly through land gateways (ports of entry) that are gateways in the sense that they are obligatory points of transit commanding access to the United States. For truck and rail flows, virtually no intermodal activities take place at land gateways, although several distribution centres are located nearby borders and along corridors. Laredo and El Paso, Texas and the Detroit/Windsor complex are notable exceptions with the presence of significant freight distribution activities.

Owing to congestion and lack of space for logistical activities near maritime terminals, the emergence of inland ports (such as satellite terminals)

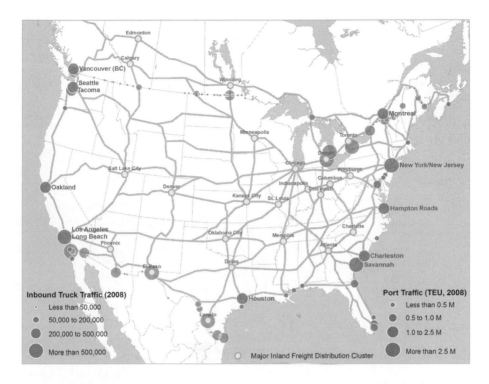

Figure 28.3   Main North American trade corridors, gateways and inland freight clusters

appears to be a significant trend, well developed in Europe but emerging in North America. Such a process is associated with changes in the organization of inland logistics.

Rail corridors

The North American rail transport system shows a high level of geographical specialization, with large rail carriers servicing large regional markets (Figure 28.4). Each carrier has its own facilities and thus its own markets along the segments it controls. The rail system is the outcome of substantial capital investments occurring over several decades with the accumulation of impressive infrastructure and equipment assets (Rodrigue and Hatch, 2009). However, such a characteristic created issues about continuity within the North American rail network, particularly in the United States. Mergers have improved this continuity but a limit has been reached in the network size of most rail operators. Attempts have been made to synchronize the interactions between rail operators for long-distance trade with the setting of intermodal unit trains. Often bilateral,

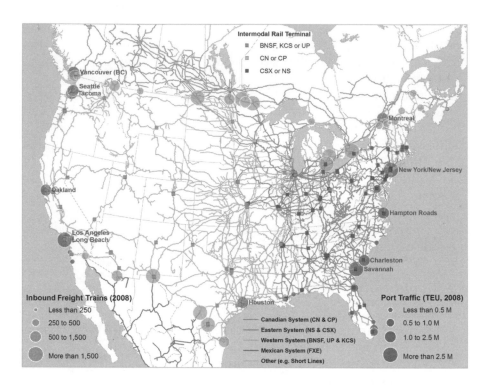

Figure 28.4 The North American rail transport system

trilateral or even quadrilateral arrangements are made between rail carriers and shipping companies to improve the intermodal interface at the major gateways or at points of interlining between major networks. Chicago is the largest interlining centre in North America, handling around 10 million TEUs per year, a location at the junction of the Eastern, Western and Canadian rail systems.

The North American system of operational intermodal rail terminals handling COFC (container on flat car) and TOFC (trailer on flat car) traffic accounts for about 206 facilities covering major inland markets. The great majority are intermodal terminals accessible by truck only, but about 20 of them are on-dock rail facilities enabling containers to be moved directly from the port to the hinterland. Most intermodal terminals are clustered around major maritime gateways (Los Angeles, New York) and intermediary locations having strong inland logistical activities and inland ports (Chicago, Memphis, Kansas City). The location of intermodal rail terminals is a balancing act between gateway location, market density, interlining and complementarity with trucking. In spite of a system controlled by only seven major operators, the great majority of inland load centres are serviced by at least two operators, which confers a level of competitiveness and offers options for regional shippers. For the western system, most load centres are serviced by both BSNF and UP, while for the eastern system, most load centres are serviced by both UP and CSX. A similar pattern is observed for the Canadian system with CN and CP. There are, however, a few notable exceptions serviced by only one intermodal terminal and with no nearby competitors such as for Halifax (CN), Salt Lake City (UP), Billings (BNSF), Albuquerque (BNSF), Amarillo (BNSF) and Prince Rupert (CN). On the opposite range of the spectrum, several locations, particularly at the interface between regional systems, have three or more rail operators (Detroit, Chicago, St Louis, Kansas City, Memphis, Dallas-Fort Worth, New Orleans and Atlanta). They are thus particularly prone to a more competitive inland terminal setting offering shipping options to both the east and the west coasts.

Air freight hubs

North America is the most important region worldwide in terms of air freight. More than half of the global volume of air freight in ton-kilometres is performed in and between North American regions (Bowen and Slack, 2006, p 41). It is also the air freight sector that was characterized by the strongest growth rates until recently. In response to the increasing demand for rapid delivery of small consignments in the courier, express and parcel services, major air freight hubs have evolved. This applies both to established airports that are engaged in freight handling and to newly emerging hubs as well, often constructed on remote airports or on the terrain of former military air bases. It is notable that in terms of throughput the Federal Express hub in Memphis, Tennessee, and the prime hub of United Parcel Service in Louisville, Kentucky are now considered the two biggest cargo airports in North America, followed by LAX/Los Angeles and New York/JFK (Bowen and Slack, 2006, p 41). Both single corporations represent the two biggest air cargo corporations worldwide, according to recent IATA-statistics, with 15 million tons of cargo (FedEx), and about 10 million tons (UPS), respectively, transported in 2008. Only these two have, by performing sustained growth and establishing their own network with hub locations, thus shifted the geography of air freight in North America significantly.

Air freight has especially contributed to the emergence of the distribution centre (DC) cluster along the Ohio River Valley, following a corridor from Ohio and Indiana to Tennessee, that hosts an ever growing number of warehouses, freight forwarding and air cargo facilities. The reasons for the tremendous growth of this region as a major distribution location are manifold. Besides the long tradition of the Midwest as a preferred manufacturing location (with certain distribution experience and competence), these locations are ideally suited to serve major markets both on the East Coast and in the Midwest. Columbus, Ohio, is within a 10-hour drive of 50 per cent of the North-American population. Starting from the Ohio Valley, about 60 per cent of the entire US population can be reached by overnight truck services along the corridor between northern New Jersey and Indianapolis. The region is characterized by offering access to major interstates and a freeway intersection, rail connections and intermodal terminals, and two airports, including Rickenbacker International Airport. Large investments of single firms have also to be taken into account, triggering 'leader–follower' impact chains. Among major corporate investments were the DCs established by Emery Worldwide (Dayton, Ohio), Lowe's Home Improvement (Allen, Ohio), UPS (Louisville, Kentucky) and Federal Express (Memphis, Tennessee). It is no coincidence that this market position is spurred by air freight carriers and integrators, since they are well suited with respect to broader structural changes in the economy.

INLAND LOGISTICS

Inland freight distribution

There have been large inland terminals in North America since the development of the continental railway system in the late 19th century. Their setting was a natural process where inland terminals corresponded to large inland market areas, commonly around metropolitan areas commanding a regional manufacturing base and distribution system. Although exports were significant, particularly for agricultural goods, this system of inland terminals was mostly for domestic freight distribution. Inland distribution expanded further with the completion of the Federal highway network and due to the advantages offered by the motor truck. The growth of metropolitan areas was accompanied by the establishment of associated distribution infrastructure, particularly linked to the demand of retail and manufacturing industries for transportation and warehousing services. Such warehouses were predominantly located in the vicinity of core urban areas. As logistics and supply chain management evolved, further changes occurred, particularly characterized by the evolution of separate distribution networks. The related nodes (DCs) were increasingly located remote from the core metro areas and thus supported further processes of deconcentration (Hesse, 2008).

One reason behind this is the tendency of logistics chains to expand from the locales of big intersections into their hinterlands; another one is the proximity of agglomerations to customers. In the course of the economy's growing demand-side orientation, distribution locations have been moving away from production and towards consumption, ie partly back towards the agglomerations. This is where clusters of distribution centres form, sometimes at single, more or less unconnected locations, sometimes planned as freight transport centres (Hesse, 2004). The locational advantage of agglomerations is less their position in an important infrastructure intersection, but rather their combination of short- and long-distance accessibility and also access to major distribution areas. Decisions on the location of new DCs are primarily based on the criteria of size and accessibility. In the past few decades, this combination of factors has brought a greater proportion of distribution uses to the areas surrounding agglomerations, as manufacturing had already done earlier. Considering the present conditions of flow-oriented economy, this movement out of the cities has become stronger because the core cities and their traffic congestion create more and more obstacles to flow-oriented distribution.

This sub- and ex-urban drift of warehousing and freight distribution, which was foreseen by Chinitz (1960) in the case of New York City, was recently analysed in more depth (Bowen, 2008; Cidell, 2009). In the United States warehousing and storage employment between 1998 and 2005 grew by 383 per cent, being the highest growth rate among all transportation subsections, and the number of establishments with more than 250 employees jumped from 26 in 1998 to 520 in 2005 (Bowen, 2008). Regarding the location of such establishments, air and highway accessibility were considered most important. The degree and direction of the spatial transformations this industry experienced have also been evidenced, with a pattern of concentration along inland ports emerging in the Midwest, the Pacific Northwest and the Piedmont (Cidell, 2009). Against the background of a strong correlation between the distribution of population and the number of freight establishments (and given that highway access is almost ubiquitously provided for in US metro areas), railway accessibility turns out to be one important factor in explaining warehousing distribution patterns per capita. Also, a certain inland (Midwest) shift of the industry is related to lower salary levels compared to metros at the East and West coasts, explaining the strong performance of cities such as Memphis or Oklahoma City. This underlines again that Chicago stands out in any regard among the metro areas studied, given its role as a prime railway hub and traditional inland gateway city (see Figure 28.4). Regarding locational dynamics within metro areas, a suburban drift of distribution establishments was also observed, with locations close to central cities attracting the establishment of DCs, particularly due to accessibility advantages.

Following the increasing extent and spatial reach of freight flows in the course of globalization and intermodalism, two main categories of inland terminals have emerged in North America. The first is related to ocean trade where inland terminals are an extension of a maritime terminal located in one of the three major ranges (Atlantic, Gulf and Pacific) either as satellite terminals or more commonly as inland load centres (eg Chicago). The second category concerns inland terminals mainly connected to NAFTA trade that can act as custom pre-clearance centres. Kansas City can be considered the most advanced inland port initiative in North America as it combines intermodal rail facilities from four different rail operators, foreign trade zones and logistics parks at various locations through the metropolitan area.

The setting of large distribution centres, often part of distribution clusters, has been a dominant trend, particularly among major retailers, which have set the standard in terms of inventory management of their supply chains. These intermodal facilities require a large array of equipment, which can vary based on the freight they handle. Large distribution centres tend to develop on the principle of internal economies of agglomeration (within the distribution centre). Logistics parks expand these advantages through external economies of agglomeration, implying that the concentration of distribution centres within the cluster, even if they concern different supply chains, has the potential to reduce an array of costs.

Added value in inland freight distribution

There are two major types of added value related to freight distribution. The first involves performing an activity that improves the efficiency of freight distribution. Added value thus results in benefits that are carried to the shippers or their customers, notably in terms of cheaper products delivered in a reliable and flexible way (see Table 28.2). The second is extracting a form of rent from the existing flows, notably through tolls and taxes. Added value results in financial gains for various levels of government, which can be used to fund infrastructure projects and improve competitiveness. There is, however, a risk of a rent-seeking behaviour where freight activities are targeted strictly in terms of a source of revenue. The 'added value' they generate for the rent seekers thus comes at the expense of the productivity of the supply chain.

North American logistics has particularly been impacted by the setting of Foreign Trade Zones (FTZs), mainly at inland ports. An FTZ is an area that is considered outside the customs jurisdiction. It makes possible to import specific categories of goods without going through customs procedures as long as the goods remain within the FTZ. In the FTZ, the goods can be transformed (eg assembled) into other goods and then 'exported' out under a different custom category. The main advantages of FTZs are thus regulatory and financial:

Table 28.2 Common added-value activities associated with inland freight distribution

Function	Overview
Processing	Operations on the goods. Includes sorting, packaging, testing, assembling.
Distribution	Operations on the cargo. Consolidation, deconsolidation, transloading or cross-docking. Assembling LTL shipments.
Customs clearance	Releasing and/or inspecting inbound cargo. Assumed by a national customs authority.
Foreign trade zone	A sanctioned site where foreign and domestic goods are considered to be outside of the customs territory. Requires bounded transport and bounded warehousing.
Container depot	Handle containers (leased or carrier owned). Transfer custody of containers between shippers. Storing and servicing/repairing containers.

- *Custom clearance.* Since the FTZ is a bounded facility, the custom clearance can be done inland instead of at the port of entry and the consignment can stay in the bounded area for an unlimited amount of time. It is likely that this can be done faster inland because the facility is less congested than a large gateway port. The consignee thus gets a better notice about the availability of its shipment and can plan its supply chain management accordingly.
- *Duties.* In spite of decades of trade liberalization, duties are still levied on international trade. With an FTZ duties are not paid until the consignment is shipped out and can be deferred further if moved to another FTZ. If a transformation (eg assembly, labelling, testing) is performed within the FTZ, this added-value activity is not subject to duties and can change the duty class of a product to a more preferential level. Commonly, duties are not levied if a product is damaged, defective or obsolete since its commercial value is considerably reduced. Thus, by inspecting products in an FTZ, the duty will be waived for any defective products. This is particularly useful for products that have a higher propensity to be damaged or defective.
- *Settlement.* For most transactions, particularly through letters of credit, the vendor is not paid until the consignment has left a facility (FTZ and/or transport terminal). An FTZ can thus be used to delay settlement until judged suitable by the consignee and also offers the opportunity to readily remove the value of damaged or defective products from the settlement.

CORPORATE LOGISTICS AND ITS ROLE IN NORTH AMERICAN FREIGHT TRANSPORTATION – THREE CASES

Wal-Mart

Corporate management in logistics and distribution has become extremely important not only for the generation of freight transportation demand, but also as a driver of organizational changes and technological innovation. Integrated supply chain management has developed in response to new modes of production, in the context of globalization, and with respect to a highly competitive market environment. Supply chain management has shifted focus from maintaining inventories aimed at approximately satisfying a demand towards a comprehensive system ensuring that supply matches more closely with demand. This is mainly to be achieved through on-demand or pull- rather than push-distribution. Thus, physical flows also involve a significant amount of information flows. Hence, major inventions in information and communication technologies were the requirement for making the new logistics systems operational. This applies particularly to the management of information flows, regarding load units (being these single items, small consignments or 20- or 40-foot containers), transport vehicles, distribution centre operations or the entire inventory management of a firm.

It is hence no coincidence that contemporary logistics activities and thus freight transportation performances are increasingly driven by corporate management, rather than by infrastructure policy or the geographical conditions for moving vehicles and handling consignments. This becomes indicative once we are discussing the case of a single corporation that is already considered emblematic for the development of 21st-century capitalism (Lichtenstein, 2006). This is the case of Wal-Mart, the US retailer that is currently ranked second on the Fortune 500 list of the largest corporations (based on turnover). Wal-Mart has achieved its position as the largest retailer worldwide – among others factors – particularly through the development of a sophisticated distribution system that has been constantly improved over time (Bonacic, 2006). The spatial expansion of the firm by placing new retail outlets was usually centred around a DC, in order to allow efficient supply of goods. As of 2009, Wal-Mart operates a network of 147 distribution centres that service its approximately 7,800 stores worldwide (4,200 of them domestic) and that receive commodities from about 60,000+ suppliers (Wal-Mart, 2009), about 80 per cent of which are located in China (Gereffi and Christian, 2009, p 579). Such an extended network requires an extreme degree of control and velocity of both inventory and flows, in order to avoid dead capital, given the marginal revenues that can be achieved in the retail industry. 'Wal-Mart revolutionized the speed and efficiency of getting products to stores through its distribution centre location strategy and cross-docking techniques. All Wal-Mart stores are typically located within a day's drive of a distribution centre, and the company works closely with its suppliers to streamline deliveries' (Gereffi and Christian, 2009, pp 576–77).

In contrast to the majority of its competitors, all distribution activities including trucking and warehousing have remained under control of the company, rather than being outsourced to service providers. Wal-Mart has always been introducing new technologies from early on, particularly those technologies that allow for an efficient flow of data and materials. This policy comprises electronic data exchange (EDI), which enabled the management to track the entire data flow, satellite systems that provided control of vehicle operations, and lastly radio frequency identification (RFID) technology that was supposed to increase inventory control through improved on-time information flow. The acceleration of average turnover allowed not only for diminishing costly inventory but also for mobilizing further interest rates before the account had to be settled. The massive expansion of Wal-Mart did not occur without affecting other companies, particularly competitors in the retail industry and also suppliers who had to follow the rather rigid imperative of the purchasing and supply chain management regimes of the retailer (cf. Gereffi and Christian, 2009, p 577). It is noted by the authors, also referring to other studies (eg Brunn, 2006; Lichtenstein, 2006), that the particular business model pursued by Wal-Mart would be essentially driven by its extraordinary power in supply chain management.

Whereas the introduction of RFID technologies have not succeeded as yet according to the firm's expectations, Wal-Mart is going to reorganize its supply and purchasing policy, following a 2005 commitment to reflect both ethical and environmental standards for achieving corporate responsibility (Plambeck, 2007). This can be read as a response to wider criticism of the company's attitude against competitors, vendors and employees articulated by the public or by community organizations (Christopherson, 2007). As part of a comprehensive scorecard approach, the firm aims at improving the overall sustainability of its products and processes, emphasizing 14 focal areas within 3 broad categories: renewable energy; zero waste; and sustainable products. One of the focal areas targets the logistics network, eg for improving the efficiency of the trucking fleet. The measures will also be undertaken as a means of maintaining the firm's profitability: 'In the first year of the program following [former CEO] Lee Scott's announcement, the logistics network achieved roughly a 25 per cent improvement in fuel efficiency, meaning almost $75 million in annual savings and 400,000 tons of CO_2 per year that did not enter the atmosphere' (Plambeck, 2007, p 4).

BNSF Logistics Park, Chicago

Distribution centres operated by the freight distribution industry are increasingly part of logistics park projects co-located with intermodal rail terminals (Rodrigue *et al*, 2010). The BNSF Logistics Park, Chicago began operating in 2002 and is entirely private, the terminal constructed by the class 1 rail operator BNSF for about 1 billion USD with ProLogis and CenterPoint responsible for the provision and management of distribution centres. Thus the world's largest rail company is in partnership with two of the largest promoters and managers of logistics space. It is a suburban logistics centre taking advantage of the principle of co-location; the rail terminal and the logistics park have been constructed at the same time, which reduces drayage considerably. A wide array of freight distribution activities is present, including free trade zones. Most of the site is a reconversion of a former Army munitions depot (Arsenal), which account for 2,200 acres (excluding the rail terminal). The rail terminal handles the largest volume in North America and is directly linked to the most important North American rail corridor, the Los Angeles–Chicago axis. The rail lines of this corridor are owned by either BNSF or UP. The terminal is therefore modern and productive with limited dwell-time and demurrage. This productivity and capacity obviously benefit the co-located activities that use such advantage in their marketing as the site benefits from massive economies of scale and excellent accessibility to the North American freight distribution system.

A large share of the real estate of 12 million square feet is leased, underlining that the business model is based upon revenue generation from the location to amortize capital investments. The main tenants are Wal-Mart (retailer with 3.4 million square feet), DSC Logistics (third-party logistics service provider; 3PL), Georgia Pacific (the world's largest wood product manufacturer in the world), Potlatch (forest products), Sanyo Logistics (distribution), Partners Warehouse (3PL), California Cartage (3PL) and Maersk Logistics (3PL). The presence of the maritime shipping company Maersk underlines the setting of a hinterland strategy pursued by several shippers around the world, which helps better manage their containerized assets. The BNSF Logistics Park is an important component for inland distribution for imports from the West Coast and its dynamics are thus strongly linked with trans-Pacific trade. About one mile north of the site, a second component is planned with 3,600 acres that have been acquired by Centerpoint, but in this case the rail terminal will be provided by UP.

CenterPoint-KCS Intermodal Center, Kansas City

With the ongoing integration of the North American economy, Kansas City has seen the emergence of a new corridor towards Mexico, often dubbed the 'NAFTA highway'. The rail operator Kansas City Southern (KCS) has been a major proponent of this corridor by establishing a Mexican subsidiary (Kansas City Southern de Mexico; KCSM) with rail terminals at the port of Lazaro Cardenas. The system is labelled KCS International Intermodal Corridor. However, the setting of this corridor requires supply chain managers to consider the Lazaro Cardenas option, thus the setting of an inland port at the end of the corridor in Kansas City to help anchor this freight. KCS and CenterPoint Properties began building a 1,340-acre inland port labelled CenterPoint-KCS Intermodal Freight Gateway in 2007, over a reconverted military base (Richards-Gebaur). This reconversion is managed by the Kansas City Port Authority which can sell or lease the land under its jurisdiction. The developer Hunt Midwest is also involved in projects related to underground warehousing facilities.

Like many inland ports in North America, it follows the landlord model where a real estate promoter seeks revenue generation through a partnership with a rail operator, building logistics activities in co-location with the rail terminal. This park is a geographically specialized inland port within the Kansas City cluster with an orientation towards Mexican supply chains or global supply chains going through Mexico. It is thus interesting to note that the complex is labelled as a gateway to underline its status as a point of entry of global trade transiting through Mexico to an inland port deep inside the United States. Like many commercial projects, the development of the inland port is divided in phases (five in this case) where facilities are incrementally provided to the location market. What is also particular to the project is that owing to its adjacency to a major interstate highway and its proximity to Kansas City (25 km south), a retailing component is planned with the sole purpose of revenue generation.

A FREIGHT AND LOGISTICS POLICY FRAMEWORK

The enormous growth of freight shipments and the associated transport needs have caused a wide range of problems and conflicts that are primarily visible in metropolitan and urban regions. These problems are due both to capacity and acceptability constraints of the current distribution system, of which the former is generally accepted as a serious challenge to policy and planning. In contrast, sustainability of freight transportation is (still) subject to minor consideration, because economic interests are often ranked much higher than social or environmental goals. Yet air pollution, noise emissions and the degradation of infrastructure (roads, bridges), mainly caused by heavy-duty vehicles, happen at a certain cost to the environment and society – not to mention the extraordinary demand for space at major gateway locations for warehousing, vehicle operations, trans-shipment, or the storage of empty containers.

Judging from the perspective of policy and planning, freight transport and logistics are an increasingly important issue, and also represent a target extremely difficult to manage. This is due to the cost-sensitive character of freight transport subject to corporate management and decision making, which is different from passenger transport where decisions are mainly made by individuals, following more than just cost-based rationalities. Freight is both an outcome and a component of highly abstract network architectures that are not necessarily open for external management, for example for governance in the public interest or in response to local issues. Freight transport remains in private interests that seek to maximize system-wide utility. Finally, the potential degree of any planning intervention depends upon the regulatory framework, which has been changing significantly over the past two or three decades, thus driving freight growth through shrinking barriers for trade and transport, falling freight rates and a highly competitive environment in the logistics service industries.

If we take a closer look at the regulatory framework and the physical operationality of the freight distribution system, the current situation appears quite contradictory, with deregulation and market liberalization on the one hand, in order to allow for accelerating freight flows, and increasing constraints due to infrastructure bottlenecks, urban density and scarce land on the other. As a consequence, there is a remarkable contrast between the fluidity of flows and the inertia of the physical infrastructure, even if we acknowledge the rising significance of information flow and managerial competence. Because transportation systems, particularly infrastructure and land supply, cannot accommodate the growing amount of freight traffic, the question is how the associated problems might be solved in future, with much higher transportation volumes in addition to the performance of the current systems.

To answer this question, it makes sense to look back and raise the issue of how municipalities and transportation planning authorities have tackled these problems in the past (see Banister, 2002). In general, transportation planning has long been focusing on passenger transportation and did not extensively develop plans and strategies for distribution. In many cases, distribution has been considered an undesirable land use at the local level, at least in economically prospering regions (in others, logistics firms have been welcomed for the sake of certain economic benefits, such as jobs, local tax revenues etc). Planning activities with respect to truck transport and rail freight have been undertaken only recently, compared to passenger transportation and the respective tradition of modelling, traffic counting etc.

The strategies of policy and planning with respect to freight distribution and logistics have changed remarkably over the past four decades. With regard to the style of policy making and intervention, different stages can be distinguished: during the 1960s, freight had not been particularly addressed by transportation planners yet, except the matters of fact that, first, infrastructure had to be provided and, second, in the case of port cities, port development in general was a major policy issue that shifted some attention to freight distribution. Planning practice in the 1970s/1980s was likely to pay more attention to freight yet mainly followed the traditional guidance of 'predict and provide', focusing on measures that were devoted to widening and expanding the infrastructure network. Not earlier than in the 1990s, the issue of intermodality emerged as a generally accepted paradigm for policy and planning. Whereas the deregulation of transport markets has substantially lowered the degree of government intervention, to some extent air quality policies have been introduced as new regulation tools, for example addressing emission standards. At the end of the 1990s and in the early 2000s, there was a substantial increase in freight-related activity at both metropolitan and national levels. As a consequence of the accelerated growth of freight transport and the rising degree of conflict, urban economists, transportation planners and the trade sector share a rising interest in freight issues. Metropolitan planning organizations and also the Federal government were developing elements of a freight-related policy framework (eg developed and distributed under the auspices of the Federal Highway Administration). This happens in order to make freight and logistics more efficient and more acceptable, by integrating freight into planning schemes and frameworks and also by offering training and education capacity.

With respect to the capacity constraints and the sustainability deficiencies of the current freight system, the need for developing a balanced framework of policy and planning measures is undoubted. Different from more traditional routines of infrastructure expansion, it would comprise a comprehensive policy approach with respect to energy, climate change, infrastructure policy and modal share, within which intermodality would play a key role. It is also time for better balancing the freight sector with community demands, for example regarding traffic generation or neighbourhood impacts of inner-city distribution centres. Regional examples such as the Seattle/Tacoma 'FAST Corridor', the Alameda Corridor or other initiatives in the metropolitan regions named above underline attempts to try to divert freight in a firmly established national trucking market. Although on paper these initiatives appear quite reasonable and promising, the existing distribution system takes time to adjust. So the modal shift they were designed for may take much longer than expected, whereas in the meantime road freight transport is growing further. Case studies may even provide evidence to suggest that attempts at freight planning are not that useful unless coming from the private sector or at least in close cooperation with it. For example, the Port Inland Freight Distribution Network of the Port Authority of New York and New Jersey has also shown a rather slow start, with much less traffic than expected in spite of subsidies and incentives. Thus modal shift strategies, either planned or left to market forces, are facing substantial inertia reflecting accumulated investments, routes and management practices.

A sound strategy for policy makers will be to favour freight distribution systems that are able to cope with changes, particularly not only those that are exclusively business related. Surprisingly, the issue is more one of adaptability and flexibility, which reflects what freight distribution systems have become, than anticipation. A national freight policy should mainly be articulated first at distributing case studies, good practice and policy experience to attract business and planning communities to put freight on the agenda, to collect data and develop strategies, and only then should plans be implemented.

A second issue is to identify strategic locations where transport investment is required to ensure adequate and reliable freight transport systems. They often correspond to congestion bottlenecks. Once these high-priority locations are identified and adjustments made to satisfy various interests, private investments should be secured by guaranteeing protection against short-sighted local nimbyism through the rationale of national strategic importance. On one hand, local opposition has been one of the most powerful forces that have impaired the development of transport systems. In California, things have even gone to the extreme; their philosophy is to build absolutely nothing anywhere nearby anything, which partially explains the growing difficulties that freight distribution is having along the West Coast. On the other hand, corporate activity in logistics and distribution still lacks more sustainable and responsible modes of management that are becoming increasingly accepted in major parts of the manufacturing industry.

Energy, climate change and North American freight distribution

Energy issues, climate change and the related environmental and economic impact will clearly affect the North American freight distribution network. Because of its high reliance on trucking and air freight to support time-based distribution, the freight distribution system is particularly vulnerable to petroleum price increases, already observed during 2008. Even more than this is the case in Europe, North American logistics and freight distribution operate on the assumption of low energy costs, and most investments in logistical infrastructures were made in such a context and with expectations that they would remain within a specific range. The fast development of the logistics industry in the 1990s became accelerated by the deregulation of most transport sectors, making the design of large-scale distribution networks attractive, with the effect of an increasing amount of vehicle miles travelled. This mode of rationalization was based on the assumption of very low energy prices, implying that energy considerations were limited in the planning and operation of freight distribution.

However, the long-term trend of rising oil prices, the convergence of supply, distribution and refining constraints will make an undeniable mark on the economic sustainability of the transport industry and force substantial adjustments. Among those, a shift to more energy-efficient modes can be expected, notably towards rail. As rail freight transport systems are already fairly congested, notably along long-distance east–west corridors, substantial investments will be required in rail infrastructures to ensure an efficient and low-energy-intensity inland freight distribution. This system could be complemented by coastal and fluvial barge systems, much in line with Western Europe. A better usage of existing resources will take place, notably in terms of existing capacity and locations, inciting innovations in the management of distribution. Intense productivity pressures will be placed on existing transport capacities, especially trucking. Location and accessibility, traditional components in costs-based assessments of transportation, will see renewed focus. Balances between modes, locations, times and costs are to be re-examined to mitigate growing mobility costs with the timely requirements of distribution. A reverse trend in logistics may take place, with several customers willing to trade more time for lower costs.

Environmental changes will be of importance for future developments, since on the one hand freight transportation, particularly the operation of trucks, contributes significantly to air pollution and related damages. According to a study commissioned by the FHWA, freight transportation is a major source of national NOx and PM-10 emissions. Particularly, freight vehicles contribute approximately half of mobile source NOx emissions and 27 per cent of all NOx emissions at the national level. Freight transportation also accounts for 36 per cent of US mobile source PM-10 emissions (ICF-Consulting, 2005). Such emissions are usually concentrated along major truck routes and close to freight facilities, such as ports and large DCs, where neighbourhoods are thus exposed to health risks. On the other hand, freight operations will be affected by the outcomes of climate change, particularly as a consequence of changing meteorological conditions such as increases in very hot days and heat waves, increases in Arctic temperatures, rising sea levels, increases in intense precipitation events and increases in hurricane intensity, which lead to the flooding of coastal roads, railways, transit systems, and runways (Committee on Climate Change and US Transportation, Transportation Research Board, Division on Earth and Life Studies, 2008). Besides mitigation policies that are discussed as means to reduce the likelihood and extent of global warming effects, adaptation policies are now increasingly considered. Hence policy makers and institutions are forced to take climate change and the vulnerability of transport systems and infrastructure into account.

CONCLUSION

North American logistics and freight distribution are adapting to the major macroeconomic changes linked with globalization, namely an acute division of production. In turn, efficient transport systems have made this modern, large-scale and network-oriented mode of production possible. Both respective interrelations are contributing to an increasing amount of freight transport. This development is causing new challenges, particularly between major North American gateways and inland freight distribution systems. In this context, an interesting question is whether there will be a certain reorientation on the global manufacturing and distribution map that reflects the rising degree of risk within the global transport network architecture. The more restricted transportation infrastructure and efficiency becomes the more attractive it will be to search for options of reorganization and regionalization of supply chains.

In the foreseeable future, the biggest momentum towards higher efficiency and sustainability of the distribution system will be provided by rising energy prices. Achieving major modal shifts from road and air freight towards rail and shipping modes could make the entire system more transport and energy efficient, so this is one of the strategies usually being developed as a response. Yet under current circumstances, both supply- and demand-side operations and requirements may delimit the needed flexibility of shippers and thus the desired change within transportation systems. However, rising transport and logistics costs will be the greatest stimulus among any other measures to reorganize the way materials flow and goods are delivered. This will trigger a phase of investment in real productive assets to guarantee future economic growth. The reliability of freight transportation infrastructures and operations is likely to be one of the top priorities.

The fact that North American logistics is a trans-jurisdictional issue involves two major dimensions. First, the commercial context is shaped by forces well outside the control and to some extent the comprehension of any political jurisdiction. Second, freight transportation and logistics are mostly a private industry and the allocation of assets is the outcome of profit-seeking and efficiency-maximizing strategies. The phase of deregulation that North American transportation went through in recent decades was mainly aimed at the national transport industry. It was not expected that because of the growing level of internationalization of supply chains, global freight shipping companies, such as maritime shippers and port operators, would play such an important role in North American logistics.

References

Banister, D (2002) *Transport Planning*, Routledge, Abingdon, Oxon

Bonacic, E with Hardie, K (2006) Wal-Mart and the logistics revolution, in *Wal-Mart: The face of twenty-first-century capitalism*, ed N Lichtenstein, pp 163–87, New York: New Press

Bowen, J (2008) Moving places: the geography of warehousing in the US, *Journal of Transport Geography*, **16**, pp 379–87

Bowen, J and Slack, B (2006) Shifting modes and spatial flows in North American freight transportation, in *Globalized Freight Transport*, ed T Leinbach and C Capineri, Edward Elgar, Cheltenham

Bretzke, W-R (2009) Supply chain management: notes on the capability and the limitations of a modern logistic paradigm, *Logistics Research*, **1** (2), pp 71–82

Brooks, M (2008) *North American Freight Transportation: The road to security and prosperity*, Edward Elgar, Cheltenham

Brunn, SD (2006) *Wal-Mart World. The world's biggest corporation in the global economy*, Routledge, London/New York

Chinitz, B (1960) *Freight and the Metropolis. The impact of America's transport revolutions on the New York region*, Harvard University Press, Cambridge/MA

Christopherson, S (2007) Barriers to 'US style' lean retailing: the case of Wal-Mart's failure in Germany, *Journal of Economic Geography*, **7** (1), pp 451–69

Cidell, J (2009) Concentration and decentralization: the new geography of freight distribution in US metropolitan areas, *Journal of Transport Geography* [Online] doi:10.1016/j.jtrangeo. 2009.06.017

Committee on Climate Change and US Transportation, Transportation Research Board, Division on Earth and Life Studies (2008) *Potential Impacts of Climate Change on US Transportation*, TRB, Transportation Research Board Special Report 290, Washington DC de Langen, PW (2004) Analysing seaport cluster performance, in *Shipping and Ports in the Twenty-first Century*, ed D Pinder and B Slack, Routledge, London, pp 82–98

Gereffi, G and Christian, M (2009) The impacts of Wal-Mart: The rise and consequences of the world's dominant retailer, *Annual Review of Sociology*, **35** (1), pp 573–91

Hesse, M (2004) Land for logistics. Locational dynamics, real estate markets and political regulation of regional distribution complexes, *Journal of Social and Economic Geography/Tijdschrift voor Sociale en Economische Geografie (TESG)*, **95** (2), pp 162–73

Hesse, M (2008) *The City as a Terminal. Logistics and freight distribution in an urban context*, Ashgate, Aldershot

Hesse, M and Rodrigue, J-P (2006) Global production networks and the role of logistics and transportation, *Growth and Change*, **32** (4), pp 499–509

ICF-Consulting (2005, accessed 6 March 2009) *Assessing the Effects of Freight Movement on Air Quality at the National and Regional Level*, study prepared for the US Federal Highway Administration, Office of Natural and Human Environment [Online] http://www.fhwa.dot.gov/environment/freightaq/index.htm

Lichtenstein, N (2006) *Wal-Mart: The face of twenty-first-century capitalism*, New Press, New York

Notteboom, T and Rodrigue, J-P (2005) Port regionalization: towards a new phase in port development, *Maritime Policy and Management*, **32** (3), pp 297–313

Plambeck, E (2007) The greening of Wal-Mart's supply chain, *Supply Chain Management Review*, 1 July

Rodrigue, J-P and Hatch, A (2009) *North American Intermodal Transportation: Infrastructure, Capital and Financing Issues*, The Equipment Leasing and Finance Foundation, Washington, DC

Rodrigue, J-P and Hesse, M (2007) North American perspectives on globalized trade and logistics, in *Globalized Freight Transport: Intermodality, e-commerce, logistics and sustainability*, ed T Leinbach and C Capineri, pp 103–34, Transport Economic, Management and Policy series, Edward Elgar, Cheltenham

Rodrigue, J-P *et al* (2010) Functions and actors of inland ports: European and North American dynamics, submitted to the *Journal of Transport Geography*

Wal-Mart (2009) *Wal-Mart: A leader in logistics*, Leaflet [Online] www.walmart.com

Index